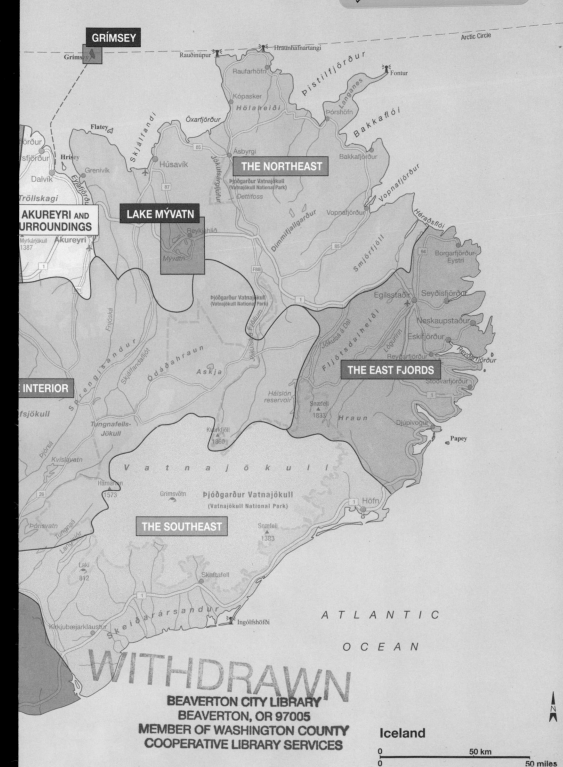

P9-CEH-528

7731 0

GRÍMSEY

Arctic Circle

Grímsey

Rauðinúpur
Hraunhafnartangi

Pistilfjörður

Raufarhöfn

Fontur

Langanes

Kópasker

Hólaheiði

Þórshöfn

Óxarfjörður

Bakkaflói

Flatey

85

Ásbyrgi

Bakkafjörður

fjörður

Hrísey

Husavík

Jökulsárgljúfur

THE NORTHEAST

Grenivík

Þjóðgarður Vatnajökull
(Vatnajökull National Park)

Dalvík

87

Dettifoss

Vopnafjörður

Trollskagi

Eyjafjörður

AKUREYRI AND
SURROUNDINGS

LAKE MÝVATN

Vopnafjörður

Héraðsflói

Reykjahlíð

Akureyri

Myrkárjökull
1387

1

Dimmifjallgarður

Smjörfjöll

85

Myvatn

F88

94

Borgarfjörður
Eystri

THE INTERIOR

Fnjóská

Skjálfandafljót

Þjóðgarður Vatnajökull
(Vatnajökull National Park)

1

Egilsstaðir

Seyðisfjörður

1020

Sprengisandur

Jökuldalur

Jökulsá á Dal

Fljótsdalsheiði

Neskaupstaður

Eskifjörður

Reyðarfjörður

Reyðarfjörður

Tungnafells-
Jökull

Ódáðahraun

Askja

Hálslón
reservoir

THE EAST FJORDS

Stöðvarfjörður

fsjökull

Snæfell
1833

1

Djúpivogur

Þórsá

Kverkfjöll
1860

Hraun

Kvíslavatn

Papey

V a t n a j ö k u l l

26

Hámarinn
1573

Grímsvötn

Þjóðgarður Vatnajökull
(Vatnajökull National Park)

1

Höfn

Þórisvatn

THE SOUTHEAST

Snæfell
1383

Tungnaá

Langisjór

Laki
812

Skaftafell

ATLANTIC

1

Kirkjubæjarklaustur

Skeiðarársandur

Ingólfshöfði

OCEAN

N

Iceland

0                    50 km
0                    50 miles

# INSIGHT ⊙ GUIDES

# ICELAND

www.insightguides.com/Iceland

# ⦿ Walking Eye App

## YOUR FREE DESTINATION CONTENT AND EBOOK AVAILABLE THROUGH THE WALKING EYE APP

Your guide now includes a free eBook and destination content for your chosen destination, all for the same great price as before. Simply download the Walking Eye App from the App Store or Google Play to access your free eBook and destination content.

### HOW THE WALKING EYE APP WORKS

Through the Walking Eye App, you can purchase a range of eBooks and destination content. However, when you buy this book, you can download the corresponding eBook and destination content for free. Just see below in the grey panels where to find your free content and then scan the QR code at the bottom of this page.

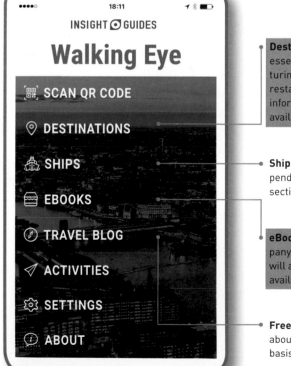

**Destinations:** Download your corresponding essential destination content from here, featuring recommended sights and attractions, restaurants, hotels and an A–Z of practical information, all for free. Other destinations are available for purchase.

**Ships:** Interested in ship reviews? Find independent reviews of river and ocean ships in this section, all available for purchase.

**eBooks:** You can download your free accompanying digital version of this guide here. You will also find a whole range of other eBooks, all available for purchase.

**Free access to travel-related blog articles** about different destinations, updated on a daily basis.

## HOW THE DESTINATION CONTENT WORKS

Each destination includes a short introduction, an A–Z of practical information and recommended points of interest, split into 4 different categories:

• Highlights
• Accommodation
• Eating out
• What to do

You can view the location of every point of interest and save it by adding it to your Favourites. In the 'Around Me' section you can view all the points of interest within 5km.

## HOW THE EBOOKS WORK

The eBooks are provided in EPUB file format. Please note that you will need an eBook reader installed on your device to open the file. Many devices come with this as standard, but you may still need to install one manually from Google Play.

The eBook content is identical to the content in the printed guide.

## HOW TO DOWNLOAD THE WALKING EYE APP

1. Download the Walking Eye App from the App Store or Google Play.
2. Open the app and select the scanning function from the main menu.
3. Scan the QR code on this page – you will then be asked a security question to verify ownership of the book.
4. Once this has been verified, you will see your eBook and destination content in the purchased ebook and destination sections, where you will be able to download them.

Other destination apps and eBooks are available for purchase separately or are free with the purchase of the Insight Guide book.

# Contents

# THE BEST OF ICELAND: TOP ATTRACTIONS

From the ethereal, magical lightshow of the aurora borealis, a glacial lagoon and the wonders of Iceland's barren wilderness areas, to the cultural attractions of Reykjavík.

△ **Northern Lights**. Visitors often come to Iceland in the darkest winter months simply to try to observe the uncanny lightshow of the aurora borealis. See page 203.

▽ **Blue Lagoon**. The extraordinary resort is set in the midst of a lava field on the barren Reykjanes peninsula. Spend an afternoon bathing in its geothermally heated, mineral-rich waters and you will emerge relaxed, re-energised and already planning your next trip to Iceland. See page 161.

▷ **Reykjavík**. Iceland's capital may be small and isolated, but it is a lively, attractive and urbane city nonetheless, with many cultural attractions. The setting, with views across to Mt Esja, is spectacular, and the nightlife is legendary. See page 141

▽ **Puffin-spotting**. See huge colonies of these curious, colourful birds on the coast at Vík and Látrabjarg, and on islands such as Akurey and Lundey (off Reykjavík), Drangey, Papey and Heimaey. See page 188.

△ **Heimaey**. Almost wiped off the map by the volcanic eruption of 1973, this quintessential Icelandic fishing port has an attractive harbour and two looming volcanic peaks. Situated on the friendly Vestmannaeyjar islands off the southwest coast. See page 185.

▷ **Geysir and Gullfoss**. Two natural wonders are a must-see countryside excursion for those on short city breaks. Geysir gave its name to all the world's geysers, although these days it is outperformed by its neighbour Strokkur. Nearby, the dramatic double waterfall Gullfoss is awesome in its elemental power. See page 175.

▽ **Ísafjörður**. The remote capital of the beautiful West Fjords region is notable not just for its setting but also for its restored 18th-century timber buildings. It is also the jumping-off point for wilderness hikers seeking to explore the deserted Hornstrandir peninsula. See page 220.

△ **Whale-watching**. Perhaps the best place in Europe to catch a glimpse of one of these majestic creatures is off Húsavík, on the north coast. See page 274.

◁ **Jökulsárlón**. The glacial lagoon features on a hundred postcards, but nothing prepares you for its ethereal beauty. Glinting blue icebergs, calved from the mighty Vatnajökull icecap, float through the lagoon on their way to the sea. See page 200.

▽ **Þórsmörk**. One of Iceland's most spectacular and inaccessible wilderness areas is sealed off by a trio of glaciers, surging rivers and steep mountainsides covered in tiny birch trees. See page 179.

# THE BEST OF ICELAND: EDITOR'S CHOICE

Stunning scenery, tumbling waterfalls, geothermal baths, outdoor pursuits and exciting nightlife – not to mention the charms of Europe's most northerly city... here are our recommendations for Iceland's unmissable attractions.

*Riding Icelandic horses.*

## UNIQUELY ICELANDIC

**Horse-riding.** The one-of-a-kind Icelandic horse is a sturdy, calm-natured breed. Farms across the country offer visitors anything from a one-hour sortie to a seven-day trek.

**Geothermal swimming pools.** Emerging from a hot tub into the frigid polar air is a memorable experience.

**Þingvellir.** Revered by Icelanders, this beautiful natural amphitheatre is the birthplace of nation. See page 169.

**Independence Day.** On 17 June Reykjavík and other places put on street parades, street theatre and music events.

**Pickled shark and brennivín.** Iceland's traditional foodstuffs are eaten with gusto during the pagan festival of Þorrablót. See page 119.

*Taking the waters at Jarðböðin nature baths.*

## SPECTACULAR SCENERY

**The coast around Vík.** Black volcanic sands, pounding Atlantic surf and jagged rocks give Iceland's southernmost point a gothic majesty. See page 181.

**Skaftafell.** Part of Europe's biggest national park area, this is prime hiking country, dominated by glaciers. See page 198.

**Snæfellsnes.** The mystical volcano here was the entrance point to the planet's interior in Jules Verne's *Journey to the Centre of the Earth*. See page 213.

**West Fjords.** Towering cliffs and remote fjords in Iceland's subarctic northwest. See page 219.

**Jökulsárgljúfur.** The impressive Dettifoss waterfall and Jökulsá Canyon are reasons to make the trip to this area in the far northeast. See page 277.

**Herðubreið.** This towering peak rises over the plain of the eastern interior, with the Herðubreiðarlindur valley an oasis of green amid desert-like surroundings. See page 309.

*The Snæfellsnes peninsula, whose focus is the Snæfellsjökull glacier.*

## SIGHTS IN REYKJAVÍK

*Leifur Eiríksson statue with Hallgrímskirkja behind.*

**Culture House.** Explore the medieval past, brought vividly to life in the saga manuscripts. See also the **Saga Museum**. See pages 147 and 152.

**Árbær Open-Air Museum.** An eye-opening experience, showing how people lived in the not-so-distant past. See page 156.

**Laugardalur.** Reykjavík's main leisure complex features a magnificent open-air swimming pool with the full range of geothermally heated hot tubs and plunge pools. See page 155.

**Harpa.** The city's controversial new concert hall is a stunning piece of architecture, with its glinting surfaces and views out to sea. See page 147.

**Hallgrímskirkja.** Visible from most points in the city, climb the tower of this striking modern structure for breathtaking views. See page 151.

**National Museum.** Recommended to anyone wishing to understand Iceland's past. See page 149.

**National Gallery.** A light and airy space in which to admire Icelandic and foreign art. See page 148.

## BIRDWATCHER'S PARADISE

**Lake Mývatn.** This volcanic lake attracts abundant waterfowl, including the world's largest population of breeding ducks. See page 263.

**Látrabjarg bird-cliffs.** Spectacular sea-cliffs, home to thousands of sea birds. See page 226.

**Grímsey.** Small island known for its abundant birdlife. See page 255.

**Króksbjarg and Bakkar cliffs.** A haven for kittiwakes and fulmars. See page 235.

**Skeiðarársandur.** World's largest breeding ground for great skuas. See page 197.

*A Skaftafell glacier.*

## VOLCANOES AND GLACIERS

**Krafla and Leirhnjúkur.** Tempt fate in one of Iceland's most explosive areas, full of craters, bubbling mudpots and smoking new lava. See page 268.

**Hveravellir.** In Iceland's barren interior, these remarkable brilliant-blue hot springs are surrounded by outlandishly coloured rocks. See page 301.

**Vatnajökull.** Europe's largest icecap and its glaciers dominate the southeast. Snowmobile tours are possible in summer. See page 198.

**Laki and Lakagígar.** Site of the largest eruption in recorded history, today spongy green moss covers the otherworldly crater row. See page 197.

**Svínafellsjökull glacier walk.** Strap on crampons and stride up a glacier on an unforgettable ice walk See page 198.

**Magni and Móði, Fimmvörðuháls.** Take a bus or super-jeep tour to see these two smoking craters, created during the first phase of the 2010 Eyjafjallajökull eruption and named after the sons of Thor. See page 180.

*Lake Mývatn.*

*Razorbills.*

*Photographing the Northern Lights from a glacial lagoon.*

Tourists at Seljalandsfoss Waterfall.

*Svínafellsjökull, an outlet glacier of Vatnajokull ice cap.*

# AN EXTRAORDINARY ISLAND

Iceland offers not only a wealth of natural
wonders, from glaciers to geysers, but also
a rich mine of history and literature.

*The reason for hereness seems beyond conjecture,*
*There are no trees or trains or architecture,*
*Fruits and greens are insufficient for health*
*And culture is limited by lack of wealth.*
*The tourist sights have nothing like Stonehenge,*
*The literature is all about revenge.*
*And yet I like it if only because this nation*
*Enjoys a scarcity of population...*
W.H. Auden, Letters from Iceland

Iceland has come a long way since the English poet Auden penned these
facetious lines in 1936. From an isolated agricultural society that many
people thought had scarcely progressed beyond the
Middle Ages, there has emerged a high-tech welfare
state with one of the highest standards of living in
the world. Yet at least one thing hasn't changed since
Auden's visit: Iceland still has a scarcity of population
(around 332,000) that leaves it with some of the greatest wilderness areas in Europe.

In fact, Iceland may be the ultimate nature trip.
Drinking water comes from pure glaciers; fish is
caught in unpolluted waters; even the lamb and cattle
graze in fields untouched by fertiliser. Most Icelanders
now live in and around the capital, Reykjavík, leaving
huge swathes of the volcanically active island – one of    *Lighthouse at sunset.*
the most recently formed on earth – quite deserted.
Dotted by steaming lava fields, icecaps, glaciers, hot pools and geysers,
the Icelandic landscape has an elemental rawness that nobody who sees
it can easily forget.

Perhaps not surprisingly, the people who live on this extraordinary
island are an eccentric breed. Speaking Europe's oldest language, little
changed since the days of the Vikings, accustomed to the endless light
of summer and Stygian gloom of the long winters, the Icelanders can be
as extreme as their homeland. Rather shy, they will rarely be the first to
talk to strangers. But once their traditional reserve is broken through,
they can be among the most friendly and hospitable people in Europe.

Which may all help explain why Iceland exerts such a powerful hold
over travellers, compelling them to return again and again.

*The solfatara, or volcanic vent, of Hverir near Lake Mývatn.*

# FORGED BY FIRE, HONED BY ICE

Iceland is one of the youngest landmasses in the world, geologically speaking. As a result, its inhabitants are used to living with change and disruption.

In geological terms, Iceland is a mere baby. No more than 20 million years have passed since volcanoes on the floor of the far northern Atlantic Ocean began to spew lava, laying the foundations of what would become Iceland. Today it is still one of the most volcanically active spots on earth – giving geoscientists the chance of observing a land still in the making.

## Movements of the earth's crust

According to the theory of plate tectonics, the earth's surface comprises a number of plates (seven major and dozens of minor plates), which "float" on the mass of magma beneath. The Andes and the Himalayas are evidence of massive collisions of tectonic plates, which have folded the earth's crust up to form great mountain ranges.

Volcanoes and earthquakes are symptoms of this vast movement, occurring at the boundaries where tectonic plates meet. These boundaries can be convergent, where the edge of one plate is forced underneath another and great slabs of the earth's surface are "lost"; or divergent, where the plates tear apart and magma rises to the surface from below, forming new crust. Iceland straddles a divergent boundary, the Mid-Atlantic Ridge, where the Eurasian and North American tectonic plates are being pulled apart. Thus, the island is literally being torn in two, at a rate of around 2cm (nearly an inch) a year – the speed of growing fingernails – with lava rising from the earth's centre to fill the gap.

## Volcanic belt

The Mid-Atlantic Ridge, running clear across the island from southwest to northeast, is marked by a belt of volcanic craters, hot

*Lava flow and plumes at the Holuhraun Fissure, near the Bardabunga Volcano.*

springs, steam springs, solfataras (areas of high-temperature activity) and earthquakes. This belt extends to a width of about 40km (25 miles) in the north, and up to 60km (40 miles) across in the south, and covers about a quarter of the country.

Not surprisingly, Iceland's rocks are almost all volcanic (predominantly basalt). The oldest rocks, from the Tertiary pre-Ice Age period, are the plateau basalts of the East and West Fjords. Slightly inland are younger grey basalts from the interglacial periods, generally appearing as open moorland with less evidence of glaciation. Further in towards the present-day volcanic zone is the palagonite formation, from subglacial eruptions in the last part of the Ice Age. Typical of these belts are tuff ridges and table mountains, the soft rock often extensively eroded by wind and water. Iceland's youngest rocks occur in and around the present-day volcanic zone.

The northwest and the east of Iceland are no longer volcanically active. Most of the rest of the island, however, conceals a seething mass of volcanic and geothermal activity. There are over 100 volcanoes in Iceland; 35 of these have been active over the past 10,000 years (recent history in geological terms!).

In the past few centuries Iceland has experienced an eruption every five years on average. Most are minor, short-lived and cause minimal damage, like the photogenic eruption of Mount Hekla in 1991 – "tourist eruptions", in local parlance. Others can cause a little more trouble, like the 2010 eruption under the Eyjafjallajökull glacier. The resulting ash cloud, which reached a height of 10km (6 miles), brought airplanes across Europe to a standstill for six days in April, with an estimated cost to the global economy of €4 billion. In May the following year, Grímsvötn,

*Eyjafjalljokull volcanic eruption.*

## THE BIRTH OF SURTSEY

The ultimate "tourist eruption" was the formation of the island of Surtsey, which began on the ocean floor just southwest of the Westman Islands in 1963. In addition to lava and ash, the Surtsey eruption produced voluminous clouds of steam as cold seawater met hot lava and instantly boiled. By the end of the eruption, the new island was 2.8 sq km (1 sq mile) in area – erosion has now reduced this to about 1.57 sq km (0.5 sq miles). The new islet was a welcome gift to scientists, a natural laboratory which offered them a chance to observe the processes by which virgin land is colonised by plants, birds, insects and mammals.

Iceland's most active volcano, followed suit; however, kinder air currents carried its 20km (12-mile)-high plume away to the northeast, causing less disruption to air traffic.

### In the shadow of disaster

Despite an apparently flippant attitude towards volcanoes, Icelanders do not forget the threat they live with. The catastrophic eruption of Lakagígar in the late 18th century poured out the largest lava flow ever produced by a single volcano in recorded history, with a volume of about 12 cubic km (3 cubic miles). As if that were not enough, it also emitted noxious gases which poisoned livestock and crops, blocked out the sun, and led to a disastrous famine. At least 20 percent of the population died.

In 1973, the subterranean peril was brought home with a vengeance, when a new volcano flared up on Heimaey in the Vestmannaeyar. It buried one-third of the town under lava and ash (see page 188).

Evidence of subterranean unrest has been felt since the mid-1970s around Mount Krafla near Lake Mývatn, an area free of volcanic activity for over two centuries. A massive eruption, which lasted from 1724 until 1729, laid waste three farms, before the lava flow halted at Rey-

to cross, scoria also creates unusual and haunting formations. A small amount is smooth, hard "ropy" lava.

## Caps of ice

In spite of its subterranean heat, Iceland has largely been shaped by cold. In the Ice Age, glaciers gouged out the fjords which cut into the coastline on the north, east and west, and sharpened the country's mountain ridges to knife-edges.

Although Iceland emerged from its glacial pall about 10,000 years ago, it remains a land

*Svinafellsjokull, an outlet glacier of Vatnajokull ice cap.*

kjahlíð church, where the congregation was praying for deliverance. Two centuries later, the earth began to move when construction started on the geothermal power station below Mount Krafla; many people concluded that man's interference with the forces of nature had set off a reaction within the earth. Mount Krafla has erupted several times since 1975, most recently in 1984, although the lava has never threatened Reykjahlíð.

It has been estimated that one-third of all the lava that has erupted on earth in recorded history has come from Iceland. As any visitor will soon discover, almost all of it is scoria, a type of basalt that is full of tiny air bubbles and is consequently very light. Loose, sharp and difficult

of glaciers and icecaps – curiously, they are believed to have been formed not in the Ice Age but during a cold spell around 500BC, reaching their largest size during the "Little Ice Age" of AD 1500–1900. Ice covers around 11 percent of the island's 103,000 sq km (40,000 sq miles). However, since 1990, all of Iceland's glaciers have been in retreat; land is currently being revealed that has been covered in ice since the 16th century.

Contrasts between heat and cold are nowhere so striking as in the glaciers that sit atop volcanoes. Some of the latter seem extinct: the volcanic crater on which the cone-shaped Snæfellsjökull glacier rests, for instance, has not erupted for 700 years.

## Melting glaciers

Eruptions from subglacial volcanoes often cause more damage than those from open-air volcanoes. Hot lava melts the ice, triggering sudden floods – *jökulhlaups* – with unpredictable results. Mount Katla, the volcano lying dormant under the glacier Mýrdalsjökull, is Iceland's largest caldera, at 80 sq km (30 sq miles). When Katla erupts, the *jökulhlaup* can be 200,000 cubic metres (7 million cubic ft) of water a second.

In 1996 a volcano in the Bárðarbunga-Grímsvötn fissure erupted beneath Vatnajökull,

*The Blue Lagoon.*

Vatnajökull, up to 1km (3,200ft) thick and 8,300 sq km (3,200 sq miles) in area, is not only Europe's largest icecap, it is also bigger than all the rest put together.

melting huge quantities of ice and scattering ash over a 100km (60-mile) area. Meltwater from the eruption flowed into a sub-glacial caldera, which began to fill. On 5 November, the water in the caldera spilled over the brim, resulting in a massive flood across the sand plain south of the glacier that swept away roads and bridges. It deposited icebergs the size of apartment blocks, which, as they melted, turned the sands into pits of quicksand. In 2015, the Bárðarbunga volcano became active again, spewing nearly 12 million tons of sulphur dioxide into the atmosphere and creating a lava field the same size as Manhattan.

Meltwater from the glaciers flows out into winding rivers, which swell whenever warm weather melts the glacial ice or when volcanic activity begins beneath the glacier. Unlike the crystal-clear rivers fed by rain or underground streams, glacial rivers carry silt from the glacier, so they are generally brownish and murky in colour. Unbridged rivers are one of the main dangers to travellers in the highlands, as the water can rise with alarming rapidity.

Iceland is no stranger to earthquakes. The stretching and straining of the earth's crust at the junction of tectonic plates inevitably produces sudden movements under pressure. Strict building regulations ensure that all man-made structures can withstand major earthquakes.

## Using geothermal heat

Living on a "hot spot" implies coexistence with natural risks. Yet the heat in the earth has also brought its own inestimable benefits. In a cold climate, what could be more valuable than endless natural hot water?

All spouting springs (geysers) in the world owe their name to the Great Geysir in Iceland's southwest, which used to spout to a height of 60 metres (196ft). The geyser spent most of the 20th century in a dormant state – earthquakes in southern Iceland in 2000 briefly gave it a fresh burst of life, but it has now returned to a more slumberous state. However, nearby Strokkur (meaning "churn") obligingly erupts every few minutes to a height of about 30 metres (100ft), and several more spouting geysers can be seen around the country.

Natural hot water bubbling irrepressibly out of the earth has been prized by the Icelanders ever since they settled the country. Ingólfur Arnarson named Reykjavík ("smoky bay") after seeing clouds of steam rising from springs in today's Laugardalur valley. These springs became the community's public laundry in later centuries, when housewives would trudge the 3km (2 miles) from Reykjavík along Laugavegur ("hot spring road") carrying their washing. The laundry springs can still be seen in Laugardalur, by the Botanical Gardens (see page 155), where one "washbasin" remains.

In 1930, geothermal energy was first piped from the springs to the town to heat a swimming pool and a school. Developing technology has made it possible to look further and drill deeper for hot water, and high-efficiency insulation means that water can be piped long distances. Reykjavík's main sources of geothermal energy lie about 30km (18 miles) from the city, at Nesjavellir and Hellisheiði; the latter is now the world's largest geothermal power station. Today 85 percent of Iceland's atmospheric heating is from geothermal sources, and almost every community

transformed into hydroelectric power (HEP), another valuable resource. The first hydroelectric power plant opened in Iceland in 1904, and today hydroelectric power stations supply some 80 percent of Icelanders' electricity.

Whatever the changes their society is undergoing, the Icelanders still live in very close proximity to nature. They take for granted an untamed, unpolluted environment that is still growing, still changing, where eruptions and earthquakes are accepted as part of the tenor of life.

*Geothermal power production.*

has its own geothermally warmed open-air swimming pool.

At Svartsengi in the southwest, superheated water (two-thirds of which is brine) from far beneath the earth's surface passes through a heat-exchange process to provide fresh water for heating, and generate electricity. A bonus is that the hot lake formed by the run-off water has developed into a popular spa, the Blue Lagoon (Bláa Lónið, see pages 161 and 162). Rich in salt and other minerals, the waters of the lagoon are reputed to be beneficial for skin conditions.

## Harnessing glacial rivers

The water that tumbles over precipices from Iceland's glaciated mountains and rivers is

### SOUTH ICELAND QUAKES

Every 100 years or so a major earthquake brings destruction to southern Iceland. In 1784 the South Iceland Quake, estimated at 7.5 on the Richter scale, wreaked destruction. In 1912 a category 7 earthquake shook the region. In June 2000, three quakes struck over the course of three days, and in May 2008 another one measuring 6.3 hit Selfoss – footage can be seen at the Folk Museum in Eyrarbakki. Experts warn that although some tension on the earth's crust was relieved, the "big one" is yet to come. In June 2016, a series of earthquakes were recorded at Katla, which, according to scientists, may suggest an eruption is imminent.

# ISLANDIA.

ISLANDIA

*emtrio*

Grims ey

A

Rauda gnupur

Rein baffri

Langanes

Q

Kolsker

Hvallaturs fiord

Flat ey

Lundey

Fulmungavig

Sumingavig

Rolla fiord

Backe fiord

Skautzug

Gunnolfnala

Vopnafiorder

Bapranes

Grimels fiord

Midfiord

Finnafiord

Sandug

Digranes

Huslley

Hvalfiord

Eya fiord

For ness

Husuig

Ryka heydir

Strand

Hof

Kurlar

Iokus a

Balanes

Surbak dalur

Modur val ler closter

Holgur dalur

NORDLEN DINGAFIOR DVNG

Munke tuere closter

Mokrufeld

Skialfiandz fiord

Bardur dalur

Grenested

Muli

Mynoti

Suar tar notn

Fodinæ sulphureæ præstantissimæ.

Skirdu closter

Reydar fiord

Garavig

Bern fiord

Sand Iokul.

Arnafelds Iokul.

His notis distinguitur limes inter vtramqz dioecesim

Aradal

AVSTLENDIN GAFIORDVNG

Fafnir

Iokuls a

Langedal.

Runa tepper

SVNDLEN DINGAFIOR DVNG.

Skalbe a.

Fiske notn

Almanhot

Hiersheyd

Iokuls a

Horns fiord

Horn

Skin eyer

Breid

SKALHOLT sedes episco palis, cui adiuncta est schola

Hekla perpetuis damnata estib.et nisib.horrendo boatu lapides euomit

Mydals Iokul.

Kirke bar closter

Brolangs eyer

P

Ingols hofds

N

Oddi

Eyafialla Iokul.

Solheima Iokul.

Medalland.

Eyrarbach

Laxma tepper

Equorum tanta hic velocitas, vt continuo cur su 20.milli aria con sirant.

Breida bolls stadur

Vacce marinæ.

Corui. et falcones albæ.

Iokul a.

Astuta vulpe cularum vena tio,in nidu volu crum nuestigandis atque diripiendis

O

Eldor

WESTMANNA EIAR

M

K

L

ILLVSTRISS. AC POTENTIS
REGI FREDERICO II DANIAE
NORVEGIAE, SLAVORVM, C
THORVMQVE REGI, ETC. PRI
CIPI SVO CLEMENTISSI
ANDREAS VELLEIVS
DESCRIBEB. ET DEDICAB.

# DECISIVE DATES

*Pytheas' trireme.*

Tryggvason, King of Norway, sends his chaplain Þangbrand to continue conversions.

**1000**
Christianity is adopted as Iceland's official religion at the annual Alþingi meeting.

**1163**
The "Stone-Throwing Summer" of violent clashes between different groups of Vikings.

**1179**
Birth of Snorri Sturluson, diplomat and saga writer.

**1230–64**
The Sturlung Age of feuds between private armies and political factions.

**1241**
Murder of Snorri Sturluson on the King of Norway's orders.

**1262**
The Alþingi agrees to allow King Haakon of Norway to collect taxes.

*Erik the Red.*

**4th century BC**
Pytheas, a Greek explorer, reports sightings of an island which he called "Ultima Thule".

**c. 6th or 7th century AD**
Irish monks start to settle on "Thule", forming small communities.

**mid-9th century**
A Norwegian, Hrafna-Flóki, tries to settle in the West Fjords. Foiled by the harsh

*Ingólfur Arnarson, the "First Settler", on an Icelandic banknote.*

winter, he calls the land Ísland (Iceland).

## Viking Settlement

**874**
Ingólfur Arnarson (the "First Settler") and his foster brother Hjörleifur Hróðmarsson settle on Iceland in the southwest and on the south coast respectively.

**930**
By 930 many other Norwegian chieftains and their families have followed and the population stands at an estimated 25,000. Creation of the Alþingi parliament, a central authority presided over by a law-speaker.

**10th century**
Erik the Red settles on Greenland and persuades numerous Icelanders to follow.

## Conversion and Feuding

**984**
Þorvaldur Koðránsson the Well-Travelled starts to convert Iceland to Christianity, often using violent means. Later Olaf

## Disaster and Decline

**1389**

An eruption of Mount Hekla is followed by smallpox and other epidemics.

**1397**

Scandinavian union of Norway, Denmark and Sweden transfers the sovereignty of Iceland from Norway to Denmark. Denmark, following Norway's example, prohibits Iceland from trading with any other countries, and agrees to send supply ships in exchange for fish.

**1469**

England and Denmark go to war over England's illegal trading with Iceland.

**1526**

A feud between the Roman Catholic bishops of Iceland's two sees, Ögmundur Pálsson of Skálholt and Jón Arason of Hólar, leads to a duel at the Alþingi.

**1541**

Denmark sends two warships to impose a new Lutheran church code through the Alþingi; former rivals Jón and Ögmundur both resist, but Ögmundur is exiled to Denmark, dying aboard ship.

**1548**

Bishop Jón is summoned by the king to Copenhagen, but instead stays in Iceland and continues his rebellion against the Protestants.

**1550**

King Christian III of Denmark orders Jón's arrest; after being captured, he is beheaded along with two of his sons.

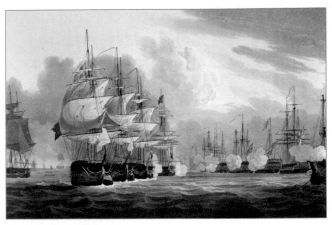

*The Battle of Copenhagen.*

**1627**

3,000 pirates land on Heimaey in the Vestmannaeyjar (Westman Islands), killing many of the inhabitants and taking others captive.

*King Christian VIII.*

**1662**

Denmark divides Iceland into four commercial trading districts which are not permitted to trade with each other, only directly with Denmark. This is reinforced by a Danish naval blockade.

**1783**

Eruption of Laki volcano in southern Iceland kills approximately 10,000

Icelanders; most deaths are due to the ensuing "Haze Famine".

**1800**

The Alþingi is abolished on the orders of the Danish king.

## A Revival of Fortune

**1801**

At the Battle of Copenhagen, the British fleet destroys the Danish Navy and confiscates the entire Danish merchant fleet.

**1809**

"Revolution" led by Jorgen Jorgensen, a Danishman serving in the British Navy, who liberated Iceland, declaring it independent. The revolution is quashed the same year by another member of the British Navy, and Jorgensen is jailed in England.

**1811**

Birth of Jón Sigurðsson, the force behind the movement for Icelandic independence from Danish rule.

**1830**

Iceland allowed two seats among 70 on an advisory body to the Danish crown.

*The Icelandic flag.*

with Denmark and a new constitution are approved, Iceland becomes a republic on 17 June. This date is celebrated each year as Independence Day.

### 1949
Iceland becomes a founding member of NATO, abandoning its "eternal neutrality".

### 1951
US military return to Iceland to set up an air base at Keflavík.

### 1952–76
Four Cod Wars (1952, 1958, 1972, 1975) with the UK over fishing rights. In 1976 an agreement is reached for a 320km (200-mile) fishing limit off Iceland.

### 1955
Icelandic writer Halldór Laxness wins the Nobel Prize for Literature.

### 1963
The island of Surtsey is created by an underwater volcanic eruption off the southern coast.

### 1973
Volcanic eruption on Heimaey island threatens to destroy it;

### 1843
Royal decree signed by King Christian VIII reinstates a consultative Alþingi of 26 representatives, with 20 elected members and six chosen by the crown.

### 1854
Trade monopoly with Denmark ended.

### 1874
Denmark gives the Alþingi autonomy over domestic affairs, but retains a veto over all it does.

### 1879
Death of Jón Sigurðsson.

### 1881–95
Benedikt Sveinsson, a campaigner for independence, calls for real self-government every year at the Alþingi; attempts to pass the proposal are foiled by the royal veto.

## The 20th Century and Beyond

### 1904
Iceland is granted home rule.

### 1911
Founding of Reykjavík University.

### 1915
Introduction of total prohibition.

### 1918
Denmark makes Iceland a sovereign state with its own flag, still with the king of Denmark as its head of state, and agrees to hold further negotiations on Iceland's status in 1940.

### 1940
With Iceland occupied by Britain and Denmark by Germany, there is no communication between them. The Alþingi announces that it has taken over the governing of Iceland.

### 1941
Iceland requests full independence from Denmark.

### 1944
Following a plebiscite at which the termination of the union

*A collision during the Cod Wars.*

an army of volunteers diverts the lava flow, preventing complete disaster.

## 1980

Vigdís Finnbogadóttir, the world's first democratically elected female head of state, becomes president. She is thrice re-elected, holding office until 1996.

## 1986

Presidents Reagan and Gorbachev arrive in Reykjavík for a summit to start talks to end the Cold War.

## 1989

Beer Day, 1 March, celebrates the end of the ban on strong beer.

## 1992

Iceland walks out of the International Whaling Commission after the country's request for a limited whaling quota is rejected.

## 1994

Iceland enters the European Economic Area.

## 1996

The Grímsvötn volcano erupts under Vatnajökull, leading to a massive build-up of meltwater under the glacier, which floods out and sweeps away chunks of the Ring Road and several bridges on the south coast.

## 2006

Iceland resumes commercial whaling, despite strong opposition from environmental groups around the world.

## 2008

The worldwide economic crisis hits Iceland particularly hard; all three of the country's major banks collapse and the country is plunged into a severe recession.

## 2009

Iceland applies for EU membership.

## 2010

In April, the ash cloud from a volcanic eruption under Eyjafjallajökull glacier brings most of Europe's air traffic to a standstill for six consecutive days; the following year, Grímsvötn erupts for five days, releasing 10,000 tons of ash per second in its most active phase.

## 2013

A European court draws a line under a five-year wrangle, ruling that the UK and the Netherlands cannot sue Iceland for the $3.8 billion losses they incurred when the Icesave bank collapsed in 2008. The Progressive and Independence parties form a coalition government, under the leadership of Sigmundur Davíð Gunnlaugsson, Iceland's youngest ever-prime minister.

## 2015

The GDP returns to the pre-financial crisis level. The

*Vigdís Finnbogadóttir.*

*T-shirt inspired by the Eyjafjallajökull eruption.*

centre-right government withdraws Iceland's application for EU membership, triggering protests in Reykjavik. The Bárðarbunga volcano erupts.

## 2016

Prime Minister Sigmundur Gunnlaugsson steps down following publication of the Panama Papers, which revealed that he had failed to declare ownership of an offshore company. Guðni Thorlacius Jóhannesson (b.1968), a historian who studied at Oxford University, becomes Iceland's youngest president. Iceland's national football team are the surprise package at Euro 2016, eliminating England en route to the quarterfinals and inspiring the nation in the process.

# ULTIMA THULE

Irish monks were the first to live on Iceland, but were soon outnumbered by Vikings who settled and started to farm the land.

A recent visitor to Iceland overheard two farmers talking passionately in a field; they were lamenting the premature death of a young man whom they were sure would have been a great credit to the country. This sorely missed individual, it transpired, was a certain Skarphéðinn Njálsson, a character in one of the celebrated Icelandic sagas, and he had been dead for all of 1,000 years.

Various versions of this story are told by travellers to Iceland, all with the same kernel of truth: Icelanders are obsessed with their history, or at least a part of it. The period they prefer to remember is between the years 930 and 1030, when chisel-jawed saga heroes threw off the tyranny of Norway's king, created a new republic, and sailed to America way before the upstart Columbus; and after all, there is little after the 13th century on which Icelanders can reflect with pleasure. The country's recent prosperity occurred only since World War II. For the previous 600 years, Iceland was a grim, depressing place: a 19th-century English visitor complained that he never once saw an Icelander smile.

This historical roller-coaster ride has tentative beginnings, with Irish monks looking for a quiet, isolated spot to meditate, and becomes substantive with the Norwegian Viking settlement, traditionally dated to 874 (although archaeological work in 2001 suggests that the date might be pushed back to 871). These same sword-wielding Vikings, who famously reduced hapless Europeans to desperate praying, then performed an astonishing volte-face. Within generations, they took up intellectual pursuits – without ever quite putting down their swords – and created a legacy of literature which scholars

*The voyage of St Brendan.*

discuss in the same breath as Homer and the Golden Age of Greece.

These transformed Vikings not only wrote down their own history, but also collected and saved the oral prehistory and religion of the whole Germanic race. They wrote in their own tongue rather than in the scholarly language of Latin, on manuscripts made of calfskin, one of the few commodities in Iceland which, like fish, was always plentiful. A great number of these manuscripts were lost or destroyed in subsequent periods of extreme hardship. Even so, those Icelandic sagas that have survived more than make up for an almost total absence of ancient monuments in the country.

## The uttermost end of the earth

The cherished history of Iceland is really quite short by European standards. As far as anyone can tell, no human had yet set foot in Iceland when, for example, the Parthenon in Athens was already some 800 years old and the capital of the disintegrating Roman Empire was being moved to Constantinople.

Possibly the earliest mention of Iceland is from Pytheas, a Greek who lived in Marseilles in the 4th century BC. He explored the north personally and returned with an account of a country called Thule situated six days' sail-

they "sought with great labour… a desert in the ocean". The Shetlands, Faroe Islands and ultimately Iceland were just the ticket. The monks are unlikely to have arrived before St Patrick's celebrated missionary work in Ireland, which began in 432.

Ireland was a redoubt of Graeco-Roman learning when the Western Roman Empire crumbled. Irish chroniclers, who were familiar with earlier writers and travellers including Pytheas, tended to embellish their work with borrowed, and sometimes counter-productive, erudition. Thus the story of St Brendan's discov-

Turf house.

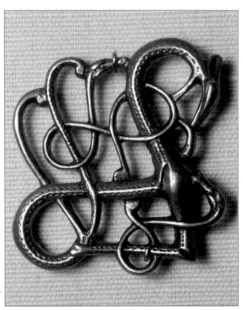

Viking brooch found in southwestern Iceland.

ing north of Britain and close to a frozen sea; whether this was Iceland, Greenland, Scotland, Scandinavia or Pytheas's overheated imagination has been debated for centuries. Later chroniclers *did* call the island Thule; but the country was variously known as Garðarshólmi, "Snowland" and "Butterland" before a Norwegian called Hrafna-Flóki came up with "Iceland", a name that finally stuck.

## Frozen gateway to hell

It was not Scandinavians who first settled on Iceland but Irish monks driven by the desire to meditate undisturbed. They set out in coracles made of hides stretched over a framework of branches. With hardly any seafaring experience,

ery of "Thule" is on the one hand made quite plausible by a description of what appears to be a volcanic eruption, possibly of Mount Hekla; but on the other hand loses credibility when St Brendan discovers that "Thule" is inhabited.

Sound information about Irish activities in Iceland is contained in the works of Dicuil, author of *On Measuring the Earth*, and the Venerable Bede. Dicuil quoted priests who said that around the summer solstice it was light enough at midnight to pick lice off one's shirt.

Since the pioneering Irish communities were exclusively male, they would not have put down roots and multiplied in the usual way. The settlements were bound to wither, but was their decline in Iceland gradual? Peace of mind would not long have survived the arrival of the 9th-century Norwegians. Ari the Learned, a 12th-century Icelandic chronicler, tells the story from the Norwegian point of view. The disembarking Vikings encountered "some Christians" who shortly afterwards "went away" because they were unwilling to live among heathens. That may be putting it mildly. Nevertheless, the Vikings were usually very candid about their atrocities, and as there is no record of anyone boasting about burying an axe in a hermit's head, scare-mongering theories about the fate of the Irish do not necessarily hold water. Sec-

Icelandic settlers, 38 are known to have been previously powerful chieftains in Norway.

Some historians believe, less dramatically, that poor economic conditions drove people abroad. Professor Munch, writing in 1859, suggested that the original settlers actually came from older Viking colonies in the British Isles, and that Scotland was therefore "the chief cradle of their race". Only a small proportion of the names in the *Landnámabók* is non-Scandinavian, and Icelanders long believed that their blood was purest Viking, but Munch's theory was quite prescient. In 2000, studies of

*The Norwegians landing in Iceland in 872.*

ond-hand accounts aside, concrete evidence for Irish monks in Iceland is lacking. No archaeological remains of any kind have been discovered; the surest mementoes of occupation are the "papar" (ie priest) place names.

## Viking Exodus

According to Snorri Sturluson, the greatest of Icelandic saga writers, the Norwegians who apparently chased the Irish away were themselves fugitives. When Harald Fairhair became the first king of Norway in 872, he immediately set about mopping up the opposition, seizing the property of defeated chieftains and so forth. Of the 400 names mentioned in the *Landnámabók (Book of Settlements)*, which lists the first

### ST BRENDAN IN ICELAND

St Brendan and crew were offshore in their boat when an inhabitant appeared: "he was all hairy and hideous, begrimed with fire and smoke". Sensing danger, St Brendan made a precautionary sign of the cross and urged the oarsmen to pull harder. "The savage man…rushed down to the shore, bearing in his hand a pair of tongs with a burning mass of slag of great size and intense heat, which he flung at once after the servants of Christ… 'Soldiers of Christ', said St Brendan, '… we are now on the confines of Hell'". He was not the last visitor to believe that eruptive Mount Hekla was the entrance to Hell.

mitochondrial DNA revealed that almost half of the women who originally settled in Iceland were actually from Britain and Ireland.

The best-known story about the early Norwegians, told in the *Landnámabók*, concerns two foster brothers, Ingólfur Arnarson (the official "First Settler" of Iceland) and Hjörleifur Hróð-marsson, who spent a winter in Iceland and were so impressed that they returned with two ships piled high with household goods. They were accompanied by family, friends and 10 slaves procured in Ireland. The two brothers parted company on reaching Iceland, Ingólfur

going to the southwest coast (and later to the site of Reykjavík) and Hjörleifur to the south, near present-day Vík.

Hjörleifur was soon faced with a rebellion by his Irish slaves because they resented having to share plough-pulling duties with his only ox. Almost all the sagas carry disparaging remarks about the character of Irish slaves, and this lot were evidently no exception. They first killed the ox, blamed it on a bear and then laid an ambush for Hjörleifur and his companions when they went to hunt the bear. As the hunters fanned out, the slaves overwhelmed them

*The Saga Museum in Reykjavík.*

## LAYING CLAIM TO LAND

The first Viking settlers laid claim to as much land as they thought they could manage, usually by throwing the pillars of the wooden high seats (a symbol of their authority) from their longboats and making their homes wherever they washed ashore. This tradition supposedly allowed the god Thor to choose the location.

The steady influx of new settlers meant rationing the remaining land by a process known as "carrying the fire". The owner of the ship bringing a group of immigrants was a chieftain or man of substance. The rest of the party would be families and attendant slaves or "thralls". The land they were entitled to was as much as could be encircled by a ring of bonfires, with the

proviso that they had to be lit with the same torch in one day and that, when burning, they were visible from one another. The criterion for women settlers – implying that some arrived independently – was the area that a two-year-old heifer could lap in a day.

The arable coastline was gradually settled in a similar pattern to that which is seen today, with most inhabitants on the coast, especially in the southwest. The interior – "nothing but ice and fire" – was out of bounds and remained so for all intents and purposes until the early 20th century. It still remains mostly uninhabited, with only a few farmers eking out a living from the starkly beautiful but barren land.

one by one. They abducted the women, piled into a boat and decamped to an offshore island.

The discovery of the hunters' bodies shocked Ingólfur. Death at the hands of a slave was such a shameful fate that he could only think that his brother's Christian tendencies had caused him to neglect his pagan sacrifices. The rebels were tracked down to their island refuge and surprised in the middle of a meal of roast puffin. Those who escaped being killed there and then were probably mindful of the penalties meted out to slaves who rose against their masters. One Irish slave, perhaps understandably unwilling to

had not long been settled, however, when the whole cycle of emigration repeated itself and for the same reasons: either land hunger, adventurism or falling foul of authority. Erik the Red was a prime example of the last. Already banished from Norway for murder, he was in turn banished from Iceland for more of the same. Having sailed off to the west and found somewhere else to settle, he then attempted to persuade others to join him. To succeed, he needed an attractive name for his new land, and in this he set a precedent for estate-agency hyperbole ever after. It was such a lush paradise, he told

*Erik the Red's son Leifur sights America.*

forgive a master for castrating him (among other grievances), had tried to cut his own throat and consequently suffered the agony of a red-hot wash basin placed on his belly with predictably gruesome results. Nevertheless, he survived – but only to be buried alive in a bog. The rebellious slaves fled to cliffs and threw themselves off. The island setting for this unpromising start to Icelandic history was Heimaey, one of the island group known thereafter as the Vestmannaeyjar (Westmann or "Irish" Islands).

### Dividing up the island

The Age of Settlement (874–930) followed these pioneering efforts, and soon the coastline was more or less fully occupied by settlers. Iceland

prospective settlers, that only one name would do: Greenland. Enough people believed him to fill 25 ships, but only 14 ships survived the voyage to the promised land.

### Vikings in America

The Vínland sagas (the *Greenlanders' Saga* and the *Saga of Eric the Red*) credit Erik's son, Leifur, with discoveries even farther afield. Old Erik would have been a partner in his son's journey, but en route to the ship leaving Greenland he was thrown from his horse and injured a foot. Leifur set sail, but his first port of call was a place so dismally useless that there was no point in stretching his imagination beyond "Helluland" ("Stoneland" – northern Labrador).

Conditions to the south improved, hence it was dubbed "Markland" ("Woodland"). Further still, he came across a climate so mild that it seemed not to require winter fodder for cattle. It was clearly a worthy contender for settlement, the more so when Leifur's German foster father returned from a sortie jabbering and "rolling his eyes in all directions and pulling faces". The German had found grapes growing: knowing what a delicious drink could made by fermenting them, he was understandably overcome by his discovery. It was thus that they gave the name "Vínland" to the future America.

when they reached Vínland and, making the false accusation that they had insulted her, ordered Þorstein ("thou miserable wretch") to kill both of them and their party of 30 men and five women. Þorstein did as he was told but drew the line at killing the women. "Give me an axe," said the ghastly Freydís.

As Freydís was soon to discover, the greatest barrier to settlement in the New World was the hostility of the natives. "They were small and evil-looking, and their hair was coarse; they had large eyes and broad cheekbones." Her crew retreated in bewilderment when attacked

*Norsemen taking possession of Iceland.*

> *Every free man was entitled to attend the meetings of the Alþingi, and the occasion acted as a magnet for the entire population.*

## The explorations of Freydís

Leifur's observations inspired a surge of voyages to this wonderful place, including one by his dreadful half-sister Freydís in a joint venture with two Icelanders, Helgi and Finnbogi. Freydís seems to have inherited Old Erik's worst characteristics – the sagas refer darkly to her "evil mind". She had married her husband Þorstein only for his money and despised him. Freydís fell out with Helgi and Finnbogi

by these tribesmen armed with catapults, a weapon new to the Vikings. Freydís snatched the sword of a man killed by a stone and faced the attackers. Yanking out a breast, she gave it a resounding thump with the flat of her sword. The Indians were as alarmed by this as the Vikings had been by their catapults. They bolted to their boats and paddled off at speed.

The lure of the land of wine was strong, but repeated attempts to follow in Freydís's wake were to prove similarly unsuccessful. Although the land was excellent, they could never live there in safety, so they made ready to leave the place and return home. Attempts continued at least until 1347, which has led to the theory that Christopher Columbus was inspired by

Icelandic stories about this distant land. These stories were probably still being recounted in seafaring circles when in 1477, according to his son Fernando, Columbus called at Iceland as a crew member of an English ship.

## The Icelandic commonwealth

Back in 10th-century Iceland, the displaced chieftains were determined never again to be relieved of their traditional authority by a single ruler. They entrenched themselves in their respective areas, or þings, and were called goðar, a word derived from "god". The com-

in promoting the development of a distinctive culture and help to explain, for example, why the language remained uniquely homogeneous without a trace of local dialects.

Although the Alþingi was the supreme spiritual and temporal authority, it was not allowed to raise a military force or to exercise police authority. Moreover, the powers of the Law-speaker were deliberately circumscribed so that the office could not be used as a springboard to monarchy; when a chieftain turned up with as many as 1,500 men to support him in a feud, there was nothing the Law-speaker could do.

*Archaeological remains in the southwest.*

monwealth Alþingi, created in 930, was a parliament whose history is almost continuous to the present day. Presided over by a Speaker or Law-speaker, it was an acknowledgement that certain matters required a central authority. Legal disputes and new legislation were settled by the Lögrétta (Law Council), the nub of the parliament, composed of chieftains and their non-voting advisers. Lesser cases were dealt with by courts for each "Quarter" of the land, made up of 36 chieftains.

The Alþingi met for two weeks every year at Þingvellir, a point roughly in the middle of the most densely populated part of Iceland and possessing a remarkable natural amphitheatre. These annual reunions were a great influence

The Alþingi therefore had considerable difficulty living up to its ideals. In 1012, for example, a litigant who suspected that his case was slipping away on a legal technicality unleashed his private army. The plain of Þingvellir was strewn with corpses before proceedings could be resumed. Litigation abounded, but the law was so complicated, and the society so riddled with vendettas, that the due process of the courts was forever on a knife-edge.

## Life in the longhouses

Settlers tried to recreate the conditions of pre-monarchical Norway as far as local conditions permitted. In Norway, farmsteads were a collection of separate wooden buildings, one for sleeping, another for cooking and so on. Although the *Íslendingabók* says that Iceland "was covered with wood between the mountains and the sea" at the time of the Settlement, its trees were quickly cut down for fuel and building, and timber was in short supply ever afterwards. The Icelandic farmstead was therefore a single unit, a row of rooms with common walls and a turf roof. Only the framework of the walls was timber; the rest was made up of stones and sod. While the Norwegian *stofa* or living-dining quarters were often large enough to accommodate several hundred guests, the

*Viking figurines.*

Icelanders could not heat such a space. Buildings became smaller and the windows fewer.

Larger farmsteads able to afford the luxury of timber imported from Norway maintained the tradition of large festive halls, which also served as religious temples. In the winter a fire was lit in a hearth at the centre of the hall, the smoke being left to find its way out through shuttered apertures in the roof. The chieftain occupied a high seat at one end with the guests lining benches on either side, their backs to the wall. "The flesh of the sacrificed animals, after being boiled in a large kettle over the fire," says a 19th-century study, "was served up to these rude banqueters, who frequently amused themselves by throwing the bones at one another, the manner in which they were placed on the opposite sides of the hall being very convenient for indulging in this elegant pastime."

Farmsteads in the Middle Ages were also equipped with an early version of the sauna, water being poured over a stone stove in the bath house *(baðstofa)* to produce vapour. The early settlers evidently made full use of water from numerous hot springs to luxuriate in hot baths.

## Early customs

Wool was the main clothing material used by the settlers, and was woven and coloured with mineral and vegetable dyes. According to the sagas, Skarphéðinn, the ill-fated young man whom we met at the opening of this history, made his entrance at one Alþingi in a blue mantle, blue striped trousers with a silver belt, and high shoes. His hair was combed back behind his ears, and round his head was a gold embroidered silk ribbon.

Like all young men, Skarphéðinn was addicted to what amounted to the national sports, horse-fighting (theoretically a contest between animals) and a kind of ball game called *knattleikur* (see box).

Marriages were arranged by the male heads of families; young men could veto the decision, but brides had no say in the matter. Once accepted as a wife, the woman acquired considerable property rights and other privileges, but these did not extend to denying the husband his concubines. The lawcode Grágas only cites three serious grounds for divorce; but the sagas suggest that either partner might terminate the marriage for a host of reasons, from physical abuse to cross-dressing.

### A VIOLENT PASTIME

*Knattleikur* was a game from the sagas, but it is hard to work out what the rules were. "Þorgrímur was unable to hold his own against Gísli, who threw him down and carried the ball away. Gísli sought again to take the ball, but Þorgrímur held it fast. Then Gísli threw him down so violently that he skinned his knees and knuckles, and blood was running from his nose... Gísli took the ball in one jump, threw it between the shoulders of Þorgrímur so that he fell forwards, and said: 'The ball on broad shoulders broke, which is not to be complained of'. At the end of the game, the two players part "not as good friends as before".

Þör ___ ___ ___
hme Jötni z Dreg
hier Midgardz Or
reidist Ymi z reid
hamarinn Miölnu
vill Liösta han þ h
ise. so sem lesa ma i d
Dæmi Saugu Er þku

# THE COMING OF CHRISTIANITY

**Although Iceland's conversion to Christianity was at times turbulent, it ushered in a period of relative stability and a literary golden age.**

On the rung of government below the Alþingi, the Icelandic chieftains fought tooth and nail to preserve their individual authority. The chieftainships were in reality more like political parties than regional entities. Dissatisfied "subjects" were at liberty to switch their allegiance – and divert their taxes – to some other chieftain, even one who lived at the opposite extremity of the land. These floating constituencies acted as a slight brake on the wilder excesses of ambitious chieftains; the rough and ready equilibrium, however, was severely tested by the advent of organised Christianity.

> Too many of the initial Christian converts in Iceland merely paid lip service to avoid paying the pagan temple tolls, which did not go down well with the chieftains for whom the tolls were a source of income.

## An Irish curse

The *Landnámabók* relates that Irish monks once lived at Kirkjubæjarklaustur ("Church Farm Cloister"); and that when they vacated the land, they left behind a curse on any pagan who occupied the site. The curse seems to have delivered, at least in the case of pagan settler Hildir Eysteinsson; he dropped dead as soon as he laid eyes on his new home.

Norwegian settlers arriving from the British islands must at least have encountered Christianity, but paganism was the new country's religion of choice. Icelandic paganism was a mixture of the old Norse deities, spirits who took on the likeness of men or beasts, and fetishes which made trees and waterfalls objects of veneration. Temples were built in holy places,

*Þorgeir, the Law-speaker at the Alþingi of AD 1,000, who decided in favour of Christianity.*

ritual taking the form of animal, and possibly human, sacrifices. One of the more concerted efforts to introduce orthodox Christianity is related in *Kristni saga* (although this is one of the less trustworthy sagas in terms of historical accuracy). Þorvaldur Koðránsson the Well-Travelled had been baptised in Germany in 981 by a Bishop Fridrek. With the bishop in tow, Þorvaldur returned to Iceland to convert his countrymen. The singing, ringing of bells, burning of incense and liturgical vestments made a favourable impression, but the number of genuine converts was disappointing.

Matters came to a head when Þorvaldur preached at the Alþingi of 984. Héðinn of

Svalbarð, an arch-opponent of Christianity, engaged comedians to mimic and poke fun at the two missionaries. Forgetting himself, Þorvaldur leapt on two of the comedians and killed them. Bishop Fridrek "bore all with patience" but was outlawed from Iceland with Þorvaldur. As they were preparing to sail, Þorvaldur spotted Héðinn sawing wood nearby: his parting shot was to kill him. "Because of this violent and unchristian act, Bishop Fridrek parted from him and returned to his native country." Þorvaldur abandoned his mission and became a travelling merchant.

## Viking converts

Christianity made greater advances under the influence of Olaf Tryggvason, the future king of Norway. Saga writer Snorri Sturluson describes him in *Heimskringla* as "the gladdest of all men and very playful, blithe and forgiving, very heated in all things, generous and prominent amongst his fellows, bold before all in battle"... although Snorri was basing this rather flattering description on an earlier hagiographical-style saga of the king. Olaf's early life gave no clue to the future. He was a full-blooded Viking marauder at the age of 12, terrorising the English coast with his fleet of five longships. Resting in the Scilly Isles, off England's southwest coast, he made the acquaintance of an elderly sage who put him on the True Path.

Olaf's conversion was electric and he returned to England in a different frame of mind, "for England was a Christian country and he was also a Christian". Olaf applied all his former Viking energies to the conversion of his countrymen in Norway. They were, in short, given no choice. As a travelling missionary he went nowhere without a few severed heads.

News of Olaf's missionary zeal reached Iceland: "It was rumoured that the people of Norway had changed religion, that they had discarded the old faith, and that King Olaf had Christianised the western colonies; Shetland, the Orkneys and the Faroe Islands." Olaf was clearly heading their way as if Iceland were just another Norwegian colony, an offensive presumption to those independent-minded settlers.

It was one such proud Icelander, Kjartan Ólafsson, who was cajoled into entering a swimming gala while on a visit to Trondheim. He found himself racing a powerful swimmer who was not content merely to beat him but ducked him repeatedly until he was on the point of losing consciousness. The graceless victor introduced himself as Olaf Tryggvason and suggested baptism. Kjartan thought it prudent to agree, as did other Icelanders who happened to be in Trondheim at the time. "When they accepted baptism," however, "it was usually for some ulterior motive, or because they regarded it as an interesting adventure."

## Brutal methods

The personal history of Þangbrand, the chaplain to whom Olaf entrusted the conversion of Iceland, was not reassuring. A 14th-century saga

*A wooden panel incised with a design depicting saints.*

of Olaf recounts: "[Þangbrand's] knowledge of the Christian doctrine might have made him a valuable man had not his violent temper and vicious habits rendered him unfit for so sacred a calling. He not only squandered the income of his parish, but he organised piratical raids to replenish his depleted stores, an unchristian conduct for which the king finally called him to account. Due repentance saved him from banishment, but he was sent instead as a missionary to Iceland."

Relying on his patron's proven formula of exemplary terror, Þangbrand won a few converts in the two years he spent in Iceland, but on returning to Norway in 999 he had to admit that the mission had not been a total success.

Olaf was furious and ordered the seizure and execution of all heathen Icelanders in Trondheim. The expatriate colony was then quite large and, freshly baptised, they were ordered to Iceland to spread the word. Their return coincided with the Alþingi of the year 1000.

Olaf was actually using Christianity as a cloak for his territorial ambitions on Iceland, and he first had to usurp the Christian party which had been developing in Iceland of its own accord. There had even been talk of the home-grown Christians setting up an alternative government, and the arrival of the Trondheim contin-

*Snorri Sturluson.*

gent in full battle array threatened to tip the country into civil war.

## A crucial decision

The *Íslendingabók*, a reliable early historical source, gives an account of the suspenseful gathering at the Alþingi. Þorgeir, the current Lawspeaker, asked for time to think. He spent a day and a night in his booth, lying in silence under an animal hide as he wrestled with the problem. Eventually he threw off the hide and made what has been described as "perhaps the most important oration ever delivered in Iceland". His speech was a masterpiece of compromise. Although a pagan, he came down on the side of the Christians, advising all parties to back

down and acknowledge that the law, and not any of them, was supreme. "It will prove true that when we sunder the law we end the peace."

The adoption of Christianity as the official religion in 1000 banned the worship of heathen gods in public, but not in private. Nor were the population required to give up their practices like exposing unwanted infants and eating horseflesh. Olaf's further plans for Iceland were never revealed because he died in battle at Svolder the same year. Olaf's Christian zealotry was his undoing. The war was the result of a grudge nursed by the wealthy Queen Sigrid of Sweden ever since Olaf first asked her to marry him and then withdrew the proposal when she declined his pre-condition: baptism as a Christian. "Why should I wed thee, thou heathen bitch?" he shouted, giving her a slap in the face to reinforce the point. "That," she replied icily, "may well be thy death." And so it proved.

Olaf Haraldsson, the future patron saint who succeeded to the Norwegian throne in 1016, appealed to Iceland's Christian leadership to tighten the loopholes which allowed pagan practices to continue. Their response was so satisfactory that he sent timber and a bell for a church to be constructed at Þingvellir, plus an English bishop, Bernhard the Book-wise, to speed up the conversion of the country.

One of the remaining obstacles to the establishment of orthodox Christianity was a shortage of priests. The chieftains regained a measure of authority by putting up themselves or equally unqualified nominees as candidates. As the choice of bishops had to be ratified by the Alþingi, the church was for a while fully integrated in the social system, and one chieftain at least "did everything in his power to strengthen Christianity". New bishoprics were set up at Hólar and Skálholt and these gradually became known as centres of learning.

## The literary Golden Age and descent into violence

Iceland enjoyed almost a century of relative peace after 1030. Long hours of darkness indoors encouraged story-telling, and the people as a whole were remarkably adept at it. An unusually large proportion of the population could read; the introduction of the Latin alphabet instead of clumsy Runic encouraged them to write as well. The Dark Ages elsewhere in Europe were characterised by clerics copying

*Today, the phrase "að leggjast undir feld", loosely translated as "to lie down under a hide", is used when someone chooses isolation to think something through.*

religious tracts in Latin. In Iceland people wrote in their own language – and about themselves.

The Icelandic sagas, universally acknowledged as one of the world's most important bodies of medieval literature, were first written down in the 12th century. This literary Golden Age, in which rich accounts of the religion, history, poetry, proverbs and imaginative tales of the Icelandic people were committed to calfskin, lasted for two centuries.

But this flowering of intellectual activity did not outstrip the country's tendencies towards political violence. The Alþingi of 1118 served as a reminder that government was still a hostage to the selfish machinations of chieftains. Proceedings against a notorious murderer named Mar degenerated into a bloody trial of strength between two chieftains which disrupted the Alþingi year after year. The general assembly passed numerous resolutions outlawing the culprits; they were laughed off.

The flaw in the legal system was that the Alþingi could not initiate prosecutions nor force its decisions on spirited opposition. A complicated web of murder led in 1163 to violent clashes in what became known as the "Stone-Throwing Summer". The combatants were said to have been driven to such rage that they were hurling stones so heavy that normal men, when they tried to clean up the aftermath, could not lift them at all.

In the course of the 12th century, the country was divided between bishops aligned with the seat of Trondheim and half a dozen clans in a state of perpetual internecine warfare. At the same time economic conditions deteriorated and, as the Icelanders had no timber for shipbuilding, they were increasingly dependent on Norwegian suppliers and shippers. Matters came to a head in the so-called Sturlung Age (1230–64), notable for its bewildering combination of horrific violence and intellectual and literary endeavour, the latter having been described as the Icelandic Renaissance.

The Alþingi's impotence in the face of feuds that were tearing apart the land's most powerful families underlined the fact that anarchy had taken over. The king of Norway was as ever ready and eager to step in and the papal legate approved, saying "it was unreasonable that [Icelanders] did not serve a king like every other country in the world." In 1262 the Alþingi submitted to King Haakon by granting him the right to collect taxes. In practice, submission left the Icelandic chieftains in control of their own affairs as before except that they were forbidden to wage war on one another. The people won a respite from constant upheaval, but by the end of the 13th century it was apparent that Iceland had started an unstoppable decline.

*View of Þingvellir valley.*

## SNORRI STURLUSON

The violence of the Sturlung Age was chronicled by Snorri Sturluson, whose family gave the Age its name. They were descendants of the saga hero Egill Skallagrímsson, and Snorri may have written *Egils Saga*. Born in 1179, Snorri married an heiress and became a Law-speaker at the Alþingi. He was despatched to Norway as a diplomat, and when he returned to Iceland in 1241 against the King of Norway's wishes, he was murdered on his orders. Snorri's undisputed memorial is the *Heimskringla*, a history of the kings of Norway whose breathtaking scope is reflected in the first words: "The face of earth inhabited by man...".

# THE DARK AGES

A combination of absolute foreign rule, trade
restrictions and a series of natural disasters
led to the darkest period in Iceland's history.

**T**he terms of Iceland's submission to
Norway were contained in the "Ancient
Covenant" and every taxpayer was
obliged to pay an annual royal tribute in
the native wool. Royal officials replaced the
*goðar*, and King Haakon appointed Snorri's
murderer, Gissur, earl of Iceland as the Free
State disintegrated. Even the weather served
as a portent: it turned colder, and all over
Scandinavia men dispensed with kilts and put
on trousers. Temperatures continued to drop,
necessitating underwear.

Gissur's "character and previous record", says
Knut Gjerset, an eminent 20th-century Icelan-
dic-American historian, "rendered him unfit to
maintain peace and order, which was his principal official duty". The *Íslendinga saga* relates
that in 1264 his enemies stormed his daughter's
wedding, killing 25 guests while Gissur hid in
a tub of whey. His revenge was to lay waste the
Rangárvellir district and then invite his enemies
to a peace conference. Their leader was executed,
whereupon Gissur announced his retirement to
a monastery. The Norwegian king decreed that
Iceland would try to survive without any earls.

*Laki volcano in Skaftafell National Park.*

## Imposing the law

Iceland clearly needed a new framework of
government, starting with a new legal system.
From 1274 to 1276, King Magnús VI, "the
Law-Mender", modernised Norway's law-code,
applying it to every part of his kingdom including Iceland. The code proved so efficient that
it served with very few amendments until the
19th century. The crown, now seen as part of
the divine order, was made the supreme legal
authority, and lawbreakers were answerable to
it, not to the injured party as previously. Murder, robbery, rape, counterfeiting, forgery and

seduction became capital offences, but judges
were supposed to administer the law dispas-
sionately. "For we are to hate evil deeds," the
judge's manual advised, "but love men by natural instinct as our fellow Christians, but most
of all their souls."

For the first time Iceland acquired a national
army rather than dozens of private armies,
although it was only 240 strong and the men
were sent to Norway in defence of the realm
against Danish and Hanseatic threats. The power
of the church was strengthened, but rested
increasingly in the hands of foreign bishops.
Church reforms required clerical celibacy; even
subdeacons who had been married for years and
had several children had to give up their wives.

Public dissatisfaction in a generally peaceful era was provoked by something that would haunt Iceland for centuries to come: the control of trade. Iceland had to trade to survive, and with no merchant fleet of its own the country was at the mercy of Norwegian merchants. The king was supposed to ensure that a certain number of ships called regularly to deliver essential supplies and take away the exports which paid for them. All too often the ships never came, which was especially disastrous if famine or natural disasters struck – and they did, with appalling frequency.

*Hverfell volcano.*

## Years of disaster

The 14th century presaged a run of calamities almost beyond belief. Hekla erupted repeatedly; each time a pall of darkness settled over southern Iceland and the following winter was unusually severe. Heavy snowfalls thawed to become devastating floods. Hekla's 1389 eruption could be felt and heard all over the island, according to contemporary accounts: "Fire arose not only from the mountain but from the woods above Skarð, the eruption being so violent that two mountains were formed with a chasm between them. In the neighbourhood hot springs welled up, forming lakes of boiling water." Smallpox and other epidemics added to the misery.

The industrious Hanseatic merchants – by then well-established on Norway's west coast – undoubtedly could and would have traded with Iceland, but the Norwegian king set a precedent later to be slavishly followed by the Danes, declaring that trade with Iceland was a crown monopoly. Iceland thus went through the extremes of either being completely neglected or facing demands for greater quantities of the prized codfish than the population could afford.

The Scandinavian union of Norway, Denmark and Sweden effected at Kalmar in 1397 transferred the sovereignty of Iceland from Norway to Denmark. The Danes were even more remote and less interested in Iceland than the Norwegians, and, in the country, conditions deteriorated accordingly: "Our laws provide that six ships should come hither from Norway every year, which has not happened for a long time," reads a plaintive message to the Danish king, "a cause from which Your Grace and our poor country has suffered most grievous harm. Therefore, trusting in God's grace and your help, we have traded with foreigners who have come hither peacefully on legitimate business, but we have punished those fishermen and owners of fishing-smacks who have robbed and caused disturbances."

## Smugglers and pirates

The unauthorised foreign traders were mostly English and their activities would be Iceland's main access to the outside world for centuries to come. They provided essential commodities in exchange for fish, which would probably have been acceptable to the Icelanders had the English not decided that they were better equipped to catch the fish themselves. This fundamental conflict of interest would continue – all the way to the notorious "Cod Wars" between Iceland and England in the 1960s and 1970s.

The activities of the English traders were therefore a mixed blessing as far as Icelanders were concerned, but to King Eric VII of Denmark, who held the trade monopoly, they were an unmitigated outrage and he protested to King Henry V of England over the illegal trade.

Pirates among the English merchants – the distinction between them and merchants could not have been finer – were quick to recognise the opportunities presented by an undefended coast, and their looting of Icelandic churches

*A violent storm in 1419 revealed the extent of illegal trade. The storm lasted only three hours, and afterwards there were 25 English ships wrecked on Icelandic soil.*

was an echo of what the Vikings had done in England. Attempts to stop the pirates were generally in vain. On one occasion, a couple of royal commissioners ordered to arrest the offenders were themselves bundled into a ship and sent to the dungeons of England.

Eric's successor, King Christian I, also tried to defend his kingdom, appointing the chieftain Björn Þorleifsson to collect customs duties from legitimate traders and to see off the pirates. Just like the commissioners before him, Þorleifsson was captured and despatched to England, along with his wife Ólöf. He managed to return to Iceland, but was killed by English pirates at Hafnarfjörður and his son captured. Ólöf paid a ransom to get her son back and then recruited an army to deal with the English. The affair escalated into a full-blown war between England and Denmark in 1469 although, ironically,

*A sea map from the 16th century.*

## WHALES, SERPENTS AND LOBSTERS

Huge whales and other mysterious creatures to be found in the remote seas around Iceland featured in numerous stories during Iceland's Dark Age. The country was so cut off at this time that there were few foreigners who were able to contradict the account of 16th-century German writer and cartographer Sebastian Münster. "In the mountain of Hecla," he wrote, "there is a great abyss which cannot be sounded and here appear often people who have recently drowned as though they were alive. Their friends beg them to come home but they reply with great sighs that they must go into Hecla and then vanish forthwith." Münster went on to describe whales

"as big as mountains... which capsize large ships and are not afraid of the sound of trumpets or of empty barrels thrown at them with which they gambol. It sometimes happens that seamen encounter a whale and if in distress cast anchor upon it thinking it to be an island... Many people in Iceland build their houses out of bones and skeletons of these whales". He also described sea serpents "200 or 300 feet long" which wound themselves around ships and "a fearful beast like unto a rhinoceros with a pointed nose and back [which] eats crabs called lobsters twelve feet long". These hefty lobsters, moreover, were said to be easily capable of seizing and strangling a man.

the illegal traders and their customers on the spot seem to have continued their prickly but profitable dealings without even noticing.

The English traders did, however, run into stiff competition from the Hanseatic League, and the Danish kings at last found an effective weapon – to play off one against the other in what amounted to an auction for limited trading concessions.

## The long decline

The auctions may have lined royal pockets but did nothing for Iceland. The cumulative effect of natural disaster and stifled trade was simply too much. The most conclusive evidence of national lethargy was that literary activity ceased. The only creativity, which did not amount to much, was the lightweight balladry of wandering minstrels.

The extent to which Iceland became dispirited and defenceless is revealed by an invasion in 1627 by 3,000 Barbary pirates commanded by a "Rais Murad" who was actually a Dutchman named Jan Janszoon. Having run wild through Grindavík, Faxaflói and the East Fjords, the pirates descended on Heimaey, one of the Vestmannaeyjar (West-mann Islands) "and overran the whole island with loud yells, massacring the terror-stricken and

*Ships off the Iceland coast, c. 1860.*

## LIVING CONDITIONS IN THE DARK AGES

Life was harsh for most Icelanders. A text excerpt from Jón Jónsson, who was probably a sheriff living in the north of Iceland during the 18th or 19th century, brings living conditions during the Dark Ages into focus: "The living room of the common peasant farmstead was usually not covered with boards on the inside. One could see between rafters to the grass-covered roof, which soon looked like ordinary sod, and from which mildew and cobwebs were hanging. The floor was uncovered, consisting only of earth trampled hard. But during heavy rains when the roof was leaking water dripped down, and it soon became a pool of mud through which people waded. The walls along which the bedsteads were nailed fast were covered with a grey coat of mildew, and green slime was constantly trickling down the walls, especially in the winter. Bed clothes were very scarce among the poor people. Old hay, seaweed or twigs did service as a mattress, and a few blankets constituted the covering." To make life even more wretched, there was a crippling shortage of firewood. In some houses the family slept on a platform with calves and lambs occupying the space underneath; this at least provided some heat which was conserved by keeping windows to a minimum both in size and numbers. A thin membrane served as glass, but it only allowed through a dim light.

helpless inhabitants". The youngest and strongest of the population were herded into their ships; the others into a warehouse which was then put to the torch. The local priest, a composer of hymns named Jón Þorsteinsson, was struck dead while kneeling in prayer; his wife and children and a second priest were taken to the ships, making a total of 242 captives bound for Africa.

The surviving priest was released the following spring to present the ransom demand to King Christian IV. He reported that many of the captives were already dead. The girls had been sold off to harems and the young men committed to lives as galley slaves. Some of the men had become pirates themselves. It took five years to raise funds to secure the release of 37 captives, but in the end only 13 got back to Iceland.

Heimaey never recovered from the decimation of its population, and it was set even farther back by the colossal volcanic eruption in 1783 which poisoned the fish in the waters around the island. A British traveller in the early 19th century related tales of a dwindling population of barely 200 souls, whose children were dying of malnutrition because they ate nothing but the oily flesh of seabirds.

## A dismal outpost

Iceland was almost oblivious of the Reformation in Europe. The people were settled, if forlornly, as Roman Catholics, and the Reformation arrived not as an intellectual awakening or rebellion against the old order but as a series of dimly understood royal decrees from Copenhagen backed by military threats.

The Church in Iceland had slipped back into old habits. "Although priests were not allowed to marry," says one of the sagas, "holy and godfearing fathers would permit them (I know indeed not with what authority) to have concubines instead of wedded wives… It was easy for the priests to get women, so that they often got the daughters, sisters and relatives of chieftains for their helpmates. Proper and lawful agreement was entered into by both parties, so that nothing was lacking of real marriage but the name."

## Feuding bishops

Old habits also affected Iceland's two bishops. Rivalry between Ögmundur Pálsson of Skálholt and Jón Arason of Hólar led to a face-off at the

Cod was Iceland's main trading commodity; others included sulphur, tallow and sheepskin, as well as the pure white Icelandic falcon, by far the best for falconry.

1526 Alþingi between Ögmundur's force of 1,300 men and Jón's 900. Full-scale battle was averted by an agreement to let the issue be settled by a duel between champions. The duel was fought on an island in the Öxará River. Ögmundur's man was declared the winner,

*Mosaic from the Hólar bishopric.*

but the next day his cathedral at Skálholt was mysteriously destroyed by fire. Ironically this softened his feelings towards Jón because he believed the latter could only have got away with arson with God at least slightly on his side.

In Denmark and Norway, the Reformation was primarily a dynastic struggle with many nobles waiting anxiously for a pretext to despoil the rich estates of the Roman Catholic Church. That ambition extended to Church possessions in Iceland too, and in 1541 two warships were despatched to the island to push a new Church code through the Alþingi, with instructions to use force if necessary.

Bishop Ögmundur, now 80 years old and blind, mounted a spirited defence, but was dragged from his bed into a Danish ship. His captors offered to release him for a ransom: his sister's money and deeds to all his property were duly handed over, but the ship sailed with Ögmundur still aboard. He is thought to have died on the voyage.

That only left Bishop Jón, Ögmundur's former adversary and by now an old man himself. King Christian III, an arch-Protestant king, took exception to Jón's continuing defiance and summoned him to Copenhagen in 1548. Jón ignored the summons and chose instead to raise a rebellion. The geriatric bishop led

*Religious imagery from the Hólar bishopric.*

100 men down to the Protestant stronghold of Skálholt and captured the Lutheran bishop, before marching on to the island of Viðey to attack the Danish administration there. On 27 June 1550, an exasperated King Christian outlawed the stubborn bishop and ordered his arrest, possibly after hearing that Jón had sent a request for military assistance to Charles V, Holy Roman Emperor.

## Demise of the rebel

One of Jón's enemies, chieftain Daði Guðmundsson, brought the bishop's crusade to an end, defeating and capturing him in battle at Sauðafell. For several days his captors debated what to do with him. A priest suggested over breakfast one morning that he knew how the prisoner could most safely be kept. Asked to elaborate, he replied that an axe and the earth would do the trick. This suggestion was at first received as a joke, but on reflection the idea commended itself. On 7 November 1550 Bishop Jón, and two sons captured with him, were beheaded at Skálholt, providing Scandinavian Catholicism with its first and last martyrs.

News of the executions aroused bitter resentment. Three masked men carrying coffins presented themselves at Skálholt and asked for the bodies. The request was granted, bells were attached to the coffins, and the cortège moved through the countryside to the chiming of church bells. The bishop was buried at Hólar and still remains something of a national hero.

The overthrow of the Catholic party soon followed Jón's death, and the king moved in quickly on its properties. He considered using the income from the confiscated lands to build schools, but decided to keep the money himself. Thereafter, one quarter of the tithes payable to the Church were to be diverted to the royal purse, as were all fines imposed in lawsuits. Other reforms were progressively introduced. Adultery became punishable by death, although only on the third offence: men were hanged, women drowned. The eating of horseflesh was banned, and persistent absence from Lutheran services was punished by flogging.

The crux of the matter was that these major changes – the confiscation of the Catholic Church's property, the imposition of new taxes, and alterations to the law – were all carried out without reference to the Alþingi or with any regard for the existing Icelandic procedure. The country was, in short, feeling the burden of absolute monarchy in Denmark, and things were to get a lot worse.

## Crushed by foreign rule

Trade was always Iceland's Achilles heel, and absolute rule in Denmark heralded a tyrannical monopoly from 1602 worse than anything that had preceded it. Iceland was obliged to buy everything it needed exclusively from court-appointed Danish trading companies at prices fixed by the company. It was a case of paying what the company demanded or doing without. With Iceland thus held to ransom, it was no surprise that the price of imports rose by

500 percent over a period in which the prices paid for home-grown products remained static. The purchase price of Icelandic fish was barely a fifth of what foreign buyers would readily have paid.

In 1662 matters were made worse by the division of the country into four commercial districts. These were prohibited from trading with one another; they could deal only with Danes and on the same Danish terms. Clandestine deals with foreign vessels were made more difficult by a Danish naval blockade and more dangerous by draconian penalties. A cer-

> *"Up till 1800," says one of the annals, "the Icelanders, both men and women, dressed according to their national style, but after that they gradually adopted Danish styles."*

tain Páll Torfason took a couple of fishing lines from an English ship in return for some knitted goods which the Danish merchants had previously declined, and lost the entire contents of his house. Holmfast Guðmundsson was flogged for selling fish to a near neighbour who was technically in another district.

The colonial administrators were nothing if not an extension of the arrogant court officials in Denmark. If they needed a horse, the first peasant they asked had to provide one. If it was a question of crossing a fjord, the nearest farmer was required to drop everything and get his boat out. A grumble meant a sound flogging.

Unsurprisingly, the authority of the ancient Alþingi was undermined and in 1800, on royal orders, it was abolished. The new law court which took over its political functions and the surviving bishoprics were concentrated in Reykjavík, the population of which was a mere 300. The sense of separate identity was all but lost.

## Litany of wretchedness

The volcanic eruptions and earthquakes which had caused havoc in 1618, 1619, 1625, 1636, 1660 and 1693 continued practically unabated in 1727, 1732, 1755 and 1783. The last in the series, the eruption of Lakagígar (Laki), is still regarded as the worst in world history, scattering ash to every corner of the globe. An account from a Scottish traveller, visiting 30 years after the eruption, listed the

Icelanders' personal losses as 11,461 cattle, 190,448 sheep and 28,013 horses. Following the human casualties of the eruption there was famine due to the haze of smoke and ash, and a smallpox epidemic. Over 20 percent of the population died as a result of the eruption and ensuing disasters.

Summing up the misery of life in 18th-century Iceland, the Chief Justice Magnús Stephensen, a young man of 21 when Lakagígar wreaked its destruction, said Iceland experienced "forty-three years of distress due to cold winters, ice-floes, failures of fisheries,

*Glacial scenery in the southeast.*

shipwrecks, inundations, volcanic eruptions, earthquakes, epidemics and contagious diseases among men and animals, which often came separately, but often in connection with and as a result of one another".

## Literary rescue

In a country where "emaciated tottering skeletons" had on occasion survived famine by boiling and eating their own clothes, it is unsurprising that literary pursuits were low on the agenda. In the early 18th century, however, the scholar Árni Magnússon (see page 87) spent 10 years gathering up Iceland's saga manuscripts. Without his foresight, who knows how many vellums might have vanished forever.

An engraving of 19th-century Icelanders.

# THE PUSH FOR INDEPENDENCE

**Upheavals throughout Europe put pressure on Denmark to loosen its hold over Iceland: by 1944 Iceland had become a republic.**

Iceland, like Scandinavia in general, missed out on the impact of the American War of Independence and the French Revolution. It didn't even feel the whiff of liberalism which passed through Denmark at the end of the 18th century under the auspices of Dr Johann Struensee.

Struensee was a German physician who was engaged to treat the half-witted King Christian VII and contrived to run Denmark personally. He introduced freedom of the press and personal liberties including the decriminalisation of adultery. His vested interest in this particular reform was the clandestine affair he was enjoying with the young Queen Caroline Matilda, sister of England's King George III. The affair was discovered, the law repealed, and Struensee's severed head was posted on a pole to advertise that the old absolutist order was back in charge.

Denmark's misfortune, broadly speaking, was to choose the losing side in the Napoleonic Wars. The British fleet destroyed the Royal Danish Navy at the Battle of Copenhagen in 1801 and then bombarded Copenhagen itself in 1807. The entire Danish naval fleet was confiscated, along with 92 merchant vessels. With Denmark's seafaring heart torn out, poor Iceland was left more isolated than ever. British merchants were eager to take over Icelandic trade themselves, and this provided the backdrop to the most bizarre chapter in Iceland's history, the "revolution" of 1809.

## An unlikely liberator

The central figure was Jørgen Jørgensen, born in Copenhagen in 1780, a son of the royal watchmaker. A brilliant but unruly student, he found himself serving in the British Navy

*A young woman in Icelandic dress photographed in the early 20th century.*

almost by accident as "John Johnson", and later changed his name officially to Jorgen Jorgenson. His early career was chequered, and he was actually on parole in England for gambling debts when he was taken on as an interpreter for an opportunistic and unofficial English trade mission to Iceland.

After one abortive trip, the traders landed in Reykjavík to find that the governor, anticipating their return, had plastered the town with notices prohibiting any trade with foreigners under pain of beheading. The governor, Count Trampe, was not just enforcing Danish policy; he happened to own the one Danish ship still trading with Iceland.

Jorgenson then came up with a bright idea: depose Trampe, reconvene the Alþingi (abolished nine years previously), declare Iceland's independence from Denmark, and make a treaty of alliance and trade with England. Some, but not all, of the English traders thought this an excellent idea. To cries of "Traitor, you'll hang for this", Trampe was marched out of his office and locked up in one of the English ships. Jorgenson could get to work.

Issuing proclamations under the self-appointed title of "His Excellency, the Protector of Iceland, Commander-in-Chief by

*Portrait of Jón Sigurðsson.*

## ROMANTICS VS RATIONALIST

The 18th and 19th centuries saw a revival of intellectual activity in Iceland. The rationalists, under the leadership of Magnús Stephensen, railed against the lack of foreign influence in the language, which had remained virtually pristine Old Norse, saying that it smacked of darkness and superstition. They advocated an intellectual *Aufklärung* which welcomed the best that the rest of the world could offer. The romantics, on the other hand, glorified Iceland's history and language. Their champion, Bjarni Thorarensen, wrote *Eldgamla Ísafold* to the tune of *God Save the King*, and his poems were mostly about heroic saga figures.

Sea and Land", Jorgenson promised the Icelanders "peace and happiness little known in recent years" and their own national flag – three white codfish on a blue background. His Excellency was just 30 years old. Backed up by 12 armed sailors, Jorgenson "liberated" Iceland by seizing the property of Danish merchants. The Icelanders were not sure how to react. The fearsome Trampe was a prisoner, but they could not be certain that he would remain so: the price of collaboration with the English if ever he regained office did not bear thinking about.

The new regime had been in existence for just nine weeks when a second British warship, *HMS Talbot*, hove into view under the command of Captain the Hon. Alexander Jones, the son of an Irish peer and not sympathetic to revolutionary activity. Jones suspected that the British government might also have certain reservations.

## The "revolution" quashed

The Hon. Alexander Jones's enquiries into what was going on – the flag was new to him, and he noticed that Jorgenson was building a fort at Arnarhóll – brought Iceland's "independence" to an end as perfunctorily as it had been created. "All proclamations, laws and appointments made by Mr Jorgen Jorgenson, since his arrival in this country, are to be abolished and totally null and void…"

In his memoirs, Jorgenson described the manner of his departure. He stepped into a fishing-boat and was rowed out to the departing warship by a crew of Icelanders: "So I went on board quietly, many of the poor natives shedding tears at my departure. It is true, indeed, that I left the island with regret. I had established liberty and freedom there without a drop of blood being spilt, or a single person committed to prison. "

He was jailed in a convict hulk on returning to England, released, imprisoned again for more gambling debts, did some sterling work for British Intelligence (at one point disguised as an Irish pilgrim), dashed off books on such weighty topics as the geography of Persia and Afghanistan, was sentenced to the gallows for selling the bedclothes from his London lodgings, was instead transported to Australia – and there served with distinction in the police force. He died in Hobart, Tasmania in 1844.

## A revival of spirit

The real price of Denmark's ultimately half-hearted alliance with Napoleon was paid at the postwar Vienna congress. Pressure from the victors forced Denmark to grant Norway its independence, albeit in a lopsided union with Sweden, and expectations rose in Iceland of a similar concession in the near future.

Visitors began to notice changes, and the foundations of Iceland's modern "cradle-to-grave" social security system caught the attention of English reformers. "We have no hesitation in saying," they reported, "that in

While parishes might keep a storehouse of emergency provisions for the destitute, the responsibility for actually looking after them was passed directly to the rate-payers. Thus, the number of paupers allocated to each depended on the value of the property owned. If the alimentor (the person who paid alimony, before the term became bound up with unhappy marriage) failed to provide adequate support, the pauper could complain to the district Þing. The alimentor who left a parish to escape the burden was liable to the kind of house-arrest known as exclusion.

*Washerwomen at the hot springs in Reykjavík, 1908.*

respect to the poor, an Icelandic parish was, to say the least, equally as well managed as an English one."

## Care for the poor

The basic principle was that any person incapacitated by age, infirmity or "misfortune" should in the first instance be maintained by the next of kin according to their ability to pay, the criterion being the value of their property. If circumstances required a pecking order, priority was given to a distressed mother followed by the father, children, brothers and sisters. If supporting some or all of these demonstrably exceeded a person's resources, the parish authorities stepped in.

The English observers thought the Icelandic system clearly superior to the English in one respect. "The Icelanders... do not charge themselves with the support of the poor without taking especial care to keep the number of paupers within due limits; a care which we have grossly neglected, and are now enduring the fearful consequences of our want of foresight."

The number of paupers was controlled by, for example, not allowing a man to marry until he had the means to support a family. Nor was a slave to be freed unless the owner could provide him with an adequate plot of land. If a freed slave became destitute through the former owner's neglect, he retained his freedom but was entitled to alimony.

*The first performance of Iceland's Thousand Years by Matthías Jochumsson, the present national anthem (now known as O God of Our Land), was given at the celebrations of the granting of home rule in 1874.*

The English observers made further notes: "Very stringent regulations were also passed to keep the poor within their respective parishes. Clothes and shoes might be given to a pauper of another parish, but any parishioner who furnished such a pauper with victuals, except he was merely passing through the parish to go to his own, rendered himself liable to the punishment of exclusion. The Icelanders also took care to make able-bodied paupers work for their living. Begging was not tolerated, especially at the Alþingi. If a beggar entered a booth on the Þingvellir plain, the booth-man might forcibly eject him, and every one who furnished such a beggar with meat, was liable to be punished with exclusion. All persons who wandered about the country for fifteen days and upwards were to be regarded as vagabonds... and punished accord-

*Reykjavík in the early 19th century.*

## A NATIONALIST HERO

Born in the West Fjords in 1811, Jón Sigurðsson, an Icelandic scholar and patriot, was educated at the University of Copenhagen. He has been called the greatest figure in modern Icelandic history. Curiously, he made his home in Copenhagen; from 1849 he merely spent alternate summers in Iceland during which time he presided over the Alþingi. His authority on Icelandic history and literature – he worked on the Árni Magnússon manuscript collection, and was president of the Icelandic Literary Society – gave his nationalist movement credibility in Danish eyes. He died in 1879, 25 years before the advent of Home Rule.

ingly. Besides other punishments to which they were liable, any one who thought proper might mutilate them in the manner practised in the East to qualify a man for the service of the seraglio" – this last sentence referring to castration.

## Unsteady steps towards freedom

Some of these comments must have been out-of-date by the time they were written. Swift social progress was obviously being made, but Iceland still had to wait until 1830 before the ripples of Norway's 1814 independence reached its shores. Even then, the concession was merely two seats among 70 on an advisory body to the Danish crown, based in Copenhagen. Prominent Icelanders such as the jurist Baldvin Einarsson protested against such feeble representation, and the romantics pressed for restoration of the Alþingi. In 1843 King Christian VIII issued a royal decree to reinstate an Alþingi consisting of 20 representatives chosen by a qualified electorate and six royal nominees. However, it was to serve merely as an advisory body on Icelandic affairs, and had no legislative power. The assemblies were not to be held at the old Þingvellir, as the romantics wished, but at Reykjavík, which would formally become the new capital.

Many felt that these gentle reforms did not go far enough, and believed the Alþingi should be held at Þingvellir, on lower franchise qualifications, and using Icelandic as the language of government. The nationalist cause was championed by the eclectic scholar Jón Sigurðsson, whose statue stands in Austurvöllur, the old town square in Reykjavík, opposite Parliament House. The nationalist movement demanded a totally independent national legislature and the ending of Denmark's final say over Icelandic judicial decisions.

Progress towards more substantial independence was delayed by Denmark's preoccupation with the Schleswig Holstein nightmare, a dispute with Prussia over the sovereignty of the frontier provinces, each with a divided population whose minorities refused to give in. Moreover, the Danish governor of Iceland, Jørgen Ditlev, was obstructive: he was suspected of applying for a private army to exorcise what he considered unlawful, pseudo-patriotic nonsense. While Denmark continued to turn a deaf ear to the fundamental issue of Icelandic independence, the trade monopoly was ended in 1854.

## The Icelandic exodus

With true independence still apparently unattainable, the newspaper *Norðanfari* suggested ironically in the 1870s that the only chance Icelanders had of tasting freedom was to emigrate en masse to Brazil or North America. As it was, Icelanders were soon leaving in such numbers that the newspaper changed its tune. People were asked to postpone their departure for a year or so in case things changed, and at the same time a number of teetotal societies sprang up. The aim was not so much a campaign against alcohol as to deny Denmark the revenue from the tax on drinks.

Under this kind of pressure, the king apparently bowed to the inevitable in 1874 by giving the Alþingi autonomy over domestic affairs, including finance. It was not quite what it seemed because he retained an absolute veto over everything the Alþingi did, but for the moment it was enough to celebrate, especially as the date coincided with the 1,000th anniversary of Iceland's settlement.

King Christian IX attended the festivities; Jón Sigurðsson was pointedly not invited, but it was said that in a private conversation afterwards the king asked him if Icelanders were satisfied with the new constitution. "As their chief wish had not been granted," he replied, "how could

*Scandinavian delegates presenting an address to the Icelanders in 1874.*

they be?". Sigurðsson recognised full independence or nothing.

## The first breakthrough

Full independence was a long time coming. Icelanders and Danes were generally talking at cross purposes. As far as the Danes were concerned, Iceland was inconceivable except as an integral part of the kingdom, although they were willing to tinker with semantics. One proposal would have made Christian IX "King of Denmark and Iceland" instead of just Denmark, with Iceland taken for granted. Iceland was in no mood for cosmetic compromise, and talk turned to secession, or what in the

20th century became known as a unilateral declaration of independence. After Sigurðsson's death, his successor, Benedikt Sveinsson, submitted to the Alþingi a proposal calling for real self-government every year from 1881 to 1895. It was twice passed, in 1886 and 1894, only to encounter the impenetrable stumbling block of the royal veto. Another breakthrough eventually came in Denmark with the election of a liberal government in 1901. Iceland's 1874 constitution was rewritten in 1903, and the following year the country received a new and improved version of home rule, including

virtue of having a common king. The arrangements were ratified by a plebiscite with 12,040 votes in favour and only 897 against. This was agreed to be valid until 1943, when Iceland's status would again be open to negotiation.

## "Occupation"

By the end of 1940, it had become impossible for Denmark and Iceland to enter into delicate constitutional negotiations. There was no contact whatsoever between them, Denmark having been occupied by Germany and Iceland by Britain. In the latter's case, strategic considera-

*Celebrations at Þingvellir to mark the 1000th anniversary of the Icelandic Parliament in 1930.*

its own Reykjavík-born Minister for Iceland in the Danish cabinet.

The saga-writers would have felt at home in the first years of Icelandic home rule as the country fragmented into a political free-for-all, various factions feuding with seemingly no greater purpose in mind than advancing self-interests. Icelanders could not agree on their relationship with Denmark either, and the impasse continued until the whole question of national sovereignty in Europe was brought under microscopic scrutiny in the peace negotiations after World War I. The Danish government then took the initiative and on 1 December 1918 Iceland became a sovereign state with its own flag, linked to Denmark by

tions had taken priority over the policy of "perpetual neutrality" which had been declared in 1915. Hitler's troops had marched into Norway and thus gained control of its immensely long Atlantic-facing coastline and ports. Iceland was a logical next step, its mid-Atlantic position being of inestimable strategic value for submarine operations and for aircraft not yet able to cross the ocean in one hop. Iceland had no military defences of its own, so Britain stepped in and "occupied" the country to pre-empt any German moves in that direction, a role later taken over by the Americans.

The British and American forces, who at times amounted to one-third of the population, were not always popular, but resentment was softened by the unprecedented prosperity that the war years brought in Iceland. The national income shot up by 60 percent on the twin strengths of construction work on American airfields and free-spending US personnel. Fish exports fetched record prices and, since they were generally paid

> Total prohibition was introduced in Iceland in 1915. The move was particularly unpopular in Spain, which had traditionally paid for imports of salted Icelandic cod with surplus wine.

to take into its own hands the conduct of all its affairs." It added that Iceland would become a republic as soon as it was possible to terminate the union with Denmark formally.

The termination of the union and a new constitution were submitted to plebiscite in 1944 and both were approved by huge majorities. The date chosen for the formal establishment of the republic at Þingvellir was, not by accident, the birthday of the great nationalist Jón Sigurðsson, 17 June.

Denmark was then still under German occupation, and many Danes felt that what amounted

*Winston Churchill leaving Reykjavík in 1941.*

for in dollars, Iceland had the means to import large quantities of American goods.

Not being able to communicate with Denmark to negotiate on constitutional changes, the Alþingi took a decision to act unilaterally: "Seeing that the situation which has been created makes it impossible for the king of Iceland to exercise the powers assigned to him by the constitution, the Alþingi announces that for the present it commits the exercise of these powers to the government of Iceland."

An Alþingi resolution made the following year went even further: "The Alþingi resolves to declare that it considers Iceland to have acquired the right to a complete breaking off of the union with Denmark, since it has now had

to a secession had been brought to fruition while they were hardly in a position to do anything about it. King Christian X sent a telegram of good wishes – it was only received after a ceremony which attracted no fewer than 20,000 people to Þingvellir on a cold and blustery day. The first president of the new republic, who was elected to a four-year term, was Sveinn Björnsson.

Iceland's neutrality did not save 352 seamen from death as a result of German actions at sea, but it was adhered to on principle when Iceland turned down an offer to declare for the Allies in the final months of the war. One of the first actions of independent Iceland was, on the cessation of hostilities, to demand the immediate withdrawal of the American forces.

# MODERN ICELAND

Since World War II Iceland has come of age
as a hardworking, modern society enriched
by a profound respect for its past.

Iceland today has all the trappings of an industrialised nation, with a sophisticated, consumer-orientated society and comprehensive welfare system. It still has one of the highest standards of living in the world in spite of its recent financial woes. It is almost impossible to imagine that, before World War II, many visitors thought Iceland to be barely out of the Middle Ages.

> The average Icelander works 2,064 hours a year, making Iceland one of the world's hardest-working countries.

## Joining the modern world

The transformation occurred almost overnight. Even so, Icelandic society did not abandon its long past, but rather adapted it to the present, replanting an ancient heritage in modern soil where it has more or less flourished since. The Icelandic language has been the bridge of centuries: the history of the Old Republic had been written down in the Middle Ages using a language which modern Icelanders can and very often do read (see page 88).

The presence of first British and then American troops in Iceland during the war, although not exactly welcome, had its brighter sides. A frenzy of road-building and development created an economic infrastructure for the postwar period. Few can deny that the prosperity brought by the war meant that national independence, declared in 1944, could be consolidated in peacetime.

More controversial was what to do after the war. Iceland's old stand of "eternal neutrality" was abandoned in 1949 when it became a

*US forces in Iceland playing cards, 1951.*

founding member of NATO. The US military had left Iceland, but returned in 1951 to set up a permanent naval air station at Keflavík. The fact that this made Iceland a major target in the event of nuclear war hardly endeared the US presence to the majority of Icelanders; nor did Icelandic men appreciate rich American servicemen floating around the countryside. But the economic argument was powerful: Keflavík provided jobs. And strict controls on marines' movements, rarely allowing them out from behind a huge wire fence, meant that not too many ran off with Icelandic wives.

Even so, Iceland never established an army of its own and also managed to maintain good trade relations with the Eastern bloc during the chilliest spells of the Cold War. Anti-Keflavík feeling flared up from time to time during the Vietnam war and was a popular cause on the political Left – but by the late 1970s it had become a principle which was costing rather than winning votes.

As a non-nuclear base, Keflavík kept its nose clean during the arms race against Brezhnev, and its role largely involved escorting "stray" Soviet aircraft back out of Icelandic airspace – there were up to 200 violations some years – and monitoring submarine movements in the area. Always keeping a low profile, the

*Cleaning cod at a fish factory.*

US military effectively disappeared from view when a civilian passenger terminal was finally opened at Keflavík Airport in 1987. Until then, all visitors who arrived in the country by air had had to land at the US military base before being allowed to tread Icelandic soil (including Mikhail Gorbachev when he arrived for the 1986 summit, see page 65).

However, in March 2006, things changed for good when the US ambassador to Iceland announced that the United States had decided to substantially reduce the size of their defence force on the island. Over the proceeding months, military operations at the Keflavík base were wound down and it finally closed on 8 September. The old barracks were used as

university accommodation to begin with, then in 2012 Verne Global opened one of the world's first carbon-neutral data centres on the site. It is predicted that within the next 10 years, this hosting of millions of computer servers will become Iceland's biggest industry.

## Riches of the sea

After World War II, the Icelandic government – with economic foresight – channelled its wartime cash-in-hand into modernising the fishing fleet, laying the foundation for a powerful industry that still exists today. Soon Iceland would be producing more income per head from fishing than Saudi Arabians did from oil.

Rich on cod income, Iceland's government grew, building an impressive system of schools, public health and social security. At the same time, Iceland's regulation of the economy had few parallels in the developed Western world. During the 1950s and 1960s, import tariffs were thrown up to protect industry, but they gradually served to foster inefficiency and higher prices for everything from fruit to toothbrushes.

It was not until the 1980s that Icelandic governments became committed, in the spirit of the times, to free-market policies. Yet throughout all of these policy changes, fishing remained the mainstay of the economy. Unfortunately, no amount of government regulation could sidestep its unpredictable nature, and fluctuations in both catches and market conditions have from time to time dealt severe blows to the virtually one-track economy.

Whenever fish catches or market prices deteriorated, the government's reaction was to devalue the Icelandic króna. This triggered an inflationary spiral in the 1970s. Wages were indexed to price rises, so that Icelanders joked that a foreign disaster was the best news: for example a flood in Brazil which ruined the coffee-bean harvest could push up prices in Iceland which would result in wage rises all round.

Although wage indexation was outlawed in 1983, loans did continue to be indexed, which put the brakes on one of the most popular national pastimes of the 1960s and 1970s: owing money. Before indexing, it was possible to take on huge debts and pray that inflation would go up enough to enable you to pay them back again. Generally it did, and whole generations bought or built the impressive apartment blocks and detached houses that decorate streets everywhere.

## The 2008 financial crisis

With inflation under control and a fish-led recovery, Icelanders enjoyed one of the world's highest standards of living for over 20 years. The country was one of the most consumer-orientated countries on earth, with Icelanders among the first to buy every new consumer durable that came onto the market. In the early years of the 21st century, cranes covered the horizon in a country-wide construction boom, Icelandic businessmen were buying up foreign businesses like children choosing sweets, and Icelandic bankers were offering incredible interest rates to overseas savers.

But this wealth was illusory: in reality, Iceland had one of the world's highest levels of foreign debt per capita, and when the 2008 financial crisis hit, Iceland's entire economy was swept away. The country teetered on the edge of bankruptcy, saved only by huge loans from its Scandinavian neighbours and the IMF.

Icelanders endured high inflation, wage cuts, redundancies, cuts in services and currency restrictions, but the country is righting itself relatively quickly. It's not all roses: unemployment stands at 6.6 percent (compared to 2.3 percent in 2007), and relations between Iceland and the UK and the Netherlands have been cool following the collapse of Icesave (a subsidiary of Iceland's national bank Landsbanki). The UK and Dutch governments reimbursed 300,000 British and 118,000 Dutch Icesave customers to the tune of £4.5 billion and €1.53 billion respectively, then pursued Iceland for the interest on the bailout. However, in 2013 a European court ruled that Iceland was under no obligation to repay the money. Despite a speedy economic recovery from the financial crisis (in 2015, GDP returned to pre-crisis levels), the fallout led to major changes in the country's political landscape. The centre-right coalition of the Progressive and Independence parties had come to power in 2013, under the leadership of Sigmundur Davíð Gunnlaugsson, who at 38 years old was Iceland's youngest ever prime minister. Controversially, Gunnlaugson formally cancelled the country's application to join the EU in 2015. The move triggered street protests and unrest in the streets of Reykjavik. In 2016, Gunnlaugsson was in the spotlight once again, as he was forced to resign from his post following the release of the Panama Papers, which revealed that he had failed to reveal his stake in an offshore company when he entered parliament in 2009.

## A healthy society

In spite of the country's financial and political woes, being an Icelander is still no bad thing. Iceland is one of the most literate countries in the world. Education levels are very high for both sexes: more than one-third of all 20-year-olds complete secondary grammar school, there are around 15,000 students at the University of Iceland, and another 3,800 Icelanders at foreign universities (not bad for a national population of only 332,000). More books are published and bought per head here than anywhere else in the world.

*Vigdís Finnbogadóttir, president of Iceland between 1980 and 1996.*

Currently, Icelandic males are at the top the world longevity tables with a life expectancy of 81.2, 2 years. Icelandic women are also high on the list, with an average life expectancy at birth of 84 years. Doctors say that the reasons include an unpolluted environment and the pure food that this offers; the outrageously fresh air of an Atlantic island on the rim of the Arctic Circle; a healthy fish-based diet; and exemplary public health care. Infant mortality in Iceland is, at 1.9 deaths per 1,000 children, among the lowest in the world, and certain aspects of preventative medicine, such as early detection of female cancers, are unmatched.

# The Politics of Fishing

**Ever since Iceland gained full independence from Denmark in 1944, the country's foreign policy has been moulded by the politics of fishing.**

Since 1944, it is the international politics of fishing more than Iceland's role as a strategically crucial – albeit army-less – component of the

*Cod still form an important part of the catch.*

NATO defence pact that have played the larger role in shaping the country's foreign policy. Indeed, the dependence on seafood earnings is such that the republic's focussed determination to repel any perceived encroachments on its fisheries resources has brought the country into a series of long-running conflicts with even its NATO allies.

A classic example of Iceland "getting tough" with an ally are the four Cod Wars with the UK between 1952 and 1976 (see page 113), centring around Iceland's proposed extension of the fishing zone around its coast. Each of the four confrontations ended well for Iceland, particularly the last , when the UK conceded a 200-nautical-mile exclusive Icelandic fishing zone.

A more recent dispute, over Icelandic vessels fishing in the Barents Sea "loophole", severely strained diplomatic relations with Norway during the 1990s. The latest spat is over mackerel fishing rights in the North Atlantic: Scotland accused Iceland of overfishing, and in early 2013 called for the EU to impose economic sanctions. Iceland shrugged off the threat, but agreed to come to the negotiating table in the autumn. However, the negotiations eventually collapsed two years later.

Iceland has also been involved in squabbles with Norway, Russia and the EU over catch quotas on migratory species such as redfish and herring – indeed fisheries issues loomed large in Iceland's long-standing determination to remain outside the EU. In the past, only the Social Democrats came out in favour of at least considering membership. Opponents of membership believed that Iceland's 1994 entry into the European Economic Area gave Iceland all the benefits of EU membership without any of the drawbacks.

This changed after the 2008 financial crash, when the desperate situation prompted Iceland to submit an application for EU membership in the hopes of greater financial security. However, it was always more a case of "needs must" than any real political conviction, and in 2013, the newly elected centre-right coalition once again put Iceland's application for EU membership on hold. Two years later, they formally withdrew Iceland's application for EU membership. The country's survival as a nation is still deeply dependent on seafood: the country's total catch value was worth 148,9 billion krónur to the economy in 2015. Anything that places this all-important industry under threat is to be discouraged, including EU membership – a 2012 poll showed that only a quarter of Icelanders were still in favour of joining.

Meanwhile, the controversial return of commercial whaling in 2006 put an issue that has long been a thorn in the side of Iceland's international relations right back under the spotlight. Having halted the practice back in 1989, Iceland walked out of the International Whaling Commission in 1992; after this it always seemed likely that whaling would resume at some point. All in all, since 2006 over 700 fin whales were killed by the Icelandic whaling company, Hvalur. For more on whaling and the controversial issues that surround it, see page 115.

## Moments of glory

In recent years, Iceland has been hitting world headlines for all the wrong reasons, but it does have its quiet moments of glory. In 1980, Icelanders chose Vigdís Finnbogadóttir as the world's first democratically elected female head of state. The former theatre director, French teacher and tourist guide took the Presidency (an office outside party politics whose function is to provide a figure of national unity), and was subsequently re-elected three times. In 2009, the new prime minister elected in the wake of the financial meltdown, Jóhanna Sigurðardóttir, was

by coming from 1-0 down to knock England out of the competition. They were eventually eliminated 5-2 by the hosts, France, in the quarterfinals. The team's determined, disciplined displays and the fantastic vocal support of the fans were mainstays of their unlikely run and they returned home as national heroes.

## Lifting a ban

On 1 March each year, Icelanders celebrate "Beer Day", in honour of the moment in 1989 that a ban on strong beer was finally abolished. Total prohibition had gone into effect in 1915; wine

*Reagan and Gorbachev in Reykjavík, 1986.*

the world's first openly gay head of government.

On a different front, Iceland was invaded by foreign journalists in 1986 when it became host to the historic Reagan-Gorbachev summit. As the mid-point between Moscow and New York, Reykjavík was deemed an auspicious meeting place for the leaders of the superpowers to discuss nuclear disarmament. Although the talks eventually stalled, they were symbolic of a breakthrough in East-West negotiations and stood as markers of the beginning of the end of the Cold War.

In 2016, the national football team's exploits captured the imagination of the world. Appearing in their first-ever European Championships, they surpassed all expectations; first by qualifying for the knockout rounds, and then

was legalised again in 1921, but, as a sop to the temperance lobby – which argued that because beer is cheaper than spirits, it would lead to more depravity – beer was not included in the vote.

The absurdity of the beer ban came fully to light in 1985 when the teetotal Minister of Justice prohibited pubs from pepping up legal non-alcoholic beer with legal spirits to make a potent imitation of strong beer. Finally beer approached legalisation in parliament – the debate and knife-edge vote were televised live and watched by huge audiences.

## Keeping traditions alive

The concern at maintaining tradition does not always seem so frivolous. An ancient and homogeneous culture of relatively few people is always at risk of being swallowed up by the outside world.

Symbolic of the changes wrought in Iceland has been the growth of the capital, Reykjavík – with only 5,000 inhabitants in 1901, by 2015

*The leap into the modern world has been fast and furious: greater changes have taken place in the past 50 years in Iceland than in the first 1,000-plus years of settlement.*

*Icelanders carrying candles in Reykjavík's annual Parade of Light procession.*

the figure was over 210,000 in the greater Reykjavík area, or some 63 percent of all Icelanders. The shift from country to city has completely altered Icelandic society: the generation of Reykjavík folk now around retirement age was largely born and brought up in the countryside, on farms or in fishing villages. Their children, now middle-aged, were born and bred in the capital, but retained some links with the outside; and the generation now at or leaving school is thoroughbred urban, most of them brought up in the "concrete lava fields" of new residential suburbs such as Breiðholt and Árbær – whose populations alone outnumber those of the largest towns outside the capital area.

These are the first Icelanders to drift away from the "classical" colloquialisms of their ancient language, which is firmly rooted in the agricultural society of yesteryear. And they are the first to have no intimate knowledge of the mainstay industries of fishing, fish processing and agriculture – hands-on experience which in the past had given Iceland a telling edge over its international competition. This lack of basic manual skills poses a threat to Iceland's few industries, a threat whose consequences few can guess.

Recognising that language is on the front line, Icelanders' defence of their ancient Norse tongue is fierce (see page 91). The same technological advances that are welcomed so warmly also pose the biggest threats. Satellite TV, for example, comes outside the jurisdiction of Iceland's legions of subtitlers, dubbers and professional and amateur word-coiners. Linguists say that the threats are becoming more subtle: borrowed words from foreign languages stand out instantly, but "hidden" foreignisms such as Anglo-Saxon syntax and thinking patterns are easier to slip into and more difficult to detect, yet undermine the very fabric of the language all the same.

Moreover, social scientists were astonished to discover in an opinion poll that a large majority of Icelanders still claim to believe in the existence of elves and spirits (see page 250). Almost all Icelanders still believe in God. Even though only a small fraction go to the Lutheran church they are all still registered at birth. At one stage during the 1960s, the Norse pagan religion was revived, although it attracted little interest at the time. Over the last few years, however, perhaps owing to rising concerns over environmental issues, the congregation has crept up to 2,400 members. The religious organisation, Ásatrúarfélagið, has its own burial ground and six priests who can conduct legally binding pagan ceremonies. In 2015, Ásatrúarfélagið began building a temple in Reykjavik.

But perhaps the real achievement of modern Iceland has been to remain essentially democratic in a personal as well as a political sense. Iceland is at once a modern technological nation and a small village writ large – a place with little crime, few class distinctions and where everybody, thanks to the old Scandinavian patronymic system still in use (see page 77), addresses one another by their first name.

Maintaining the old traditions
is a preoccupation in today's
globalised society.

*Admiring Lake Lögurinn.*

# THE ICELANDERS

Today's Icelanders, a product of their landscape and history, are looking to the future with determination.

Probably the first thought that occurs to many visitors as they drive through the desolate lava plain that separates Keflavík airport from the capital, is: "Very impressive – but why would anyone want to live here?"

The inhabitants of a country often tend to reflect their environment. The Danes, for example, live in a flat, fertile country, and are by and large an easy-going, laid-back bunch. Their Icelandic cousins, however, do not really know how to relax and enjoy life. The visitor may be puzzled at how Icelanders can be completely uninhibited one minute, yet stubbornly taciturn the next; at how such a practical nation could produce so many poets, writers and musicians; and at how such hard-working souls, obsessed with the benefits of good honest labour, could be drowning in such a financial quagmire.

But in these tendencies towards extremes, excess and unpredictability, the Icelanders are only reflecting their homeland. Anyone would be a little crazy living in this world of glaciers

*Fishing is hugely popular in Iceland, both as a hobby and a job.*

> "Somewhere, in all these rocks and stones, is my home."– Nationalist poet Pétur Gunnarsson

and flowing magma, where the sun shines all night in summer but winter is long, dark and cold, and where its very people transformed themselves almost overnight from a near-medieval society into one with admirably high living standards.

Icelanders have a reputation for being rather dour – but this quality does not go too deep. When the days get longer and lighter and the sun shines, however weakly, the entire nation can be seen to undergo a metamorphosis. Out come the pavement tables outside the cafés, the bottles of red wine and barbecues. Some people even manage to stop working overtime.

## Medieval to modern

Icelanders have an extremely strong national identity, and a cultural heritage of which they are very proud. The constant suspicion that the outside world thinks them small and insignificant, coupled with having been isolated for so many years, sometimes makes them seem insular and absurdly patriotic. They are prone to harp on the nation's illustrious past, "cashing cheques on deeds committed 700 years ago," as writer and scholar Sigurður Norðal put it.

Yet no one can deny that the Icelanders are a resilient bunch, having survived all sorts of calamities – both natural and induced – throughout the centuries. When the independence struggle began in the 19th century, Iceland was still deep in the Dark Ages. There were no roads and very few stone-built houses. But in a single generation, around the time Iceland gained self-government in 1918, the society moved, with no apparent difficulty, straight into the 20th century.

much the importance of the whale-hunt, but the questioning of Iceland's right to self-government that raises the national hackles.

## Social changes

Their fierce patriotism can give Icelanders a rather inflated view of the country's importance on the world stage. They are very sensitive to slights to their national pride, and react strongly to any real or imagined threats to the community. This characteristic can sometimes manifest itself in an unpleasant way – such as the ban on black servicemen which the Icelan-

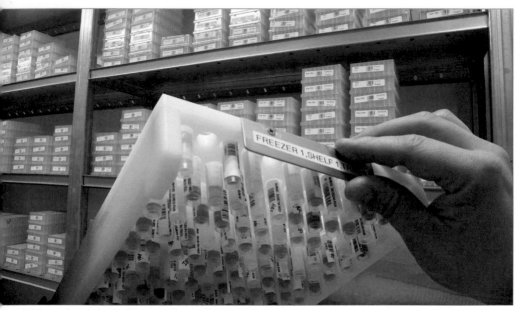

*DNA samples – Iceland is big on genetic research.*

One of the most oft-cited reasons for the speed of this transition was the high standard of education in the country. While the people were poor, they were never ignorant. Nearly all of them could read and write, and quite a few could speak foreign languages.

Another is the strong sense of national identity and community. Icelanders have had to learn to stick together through necessity and overcome impossible odds. Thus, in the so-called Cod Wars with Britain in the 1960s and 1970s, this country without an army took on and defeated a world power that was threatening its interests and livelihood. A similar motivation lies behind the stubborn stand on whaling (see pages 64 and 115). It is not so

dic government secretly insisted on imposing when the NATO military base was established at Keflavík during the 1950s.

Iceland's racial make-up is around three parts Nordic to one part Celt. Today people are much more cosmopolitan, but before the 1960s a black person walking down the street in Reykjavík was invariably followed by a crowd of excited children. In fact, Icelanders are generally free of racism. In 1989, when 5,000 foreign citizens were already resident in the country (making up 2 percent of the population) a survey showed that a vast majority supported the idea of people of different races settling in Iceland. A large number of Icelandic couples adopted Vietnamese orphans during the Boat People crisis, and few of these children have experienced anything but a warm welcome into the community.

The homogeneity of Iceland's population, teamed with genealogical records that stretch back for a thousand years, brought the country to the fore in the field of population-based molecular genomics. In 1996, the first firm specialising in such research, deCODE Genetics, was founded in Reykjavík by ex-Harvard professor Kári Stefánsson. In its first two years deCODE grew exponentially, attracting foreign investors and generating considerable attention

> *In the pre-war years Hitler and his Nazis assiduously courted the Icelanders as an example of a "pure Aryan colony"; to the country's credit few people took any notice of this dubious flattery.*

within the international medical community. However, although its research was revolutionary, its financial path has been rocky, leading *Newsweek* to dub the company "the world's most successful failure".

deCODE received a mixed response from Icelanders themselves, although by 2013, 140,000 citizens (43 percent of the entire population) had participated in research for the company. While deCODE's efforts and vision have been applauded – it has discovered genetic risk factors for dozens of common diseases, including Type 2 diabetes and stroke – the company was surrounded by controversy from the start. Ethical questions were raised, such as whether a single private company should have exclusive rights to personal medical information. There were also fears that the confidentiality of medical records might be violated; and wider concerns about how DNA-based risk assessment tests, created using the results of this Icelandic research, might be employed in the future. These issues arguably became even more pertinent after deCODE was purchased by US-based biopharmaceutical giant Amgen in late 2012.

## Looking to foreign shores

One of the many paradoxes typical of Icelanders is that along with being insular, they are insatiably curious about the outside world, even to the most obscure detail. The only epic

poem that has ever been written in honour of the medieval Albanian hero Count Skanderbeg was composed by an otherwise unknown Icelandic clergyman in 1861.

Icelanders lay great store by being cosmopolitan and well-travelled – "sailed", as they put it. This dates back to the days of the sagas when every self-respecting Viking started off his career by journeying abroad, returning home laden with renown and gifts from European royalty. Young modern-day adventurers also have the community's blessing to quit the nation's shores and try their luck at seeking

*Björk has proved herself one of Iceland's major exports.*

fame and fortune in foreign lands. They are said to be *að gera garðinn frægan*, "winning renown for the old homestead."

## The Björk phenomenon

No one has done that with as much panache as Björk Guðmundsdóttir, who has done more to promote her home country than any

> *The world's first Basque dictionary was written by a farmer in a desolate part of northwest Iceland – he had learnt the language from Basque sailors who came to fish off the nearby coast.*

advertising campaign. Björk became a household name in Iceland at age 11, when she released her first solo record. During her teens and early twenties she sang with a handful of bands before becoming a founding member of The Sugarcubes, who were catapulted to stardom all over the world largely on the strength of Björk's inimitable vocal style.

Björk has since won the widespread acclaim and respect of fans and critics alike for her solo career, picking up over 90 awards for her unique and experimental music (including the 2011 AIM Independent Music Awards for

*A still from the film Children of Nature (1991).*

outstanding contribution to music) and acting career (including Best Actress at the Cannes Film Festival in 2000 for her role in director Lars von Trier's *Dancer in the Dark*). In 2015, the Museum of Modern Art held a large retrospective exhibition dedicated to Björk, who released her 9th album, *Vulnicura*, in 2015.

## Other cultural exports

Björk's success in the international arena has flung open the doors for other Icelandic musicians to become better known internationally. Talent scouts from every corner of the globe have made their way to this tiny north Atlantic island to see who else might be hiding. A number of musicians and bands have since landed deals with foreign recording companies, notably Indie band Sigur Rós, and Of Monsters and Men, whose debut album, *My Head Is an Animal*, stormed the international record charts in 2011. Emiliana Torrini has also gained well-deserved fame across the world.

In the classical sector, Icelanders have also excelled. The Iceland Symphony Orchestra has won great critical acclaim in the recent past, not least for their recordings of the works of the composer Jón Leifs. Leifs, who died in 1968 and whose unconventional – but decidedly Icelandic – sound was shunned by the establishment for decades, has recently been "discovered" by Icelanders and foreigners alike. Meanwhile, the opera singer Kristján Jóhannsson – a former Akureyri native and ex-motor mechanic – has sung in major roles at the world's top opera houses.

Another heavyweight figure on the Icelandic cultural scene is filmmaker Friðrik Þór Friðriksson. His film *Children of Nature*, written in collaboration with Iceland's literary golden boy Einar Már Guðmundsson, was nominated for an Academy Award in the Best Foreign Film category, in 1992. Although it did not win, it helped pave the way for Friðriksson abroad. Friðriksson has been named one of the most influential filmmakers in Europe, and his films have won awards at numerous international festivals throughout the world: the latest to do so was *Mamma Gógó* (2010), a personal piece about his mother's development of Alzheimer's disease. Another respected Icelandic director, Baltasar Kormákur, has had a hand in several crowd-pleasers that have made it onto international screens, most famously the comedy *101 Reykjavík*, the detective film *Jar City* and the thriller *The Deep*, nominated for the 2013 Academy Awards for Best Foreign Language Film. More recently, *Life in a Fishbowl* by Baldvin Zophoniasson – an up-and-coming Icelandic director – has made waves across the cinematic world, as Iceland's candidate for the Best Foreign Picture Award for the 2015 Oscars. Recently Iceland has been a popular location for many international films, as well as the award-winning series, Game of Thrones.

Readers with children may be familiar with the TV programme *LazyTown*, responsible for lowering childhood obesity rates in Iceland and boosting vegetable sales by 20 percent, and now broadcasting its healthy-lifestyle message to kids in over 100 countries. Its creator, gymnast Magnús Scheving, also stars in it as the hero Sportacus.

Icelanders are also terribly proud of their three Miss Worlds. As if to give credit to the common notion that Icelandic women are among the most beautiful in the world, two Icelandic women were awarded the Miss World title within three years of each other: Hólmfríður Gísladóttir in 1985 and Linda Pétursdóttir in 1988. Unnur Birna Vilhjálmsdóttir repeated their success when she was crowned in 2005. Meanwhile, Arna Ýr Jónsdóttir, who was Miss Iceland 2015, was voted Miss Euro 2016.

The creator of Harpa Concert Hall's glittering façade, Ólafur Elíasson, is a Danish-Icelandic artist who is internationally renowned for his installations, which play with elemental forces: for example, *The Weather Project*, which appeared in the Turbine Hall of Tate Modern, London, and his unearthly *New York City Waterfalls*.

## Sports and business

Two Icelanders have taken the title "World's Strongest Man" four times each: Magnús Ver Magnússon and Jón Páll Sigmarsson, who died in 1993 at the age of 33. A colourful character, Jón Páll had his status as national hero reinforced by the documentary film *Larger than Life*, which broke Icelandic box-office records on its 2006 release. Follow in the footsteps of these giants is Hafþór Júlíus Björnsson, who finished third in the 2012 competition and second in 2014, and Benedikt Magnússon, current holder of the world record for a raw deadlift.

A few other Icelanders have made the transition into the international sphere, most notably footballers, such as Eiður Guðjohnsen – who had a distinguished career at Chelsea in the English Premier League before moving on to Barcelona, Monaco, Club Brugge, Bolton and many other clubs – and Gylfi Sigurðsson, who has recently returned to Swansea City, after a two-year spell with Tottenham Hotspur. Ágúst Sigurvinnson has also had a successful career in Germany. Aron Gunnarsson (Cardiff City) and Johann Berg Gudmundsson (Burnley) are current making a name for themselves in Britain.

Iceland established a brief and unlikely influence in the English game in 1999, when England's oldest premier-league club Stoke City was bought up by a consortium of Icelanders, spearheaded by fruit-and-vegetable distributor Gunnar Þór Gíslason. Then 2006 saw the £85-million takeover of West Ham United by businessmen Eggert Magnusson and Björgólfur Guðmundsson, but the 2008 crash put an end to Icelandic club ownership in Britain.

Until Euro 2016, Iceland's national football team had never played in an international tournament. Led by Heimir Hallgrimsson, a dentist from Heimaey, Iceland quickly became a global sensation, drawing their first game with Cristiano Ronaldo's Portugal and advancing through their group, to knock out England before being knocked out at the hands of the hosts, France. Amazingly, more than 10 per cent of Iceland's population travelled to France to

*Icelandic actor and Game of Thrones star, Julius Bjornsson.*

support their team. Tens of thousands of fans took to the streets of Reykjavik to welcome home the returning heroes.

A handful of Icelandic companies have not only excelled in the international business arena in the recent past, but continue to flourish in spite of the country's financial calamities. Össur has been carving out a name for itself as a leading researcher and producer of prosthetics. Another is Marel, a top developer and producer of high-technology scales and software for the food processing industry. Other Icelandic entrepreneurs have their eye on cutting-edge technology. The country's cold climate and green energy mean it is a prime site for server farms: Nordic IT company Advania and Verne Global both opened Icelandic datacentres between 2010 and 2012.

Whenever an Icelander "makes it" on the international level, the entire Icelandic nation basks in his or her success. These people often achieve larger-than-life status in their home country; never mind that they may be queuing in front of you at the supermarket.

## My people and your people

Icelanders often claim that theirs is a classless society. This claim has some basis in that there is certainly a lot of class mobility. But there

*A black and white Icelandic lamb.*

exist, like everywhere else, disparities of income and status: some families are considered older and are more "aristocratic" than others. Generally speaking, Icelanders are obsessed with their genealogy and most can trace their ancestry back at least six or seven generations. Some even have family tables that go back beyond the age of Iceland's settlement into the realm of legend – perhaps with a Norse god or two sitting proudly at the top of the family tree. The common enquiry "who are his people?" is not just snobbery, however. It is a relevant question in a society where everyone is related to everyone else in the tenth generation.

The national inferiority complex also comes into play – and it has obviously been around for some considerable time. The author of the 12th-century *Landnámabók (Book of Settlements)*, which charted the progress of the first pioneers who came to Iceland, stated his purpose in writing as follows: "so we would better be able to answer foreigners who upbraid us for our descent from slaves or scoundrels if we knew our true origins for certain."

## Small-scale society

Despite remnants of old snobberies, modern-day Iceland is on the whole an informal, egalitarian and familiar society. Everyone from the President down is addressed by their first names. Jón the doorman greets Jón the eminent politician with a cheery hello – they come from the same fishing village and are probably second cousins. As you shower after an early-morning dip in the local swimming baths, there might be a famous pop star getting changed in the cubicle next to you. But Icelanders do not identify easily with the idea of fame, with its paraphernalia of bodyguards and exclusiveness. They are used to everyone being accessible. The President grants interviews to any member of the public who wishes to see him and top sportsmen and pop stars usually have to keep their day jobs, as few can afford to go professional.

And it is very easy to be famous yourself. Anyone with application and talent can stand for parliament, present a television programme, set up an art exhibition or play in a football team. Anyone can be a published author – and usually is. One in 10 Icelanders publishes something in the course of their life and writing a book is considered almost a form of National Service. If you fail to hit the headlines in your lifetime you will at least do so after your death. Even the most obscure person can be sure of at least one long obituary, with a photo, in the newspapers on the day of their funeral. Pillars of the community may run to several pages over many days.

The concept of being a participating member of society is very strong. As a Japanese academic who settled in the country noticed: "Everyone is equal, so everyone is important. Everyone is a participant in society, it isn't possible to opt out, to deny your responsibility." Just as being a member of the community is an honour, being excluded from it is the worst possible dishonour. In the Saga Age, criminals were not killed or imprisoned, but outlawed – made outcasts from their society.

Every individual matters and in return is obliged to participate. Iceland supports two daily newspapers, two major TV channels, a national theatre and opera plus dozens of orchestras, art galleries, theatre companies, radio stations and museums. None of these could hope to survive unless individuals visited the theatre at least once a year, took two newspapers, supported the arts, and so on.

## Spending and debt

Surveys have shown that in many areas Icelanders are closer to the US in their attitudes than to Europe. Icelanders are believers in market forces. In their personal tastes, they have a slight tendency towards ostentation, glamour and displays of wealth. But this materialism is partly a matter of economic survival. Importers and retailers would go out of business unless every household found it an absolute necessity to purchase the newest model laptop or flatscreen television, or whatever is the latest strange gimmick to seize, albeit briefly, the nation's collective imagination. As the late Nobel-prize winning author Halldór Laxness once declared, "it is, in general, expensive to be an Icelander."

The spend, spend, spend mentality was encouraged by an economy plagued through the years by soaring inflation. Icelanders tended to be compulsive in their spending habits and are renowned for scooping up the latest gadgets. "Keeping up with the Joneses" is a national pastime, and some Icelanders have appeared to continue with these spendthrift ways regardless of the country's financial crisis – old habits obviously die hard.

The nation has always been gripped by a collective compulsion to work all the hours that God sends. Icelanders are fierce devotees of the Protestant work ethic – no doubt a throwback to the days when a person's worth was measured in the number of hours of hard labour they could deliver per day. Moonlighting is extremely common, and many people managed to hold down two or even three jobs at the same time (at least before the crash). As a result, they are always doing things at the last minute and are late for everything: unpunctuality is one of the country's vices.

## Working hard

It has often puzzled foreigners why Icelanders devote so much time, money and effort to building palatial houses equipped with state-of-the-art furnishings when they are always at work and therefore never at home to appreciate them. But work is not just a way of getting money: it is an end in itself, a means of gaining self-respect. Although the Icelandic welfare state is fairly comprehensive, it is seen as something of a shameful thing to claim money off the state. "The comprehensive ability to work is the hallmark of the Icelander, whether a desk-bound intellectual, a farmer or a fisherman," comments anthropologist Finnur Magnússon.

*Harpa Concert Hall, Reykjavík.*

## ICELANDIC NAMES

The continued widespread use of the patronymic system, whereby a surname is derived from the father's christian name, is an ancient Scandinavian custom. "Son" or "daughter" is tacked on; thus Björk Guðmundsdóttir is Björk, daughter of Guðmundur. Her brother would be Guðmundsson. Some families have family names, but they are often of foreign origin: Zoega, Schram and Petersen. It used to be possible for family names to be bought for cash by up-and-coming parvenus who considered them smarter and more aristocratic; now it is not permitted to take a new family name. The tradition makes things easier for anyone tracing family roots.

This devotion to the Protestant work ethic was demonstrated during the World War II. "British work" – employment that was offered by the English military forces occupying the country – was despised by the Icelanders as fit only for layabouts and degenerates. The reason seems to have been because it was too easy and well-paid.

This extreme work ethic and pride in a job well done made the 2008 financial crisis even more galling for Icelanders. For individuals to have worked so hard, and yet to be left with impossible debts, was desperately hard to swal-

*Reykjavik Gay Pride.*

low. Uncharacteristic amounts of wrath were directed at the bankers and the government, and Icelanders also ruefully examined their own behaviour. But people here are used to weathering storms and pulling together in the face of adversity, and smouldering resentments and lifelong grudges are not in the nation's character. In the 2013 elections, the parties widely blamed for the crash were once again voted back into government.

Although Icelanders are gritty, resourceful and thrive on work, they have always had a secret fascination for a more bohemian lifestyle. Hard-nosed businesspeople will occasionally take the time to hang out philosophising with the regulars in one of Reykjavík's innumerable coffee-bars, and even publish a book of poems on the quiet. In Iceland, poets and artists are respected and admired, and seem to have a special dispensation to lead a ramshackle, layabout lifestyle. As Laxness put it ironically, "since time immemorial, the Icelandic nation has had to battle with men who call themselves poets and refuse to work for a living."

However, it must be admitted that in most cases the old Protestant work ethic tends to win out. Back in the 1960s, Icelandic hippies, although they were quite adept at tuning in and turning on, never really got the hang of dropping out. The real diehards had to head over to Copenhagen if they wanted to bum around in style – back home in Reykjavík they would have been too embarrassed not to have a job.

## Playing harder

Icelanders take their work seriously but are equally single-minded about their play. An inability to do anything in moderation is in fact one of the most characteristic national traits, as is demonstrated by a trip to downtown Reykjavík on a Friday or Saturday night (see page 150). This excess, however, is also partly explained by the high price of alcohol – it is too expensive to indulge in every day so many people prefer to save up for one almighty binge at the weekend.

Most Icelanders also have an odd flibbertigibbet streak, and are very quick to latch onto new trends, which sweep across the entire nation with lightning speed. Every household in Iceland has its sunbed, barbecue, footspa, new-age crystals, trampoline and set of knitting needles stuffed in a cupboard or garage somewhere, the detritus of crazes past.

## Non-violent society

The Icelanders are intrinsically a gentle people, and, despite having a fair share of the prevailing 21st-century social plagues – including drugs, porn, latch-key kids and so on – society is essentially non-violent, and Reykjavík is one of the safest capitals in the world. Even boxing was banned until as recently as 2002 – Icelanders prefer the far more elegant ancient sport of *glíma* (which resembles sumo wrestling).

The lack of serious crime means that society can be rather at a loss as to how to treat its more anti-social and violent elements. Even the most vicious of criminals rarely gets sentences of more than seven years, and the lenient sentencing in sexual abuse and incest cases – in which the perpetrator often escapes any sort of rehabilitation – has been criticised in recent years. Progressive and forward-looking as it may be, Iceland still seems to prefer to turn a blind eye to some of the more "sensitive" issues.

The other side of the coin is that, in general, Icelanders are broad-minded and tolerant about most things. In June 2010, for example, a bill was passed giving all couples the same marriage rights regardless of sexual preference, allowing gay couples to get married in church. Single mothers are admired rather than frowned

Above all, Icelanders also have a greater respect for family ties than many other societies. They take care of each other – there are few neglected grannies and grandpas left to fend for themselves in high-rise blocks. Icelanders put family as their top priority, above friends, free time and even their beloved work. Social cohesion and inclusion are the norm: in the 2013 OECD report, 45 percent of Icelanders said they had helped a stranger in the last month; while 98 per cent were confident that a family member or friend would help them out in a time of need.

*The popular Pravda Bar, Reykjavik.*

> *The Woman of the Mountains is a quasi-supernatural persona who plays a similar role in the national psyche to Marianne in France and John Bull in England.*

upon: everyone is happy to welcome children into the world whether they have two resident parents or one. Although a few moralists have predicted imminent destruction of the social fabric from such a lax set-up, marriage, which for many years was seen as irrelevant, is coming back into fashion – even though many bridal couples have their own offspring acting as bridesmaids and pageboys.

## Iceland's women

In recent times the Icelandic woman has become somewhat of an archetype, combining Nordic beauty with physical and spiritual strength. The popularity of this image undoubtedly received a boost through the three Miss World titles and the election, in 1980, of Vigdís Finnbogadóttir to the office of President. At the time of her election Vigdís was a single mother with an adopted daughter and, as such, represented a new era. She was also a survivor, having triumphed over breast cancer. In short, she combined femininity with strength, and common sense with strongly held personal views, albeit ones that she was not permitted to voice publicly by virtue of her office.

In fact, women have always played a forceful role in Icelandic society. The sagas and old tales are full of strong, matriarchal figures – from Aud the Deep-Minded, one of the greatest of the pioneers, to the irascible Bergþora, Njáll's wife (see page 92). Ancient lawbooks indicate

> There are fewer atheists than in any Western country except the US – 97 percent of Icelanders say they believe in God, although only a fraction attend church regularly.

Icelandic women first hit the international headlines in 1975, when they marked the beginning of the United Nations Women's Decade by going on a one-day mass strike to remind their menfolk of the essential role they played in society. Secretaries downed note-pads, bank-clerks and teachers stayed at home, mothers handed babies over to bewildered fathers – and the country was brought to a standstill.

When the Women's Decade drew to a close in 1985, a second walk-out was staged. Then-President Vígdis joined the protest, causing a constitutional crisis by refusing to sign a decree

*Hornid Restaurant, Reykjavik.*

that the medieval Icelandic woman enjoyed a great deal more emancipation than the majority of her European counterparts. She had equal rights in marriage, could own property and could even hold a *goðorð*, or chieftainship.

## Feminist advances

The women of Iceland are veterans of mould-breaking feminist activity. Iceland was one of the first countries in the world to introduce female suffrage: women were given the right to vote in municipal elections in 1908 and general enfranchisement in 1915. Between 1908 and 1922 a number of women-only panels of candidates were put forward for municipal and parliamentary elections, with considerable success.

that would force striking air stewardesses back to work. Male government ministers eventually forced her to sign, but her stand was much appreciated by her female compatriots.

In 1983, Iceland became the first country to elect a women-only party to parliament. The Women's Alliance (WA), a grass-roots radical movement with no leaders and an economic model based on the concept of "the thrifty housewife," had three of its members elected only a couple of months after the party was formed – and doubled its support at the following election. Support for the WA went down in the 1990s, however, mostly due to internal disagreements and the party formally disbanded before the 1999 elections.

## Icelandic women today

In 2009 Iceland elected prime minister Jóhanna Sigurðardóttir, who is not just the country's first female prime minister but is also the world's first openly gay head of government. The post-crash government was obviously preoccupied with financial concerns, but it still found time to ban strip clubs in March 2010, for feminist reasons – Jóhanna specifically stated that the intention of the law was that women would be treated "as equal citizens rather than commodities for sale".

Of the current centre-right coalition government, exactly half of the cabinet are women.

in years 2009– 2015. So what has made this remote island in the North Atlantic such a hotbed of feminist activity? Dr. Guðrún Agnarsdóttir says the low population is highly relevant. "A small community expects a lot from each individual, and each individual's contributions are also more likely to be noticed and appreciated." Supreme Court judge Guðrún Erlendsdóttir considers it very important that women in Iceland have always kept the old Norse tradition of retaining their natal surnames when they marry. But the factor that all eminent women in Iceland

*Austurvöllur Square, Reykjavík.*

The balance of the sexes is also reflected in parliament, where nearly 40 per cent of MPs are women.

About seventy per cent of students in university education are women; it is perhaps significant that single mothers are given plenty of support – the University of Iceland, for example, has several on-campus crèches and kindergartens. Paternity leave is among the most generous in the world, with fathers entitled to the same amount of time off as mothers.

The Global Gender Gap Index, which lists countries according to gender equality based on economic opportunity, politics, education and health, ranked Iceland first in the world

mention when asked about their emancipation is the sea. "Icelandic women are strong because the wives of seafarers have to be," says former President Vigdís Finnbogadóttir.

Indeed, this tradition of holding the fort stretches right back to the Viking era, when women would be left in control of the farms while the men went pillaging and raiding. Today, women play a vital role in the economy. Almost 88 percent of women work in either full or part-time employment. One of their main grievances is that their salaries are still on average 10 percent lower than that of men, and that like women elsewhere in the world, they still have to do most of the work in the home as well as outside it.

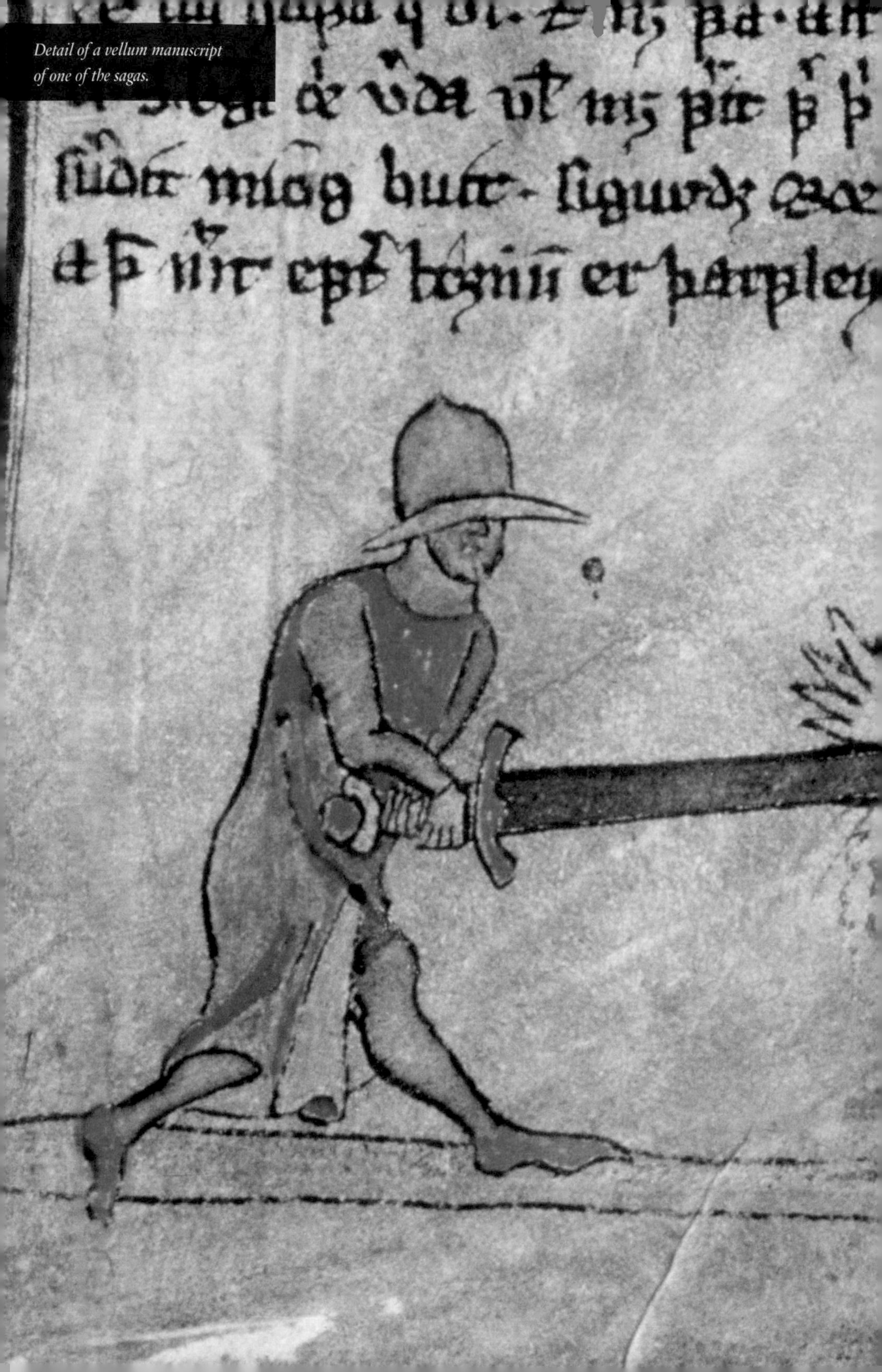

*Detail of a vellum manuscript of one of the sagas.*

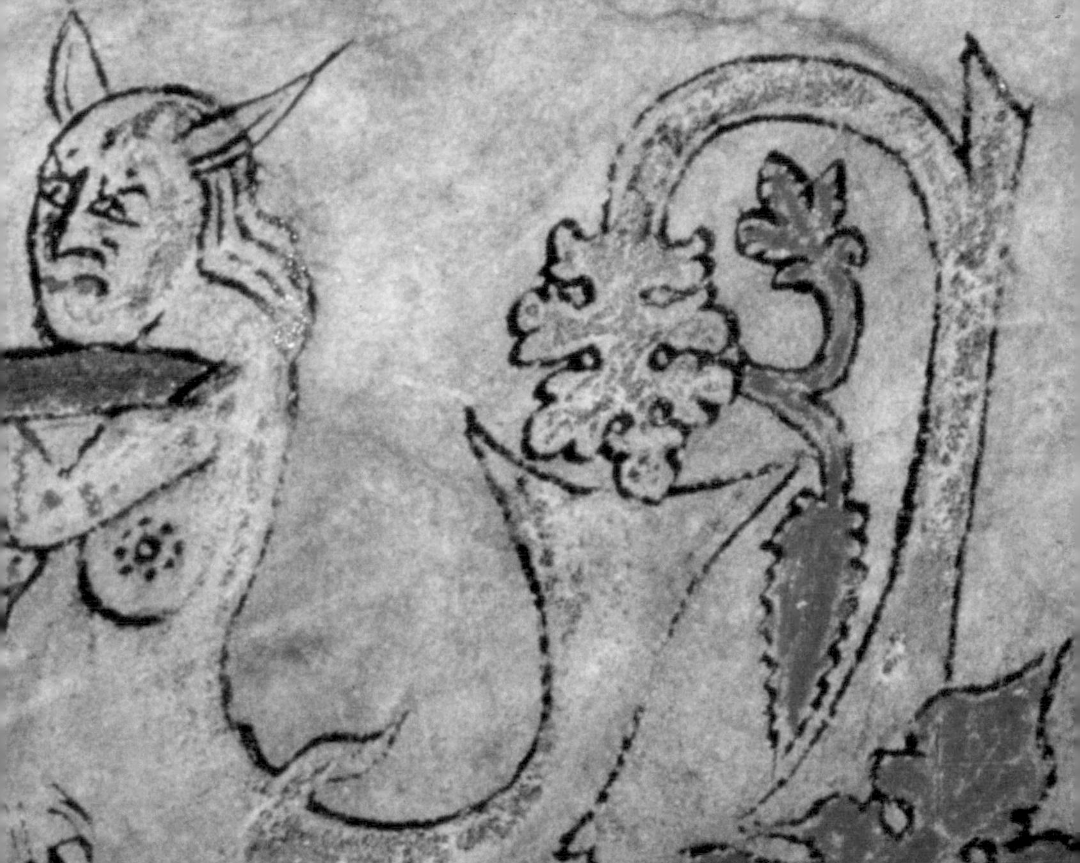

# ICELANDIC LITERATURE

Iceland has a proud literary and linguistic heritage, most famously captured in the medieval sagas which tell of the early settlers, their lives, families and struggles.

The rich literary tradition of Iceland, in tandem with the preservation of the purity of the language, is of great importance to the national identity. Above all, the Icelandic saga is one of the world's most astonishing literary achievements and an important contribution to European culture. The anonymous 13th-century saga authors, who lived in a desolate northerly island in the midst of a raging civil war, were the first Europeans to write prose in their own language rather than in Latin. Why the sagas were written, where the balance lies between history and fiction, who composed them, no one knows. But the greatest of them – the romantic *Laxdæla Saga*; the thrilling adventures of the two outlaws Gísli Súrsson and Grettir; the tale of the rogue warrior-poet Egill Skallagrímsson; and above all the magnificent epic *Njáls Saga* (see page 92) – can hold up their heads proudly in the midst of any literary company from Homer to Shakespeare.

Classified under the term "saga" – which in Icelandic simply means "story" – are countless historical chronicles, romances, legends, and lives of kings and holy men. Best known are the family sagas – 40 or so chronicles about various Icelandic families in the years following the land's settlement. The events they describe therefore occur around 200 to 300 years before the sagas were written, but until the 20th century they were taken as undisputed historical fact, passed down the generations orally until being finally recorded on manuscript. More recent scholarship, however, holds that they are basically works of fiction. The identity of the authors remains a mystery, although the chieftain Snorri Sturluson (see page 43), author of *Heimskringla*, the history of the Norwegian kings, is generally acknowledged to have also written the saga of Egill Skallagrímsson.

*An illustration of the blind Höðr killing Baldr, from an 18th-century manuscript.*

## Bloody chronicles

To summarise a saga storyline is almost impossible. They are great epic sprawls, which span many generations with dozens of characters and sub-plots. One 18th-century Icelandic scholar summed them up with the sardonic epigram "farmers at fisticuffs". He has a point – much of the action centres around blood-feuds, killings and conflict – but there is much more to them. They were written at a time of social chaos, when Iceland, North Europe's first republic, was being brought under the rule of foreign monarchs because of internal power struggles and conflicts. They contain a retrospective warning to the authors' contemporaries. As

Njáll, the sage-prophet hero of *Njáls Saga*, says: "with laws we shall build our land, but with lawlessness it shall be laid waste." At the same time, there is a certain nostalgia for a heroic golden age where men fought for personal honour rather than power and politics.

Bearing in mind that Iceland was being subjugated to the Norwegian king, there is a rather wistful recurring theme of Icelanders being feted and honoured at foreign courts, and being showered with gifts by, or getting the better of, various European monarchs. In the short saga of Halldór Snorrason, for example, the epony-

courage and honour the greatest virtues. "Better to die honourably than to live on in shame," as *Flóamanna Saga* puts it.

Fate plays the strongest role in determining men's actions. Tragedy is usually the result of *ógæfa*, meaning more or less "ill luck".

The sagas are written in a highly distinctive terse and economic style. The dry, laconic viewpoint, both of the narrative and the characters, sometimes borders on parody. One dying Viking's words, as he has a spear thrust into his gut, were "I see the broad spears are now in fashion."

*The Saga Museum, Reykjavík.*

mous hero actually forces the Norwegian king Harald Hardrada at swordpoint to hand over his rightful bounty.

## Morality and fate

The saga narrators make few moral judgements, and the sagas themselves are not concerned with good and evil in the modern sense. Most of the characters are mixed, and unmitigated villains are rare – the cunning lawyer in *Njáls Saga*, Mörður Valgarðsson, is one of the few that spring to mind (for more on characters, see page 94). Despite being composed in a Christian society, the sagas portray the old pagan Viking morality. Oathbreaking, meanness and cowardice are the worst sins; open-handedness,

## The long journey home

The sagas themselves play a key role in the national psyche – they are symbolic not only of the nation's heroic past and literary achievements, but also of its survival. Many of the original vellums were hunted down and removed to the University of Copenhagen in Denmark during the 17th and 18th centuries. The most famous and indefatigable collector was Árni Magnússon (see box).

As Iceland began to claim self-rule from Denmark in the late 1800s, it became a matter of intense national importance that the country's literary heritage should be returned after centuries of "exile" overseas. When the country became independent in 1944, ownership of the manuscripts was contested. After years of internal debate and two domestic legal cases, Denmark agreed in 1961 to return the bulk of the manuscripts, hanging onto those relating to other Scandinavian countries. A decade later the first two books – the precious *Codex Regius* (containing the Poetic Eddas) and *Flateyjarbók* (the most important collection of sagas) – crossed the Atlantic in a Danish naval frigate. On 21 April 1971, thousands of spectators flocked to Reykjavík harbour to watch the manuscripts' arrival, carried ashore by naval officers in a solemn ceremony.

Since that day, 1,807 manuscripts have been returned by successive Danish governments. The Icelandic Manuscript Institute, founded in 1961 to take on the responsibility of caring for the books, is now known as the Árni Magnússon Institute for Icelandic Studies, named after the great Icelandic researcher.

## Sagas in modern Iceland

Numerous phrases from the old sagas spring readily to the lips of many modern Icelanders. For example, *"Fögur er hlíðin"* ("how fair the slopes are"), the first line of Gunnar of

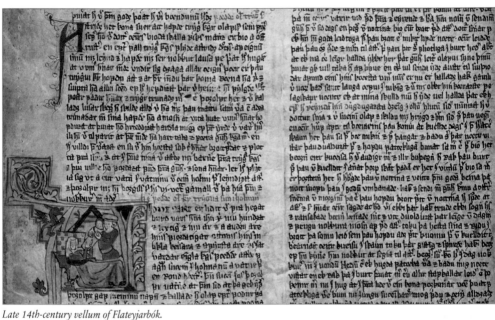

*Late 14th-century vellum of Flateyjarbók.*

## A LIFE'S WORK

Árni Magnússon was an Icelandic scholar who devoted his life to the vast number of vellum saga manuscripts that were taken away to Denmark during the days of colonial rule. Educated in Denmark, Árni returned to Iceland in 1702 to conduct a census and spent the next decade obtaining every medieval document that could be bought, and laboriously copying out the rest.

Árni's almost supernatural knack of sniffing out manuscripts has become legendary: on one occasion he discovered a vellum that had been made into a template from which to cut out waistcoats! Árni took back with him 55 cases full of manuscripts. As one of the leading scholars in Scandinavia, he was able to

continue the task from his post as Secretary of the Royal Archives in the University of Copenhagen, using his considerable influence to amass the world's best collection of Old Icelandic documents.

Tragically, fire swept through Copenhagen in 1728 and although Árni pulled most of his manuscripts from the flames, many were lost. Modern historians believe that the best parts of the collection were probably saved, but the trauma may have been too much for Árni, who died 15 months later. The research institute in Reykjavík named after him still keeps most of the manuscripts, but only a few are on view; the Culture House in the city centre has the largest public display.

Hlíðarendi's lyrical speech, when he decides not to go into foreign exile but instead to stay in his beloved homeland and face his doom, has been a patriotic catchphrase since the 19th-century struggle for independence. One of Njáll's famous sayings, *"með lögum skal land byggja"* ("with laws shall we build our land") was a punning slogan of a leading Icelandic record company – *"lögum"* can also mean "tunes".

Heroes and villains of the sagas live on in the language. A large boulder is known as a *Grettistak* after the strongman's ability to lift such

*Snorri's pool at Reykholt.*

things, and a liar is known as a *lygamörður* after the villain of *Njáls Saga*, Mörður Valgarðsson.

## Saga sites

Although the sagas are a complex mix of fact and fiction, their events can usually be pinpointed to actual places. There are usually no concrete remains at these saga sites, but it is still fascinating to visit valleys, hills and islands that resonate with the echoes of these ancient tales.

Reykjavík's 871±2 Settlement Exhibition (see page 145) is the location of Iceland's best-preserved Viking longhouse, inhabited between AD 930 and 1000, and an intriguing stretch of turf wall that seems to predate the official Settlement. However, perhaps the best-known saga

> Iceland publishes more books per capita than almost anywhere in the world, and a surprising number of prize-winning authors have risen from its tiny population. Unesco designated Reykjavík a City of Literature in 2011.

site is Snorri's pool at Reykholt in the west of Iceland (see page 209). Also in the west are the remains of Erik the Red's farmstead Eiríksstaðir, in Haukadalur valley. Excavations from 1997–9 proved that ruins of a turf lodge there date from between 890 and 980 (see page 215). Today a reconstruction of Erik's home has been built close to the archaeological remains.

In northern Iceland, the outlaw Grettir Ásmundarson, hero of *Grettir's Saga*, spent several years hiding out on the sheer-sided island of Drangey and once swam from Drangey to the hot spring Grettislaug (see page 235) on the mainland.

The setting for *Hrafnkells Saga* is the farm Aðalból (see page 289) in the east of the country, whose owner offers a guided walking tour of sites associated with the saga; while in the southwest, the Rangárvallasýsla district provides the background for *Njáls Saga*. Visit the Saga Centre in Hvolsvöllur to discover local sites connected to the story (see pages 92 and 178).

## Keeping the sagas alive

Unlike most ancient literature elsewhere, which was composed and enjoyed by a small and privileged elite, the sagas have always been the property of the common people. Also uniquely, because the Icelandic language has remained so little changed since medieval times, they remain accessible to the ordinary people of Iceland in their original language. The sagas are still read and enjoyed: nearly every Icelander is familiar with the characters and plots of the major works.

## Other Icelandic literature: poetry

The Icelandic literary tradition extends far beyond the hallowed sagas, however. The golden age of Icelandic literature, beginning around 1100 with the historical chronicle *Landnámabók* (*Book of Settlements*), was one of the richest and most diverse in medieval Europe. Even more invaluable for providing a feeling of the way of life, thoughts and priorities of these people, is the poetry they have left behind them. Icelanders were, from the start, poets. Between the 9th and 13th centuries there were 100 Icelandic poets working around the courts of Europe; after the end of the 10th century the position of court poet in Scandinavia was held only by Icelanders.

The poet or *skáld* had an elevated, even mystical status. He was entrusted with preserving the tribe's deeds in his poems, and raising morale with heroic verse. The Icelandic *skálds* have always been important members of society. Many, for example, took an active part in the independence struggle – and poetic talent has always been regarded as the sign of a noble personality.

through hard years of poverty. Since medieval times, Icelanders have always been able to read and write – children could not be confirmed until they were literate – and learning has been held in high esteem. Foreign travellers wrote of being addressed in Latin and ancient Greek by filthy, half-starved natives, and taken into huts to look at priceless manuscripts.

## Poetry and politics

In the 19th century, with improving social conditions and a growing independence movement, the *skáld* came back into his own. The poet

*Drangey island, the setting of Grettir's Saga, during midnight sun.*

The Eddic poems, like those by the *skálds*, were composed in accordance with strict rules of internal rhyme and alliteration, but are much more accessible. Dealing with heroic or mythological subjects, they were written down at the same time as the sagas, but most were probably composed much earlier. Poems such as *Hávamál* give a vivid insight into the Viking mind, revealing a people preoccupied with honour who were sociable, generous but highly pragmatic: "Cattle die, kindred die, we ourselves also die," runs one oft-quoted line, "but the fair fame never dies, of him who well deserves it".

Iceland's loss of independence (see page 45) dampened creativity, although the old language and literature remained treasured

Jónas Hallgrímsson, born in 1807, reached the hearts of his people as no one else has before or since. Known as "the nation's beloved son," he was the first Icelander to have a statue raised to his memory by his countrymen. A Romantic in the high tradition, he was at the forefront of the struggle for independence from Danish rule, and his poetry is full of love for his native land.

Jónas was a poetic radical; like Wordsworth, he wrote in the common tongue rather than high-flown poetic simile. He was also a highly qualified botanist, and travelled round the highlands each summer, collecting material for a comprehensive account of Iceland's natural history – a huge task he was never to complete. From rural North Iceland, Jónas spent much of his adult life in Copenhagen where he wrote some of his best work, including *Ísland*, a testimony to former glories and a call for a better future that every Icelander knows by heart:

> *Iceland, happy homeland,*
> *fortunate frost-white mother,*
> *where is your ancient honour,*
> *your freedom and deeds of renown…*

He suffered much hardship and exposure during his explorations, and these, together with poverty and drink, took a heavy toll on his health. He put the seal on his reputation by dying a true poet's death – young, poverty-stricken and alone.

*The late Halldór Laxness.*

## Contemporary voices

By far the most important modern literary figure is Halldór Kiljan Laxness, winner of the 1955 Nobel Prize for Literature, who died in 1998. Laxness broke away from the idealisation of peasant life prevalent in Icelandic writing, portraying the dark underside of rural life, which caused resentment amongst those who felt he was presenting Iceland in a bad light. He also played around with language, changed spellings, used street language and made up or even borrowed words – also considered unpatriotic acts. His best-known creation is Bjartur of Summerhouses, the peasant crofter hero of *Independent People*. Stubborn, infuriating, hamstrung by debt, but nevertheless "the most

independent man in the country", Bjartur is a sly dig at the "archetypal" Icelander.

But, in his own way, Laxness was as fervent a patriot as any. His novel *Iceland's Bell*, set in the 18th century, contains references to the contemporary independence struggle. The postwar *Atom Station*, from the time of the NATO airbase controversy, contains pointed criticism of the politicians who were ready to sign away their country's independence out of greed. *World Light* is another epic dealing with a slippery mass of themes: human weakness, aspiration, and the poet's role in society. Laxness was a prolific writer and his creations evolved alongside his own complex psychological, spiritual and political development.

> Nordic Noir is alive and well in Iceland. Arnaldur Indriðason's crime fiction is bestselling, and his Jar City was a film hit. Yrsa Sigurðardóttir's thrillers, featuring feisty lawyer Þóra Guðmundsdóttir, have been translated into English.

Pétur Gunnarsson, one of the first "urban novelists", innovated the use of colloquial, humorous first person narrative. Þór Vilhjálmsson makes use of fragmented language and cultural reference to come to terms with modern life, while Guðbergur Bergsson criticises the American-worshipping culture of the postwar period through absurd humour. Among women writers Svava Jakobsdóttir has developed a unique brand of surreal feminism, while the lyrical narrative method of Vigdís Grímsdóttir is much admired.

There have also been great innovations in poetry. The *atomskálds* of the 1950s caused a storm when they broke all the old rules and began to write in free verse. Continuing the prose-poem feel, poet and novelist Sjón was awarded the Nordic Council Literature Prize for his book *The Blue Fox* (2005), and his novel *From the Mouth of the Whale* was shortlisted for the Independent Foreign Fiction Prize 2012. His latest novel, *Moonstone – The Boy Who Never Was*, was published in the UK in 2016. But modern or traditional, the latter-day *skálds* of Iceland still take their responsibilities seriously. They are above all guardians of the holy trinity: language, land and nation.

# The Icelandic Language

**Icelanders know in their heart of hearts that their language is, as the poet Einar Benediktsson said, "more noble than that of any other nation".**

To the Icelander, the mother tongue is far more than just a method of communication: it is the essence of culture, and its nurture and preservation is inextricably tied up with the survival of national identity and pride.

Icelandic is one of the North Germanic family of languages, its nearest relatives still in use being Norwegian and Faroese. Thanks to centuries of comparative isolation, it is still very similar to old Norse, the language that was spoken by most of Northern Europe during the 7th to 11th centuries, and is the only language to still use the old runic symbols of ð (eth) and þ (thorn). Although no longer isolated, the language continues in its unaltered state – for Icelanders will fight to the death against any influences which might corrupt or change their beloved mother tongue.

## Preserving an ancient language

What would be regarded in other countries as normal linguistic development is seen as a national disaster in Iceland. There is, for example, "dative sickness" – a debilitating contagious disease which causes sufferers to put nouns which should be in the nominative or accusative case into the dative. Like most ancient languages, Icelandic is a complex minefield of case endings, subjunctives and inflections which can catch out many native speakers, let alone foreign students. Nevertheless, any grammatical slip-ups are considered social solecisms, and if committed by a guardian of public linguistic morals, such as a radio-show host, a grave offence.

In the spirit of individuality typical of Iceland, foreign influences on the language are kept strictly in check, and great care is taken to prevent Icelandic becoming diluted. Icelanders have no truck with such international loan-words as "radio", "telephone" or "computer", which have infiltrated many other languages; instead academic committees are set up to find proper, Icelandic words for these various new-fangled phenomena, using combinations of old words, or reappropriating words that have fallen out of usage. Thus, the computer was christened *tölva* – a mixture of the word *tala* ("number") and *völva* ("prophetess"). The telephone became *sími*, from an ancient word meaning "thread". A helicopter is a *þyrla* or "whirler"; a jet aircraft is a *þota* or "zoomer"; and electricity is the rather lovely *rafmagn* or "amber-power". The practice even extends to scientific language, which is kept as firmly non-Latin as possible. The general public joins in the fun of "word-building", and a raging debate almost always seems to ensue.

Some of these neologisms are wittily creative. Margarine is merely *smjörlíki* ("butter-like"); an echo is *bergmal* ("rock-talk"); and the post-Freud-

*Kiosk in the East Fjords.*

ian figure of the voyeur is cut down to size in Icelandic as a *gluggagægir*, the name of one of the 13 traditional harbingers of Christmas, who used to spy in through farm windows.

Another way in which tradition is preserved is in people's names: a surname is derived from the christian name of one's father or mother – hence Eiður Sigurðsson is the son of Sigurð, while Björk Guðmundsdóttir is the daughter of Guðmundur.

Icelandic is known as the Latin of the North, not only because the language itself has remained unchanged – it has also preserved, in its literature, the ancient Norse culture. Because it is almost unchanged since the Middle Ages, it makes the medieval sagas readily understandable to the modern Icelandic reader.

# In Pursuit of Njáll

The best place to start a saga tour is at Hlíðarendi, Gunnar's farm and the focus of the first part of Njáls Saga, which is widely considered to be one of the greatest Icelandic sagas.

The action of Njáls Saga – the most widely read saga today – takes place in a small stretch of the

*Flosi attempts to entice Njáll's wife from the house.*

southwestern coastal plains between the Rangá and Markarfljót rivers. Written by an unknown scholar in the 13th century, Njáls Saga is the rip-roaring tale of a 50-year blood feud.

Njáls Saga is divided into three parts. The title character, Njáll Þorgeirsson, is the most skilled lawyer in Iceland, blessed with second sight and universally respected for his fairness and integrity. A farmer who never raises his sword in anger, he is bound by the strict codes of family loyalty and honour. Oddly, Njáll plays a small role in much of the saga, reacting to rather than shaping events.

The first part of the saga concerns Njáll's friendship with the greatest champion of the land, Gunnar. Gunnar's farm, Hlíðarendi, is set above the marshy Rangá plains on Route 261 (turning south from the Ring Road east of Hvolsvöllur; see page 178). It now consists of a few white buildings and a pretty church among some trees in a mellow, peaceful landscape.

Gunnar could fight so skilfully that "he seemed to be brandishing three swords at once". He was a fair-minded fellow, slow to anger and keen to avoid trouble. His problems began when he married the beautiful, manipulative Hallgerður Long-Legs, who had arranged the demise of two previous husbands for slapping her face.

## A feud begins

Hallgerður started up a feud with Njáll's equally uncompromising wife, Bergþóra. Each of the women ordered the murder of the other's slaves in an escalating feud that the friends Njáll and Gunnar refused to be drawn into. Relatives of the victims became involved, until Gunnar was prosecuted at the Alþingi for butchering some assailants in self-defence. Sentenced to outlawry for three years, he was riding away from Hlíðarendi when his horse stumbled and he looked back. "How lovely these slopes are," he said, "more lovely than they ever seemed to me before, golden cornfields and new-mown hay. I am going back home, and I will not go away."

## Treacherous Hallgerður

The decision was fatal. Gunnar's enemies soon surrounded the farm, although he kept them at bay with his bow and arrow until his string broke. Gunnar asked his wife for two locks of her hair to plait a new bowstring, but Hallgerður refused, reminding him of a slap he had given her years earlier, and calmly explaining that she doesn't care if he holds his enemies at bay for a long time or a short one. Gunnar's reply to this death sentence is one of the sagas' most famous lines: "To each his own way of earning fame… I will not ask you again." Gunnar took many of his enemies with him, but ultimatley, they were slaughtered.

## The ambush of Þráinn Sigfússon

The bloodshed was far from over. Njáll's three sons – Helgi, Grímur and the eldest, Skarphéðinn – helped take vengeance on the killers of Gunnar. But they also wanted to kill Þráinn Sigfússon, a vain relative of Gunnar's who had been present at an earlier ambush. South of

Hlíðarendi, half way between Gunnar's home and Njáll's on the rough but passable Route 250, is a rounded hill in the middle of the plain. Today called Stóra-Dímon, it was in Njáll's time known as Rauðaskriður, or "Red Skree", and is where the three Njálssons lay in wait one winter's morning in 995 for Þráinn Sigfússon and his friends.

The ambush was spotted, and it looked as if Þráinn would get away, but Skarphéðinn leapt onto the glassy ice of the Markarfljót, skidded downstream "as fast as a flying bird", and finally buried his axe in Þráinn's head. The gymnastic

Gunnar and plotted to destroy Njáll's family. His chance came when arrangements for a money settlement over Höskuldur's murder fell through at the Alþingi. Höskuldur's kinsman, Flosi Þórðarson from the Skaftafell area, was just about to accept a deal from Njáll when Skarphéðinn insulted him, even going as far as suggesting that he was regularly sodomised by a troll.

## Bergþórshvoll

Follow route 252 to the site of Njáll's farm, Bergþórshvoll. The modern farmhouse is uninspiring, but you can still see the three hills of the

*Bergþórshvoll is an important setting in Njáls Saga.*

Skarphéðinn managed to swoop off to safety before anyone realised what had just happened.

Njáll was horrified when he heard of the killing. He organised a settlement at the Alþingi and even adopted Þráinn's orphaned son, the cherubic Höskuldur, to smooth things over. Höskuldur grew up to take over the farm Ossabær, which is now a ruined site on Route 252 heading south, but the Njálssons grew jealous of him. One day the three sprung upon him without warning in a corn field and cut him down.

## Mörður Valgarðsson

Putting the Njálssons up to this butchery was the diabolical Mörður Valgarðsson, who loathed

saga; on a clear day, the snow-covered peaks on the horizon make a spectacular sight. Having stuck by his bloodthirsty sons, Njáll spotted Flosi with 100 men bearing down on the farm. Instead of fighting, he ordered them all to retire to the house – effectively committing suicide, since Flosi promptly set the place on fire. Njáll and his wife refused an offer of mercy, preferring to die with their three sons. Only Kári Sólmundarson escaped.

Interestingly, several archaeological digs that have taken place at Bergþórshvoll during the 1920s and 50s have found evidence that suggests that a Saga Age burning did occur (the accepted date is 1011), indicating that the story may well be true.

# HEROES AND HEROINES OF THE SAGAS

**The sagas are populated with memorable and vividly drawn characters that are very human in their desires, actions and frailties.**

One of the recurring themes of the Icelandic sagas is the difference between the fortunate "light" heroes and the unlucky "dark" heroes. The romantic Kjartan Ólafsson of *Laxdæla Saga* is an archetypal light hero – handsome, accomplished and brave. In a similar mould is Gunnar of Hlíðarendi in *Njáls Saga*: "He was a handsome man...extremely well-bred, fearless, generous and even-tempered... It has been said that there has never been his equal."

The conventional romantic hero pales against the enigmatic figure of the dark hero. Like the warrior-poet Egill Skallagrímsson, they are often ugly, awkward, complicated men, at odds with society. Egill ("thick-necked and big-shouldered, hard-featured, and grim when angry") is a boastful bully, prone to rages, who commits his first killing at the age of six. At the end of a long and brutal life, his family prevent him from starting a fight – just for the fun of it – at the Alþing. The old man, now bald and blind, buries his silver in a fit of pique, along with the two servants who helped him to hide it.

The saga women were no less formidable than their male counterparts. *Njáls Saga* contains two bloodthirsty and ruthless women – Hildigunnur and Hallgerður Long-Legs. But queen of these indomitable women is Guðrún Ósvífursdóttir, heroine of *Laxdæla Saga*, who marries four times in the course of her stormy career, and ends her days as Iceland's first nun.

*For centuries, the Alþingi, the national assembly of the Icelanders, took place on the plains at Þingvellir, the scene of many of the events recounted in the sagas.*

*Antihero Egill Skallagrímsson, poet, warrior and farmer.*

*A Thor amulet. During the course of the sagas, the heroes converted their faith from the worship of Odin and Thor to Christianity – a cause of many disputes.*

*Saga Museum, Reykjavík.*

*Turf farmhouse museum, Glaumbær.*

*Wood panel depicting Odin being swallowed by Fenrir.*

## HISTORY AND FICTION

In the Middle Ages the Icelanders were the historians of the North. The surviving saga manuscripts by anonymous authors preserve most of our present knowledge of North European history and learning during this period. At the same time they sketch the outlines of Nordic identity. In a sense, they are frontier literature, in which the descendants of the settlers reflect on their origins, legends and back upon the settlement period as a golden age, with a well-functioning commonwealth of free chieftains.

The sagas were intended not only as a record of events but also as entertainment. Their authors therefore added a generous pinch of fiction to these tales of families and feuds. This mixture is probably what has given them their enduring appeal. Passed down through generations of Icelanders retelling saga tales on a winter's night, they are still a central part of the national consciousness.

*Grettir the Strong is the "dark" hero of Grettis Saga: an outlaw, strong and courageous, but quarrelsome and extremely unfortunate.*

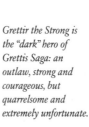

*Dynjandi waterfall, West Fjords.*

# LIVING WITH THE ENVIRONMENT

Iceland is a place of extremes, from long nights in winter and even longer days in summer, to heavy snow, to the threat of volcanic eruptions.

The English traveller John Stanley, who visited Iceland in 1789, commented: "I pitied the poor Icelanders who could not like swallows gather themselves together for a flight to a climate less hostile to the comforts of human existence. What the Icelanders can enjoy deserving the name of happiness during the long winter I cannot imagine."

There is less reason to pity the poor Icelanders these days. Warm, centrally heated houses have taken the place of damp turf huts, electric light docs much to compensate for long hours of darkness, and powerful snow-ploughs mean that only the most isolated settlements are cut off during the winter months.

In fact, during winter, the inhabited areas around Iceland's coast do not experience the bitter extremes of cold that the country's name would suggest. Unlike most other countries at this latitude, Iceland is washed by the warm waters of the Gulf Stream and moderate south-westerly Atlantic winds.

*Lighthouse on the Reykjanes Peninsula.*

Although summers are chilly by most standards, Icelandic winters are milder than in more southerly places such as New York or Moscow. It is unusual for temperatures to fall below −10°C (14°F) in Reykjavík.

## The dreaded wind and rain

Even so, as any visitor to Iceland will quickly find out, living with the climate here is still no picnic. The same Gulf Stream and mild winds that bring moderate weather run up against the Icelandic mountains and the icy polar air to create some wretched weather of wind and rain. Although there are the occasional freak summers, Reykjavík normally enjoys only one completely clear day every July. In January, the average goes up to three.

The combination of gales and rain renders umbrellas completely useless, and locals joke that Iceland is the only place where rain falls from all directions – including a horizontal one. Even so, it is not uncommon to see Icelanders wandering around without any protection during heavy downpours. Ask them why and they might shrug: "It's rained here since I was a child. I don't even notice it any more."

The weather is worst around the southwest, improving markedly around Akureyri, the north and east. But the true norm for Icelandic weather is its sheer unpredictability, shifting rapidly from clear to miserably wet, then back again, several times in the course of a single day.

## The polar night

Despite the blessing of the Gulf Stream, the Icelandic winter is still a cold, long and miserable affair. At this high latitude, it is also particularly dark. Iceland's mainland lies south of the Arctic Circle (only part of the northern island of Grímsey is within its bounds), and so avoids the extreme months of darkness endured by northern Greenland and the Arctic icecap.

golden plover (*lóa*) – the "harbinger of spring" – are reported extensively in the local press. By the middle of May the grass is turning green, birds are nesting and wild flowers are appearing. When summer truly arrives in June, the long winter wait seems almost worth it. Although temperatures are hardly tropical, between 12–15°C (54–60°F), the sun shines almost all night.

Strictly speaking, it is only above the Arctic Circle that the true "midnight sun" occurs, where the sun never dips below the horizon. This can be seen on the island of Grímsey, from

Boats at Heimaey harbour.

Even so, things here are quite bad enough. During December and January there are no more than five hours of daylight a day anywhere in the country.

That's when Icelanders begin to suffer from *skammdegisþunglyndi*, "short day depression". As some sort of compensation, winter is the time when the ghostly aurora borealis (northern lights) is visible – shimmering green and mauve waves of astral electricity flickering in the starry sky.

## Waiting for the sunshine

Across the country, Icelanders wait impatiently each year for signs of spring. The first sightings of migrating birds, particularly the

the mountains close to Ólafsfjörður or from the northeast coastline near Raufarhöfn (the northernmost point of the mainland, just 2.5km/1.5 miles south of the Arctic Circle). However, even without the true midnight sun, real night never falls during June and July. The sun only just skims below the horizon at midnight: an extended dusk is the only sign of the day's passing, and the stars cannot be seen until August.

## Summer fever

Foreign visitors have often commented that Icelanders remind them of hibernating animals, sleeping in winter and letting rip in summer. June and July – and, to a lesser extent, August – are the times when Iceland's national parks are filled to overflowing on weekends and when the country's interior is criss-crossed with frantic drivers speeding around in their huge-wheeled vehicles. The *joie de vivre* is contagious and normal rules go by the board, with even very small children playing out in the street until midnight. Visitors often find these endless days difficult to cope with: it's not easy to sleep when the sun is glistening through the window. However, there are advantages: photographers will find the golden light of the early mornings and late nights in Iceland at this time of year particularly beautiful.

In the absence of an army, the NCD is also responsible for conducting rescue operations in the event of other natural disasters; storms, avalanches, floods and volcanic eruptions are all major threats.

On average, there is a volcanic eruption somewhere in Iceland every five years. During the 20th century there were more than 20 eruptions, many of which occurred unseen, deep beneath the mighty glacier Vatnajökull. No one, however, failed to notice two of the most famous – the one off the south coast in 1963, which formed a completely new island,

*Keeping the roads open can prove a major challenge.*

At any time of year, Iceland's unpolluted arctic air makes visibility almost supernaturally clear. Far away objects often seem deceptively close: on a fine day in Reykjavík, for example, the distant icecap of Snæfellsnes seems only a few miles away.

### Treacherous seas, unstable land

The ocean is the source of Iceland's livelihood, but it can also be a killer. Despite enormous improvements in safety aboard fishing vessels, the life of the fisherman remains a dangerous one.

Nor is one safe on Icelandic dry land, either. Scientists at National Civil Defence monitor each tiny seismological tremor with concern.

*Swimming baths are one of the main focuses of social life in Iceland, and many of the country's most important decisions are made in lunchtime hot pool sessions.*

Surtsey; and 10 years later, the eruption on the Vestmannaeyjar (Westman Islands). Suddenly, in the middle of the night, what was believed to be an extinct volcano on the inhabited island of Heimaey began to erupt. Fortunately, the fishing fleet was moored in the harbour that night, and every one of the 5,300 inhabitants of the island was successfully evacuated to the mainland (see page 188).

A much more devastating eruption was that of Lakagígar in 1783, especially as the country's inhabitants could not then call upon modern technology to aid them. The lava flow, produced by some 100 craters in a volcanic fissure more than 25km (15 miles) long, was the greatest ever recorded in human world history, and it eventually covered an area of 565 sq km (218 sq miles). It was Iceland's most cataclysmic natural disaster, and the eruption together with the Haze Famine that came in its aftermath, caused the deaths of thousands of people (see page 51).

Another old enemy is erosion. Iceland was once, according to the old chronicles, heavily forested, but now there is a startling absence of trees, and most natural vegetation is scrubby tundra. The lack of trees means there is little to bind the soil, which is bad news on a such a windswept island.

## Exploiting the volcanic landscape

A natural force can occasionally be tamed and made to earn its keep. Iceland's homes have been provided with cheap and environmentally friendly hot water and heating for the past 70

*Hverir geothermal field, Lake Mývatn.*

### TO THE RESCUE...

Iceland's unpredictable weather can have dangerous consequences. Trippers and mountaineers should notify the National Association of Rescue Groups of their journey before they set off. This fine body of volunteers will organise search parties if travellers do not return to base on schedule. They don't take kindly, however, to risking life and limb rescuing people who have got into trouble through sheer foolhardiness, so make sure that you take sensible precautions, such as not venturing onto a glacier alone, or climbing unknown mountains or walking in unfamiliar areas except with an experienced guide.

years by geothermal energy – water heated naturally under the earth's crust. This water is also used to heat the acres of greenhouses, used for growing fruit and vegetables, especially tomatoes, bananas and mushrooms, in the towns of Hveragerði, Reykholt, Laugarás and Flúðir – the country's market-gardens under glass.

Geothermal energy is also the reason that Icelanders can enjoy an open-air swim on the most bitterly cold and snowy morning – and soak afterwards in a 45°C (113°F) hot pool. Swimming in Iceland is not so much a hobby as a way of life, and the geothermal pools have a total attendance of around 1.6 million people a year. Icelanders have been used to regarding their geothermal water as a bottomless pit

– one swimming pool, for example, uses up 1.3 million tons of water a day – but there are indications that the reserves in Reykjavík may be drying up because of overuse.

Hydroelectricity supplies around 80 percent of Iceland's power, much of this being used in aluminium smelters near Hafnarfjörður, Akranes and Reyðarfjördur. In the past, damming rivers for hydroelectricity has caused environmental concerns; but many argue that Iceland's glacial rivers still have plenty of untapped potential. And with so much surplus energy, it seems logical to try to export some

*Keeping your car from skidding on the icy roads is a concern.*

of it abroad. The practicalities of laying underwater electric cables to Scotland, Germany and even Canada have been discussed for over 20 years, and in 2012 the UK energy minister, Charles Hendry, travelled to Iceland to discuss the topic further: the proposed Iceland–UK cable would be the world's longest at around 1,500km (900 miles). A growing worldwide demand for electricity coupled with the development of ultra-low resistance wires mean that schemes such as these will probably become a reality within the next decade.

Tourism saw a rapid increase between 2002 and 2015, with over 1 million visitors during the latter year.. It is one of the island's most important industries, bringing in 31 percent of the total foreign currency earnings. However, the environment, seemingly so rugged and powerful, is actually extremely fragile – and the authorities are as a result not keen to see it grow out of control. "Iceland isn't open safari country," says Þóroddur Þóroddsson of the National Conservation Council. "We want tourists who are sensitive to the environment."

## Keeping the roads open

Although Iceland does not fully merit its chilly name, winters are prolonged and snow can be heavy, but this does not discourage the Icelanders from travelling as much as possible all year round. A few decades ago, the sea was the most important route for travel between Iceland's dispersed coastal communities. Roads hardly existed, and the coastal boats transported passengers and goods alike. Today, however, overland travel has become the norm.

A vastly improved road system means that land travel is possible throughout the year, albeit a little difficult at times. If the road network seems, to the outsider, to be a series of primitive narrow roads, at times dispensing altogether with the need for tarmac, the outsider should bear in mind that it is a huge, and vastly expensive, transport network for such a small population in such a large country. The quality of the roads has advanced by leaps and bounds since the 1960s, and every year further stretches of unsurfaced track disappear under a layer of tarmacadam.

Policy laid down by the Ministry of Communications aims to keep all major roads passable, as far as possible, throughout the winter months: the first priority is given to keeping open routes between centres of population within each region. These are generally cleared every working day, and even more frequently in the event of unusually heavy snow. Roads out of Reykjavík, north to Borgarfjörður and east to Hvolsvöllur, for instance, are very rarely closed to traffic for more than a few hours at a time.

The second-highest priority is placed upon keeping clear roads linking one region to the next, such as the South to the East Fjords, or the route from Akureyri to Reykjavík. These roads are cleared two or three times weekly on average.

Minor roads, however, are cleared less frequently, if at all. Mountain tracks across the interior are normally closed by snow by the end of

October. Although these roads are largely free of snow again by May, meltwater turns them into impassable seas of mud, and they are only reopened once they are dry enough to sustain traffic, usually in late June or early July, after assessment by the Public Roads Administration. This body closely monitors traffic on the highlands; unauthorised travel on the muddy roads in early spring can cause severe damage, and offenders are subject to heavy fines.

Although all efforts are made to keep the road network functioning, ordinary family cars will struggle with winter driving conditions.

*Dog-sledding in winter.*

Icelanders have therefore taken enthusiastically to large four-wheel-drive vehicles and wintertime travel in the souped-up, giant-wheeled versions of these cars has become a popular hobby.

## Alternative routes

Some major routes over highland passes – such as those into the mountainous West Fjords – are subject to such heavy snowfalls that they cannot necessarily be kept open through the winter, and they may be closed for weeks or months. Alternative routes at lower altitudes remain open, and in some regions the sea route provides the main winter link between communities. In the West Fjords in particular, travel by sea still remains almost as important as in the past.

Air travel is of unusual importance in Iceland, and even more so in winter. It takes about five hours to drive the 389km (243 miles) to Akureyri from Reykjavík, in good conditions. By air, you can get there in 45 minutes. In winter, with uncertain road conditions, the comparison becomes even more favourable. Flights are relatively rarely cancelled, although there can be delays, and Icelandic pilots attain great expertise in taking off, flying and landing in difficult, icy conditions.

The air route is also, of course, the emergency route into and out of most communities during the winter months. Scheduled flights operate frequently to major centres such as Akureyri, Ísafjörður and Egilsstaðir, and less often – although still regularly – to a host of small centres around the country, where there may be no more than a landing strip and a windsock to indicate the "airport".

## Icy conditions

Snow is not the only hindrance to winter travel, though. Roads are often dangerously icy, mainly because of a tendency for Icelandic temperatures to hover around freezing point for much of the winter. The temperature may be 2–3°C (35–38°F) when snow falls, then warm up to reduce the snow to the consistency of a smooth mush. The thermometer might then plummet to −10°C (14°F) and the mush freezes, smooth as a skating rink.

Winter tyres are compulsory from 1 November to 14 April, even in towns, where

> Iceland has more than 13,000km (8,000 miles) of roads, and approximately 8,000km (5,000 miles) of them are classified as major roads.

all roads are cleared regularly in snow, and salted to reduce ice. Many Icelanders opt for studded tyres, which give a better grip on icy road surfaces, although braking remains a problem on slippery roads. Heavy-tread snow tyres offer better braking, but may not provide enough grip for driving up slippery slopes. If you want to learn how to handle a car in a skid, Iceland is the place. With roads this slippery, you learn fast.

*Stopping to admire the scenery at Borgarfjörður-Eystri.*

# Environmental Protection

**A land of some 100,000 sq km (38,610 sq miles), and only 332,000 people, with clean air and clean water, Iceland was relatively slow to see the need for conservation.**

In today's interdependent world, Iceland is facing a dilemma – how can its pristine environment and outstanding natural beauty be protected

*Iceland's glaciers are under threat from rising temperatures.*

from the ravages of industrialisation and global warming? It's a problem that has vexed the Icelandic people and which has attracted attention from environmentalists the world over.

Increasing awareness has resulted in measures to reverse soil erosion, limit gravel mining in volcanic areas, and regulate the fishing that is essential to the economy. Other advances are stricter limits on off-road driving, and even cycling on mountain tracks.

## Dams and smelters

Aluminium processing is an energy-intensive business, and since the 1960s, foreign companies have been attracted to Iceland's renewable

energy sources to power their smelters. Rio Tinto Alcan still operates the first ever aluminium smelter, built near Hafnarfjörður in 1969; while the American-owned Norðurál runs the smelter built in 1998 near Akranes. However, when, in 2003, the Icelandic government approved the building of a gigantic dam in an area of the uninhabited interior of the country known as Kárahnjúkur, the environmental movement gained a whole new *raison d'être*. The country's biggest ever construction project centred on a highland valley on the northeastern edge of the mighty Vatnajökull glacier, one of Europe's last areas of untouched wilderness and summer breeding grounds for the rare pink-footed goose.

The project, an immense complex of reservoirs, tunnels, shafts, canals, embankments, roads and five dams, provides the power for an American-owned aluminium smelter 75km (45 miles) away, in Reyðarfjörður in the East Fjords. Within this region, most people strongly supported the project, as the aluminium smelter generated badly needed jobs. Elsewhere, however, people were less enamoured. The filling of the largest dam triggered one of the biggest demonstrations in Icelandic history, when 15,000 protestors, led by former president Vigdís Finnbogadóttir, marched to the doors of the Icelandic parliament. Opponents claimed that the then-government was wilfully selling off the country's pristine nature for short-term profit – after the immense Kárahnjúkur project, two other major smelters, at Húsavík and Helguvík, were also planned. Following the 2008 crash, a new Left-Green coalition government came into power with a manifesto that emphasised the importance of long-term environmental protection. Several controversial proposals, including the two new smelters, and a plan to dam the lower part of the Þjórsá river, were shelved, bringing a modicum of hope to Iceland's environmentalist movement. These hopes were dimmed when the pre-crash incumbents were returned to political office in April 2013, creating renewed fears that the smelters and dams had simply been put on a four-year hold.

## Wearing away the soil

Land erosion is a problem in many countries, but in Iceland it presents a major environmental challenge. Human occupation since the time of the Settlement has caused more damage to the natural environment than in any other country in

Europe. Iceland has lost 50 percent of its original vegetation and 95 percent of its tree cover, with the result that two-thirds of Iceland's terrain is now subject to erosion, ranging from slight to extremely severe.

The first settlers unwittingly began this gradual destruction when they introduced sheep to the land, which steadily grazed away entire areas of vegetation. Population growth soon put additional pressure on the country's fragile ecosystem: trees, which once held the soil in place and sheltered smaller plants from the heavy sea sprays, were felled to provide fuel and building timber.

Today, serious efforts are underway to reverse the damage. The Soil Conservation Service of Iceland (SCS) and the Iceland Forest Service (IFS) were created as far back as 1907 to rescue the country from desertification. The IFS oversees the plantation of tough species such as larch, birch and spruce, whose roots keep the fine sandy soil from blowing away. The soil reclamation project known as Hekluskógar (Hekla Forests), currently underway around the Hekla volcano in the south of Iceland, is the biggest such programme in Europe. Its aim is to stop the spread of the ash desert around the volcano, with landowners and volunteers planting 90,000 hectares (222,400 acres) of birch forest and willow scrub.

In June, visitors can't fail to notice the swathes of purple-blue lupins that bloom all over the country. The flower has been used extensively since the 1950s to cover vast barren areas, pinning down the fine soil and fixing it with nitrogen. However, the lupins' spread has been too successful in some places, where it has invaded delicate heathlands and displaced native vegetation. Today there are battles to eradicate the plant from sensitive spots such as Skaftafell, in Vatnajökull National Park.

## The marine environment

Control and regulation of the seas and fish stocks off Iceland is at least as important to the country as on-land conservation. During the Cod Wars with the United Kingdom in the 1970s, the government set a 322km (200-mile) limit for its territorial waters. The extended fishing zone was not just to prevent competition from foreign vessels; it was partly created so that the government could more easily control how much fish was caught.

After several years of bumper catches, with the cod take nearing 508,000 tonnes (460,000 US tons) in 1982, cod stocks then became dangerously low. A complex quota system was introduced in 1984, with the intention of limiting the catch and the preserving the population. Every fishing vessel now receives an annual quota, specifying how many tons of each fish it is allowed to haul in. The system took some pressure off cod stocks by increasing the number of other species fished. Over 20 years later, and there are now signs that cod numbers have now started recovered a little since their all-time his-

*Geothermal power production on the Reykjanes Peninsula.*

torical low in 1993. However, many other commercially caught species are now being overfished themselves.

## Europe's biggest national park

Iceland has more than 80 protected nature reserves, and until recently had four national parks – Þingvellir, Snæfellsjökull, Skaftafell and Jökulsárgljúfur. In June 2008, the latter two were joined together to form the Vatnajökull National Park, Europe's biggest at 12,000 sq km (4,633 sq miles). The park covers over 11 percent of Iceland, including the whole of the Vatnajökull icecap. Its creation was largely a political move to draw attention to Iceland's fast-melting glaciers.

*Enjoying a whale-watching expedition near Húsavík. Inhabitant species include the minke, humpack and blue whale.*

*Crates of the day's catch packed in ice for freshness.*

# HARVESTING THE SEA

**Fishing has provided food, employment and wealth for Iceland for centuries; the challenge now is to avoid over-exploiting the limited resources of the sea.**

"Life is saltfish," wrote Iceland's Nobel Laureate, the late Halldór Laxness, in the 1930s. At the beginning of the 21st century, with the country's economy dependent on the sea more than ever before, life is still saltfish, but it's also canned fish, smoked salmon, frozen shrimps and caviar.

Fish has been an important export item from Iceland ever since the stockfish trade to Britain commenced in the Middle Ages. But fishing only began to outpace agriculture in economic status with the advent of motorised fishing vessels around the start of the 20th century.

And while improvements in vessel technology soon made fisheries into Iceland's mainstay national industry, at the same time they intensified the threat of overfishing by foreign deep-sea fleets, which escalated until the famous Cod Wars with Britain.

## Fishing and fortune

The first 30 years of the 20th century were a time of intense, fisheries-led economic growth, with almost 90 percent of the nation's income coming directly from the sea. Iceland was gradually escaping from Danish colonial rule, and economic independence was an obvious prerequisite for true political independence. Iceland's fishing industry has been coloured by fierce nationalism ever since.

Salted whitefish – mainly cod, sold to Spain – and iced whitefish and herring, sold to the UK and northern Europe, were the mainstays of Icelandic fisheries right up until World War II. Dependence on those few markets had its limitations: for example, Spanish wine producers threatening to ban imports of saltfish were able to "twist Iceland's arm" into lifting a six-year alcohol prohibition in 1921. Later, the

*A fisherman sporting traditional clothing, Bolungarvik.*

collapse of the fish market in the Great Depression devastated Iceland's economy.

## The fish boom begins

Unemployment ran high right up until World War II, when Iceland suddenly became the only large fish-producer in the whole of northern Europe. Icing their catches, Icelandic fishing vessels sailed directly to Britain, often suffering fatalities from U-boat attacks. Meanwhile, superior freezing technology was developed. This would become the key to the postwar fisheries boom, which targeted both the UK and American markets.

Iceland made good money during the war and allocated funds for the modernisation of the trawler fleet, and an era of larger catches and more diverse markets began. Frozen block and fillets went to both sides of the Atlantic. During the Cold War, Iceland kept good trading relations with Eastern Europe, and the Soviet Union became a major buyer of products such as salted herring. Meanwhile, the diversification which remains the key to Iceland's survival as a specialist fish-producing nation began.

Of increasing importance in this environmentally conscious age is the cleanness of Iceland's fish. The fishing grounds are far enough from the industrial centres of Europe and North America to remain very pure, while the small local population and absence of large-scale manufacturing industries keep "home-grown" pollution to a bare minimum. Iceland even exports the technology for catching and handling fish: in some specialist areas, such as the electronic weighing of fish at sea using scales that automatically compensate for the roll of the boat, Iceland is a world leader.

## Surviving in a high-risk industry

Seafood is, however, a notoriously shaky business – size of catches can never be taken for

*Fresh cod arrivals on the Reykjanes Peninsula.*

### RICHES FROM THE SEA

Situated in the North Atlantic where warm Gulf Stream waters merge with cold Arctic currents, Iceland's relatively unpolluted fishing grounds offer near-perfect conditions for a huge variety of marine species. These include demersal (bottom-feeding) fish, led by cod, haddock, redfish (ocean perch), saithe (pollack), ocean catfish and flatfish such as Greenland halibut and plaice. There are also shellfish such as shrimp, scallops and Norway lobster (nephrops or scampi tails). Finally there are river-migrating fish, such as wild salmon, trout and Arctic char, as well as pelagic (topwater) fish including herring and capelin.

granted and prices fluctuate far more than in land-based food processing. Unstable as its economy has been, Iceland buffered itself against heavy market shocks by shrewdly spreading its coverage and its product range.

The US was Iceland's main buyer of frozen fish from the 1970s to the mid-1980s, until a sliding dollar made Europe a more attractive proposition. Today, Iceland's biggest European customer by far is the UK, followed by Spain, Norway, France and the Netherlands. The most important sales to the UK are of frozen cod, followed by haddock; Spain favours split saltfish; Norway buys quantities of fishmeal and fish oil; France buys cod and redfish; and the Netherlands are partial to haddock, plaice and lemon sole.

> *Although only around 5 percent of the Icelandic population is employed in the fishing industry, fish make up some 40 percent of Iceland's total export earnings.*

Nigeria has shot up the market table recently, and is Iceland's biggest buyer outside Europe. Japan, the world's largest seafood market, became important for Iceland in the 1980s, yet hardly competed with established lines sold elsewhere. The oriental taste is for flatfish, whole-frozen redfish (Europeans and Americans prefer fillets), shell-on shrimp (the British and Danes prefer peeled), and previously unexploited delicacies such as capelin roe, whole-frozen female herring, cod milt (sperm) and sea urchins.

At least in terms of demand, and of income, the future looks promising. Awareness of the healthiness of a protein-rich, low-cholesterol seafood diet, backed by the clean image of the waters where Iceland catches its fish, look set to keep demand buoyant well into the 21st century. The worldwide call for fish, an ever-more expensive product thanks to decreasing stocks, saw Iceland adding a further 35 vessels to its fishing fleet in 2012 to meet demand.

Fisheries constitute 40 percent of Iceland's total export value and 12 percent or the country's GDP, even though only 3.1 percent of Iceland's population is employed on fishing vessels and 2.2 percent in land-based processing plants.

## The Cod Wars

The big problem since the start of the 1990s has been supply. Major stocks are at or beyond the maximum level of safe harvesting, and with a fleet powerful enough to vacuum-clean the ocean floor in a couple of weeks, the industry is being forced to scale down its operations. This is not a new problem. Overfishing by foreign fleets was a strong fear in Iceland in the early postwar period. The traditional 5km (3-mile) exclusive fishing zone around Iceland's coast was extended to 6.5km (4 miles) in 1952, and even though this seems like a drop in the ocean now, it sparked massive protests and a temporary ban on fish imports from Iceland in the UK. The first real "Cod War" began in 1959 when Iceland upped its territorial waters to 20km (12 miles) and Royal Navy frigates were sent in to protect, unsuccessfully, British

trawlers from being evicted or arrested by Iceland's tiny coastguard force.

Eventually the dispute was resolved, only to be followed by successive extensions to 80km (50 miles) in 1972 and 330km (200 miles) in 1975. This renewed more ferocious clashes, although no fatalities ever occurred. While the British gunboats rammed coastguard vessels and fired shots over their bows, the ultimate deterrent in the Icelandic arsenal was the dreaded "clippers" – rather like garden shears – which were used to cut trawls from British vessels, removing both their nets and

*Harðfiskur, or hard, wind-dried fish, is a popular snack and great for taking on trips thanks to its lightness.*

their catches. Some of these clippers are now proudly, if rather mock-heroically, on display in the National Museum in Reykjavík.

On one occasion, the world's press almost outnumbered the naval ratings when a British frigate and Icelandic gunboat had a confrontation on the high seas. Fortunately, the opposing captains had a keen sense of occasion and the ensuing exchange was not of shots but of Biblical quotations which were delivered broadside by loudhailer. Initially taken aback, journalists managed to salvage just enough Scripture knowledge to award the result to the Icelandic team.

More considered formal arguments gradually swung international opinion over to Iceland's

The territorial waters limit that Iceland established in the 1970s has since become a standard for international marine legislation.

point of view, and a "truce" was eventually agreed in 1976 – by which time the UK itself had announced its own 330km (200-mile) limit.

Disputes continue to this day, this time in the form of a brewing 'Mackerel War.' Although Iceland reduced its mackerel quota by 15 percent in 2013, the Scottish fishing industry believes

*Wafer-thin smoked salmon.*

Iceland is still taking more than their fair share of the fish – Scotland's most valuable catch. The European fisheries commissioner intervened, warning Iceland's government that it needs to come to the negotiating table or face sanctions. Iceland has so far rejected the threats and the contentious issue has yet to be solved.

## Protecting the sea's bounty

Part of the philosophy behind extending the fishing zone was not just to prevent foreign fishing, but to be able to control how many fish were caught. After several years of bumper harvests, with the cod take nearing 508,000 tonnes (460,000 US tons) in 1982, the time came to put the brakes on Iceland's own fleet. Even as

the Cod Wars were in full swing, Iceland had learned that it could overfish all by itself: the "herring boom" in the Northeast collapsed in the late 1960s when the fish virtually disappeared from one season to the next.

When cod numbers plummeted in a disconcertingly similar manner, a complex quota system was introduced in 1984. Today, the Ministry of Fisheries and Agriculture keeps a close eye on fish stocks, checking to see that numbers look healthy. It then grants each fishing vessel a tonnage quota for individual species of fish. Boat owners are free to swap or trade their quotas among themselves to maximise efficiency – and to make money.

Many skippers claim they have been transformed overnight from heroic hunters into accountants. Unfortunately, years of poor spawning have forced the government to cut quotas regularly. Tradeable quotas have become a claim on a scarce resource, and the value of "paper fish" – the cod swimming unsuspectingly with a quota on its head – has grown at a rate that would draw looks of disbelief even from people who habitually play the money markets.

## Future of the fishing industry

Following the 2008 financial crisis and collapse of the króna, Iceland applied for EU membership. Previously this would never have been seriously considered, mainly because prohibitive EU quotas would have a detrimental effect on the country's all-important fishing industry. Even after the application had been submitted, though, lively for-and-against debates continued. By January 2013, support for EU membership had waned to the point where a parliamentary proposal to suspend the application was passed – the biggest issue being the knotty topic of the country's fishing rights. Iceland eventually dropped its EU application in 2015; one year later fishery minister Gunnar Bragi Sveinsson bluntly stated that Iceland "would never join the European Union". The Icelandic government strongly believes that it is more than capable of managing its fishing stocks, and that it will be better off outside the Union. This point of view may well be justified by the fact that previously depleted Icelandic cod and haddock numbers have been replenished in recent years. As a result ,cod and haddock for fishing quotas 2015/2016 were increased by 10 and 20 percent respectively.

# Whaling

**Most Icelanders regard the harvesting of the seas around their country as a virtual birthright and are strongly pro-whaling.**

Whaling is a topic that arouses passionate feeling in Iceland today – a 2009 Gallup poll found that 77.4 percent of Icelanders support the commercial hunt.

When a 20-year global moratorium on whaling was introduced in 1986, Iceland continued whaling, exploiting a loophole in the legislation that enabled it to whale for "scientific" purposes. By 1989, when Iceland stopped all whaling amid a domestic political furore, 292 fin whales and 70 sei whales had been killed for "research".

## The hunting continues

It was widely expected, though, that Iceland would resume whaling when the time was right. Indeed, in 1992 the country pulled out of the International Whaling Commission (IWC), of which it had been a founding member. It cited growing frustration with a new protocol that would reintroduce commercial hunting under strict international limits. Iceland then set up a rival organisation with Norway, Greenland and the Faroe Islands in the hope of challenging the power of the IWC. However, after 10 years, Iceland rejoined the IWC, registering at the same time a reservation to the commission's moratorium on whaling.

Amid international outcry, the Icelandic government announced in 2003 that it would catch 36 minke whales for "scientific research", later selling the meat commercially to the neighbouring Faroe Islands, whose government claimed it was exempt from a ban on importing whale meat. Conservationists feared that this was a first step towards the full resumption of commercial whaling.

Sure enough, in late 2006, the government announced that Iceland would resume the commercial hunting of whales. The Icelandic fisheries ministry issued a statement claiming that it would keep catches within sustainable limits. Initially the quota was set at 30 minke whales and nine fin whales per year. Ministry research recommended that up to 229 minke whales and 154 fin whales could be caught sustainably in

the 2014 season. In 2015, Icelandic whalers killed some 155 fin whales and 29 minke whales. Whale catches currently end up in domestic supermarkets and on restaurant menus, where the meat is mostly eaten by curious tourists. Some of it is also exported to Japan. To many outside observers, the 2006 decision to resume hunting might have appeared self-defeating. Iceland had been gaining a reputation abroad as one of Europe's premier whale-watching destinations, and tourist leaders were quick to point out to the government that butchering whales for a not-particularly-buoyant food mar-

*A whale is hosed down before being skinned.*

ket was totally at odds with the nascent whale-watching industry. Iceland's fragile economy could ill afford any form of international boycott, be it from tourists choosing to take their holidays elsewhere, or from anti-whaling nations refusing to import Icelandic fish and fish products.

However, the worst fears of the tourist industry do not seem to have materialised. Tourist numbers have continued to rise dramatically since 2006, and the whale-watching industry is also booming, with around 175,000 visitors each year joining a tour. The whale-hunting situation looks unlikely to change in the near future, as the government insists that whale-hunting in Iceland is "science-based, sustainable, strictly managed and in accordance with international law".

# LIFE ON
# THE LAND

With a short growing season and land of variable fertility, the Icelanders have come up with inventive and successful ways of farming.

In the early 20th century, Iceland's farmers still lived much as their forebears had done for 1,000 years: they kept their sheep, grazed them in summer on the highlands, cut the hay in summer, rounded up the animals in autumn. After the autumn slaughter, some of the livestock were foddered on hay through the winter, while the meat was salted, smoked and otherwise preserved. During the winter, wool was knitted and woven into clothes for the household.

Around 100 years ago, with Home Rule granted by Denmark, things began to change rapidly: aided by the cooperative movement, farming developed from a subsistence activity into a business. The countryside was transformed. Some of the most marginal regions became totally depopulated. Young people left in droves to seek education and a better life (and mechanisation meant far less labour was needed anyway). Roads and telephones made isolation a thing of the past.

There are still some 3,200 working farms in Iceland, but farmers are plagued with problems, from desertification to over-production of lamb and milk. A quota system was introduced in the 1980s, although this has meant that over the last 30 years, many smaller farms have become economically unviable. Some survived by tapping into the tourism boom, with farm-stay holidays a potentially lucrative business (after all, there are no quotas on tourists).

The future is likely to bring greater competition. Protectionist legislation and heavy government subsidies have hitherto helped farmers survive, but these are likely to be threatened in future by Iceland's participation in the European Economic Area formed by EFTA (European Free Trade Association).

*Gathering colourful guillemot eggs.*

*Cows first arrived on Iceland in the 10th century, having been brought over from Norway.*

*The roofs of rural homes were traditionally turf-clad for insulation. The memory of a time when all Icelanders lived off the land still grips the national imagination, but in reality the rural life was often one of hardship and struggle against an unforgiving environment.*

*Farmer leading sheep to be sorted.*

## SUPPLEMENTING THE DIET

Iceland's dramatic sea-cliffs, clustered with millions of birds, were once known as "pantries", and Icelanders would often have gone hungry had they not had the nourishment of these natural food stores. In all the areas where sea-bird colonies are found, men would clamber down the near-vertical cliff-faces, gathering eggs from the nests. Today sea-birds' eggs are still gathered in some quantity. Sprang, the art of swinging nimbly down a cliff-face on a long rope, is still a much-practised skill in the Vestmannaeyjar (see page 184).

Regarded as a great delicacy by many, sea-birds' eggs are commonly eaten in coastal villages in season, and are sold in supermarkets. The eggs of the guillemot are most often sold commercially. Other species were also hunted for food, and still are today, notably puffins and guillemots. Other than sea birds, the goose, wild duck and ptarmigan are practically the only birds hunted for human consumption.

*The fairytale hues of guillemot eggs, the type of sea-birds' eggs most frequently sold.*

*Tractor amid stunning scenery.*

*Ruin in the West Fjords.*

# FOOD AND DRINK

A unique line in traditional delicacies provides variety from the ever-present, but high-quality, staples of fish and lamb. A plentiful supply of cosy restaurants makes eating out a pleasure.

Icelandic food is based on fish and lamb, the two ingredients most readily available in the country. Throughout the centuries they have been boiled fresh, and smoked, salted, pickled or dried to store for the winter months.

The fish is likely to be among the most exquisite you have ever tasted. Indeed, many Icelanders simply refuse to eat fish when they go abroad because it just doesn't taste the same as it does back home. Fish generally arrives in the shops a matter of hours after it has been landed and is accordingly juicy, tender and fresh. Haddock and halibut are often boiled or grilled and served with a prawn sauce or simply with butter. Salmon and trout are served fresh or smoked – traditionally using dung. Thin slices of smoked fish are served with hot spring-baked rye bread. Try herring, smoked, pickled or the tinned variety in mustard or garlic sauce. Nothing is wasted and you will find cod's cheeks and roe alongside salmon and prawns on the fish counter.

When it comes to lamb, there's the tender smoked variety, often served in the home with pickled red cabbage and sugar-browned potatoes, as well as regular lamb chops or steaks. In fact, whatever form it comes in, Icelandic lamb, although rather expensive, is delicious since sheep are left to wander freely in the mountains all summer long, grazing on the herb-rich pastures.

Chicken and beef are also popular. Chicken has become increasingly so in recent years with the rise in fast-food outlets and oriental restaurants even though it remains one of the most expensive meats available in Iceland.

## Traditional delicacies

Whalemeat (*hval*), mostly from minke whales, is commonly found on tourist menus. It is usually soaked first in milk to extract some of the

*Traditional Reykjavík restaurant.*

oil, and then served as medallions or steaks. It tends to be an expensive meat product due to the high costs associated with whaling. There are also ethical issues to be considered: the Whale and Dolphin Conservation (WDC) and the International Federation for Animal Welfare (IDAW) both strongly advise visitors against consuming whalemeat. Only an estimated 5 percent of Icelanders eat it regularly, so

*Traditionally served with potatoes, white sauce and peas, hangikjöt – smoked mutton – is a festive Christmas and New Year dish, but is eaten eagerly at any time of the year.*

one of the main markets for the products of the country's controversial whale hunts are tourists.

Sea birds, particularly puffin *(lundi)* and guillemot *(svartfugl)*, which once saved destitute Icelanders from starvation (see page 117), are now considered something of a delicacy. A particular favourite is smoked puffin, accompanied by a delicate blueberry sauce. Seemingly Icelanders have no qualms about eating their national bird – after all, salted or smoked, puffins were one of the dietary staples of centuries past.

Many other traditional foods have survived to this day and are as popular as ever. Adventurous

served up at the þorrablót feast either in halves or off the bone and pressed into a kind of pâté. Accompanied by mashed turnips, it tastes better than it looks – even, surprisingly, the eyes. Pride of place goes to pickled rams' testicles, pressed into a nightmarish cake. Not a dish for the faint of heart, but oddly digestible in small quantities.

Guts, blood, fat and a dash of meat for form's sake, nattily sown up in sheep's stomachs, create another dish appropriately called *slátur* (slaughter). *Slátur* is not confined to the midwinter feast; it is eaten regularly in Icelandic homes. The dish comes in two varieties: *lifrarpylsa*,

*Fish dish on offer in the East Fjords.*

types in search of authentic food and blessed with a cast-iron stomach will relish the midwinter þorrablót feast (mid-January to mid-February, although many items are available all year). The feast is largely an act of homage to the old methods of preserving food. One of the best places to sample a þorrablót menu is at the Fjörukráin restaurant in Hafnarfjörður (see page 159), just outside Reykjavík. Here you really can pretend you're back in Viking times and sample the strangest of dishes, washed down with generous amounts of beer or schnapps. Almost everything a sheep can provide ends up being eaten: don't be surprised to spot *svið*, a whole sheep's head, burned to remove the wool and then boiled, staring at you from your plate. This delicacy is

which means "liver sausage" but isn't, and the darker, fattier *blóðmör* or blood pudding, which is like Scottish haggis without the spice.

One of Iceland's most notorious food rituals is the ceremonious intake of rotten shark *(hákarl)* and schnapps. After being buried for three months or so, shark becomes acrid and ammoniac; rubbery and rotten, it is washed down in small cubes with ample quantities of the Icelandic spirit, *brennivín* (see page 121). A few nips beforehand for courage's sake is not a bad idea either! Icelanders view eating *hákarl* rather like the dark midwinter itself. It strikes an emotional chord deep within the soul; and once over, the joy of having survived makes life seem instantly brighter again.

## Dairy products

Cows in Iceland feed on fresh grass, free from pesticides, and are raised without the use of growth hormones and antibiotics. Well worth a try as a snack or dessert is *skyr*, a rich type of curd, high in calcium and low in calories, which resembles a thick, creamy yoghurt in consistency. Competition from flavoured yoghurt and ice cream has led dairy producers to create a number of varieties of *skyr* such as blueberry, pear or vanilla. However, the genuine article is still sold unflavoured, ideally with cream stirred in and topped with wild crowberries.

*Súrmjólk*, soured milk, is eaten at breakfast with brown sugar. If you want normal fresh milk, choose the cartons marked *nýmjólk* (full-fat) or *léttmjólk* (semi-skimmed). *Mysingur* is a sweet spread made from whey which is popular with children. Those with a sweet tooth will also love rich Icelandic ice cream, which is sometimes made and sold directly from the farmhouse – look out for signs when you're driving in dairy country.

Icelandic cheeses are generally mild Gouda-type varieties, and are rarely matured. There is no tradition of cheese-eating after dinner, as found in some European countries.

*Delicious dessert in Reykjavík.*

*Brennivín, the lethal local spirit.*

### EATING OUT

Dining out in Iceland has undergone tremendous changes in the past 20 years. Many young Icelandic chefs have sought training abroad, then returned home to apply their new-found gourmet knowledge to traditional ingredients. As a result, Reykjavík's restaurant scene has been transformed, and dining out here is now a real treat.

Iceland takes utmost pride in its fresh fish and lamb, but there is also a growing local-food movement with a strong emphasis on seasonal, organic ingredients. Langoustines from Höfn; reindeer and pink-footed geese from the eastern highlands; shrimp from the north; seabirds' eggs taken from cliffs around the country in spring; and crowberries, blueberries and wild mushrooms picked in early autumn all feature on Iceland's menus and are worth savouring.

Prices are not low in Iceland's better restaurants – but you are paying for excellent meals made with high-quality ingredients. In Reykjavík, many restaurants also offer good-value fixed-price tourist menus or buffets in summer, which include a soup or starter followed by a fish or meat main course and coffee. Prices are lower at lunch. Children under six usually eat for free and 6- to 12-year-olds pay half price. It is rare, though, to find special offers outside the capital, where good-quality dining is thinner on the ground.

## Breads and pastries

Although sandwiches are generally served on white or wholegrain sliced bread, rye is a popular ingredient in bread-making. Healthy, filling rye bread is often consumed at breakfast with toppings of ham, cheese, pâté or jam. Rye is also the key ingredient in *flatkökur*, which as the name suggests are flat, rounded, unsweetened pancakes with a somewhat smoky taste. These can be found in most corner shops and supermarkets and are a good source of fibre and excellent for picnics. Iceland's cakes and pastries have a heavy Danish influence, and are devoured with cream (and gusto) over cups of strong coffee. Popular varieties include a square-shaped Danish pastry with gooey vanilla filling, cinnamon buns (*snúður*), layer *cake (lagkaka)*, and traditional twisted Icelandic doughnuts known as *kleinur*.

## Fruit and vegetables

Iceland proudly boasts of bananas that are grown in greenhouses in the south of the country, but most fruits and vegetables are still imported. Unfortunately, long transit times take their toll on the freshness of the produce on offer, particularly in smaller countryside supermarkets; onions, especially, can be rotten on the inside. The high cost of importing fruit and veg means that customers pay lofty prices for these unhappy-looking specimens.

Tomatoes and cucumbers are grown under glass in Iceland in places such as Reykholt, Flúðir and Hveragerði, and so tend to be less woeful than other produce. Rhubarb is one of the few vegetables that thrives in Iceland's climate. It is harvested in late spring, sometimes appearing on dessert menus in Reykjavík.

Vegetarianism, whilst not unknown, is not something Icelanders particularly adhere to. Vegetarians will be fine in Reykjavík, where there is one vegetarian restaurant that opens for lunch and dinner, a few veggie/vegan cafés and several health-food outlets offering a more promising selection of non-meat-based meals than the city's mainstream eateries. Outside the capital, most restaurant menus have one vegetarian option – almost always a pasta/cheese/tomato dish, which can get tedious. Vegans will generally be limited to self-catering.

## What to drink

Coffee is the national drink of Iceland, consumed from early morning to late at night, at home, at work or even walking down the street. Refills are usually included if you buy a cup of standard coffee in a café, and some petrol stations have a free jug on the counter for their petrol-buying customers. In recent years, there has been a veritable explosion in the coffee culture in Iceland and it's now possible to get expertly brewed espressos, cappuccinos and lattes.

Traditionally, drinking alcohol mid-week has not been part of Icelandic culture, although it is becoming more common to have a glass of wine or beer with a meal when dining out. A strong Protestant work ethic is usually cited

*Danish rye bread accompanies a platter of fish, smoked lamb and more.*

as the cause… along with the inflated price of alcohol. The bottle that is expensive enough at the state liquor store will invariably be around three times higher in price at a restaurant. Even house wines generally cost around ISK700–1,000 per glass, and a decent bottle of wine in a good restaurant will cost upwards of ISK5,000. Beer, whilst not exactly inexpensive, is generally a more affordable ISK800 to ISK1000 per half litre.

Iceland's local home-produced drink is *brennivín* ("burnt wine"), a caraway-seed-flavoured spirit that is drunk icy cold. It is generally referred to as "Black Death", which gives an idea of its strength. You have been warned.

A bird-watching group gathers on the dramatic Krísuvík Cliffs.

# A NATURALIST'S PARADISE

**Iceland is home to, or a stopping-off point for, a wide variety of birdlife; and although it has only one indigenous land mammal, the Arctic fox, there are a number of introduced species as well as seas rich in marine mammals.**

A ny traveller to Iceland with even a vague interest in birdlife should bring along a pair of binoculars and a good ornithological guide. Around 70 species of birds breed annually in every corner of Iceland (including year-round residents and those which migrate to Iceland each spring), while more than 370 different species have been seen in the country at one time or another.

Some species regularly winter in Iceland before flying further north to breed in summer. For others, Iceland is merely a stopping off point on their migration journey. Many are accidentals – individual birds which have drifted across the ocean on prevailing winds. Those of North American origin are of great interest to European bird-watchers and mostly occur in the south in autumn.

Seventy breeding species is not a great deal, but the actual bird population is numerically large: some of the commonest species, like the puffin, are present in millions. The Icelandic environment is particularly favourable to sea birds, which make up around 25 of the country's breeding species (see page 228), but is less welcoming to passerines (perching birds) whose principal food source – insects – is in short supply. While just over two-thirds of the world's birds are passerines, they comprise only one seventh of Iceland's avian population.

Most of Iceland's birds are also found in Scandinavia and Northern Europe. Three species,

*An Arctic fox, Iceland's only indigenous land mammal, in its brown summer coat.*

however, are American: the Barrow's goldeneye; the great northern diver or common loon; and the harlequin duck, which breed practically nowhere else outside North America.

## Heralds of spring

Both the Arctic tern and the golden plover are migratory birds commonly regarded as harbingers of spring. The golden plover, which generally arrives in early April, is a particular favourite with Icelandic poets:

*Lóan er komin að kveða burt snjóinn/kveða burt leiðindin, það getur hún./Hún hefur sagt mér að senn komi spóinn,/sólskin í heiði og blómstur í tún.*

> *Even those who cannot tell a hawk from a handsaw may find themselves flicking through ornithological guides: Iceland promises first-time and dedicated "twitchers" endless pleasure.*

"The plover has come and she'll sing away winter / Drive off all sorrow as only she can / She says that the whimbrel soon will be coming / Sun on the valley and hayfields in bloom" – by Páll Olafsson (1827–1905).

The Arctic tern, which usually appears in early May, is one of the wonders of the ornithological world. It migrates each spring from Antarctica, 17,000km (10,500 miles) away. The arctic tern is a graceful flyer, often seen hovering over water. It also makes unnerving "dive-bombing" attacks on humans who enter its nesting colonies in June and July,

prime puffin-watching spot, and you'll still see birds there in season; but today the best places to see puffins are in the northwest on Vigur island near Ísafjörður and Grímsey near Hólmavík; in the north on Drangey and Grímsey; and in the southeast on Papey. These unusual birds do not simply build a nest – they dig a burrow, up to 1.5 metres (5ft) deep, where a single egg is laid. On the sea cliff, puffins are usually found nesting at the top, where a little soil and vegetation provides the space to dig. Puffin pairs will return year after year to the same burrow. After the 1973 eruption on Heimaey island, many returned to find their

*Atlantic puffins catching fish.*

screeching "*kría*!" (also the bird's name in Icelandic).

The puffin is Iceland's commonest bird, with a population of 8–10 million. The comically dignified stance of this decorative bird has earned it the nickname of *Prófastur* (the Dean). Around the third to fourth week of May each year, puffins start flying ashore for the breeding season, after spending the winter out on the North Atlantic. Their main breeding grounds are on sea-cliffs and low-lying offshore islands. Warming waters around Iceland mean that the sandeels that the puffins feed on have moved further out to sea, and several puffin breeding colonies have suffered a crash in numbers in recent years due to food scarcity. The Vestmannaeyjar were once a

burrows buried under a thick layer of lava. Rather than nest elsewhere, they tried to burrow to their old nesting places; some died in the attempt.

## Rare birds

One of the most famous of the island's bird species is, sadly, extinct. The great auk (*Pinguinus impennis*) was a big, awkward, flightless sea bird, about 70cm (27ins) high, and very tasty, according to the fishermen who hunted it for food. The last breeding pair of great auks was killed on Eldey in 1844 (see page 229).

An endangered species still native to Iceland is the gyrfalcon, the largest of all falcons at 51–60cm (20–23ins) long. About 300–400 pairs are estimated to breed each year. The gyrfalcon has a colourful history as one of Iceland's most prestigious and valuable exports. Due to their skill and manoeuvrability in the air, gyrfalcons were prized as hunting birds and made gifts fit for kings and princes. In medieval times, up to 200 trained birds were exported each year, and in the 16th century the king of Denmark (who also ruled over Iceland) claimed a monopoly on the trade, which made a significant contribution to the royal coffers.

Although falconry largely died out in Europe by the 18th century, it continues in other parts of the world. Even today, an illicit trade in hunt-

protective white colouring in winter. Humans share the falcon's taste for ptarmigan, which is part of the Icelanders' Christmas dinner and traditionally hunted on the heathland of Þingvellir National Park (see page 169). Ptarmigan numbers fluctuate, but there is a concern that the bird is in decline: hunting was banned in 2003 and 2004, and the length of the hunting season has been progressively reduced since then, from two months down to nine days in 2012.

Iceland's most numerous bird of prey is the merlin. Smaller than the gyrfalcon at 27–32cm (10–12ins) long, the Icelandic merlin is a

*The volcanic island of Heimaey.*

ing falcons exists, and isolated attempts have been made to steal falcon eggs and chicks and smuggle them out of the country. The smugglers (including, on one occasion, a German "tourist" with two chicks hidden in his luggage) have been apprehended and heavily fined. Iceland's gyrfalcons enjoy special protection: their nesting places are kept secret, and carefully monitored. No one may approach the nests, or photograph them, except by permission of the Ministry for the Environment and Natural Resources.

The gyrfalcon lives in close community with its preferred prey, the ptarmigan (*Lagopus mutus*). Considerably smaller at 35cm (13ins) than its European relatives – the red and black grouse and the capercaillie – the ptarmigan adopts

unique subspecies, *Falco columbarius subaesalon*. It lives mostly on passerines such as redwings, wheatears and meadow pipits.

## Lord of the skies

The largest of Iceland's birds of prey is the rare white-tailed eagle, up to 90cm (3ft) long, with a wingspan of up to 2.5 metres (8ft). This is a

*The lake (Tjörnin) in Reykjavík is a natural habitat for wild birds. As well as a variety of ducks, geese and swans, it also has a breeding colony of arctic terns and the occasional red-necked phalarope.*

close relative of the bald eagle, the US national bird. During the early 19th century, there were 200–300 breeding pairs in Iceland. The bird was accused, however, of carrying off lambs, and it certainly disturbed eider colonies by taking both eggs and chicks. A bounty was offered for eagles, and they were shot and poisoned by farmers and eider breeders until, in 1920, only 10 pairs remained. Since 1913 the eagle has been fully protected by law, and is making a slow recovery. Today, breeding pairs number around 70, with nesting sites kept a strict secret.

*A black guillemot on Flatey island.*

## By the sea

Iceland's coast and offshore islands provide marvellous opportunities to birdwatch at close quarters. The islands of Breiðafjörður, for instance, teem with shag and cormorant, along with the occasional white-tailed eagle. The grey phalarope – much rarer than its red-necked cousin – also breeds there. On sightseeing cruises from Stykkishólmur, birdwatchers can sail in close to the birds.

Bird-cliffs are found around the country, although the mixture of species nesting on the cliffs varies from region to region. The common guillemot, for instance, prefers the north, while the Brunnich's guillemot is found most often in the south. The cliffs provide ledges and hollows not only for the ubiquitous puffin, but also for fulmars, kittiwakes, guillemots and razorbills.

Látrabjarg, at Iceland's westernmost point, is one of the world's great bird-cliffs. An imposing 16km (10 miles) long, the cliffs soar 500 metres (1,600ft) up from the sea – however, they are so straight and sheer that it is can be quite difficult to see nesting birds from their tops. The cliffs that fringe Hælavíkurbjarg and Hornbjarg, in the far northwest, are less accessible, but certainly no less spectacular. Other bird-cliffs can be seen on the Vestmannaeyjar (accessible by sightseeing cruises from the main island, Heimaey), Krísuvíkurbjarg on the southwestern peninsula, Reykjanes, and around the town of Vík on the south coast. The Snæfellsnes peninsula, in the west, is also an excellent area for viewing cliff birds and other sea-bird species.

> The Þjórsárver wetlands, in the heart of the highlands, are one of Iceland's largest breeding sites of the pink-footed goose, with around 6,000 to 10,000 breeding pairs.

Grímsey island, 40km (25 miles) off the north coast, was until recently the only Icelandic habitat of the very rare little auk, which was so well protected by law that you needed to obtain a permit simply to approach the nesting area. The bird has not bred here now for several summers, although it is still a winter visitor. About 16,000 pairs of gannets nest on Eldey island off the Reykjanes peninsula, the fourth-largest gannet colony in the world. Eldey is a closely protected bird sanctuary, as well as being a remote, sheer-sided, 77-metre (253ft)-high hyaloclastite plug – two webcams have been installed so that visitors can watch the birds (see www.eldey.is).

Bogs, marshes and wetlands also provide important habitats for many species of birds, including the whooper swan, the greylag goose, and waders like the whimbrel and golden plover.

## Accidentals

The southern coast of Iceland is a particular favourite with birdwatchers who are on the lookout for exotic "accidentals", lost birds that have flown from North America and mainland Europe. Breiðamerkursandur, a wasteland of glacial sand south of Vatnajökull glacier, is one of the world's main breeding areas for the great skua, a fascinating bird to observe as it makes its piratical attacks on other birds.

In the Skaftafell area of Vatnajökull National Park, another excellent location for bird-watching, the wren is particularly common. Though the smallest of all the Icelandic birds at 12–13cm (5ins), it is larger than wrens in nearby countries, and is defined as a special subspecies, *Troglodytes troglodytes islandicus*.

One Icelandic bird you cannot expect to see is the water rail. This extremely shy species is so wary and elusive that it has hardly ever been photographed, although its call may be heard in its typical habitat, reedbanks edging marshy lowlands. Wholesale draining of marshland has slowly but surely been destroying the water rail's habitat, and it is also an easy prey for the fast-moving and bloodthirsty mink, so its call may not be heard in the marshes of Iceland for very much longer.

## Mammals in the wild

Iceland was never connected to any ancient land mass, so it's hardly surprising that it has few native animals – although a variety of marine mammals have been established on its

*White-tailed eagle in flight.*

### BIRDLIFE AT LAKE MÝVATN

Lake Mývatn, in the north, is a unique natural phenomenon; a large lake, 37 sq km (14 sq miles) in area, yet only 1–4 metres (3–13ft) deep. It is also fed by underground hot streams from the adjacent active geothermal and volcanic area, which raise the temperature higher than one would expect both at this northerly latitude at an altitude of 277 metres (908ft). Even in severe winters, the lake never freezes completely.

This benign environment means that Mývatn is a paradise for ducks, and all of Iceland's duck species save the eider are found breeding here. Most common is the tufted duck, then the scaup and wigeon. Mývatn is also the only known European breeding area for Barrow's goldeneye. Other common species include the common scoter, red-breasted merganser, long-tailed duck, gadwall and teal, while the mallard and pintail are less common. The goosander, shoveller and pochard are rare. The harlequin, which likes fast-flowing waters, is found on the adjacent Laxá river.

Many other bird species are also found in the unspoiled countryside around the lake. The Slavonian grebe nests at Mývatn, and the short-eared owl on nearby marshes, along with snipe and red-necked phalarope. Merlins and gyrfalcons nest in the nearby mountainous areas. And don't forget the 40 species of midges that hum their way through this rich region.

coasts for millennia. The only land-based Icelandic mammal to pre-date the human settlement of the country is the Arctic fox *(Alopex lagopus)*, which is thought to have walked to Iceland over the frozen sea during the Ice Age. Two variants exist: the "blue", relatively rare in other Arctic areas, comprises about two-thirds of Iceland's fox population; it is dark brown in summer, and turns a lighter brown in winter, with a bluish sheen. The "white" variety only lives up to its name when in winter camouflage; its summer coat is greyish-brown with a grey or white belly. Exceptionally well insulated, the

*Harbour seals.*

Arctic fox grows a thick and furry winter coat, including fur on the soles of its paws.

Icelandic farmers long blamed foxes for the deaths of lambs and eider ducks, and have trapped or shot them since the Settlement (see page 33). Research has shown, however, that they pose little threat to livestock. The fox is hunted across the country to control numbers, apart from in Hornstrandir nature reserve in the Westfjords, where it enjoys protected status and has consequently become quite fearless. In spite of the hunts, numbers have increased six-fold in the last 30 years. In some areas, red foxes from commercial fur farms have escaped to the wild and mated with native Arctic foxes, producing hybrids.

## Rodent residents

Iceland has several naturalised mammals introduced, deliberately or not, over the years. Four rodent species have settled here, arriving as stowaways on ships. These are the long-tailed field mouse or wood mouse *(Apodemus sylvaticus)*, house mouse *(Mus musculus)*, brown rat *(Rattus norvegicus)* and black rat *(Rattus rattus)*. The house mouse, brown rat and black rat are only found in and around urban areas; of them only the brown rat is common.

The long-tailed field mouse (a uniquely Icelandic sub-species, *Apodemus sylvaticus grandiculus*) certainly merits its name, with a tail as long as its body (8–10cm/3–4ins). It is found both near human habitation and in remote areas; eats mostly plants, berries and fungi, as well as small insects; does not hibernate; and sometimes takes shelter in houses and outbuildings in cold weather.

Both the house mouse and long-tailed mouse are long-established residents in Iceland, probably dating back to the original settlement. Some zoologists believe that the long-tailed mouse must, like the fox, pre-date human habitation, as 1,000 years would not account for the development of this sub-species' differences from its mainland cousins. The brown rat is believed to have arrived in 1840, and spread rapidly to every region. The black rat has been sighted from time to time since 1919, but is not firmly established.

Another addition to Icelandic fauna was accidentally introduced into the wild. The American mink *(Mustela vison)* was brought to Iceland in the 1930s, and there are now 24 fur farms: like the red fox, a number of animals escaped. Within 35 years, the species were firmly established over almost the whole country, causing havoc among nesting birds such as puffins, guillemots, ducks and eiders by taking eggs and chicks. Mink numbers peaked around 2003, but then went into decline – possibly due to a reduction in bird numbers and/or increased competition from Arctic foxes.

## Imports from Lapland

Another of Iceland's wild mammals is a reminder of a well-meaning but misguided attempt to alter the Icelandic way of life. Several dozen reindeer *(Rangifer tarandus)* were introduced from northern Scandinavia in 1771–87, when Icelanders lived in penury, on the verge of starvation. The beasts were imported so some

*Examples of Iceland's wild mammals, which are at times hard to spot in the wild, can be viewed at Reykjavík's zoo.*

Icelanders could adopt the existence of the nomadic Sami people. The experiment did not work and the reindeer reverted to the wild, adding an exotic touch to the uplands, and some meat to hunters' tables.

By 1817, reindeer were widely distributed in many areas, and their growing numbers gave

descend to lowland farms and villages in search of adequate grazing.

Attempts have been made to introduce the musk ox (*Ovibos moschatus*) and mountain hare (*Lepus timidus*) into Iceland, with no success.

## Mammals of the sea

Iceland's rugged coast sustains a range of marine mammals. Seals are most likely to be spotted, with two species, the common or harbour seal and the grey seal, breeding in Iceland. The country boasts about half the world population of harbour seals, which can often

*Humpbacks are one of the more common species found in Icelandic waters.*

rise to fears that they were overgrazing the upland pastures, traditionally sacrosanct to the sheep. A royal charter of 1817 permitted unlimited hunting of the animals, except for juveniles under a year old. Half a century of indiscriminate slaughter left the reindeer stocks in a poor state by 1882, when hunting was restricted.

Thanks to a total hunting ban from 1901 to 1940, the herds made an excellent recovery, and the population is now maintained at about 3,000. Herds are found only in the mountains and valleys in the east of Iceland. They graze on mosses, fungi, lichens and grasses, but will also nibble shoots of shrubs and young trees. The shy creatures can rarely be spotted in summer, but in the depths of winter they sometimes

be seen sunning themselves on the black sands of remote fjords. Five other species breed on Greenland and the polar ice floes, and make occasional visits to northern Iceland: they include the ringed, bearded, harp and hooded seals, and the Atlantic walrus.

Medieval Iceland was famous for the whales off its coast, and today whale-watching tours do a booming business. Most typically spotted off Icelandic are minke whales and harbour porpoises; the latter are usually seen in pods of 3–10 animals, but sometimes in their hundreds. Other commonly seen species include humpback (easy to spot as they raise their tail flukes vertically before diving), fin and killer whales; and, less frequently, blue, sperm and pilot whales.

A climber scales the wall of an ice cave in winter.

*Kayaking in arresting surroundings, Hornafjordur fjord.*

*Ásbyrgi canyon, the northeast.*

# INTRODUCTION

**A detailed guide to every region of Iceland, with principal sites clearly cross-referenced by number to the maps.**

*Sculpture at Arnarstapi.*

Iceland is one of the world's most spectacular destinations, with vast empty landscapes illuminated by sparkling, clear subarctic air and cosy fishing villages sheltering from Atlantic storms beneath gargantuan cliffs. It's a paradise for anyone with a love of nature and the great outdoors, lent a surreal edge by the presence of the restless tectonic activity beneath.

Reykjavík is a pleasantly small, personable and lively capital city, the perfect base for exploring the so-called "Golden Circle", which includes some of Iceland's best-known natural spectacles such as the waterfall Gullfoss, the eponymous Geysir and Iceland's historical centre, Þingvellir. Also within easy reach is the amazing Blue Lagoon spa resort. Beyond the black sand beach at Vík, Iceland's southernmost point, lie Iceland's most accessible glaciers and Skaftafell, part of the immense Vatnajökull National Park and a favourite hiking spot among locals.

North of Reykjavík is the historic Snæfellsnes Peninsula, the setting for many an Icelandic saga, while further north lies the remote, windswept West Fjords region with some of the wildest (and wettest) landscapes in Iceland.

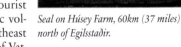

Akureyri, Iceland's only large town outside of the capital, is the jumping-off point for exploring the North. Nearby Lake Mývatn is Iceland's most popular tourist spot outside the "Golden Circle", where dramatic volcanic activity can be seen at close range. In the Northeast is Jökulsárgljúfur, another awe-inspiring section of Vatnajökull National Park, whose series of canyons leads to Dettifoss, Europe's most powerful waterfall. The East Fjords region holds tiny fishing villages and rugged scenery that manages to retain its character despite the new Fjarðaál aluminium smelter.

*Seal on Húsey Farm, 60km (37 miles) north of Egilsstaðir.*

Finally, there is the interior – an area quite different from the rest of Iceland. Almost all coastal roads are passable in two-wheel drive cars; but routes through the interior demand four-wheel drive or a specially designed touring bus. The coast has hundreds of villages and farms offering accommodation; in the interior, camping or bed-/floorspace in a basic mountain hut are the only options. Weather by the coast is relatively warm, if often wet; temperatures in the interior can plunge to dangerous levels without warning.

Arctic Circle

G r e e n l a n d   S e a

Straumnes

Hornstrandir

Bolungarvík

Suðureyri

Drangajökull
925

Ísafjörður

Norðurfjörður

Rifsnes

Málmey

Hof

Skagaströnd

Saúðákrókur

Pingeyri

Kópur

Arnarfjörður

G l á m a

Húnaflói

Blönduós

Bíldudalur

Hólmavík

Patreksfjörður

Bjargtangar

Barðaströnd

Brjámslækur

Skáleyjar

Flatey

Króksfjarðarnes

Hvammstangi

Hop

Breiðafjörður

Laugar

Borðeyri

Blöndu

Búðardalur

Stykkishólmur

Hvammsfjörður

Hellisandur

Öndverðarnes

Ólafsvík

Grundarfjörður

Eiriksjökull

Kjölur

Þjóðgarður
Snæfellsjökull
(Snæfellsjökull
National Park)

S n æ f e l l s n e s

Norðurárdalur

Arnarvatnsheiði

Langjökull

Hvítárvatn

M ý r a r

Hvítá

Bogarnes

Miðsandur

F a x a f l ó i

Akranes

Hvalfjörður
Tunnel

E s j a

Þingvellir

Þjóðgarður Þingvellir
(Þingvellir National Park)

Gullfoss

Reykjavík

Hafnarfjörður

Þingvallavatn

Búrfell

Sandgerði

Keflavík

Vogar

Þríhnúkagígur

Hveragerði

Hekla
1491

Fjallab

Keflavík
International Airport

Njarðvík

Reykjanesfólkvangur

Ölfusá

Vatnafjöll

Blue Lagoon

Selfoss

Eldey

Grindavík

Þorlákshöfn

Hella

Myr
Jök

Hvolsvöllur

A T L A N T I C

Markarfljót

Eyjafjallajökull

Landeyjarhöfn

Skógar

O C E A N

Vestmannaeyjar

Heimaey

Surtsey

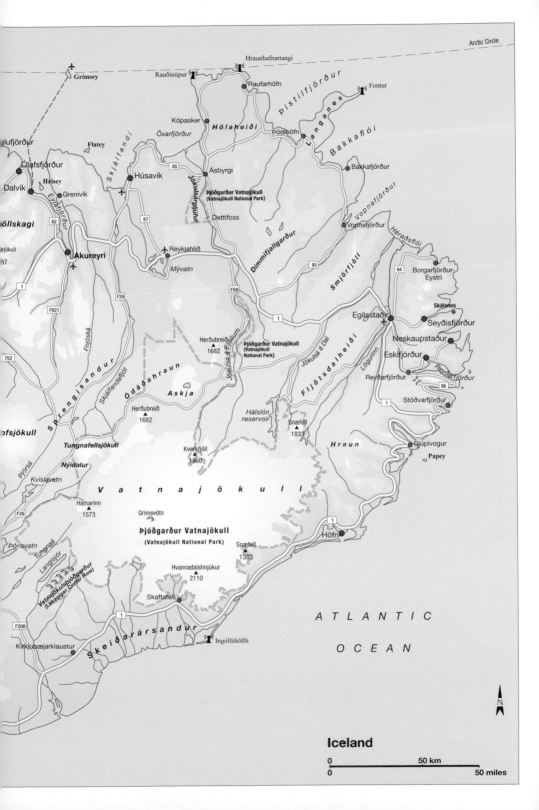

Arctic Circle

Hraunhafnartangi

Grímsey

Rauðinúpur

Raufarhöfn

P i s t i l f j ö r ð u r

Fontur

Kópasker

*H ö l a h e i ð i*

L a n g a n e s

Öxarfjörður

Þórshöfn

Flatey

*S k j á l f a n d i*

B a k k a f l ó i

lufjörður

85

Ásbyrgi

Bakkafjörður

Ólafsfjörður

Húsavík

Dalvík

Hrísey

Grenivík

Þjóðgarður Vatnajökull
(Vatnajökull National Park)

*J ö k u l s á r g l j ú f u r*

V o p n a f j ö r ð u r

öllskagi

82

*E y j a f j ö r ð u r*

87

*Dettifoss*

Vopnafjörður

*H é r a ð s f l ó i*

rjökull

Akureyri

Reykjahlíð

D i m m i f j a l l g a r ð u r

S m j ö r f j ö l l

Borgarfjörður-
Eystri

85

94

1

Mývatn

F26

F88

**Skálanes**

F821

1

Egilsstaðir

Seyðisfjörður

*F r i ð s k á*

Herðubreið
▲
1682

Þjóðgarður Vatnajökull
(Vatnajökull
National Park)

*J ö k u l s á á D a l*

Neskaupstaður

752

*S p r e n g i s a n d u r*

*S k j á l f a n d a f l j ó t*

*Ö d á ð a h r a u n*

*A s k j a*

*J ö k u l s á á F j ö l l u m*

*L a g a r i n n*

*F l j ó t s d a l h e i ð i*

Eskifjörður

Reyðarfjörður

*R e y ð a r f j ö r ð u r*

96

Herðubreið
▲
1682

*Hálslón
reservoir*

Snæfell
▲
1833

1

Stöðvarfjörður

ofsjökull

**Tungnafellsjökull**

Kverkfjöll
▲
1860

*H r a u n*

Djúpivogur

**Nýidalur**

*Þ j ó r s á*

Papey

Kvíslavatn

*V a t n a j ö k u l l*

F26

Hamarinn
▲
1573

Grímsvötn

Þjóðgarður Vatnajökull

Þórisvatn

*Tungnaá*

*Langisjór*

(Vatnajökull National Park)

Snæfell
▲
1383

1

Höfn

Vatnajökulsþjóðgarður
(Lakagígar Crater Row)

Hvannadalshnjúkur
▲
2110

F208

Kirkjubæjarklaustur

*S k e i ð a r á r s a n d u r*

Skaftafell

1

Ingólfshöfði

A T L A N T I C

O C E A N

N

**Iceland**

| 0 | 50 km |
| 0 | 50 miles |

*The twinkling city in winter.*

# REYKJAVÍK

The world's northernmost capital is a bright, colourful city. Rich in cultural attractions and with a vibrant nightlife, Reykjavík also has parks and wildlife areas surprisingly close to its centre.

**V**isitors are often unsure whether Reykjavík is a scaled-down city or scaled-up village. Housing around one-third of Iceland's population, it is the undisputed political, business, cultural and intellectual centre of the country, with a sparkling new world-class concert hall, Harpa, and some small but state-of-the-art museums. Yet Reykjavík retains a certain slow pace and almost rustic charm that makes it unique amongst the world's capitals. Drivers on the one-way shopping street Laugavegur will often stop in the middle of the road to chat to friends, while a queue of cars waits patiently behind. In the summer, whales swim in the bay, people picnic outside their parliament, and kids play in the streets until midnight.

From the higher elevations the eye is drawn across the bay to the flat-topped mountain of Esja, often snowbound, its cold grey bulk a constant reminder of the subarctic location. It was here that the "official" settlement of Iceland began, after a few false starts, in the late 9th century AD. For centuries there was little to distinguish it from any other cluster of farms elsewhere in the country, although the strands of its noble fate had already been woven: while the practical details of settlement and development were entrusted to man, the site itself was originally chosen by the pagan gods. Ingólfur Arnarson, who has been given the title First

Settler of Iceland, brought with him from Norway not only his family and cattle but also the high seat that was the symbol of the homestead. Following established Viking custom, Ingólfur dutifully tossed overboard the pillars on which the high seat was mounted – wherever they washed ashore, that was where the gods willed him to live.

It took over three years for Ingólfur's slaves to find the pillars, while the Viking himself stayed temporarily in the south, but eventually they turned up on the shores of what is

*Jón Sigurðsson statue.*

**Main Attractions**
Reykjavík 871±2
  Settlement Exhibition
Harpa Concert Hall
Nightlife
Culture House
National Museum
Hallgrímskirkja church

*One-off boutiques abound.*

now Iceland's capital. One of the slaves, less than impressed with the gods' choice, snapped that "to no avail we have crossed fine districts to live on this outlying wilderness", and ran off with one of Ingólfur's maidservants. But the other slave, Vífill, was given his freedom; he lived at Vífilsstaðir, now the site of a sanatorium, between Reykjavík and neighbouring Garðabær, just to the south of the city. Ingólfur himself submitted to the gods' judgement and probably built his house in the old city centre, with a view of the duck-filled lake, Tjörnin.

## In the shadow of steam

The First Settler, Ingólfur, named his new home Reykjavík (Smoky Bay), after clouds he saw rising from the ground, probably in what is now the Laugardalur area. The "smoke" was steam from geothermal springs – ironically, the same "smoke" that today makes Reykjavík an almost completely pollution-free city.

As for Ingólfur, he still has a presence in the shape of one of the statues so characteristic of the capital (by

Einar Jónsson, 1874–1954). The First Settler is now perched atop **Arnarhóll hill**, next to Government House, his back turned upon the Culture House (see page 147). The statue gazes across the harbour to where, on a clear day, the glacial cap of Snæfellsjökull glimmers mystically on the horizon, some 100km (60 miles) away to the north.

## Reykjavík today

For a visitor, the old city centre is definitely the most charming part of the capital. Well-to-do residential streets, with their brightly coloured, corrugated-metal-clad houses and mossy lawns enclosed by picket fences, run alongside the shops, cafés and galleries of the main commercial thoroughfares. In contrast to the compact centre, Reykjavík's sprawling suburbs extend eastwards for mile after mile, all drab apartment blocks and busy roads.

The city as a whole has been undergoing a transformation in the past 15 years. Whereas visitors to Iceland once considered Reykjavík little more than a stopover en route to the country's undisputed main attraction – the landscape

– the capital has now earned its stripes as a destination in its own right (a process encouraged by the availability of cheaper flights since the turn of the 21st-century). Its energetic and distinctive cultural scene is a constant source of fascination. After all, what other city with a population of 120,000 has an internationally acclaimed symphony orchestra, two major professional theatre companies, numerous independent theatre groups, an opera company, a national ballet and both a national and municipal art gallery? On top of this, dozens of smaller independent galleries and venues offer continuous exhibitions, recitals and performances throughout the year, and an annual arts festival attracts numerous renowned artists of international standing.

Reykjavík nightlife has also been discovered by visitors from around the world eager for something different and vibrant. The city's reputation as a "happening" place has largely grown out of the success of pop diva Björk since the early 1990s and the roster of international stars that have since taken to visiting the country.

Unlikely as it may sound, Reykjavík has also become increasingly popular as an attractive option for the cosmopolitan shopping enthusiast. Icelandic design favours the clean lines and cool functionality of modernist Scandinavian products, but tends to use local materials and be infused by a darker spirit. Unusual and unmistakeable, Icelandic design is on the rise, and the city has a wide range of one-off shops selling homeware, clothing and jewellery, all within a relatively small geographical area. The **Iceland Design Centre** (Aðalstræti 2; www.icelanddesign. is; Mon–Fri 9am–5pm) is an information centre where you can learn about Icelandic design and architecture. The centre also hosts events, exhibitions and conferences dedicated to local design.

## Around Austurvöllur

The old city centres around the small plaza of **Austurvöllur** ❶ ("eastern field"), today a tidy green area laid out around a statue of the nationalist hero Jón Sigurðsson. It is said that the first Viking settler Ingólfur Arnarson actually grew his hay here.

*Enjoying the sun in Austurvöllur Square.*

### REYKJAVÍK'S RISE

For centuries after settlement, Reykjavík remained little more than a few farmhouses. In a census taken in 1801 its population was a mere 301 souls, mainly spread between the lake and the Old Harbour where the shops and offices of the old city centre now lie. The population was presumably even less in 1786, when Reykjavík was first granted a municipal charter as an official trading post. In 1901, Reykjavík still only had 5,000 inhabitants. The sudden leap to today's 120,000 has occurred mostly since World War II, as tens of thousands of provincial Icelanders moved to the capital in search of better job prospects and a more cosmopolitan way of life. However, Reykjavík's gain has been the countryside's loss: many areas are suffering decline as a result.

The grey basalt **Parliament Building** (Alþingishúsið) ❷ on Austurvöllur was custom-built in 1880–81 to house the ancient assembly. After more or less continuous operation in nearby Þingvellir (see page 169) since the year 930 (albeit mostly as a court, because Iceland lost its independence in 1262), the Alþingi moved to Reykjavík in 1798. The building visible today was built to house it during the upswell of the 19th-century nationalist awakening.

Excavations around the Parliament Building, carried out between 2008 and 2016, have unearthed yet more Viking remains. The site is unusual in that it appears to be an industrial area – the first ever found in Iceland. Archaeologists believe they have discovered the walls from the Old Harbour, dating back to 1913, the remains of an iron smithy, a carpentry and stonemason's workshop, and possible wool- and fish-processing facilities, in continuous use from the 9th to the 11th century.

The old city boundaries are roughly marked by Suðurgata to the west, Hafnarstræti to the north, Lækjargata and Fríkirkjuvegur to the east and Hringbraut to the south. Street names give some hint of the way Reykjavík looked in the 19th century and before. The traffic artery of Lækjargata ("brook street"), for example, followed

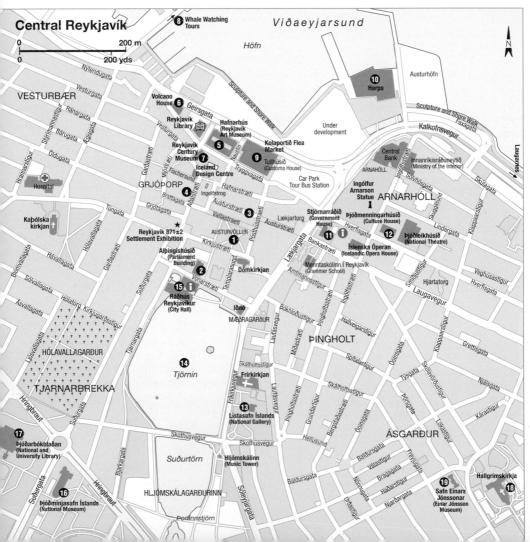

Central Reykjavík

a stream between the shore and the lake; eels were caught here once, but it is now buried beneath asphalt and flagstones. Today's main shopping street of Laugavegur ("pools road") points the way that women followed on foot or horseback to the Laugardalur hot springs to do their washing.

Austurstræti ❸ was once the city's most easterly point – the street's maidens were immortalised, like distant cousins of Heine's *Daughters of the Rhine*, by Tómas Guðmundsson (1901–83), Iceland's first urban poet. A plethora of pubs and restaurants on Austurstræti, Hafnarstræti and around Laugavegur lends a boisterous atmosphere to downtown Reykjavík by night, creating a beehive of activity more in keeping with a city many times the size. Nightlife begins late and lasts until morning. Bar prices are high and most nightlifers "warm up" with a few drinks at home before taking the plunge. The "in" spots tend to change regularly; what was hip today may be passé tomorrow. Queues are quick to form when the action gets underway.

## Aðalstræti

Reykjavík's oldest buildings are on **Aðalstræti** ❹ ("main street"). In the 18th century, Aðalstræti was earmarked by High Sheriff Skúli Magnússon (nicknamed "the Father of Reykjavík") for a crafts and trades development project. An unusual effort to catch up with the outside world, it was a scheme for creating cottage industries – wool-dyeing, knitting, weaving, etc. Although it folded, the project left not only inspiration, ambition and skills, but also the capital's earliest surviving architecture.

The most tangible signs of Iceland's Viking settlement can be seen at the **Reykjavík 871±2 Settlement Exhibition** (Landnámssýningin; http://borgarsogusafn.is; daily 9am–8pm; guided tours Jun–Aug Sat–Sun at 11am) at Aðalstræti 16. Here you'll find the remains of an oval-shaped Viking-age farmhouse just below the current street level. With

a hearth as its central point, the farmhouse covers around 85 sq metres (915 sq ft) and is thought to have been occupied until around AD 1000. Another intriguing structure is a modest-looking piece of turf wall to the north of the hall: the layer of volcanic ash which lies just beneath the ruins has been dated to AD 871, three years before the conventional Settlement date; but the wall lies underneath the tephra layer.

Between the museum and the **tourist office** at Aðalstræti 7, is the oldest surviving building in the (street-level) city, built in 1764 to replace a 1752 weaver's shop that had burnt down. Its history is dotted with larger-than-life characters, including one-time owner Bishop Geir Vídalín (1761–1823). A cleric famed for his hospitality, Bishop Vídalín left an immortal dedication to the city's nightlife: "There are two places where the fires never die down – Hell and my house." Burning a hole through his wallet in the process, Vídalín won the dubious honour of becoming the only bishop in ecclesiastical history to be declared bankrupt. The building now contains the large design shop

*Austurvöllur Square architecture.*

**Kraum** (www.kraum.is), showing off the best of Iceland's talent. On show across the road, beneath a thick layer of clear plastic, is one of the old wells that used to provide Reykjavík's residents with drinking water. Relics dating back to the Settlement have been found to the right of the well, at the corner of Aðalstræti and Túngata.

## The old and new harboursides

Parallel to Austurstræti, Hafnarstræti ("harbour street") is no longer on the harbourfront – it was superseded by Tryggvagata, built during World War I on gravel and sand dumped to extend the waterfront, then by the modern Geirsgata, which is now on the harbourfront. Hafnarstræti houses the customs office, tax office and a couple of pubs, but the houses on the southern side of Hafnarstræti date back to the 19th century. At Tryggvagata 17 is **Hafnarhús** ❺ (http://artmuseum.is; daily 10am–5pm, Thu until 10pm), one of three galleries belonging to the Reykjavík Art Museum, situated in the stylishly renovated former warehouse of the Port.

*A designer boutique.*

LISTASAFN REYKJAVÍKUR

Reykjavik Art Museum

Just down the road, beyond the Reykjavík City Library, is **Volcano House** ❻ (tel: 555 1900; http://volcanohouse.is; daily English screenings on the hour 10am–9pm; free interactive exhibition), a small, specialist cinema which shows a 40-minute documentary about the 1973 Heimaey and 2010 Eyjafjallajökull eruptions. Walk up Vesturgata instead, and you'll find the **Reykjavík Century Museum** ❼ (www.reykjavik centurymuseum.com; closed until further notice at the time of writing), which includes the state-of-the-art Reykjavík Walk virtual simulation, which time-travels you through the city streets, showing you how they have changed between 1912 and now.

On the other side of Geirsgata is Reykjavík's main harbour, from where two companies, Elding (www.elding.is) and Special Tours (www.specialtours.is) run **whale-watching tours** ❽ (daily Apr–Oct, times vary – see websites for sailing schedules) in Faxaflói, the bay which lies between the capital and the Snæfellsnes peninsula. Minke whales, white-beaked dolphins and harbour porpoises are the most common cetacean species spotted on the tours, though there's also the chance of seeing humpbacks, killer whales, sei and blue whales. In puffin-breeding season (mid-May–mid-August), the boats sail past the rocky islands of Lundey or Akurey, which are home to up to 30,000 puffins, giving you a chance to see these comical birds at close quarters. **Kolaportið Flea Market** ❾ (www.kolaportid.is; Sat–Sun 11am–5pm), situated on Geirsgata, across from the harbour, is a small but cheerful occasion selling clothes, books and other assorted odds and ends. The food section is a must for anyone who is curious about traditional Icelandic fare; here are featured the tasty *harðfiskur* (dried fish), *hákarl* (cured shark), *síld* (pickled herring) and *hrútspungar*, the infamous pickled rams' testicles, as well as a wide range of other culinary novelties and delights.

Just across the busy lanes of traffic is one of Reykjavík's newest and most

most jaw-dropping buildings, the **Harpa Concert Hall** ⑩ (tel: 528 5000; http://en.harpa.is; building daily 10am–midnight, box office Mon–Fri 10am–6pm, Sat–Sun noon–6pm). Hugely controversial at the time of its construction, this ISK28-billion-krona structure was only half finished when the financial crash struck, when money was so tight that once-affluent Icelanders were queuing at soup kitchens. It looked as though the half-finished shell would remain that way, since its main financier was the now-bankrupted owner of the Landsbanki bank – but the city and the state stepped in, and the hall finally opened in May 2011; in 2013, it won the Mies van der Rohe Award, the European Union Prize for Contemporary Architecture.

Now that it *is* here, you can't help but admire the vision and tenacity that brought such a beautiful building into being. The exterior is a wonder of glass, designed by artist Ólafur Elíasson to resemble the mosaic-like basalt columns found scattered throughout Iceland, and its glittering polygons reflect the sea and sky in a kaleidoscopic lightshow. Inside it has four concert halls, from the main auditorium Eldborg, which seats 1,800, to tiny Kaldalón, used for lectures and more intimate concerts. Iceland's Symphony Orchestra, the Icelandic Opera, the Reykjavík Big Band and the Reykjavík Chamber Orchestra all perform here regularly, and there are daily guided tours of the building at 3.30pm (May–Sep at 11am, 1.30pm, 3.30pm and 5.30pm).

## Humble beginnings

Iceland's **Government House** ⑪ (Stjórnarráðið) stands on a small grassy bank overlooking Lækjartorg square, a stone's throw downhill from First Settler Ingólfur's statue on Arnarhóll. Built between 1765 and 1770, which makes it one of Reykjavík's oldest buildings, this unassuming whitewashed structure now houses the offices of the Prime Minister, yet it began its days less gloriously, as a prison workhouse. This building also

housed the offices of the President of the Republic until 1996, when they were moved to premises at Sóleyjargata 1.

Behind the National Theatre on Hverfisgata is the **Culture House** ⑫ (Þjóðmenningarhúsið; www.culture house.is; May–15 Sep daily 11am–5pm; winter closed Mon), part of the National Museum of Iceland. This excellent museum contains a well-conceived exhibition of Iceland's ancient sagas and other medieval manuscripts and artefacts, displayed in sealed glass cabinets and dimly lit to aid their preservation. A visit here is a trip into a different world: swirling, flamboyant characters seemingly leap from every page telling the tale of life in the North Atlantic during the stirring Viking age. Upstairs, regularly changing exhibitions focus on different aspects of the country's heritage: past themes have included everything from the explosive creation of the island of Surtsey (see page 20), to drawings of subarctic flora, to the emigration of Icelandic Mormons to North America.

Further along Lækjargata, on the same side as Government House,

*Parliament Building.*

*Strolling in Reykjavík.*

**TIP**

The Reykjavík City Card – available for 24, 48 or 72 hours – is good value if you plan to visit several museums and galleries, and unwind in one or more of the city's seven thermal pools. Bus travel is included in the price. See page 319.

*Reykjavík 871±2 Settlement Exhibition.*

stands a row of houses built in the mid-19th century. These narrowly escaped demolition some years ago and have been renovated; they now house two restaurants and the privately run tourist information centre known as the **Icelandic Travel Market** (www.icelandictravelmarket.is; the government Tourist Information office is on Aðalstræti 2, see page 145). Further still, shortly before Tjörnin lake, the stately **Reykjavík Grammar School** (Menntaskólinn í Reykjavík) presides over the streetscape. This was the first school of its kind in the country and among its alumni are two Nobel Laureates: Halldór Laxness (literature, 1955) and Níels Finsen (medicine, 1903).

The **National Gallery** ⓭ (Listasafn Íslands; www.listasafn.is; 15 May–15 Sep daily 10am–5pm, 16 Sept–14 May Tue–Sun 11am–5pm), overlooking the lake at Fríkirkjuvegur 7 and next door to the grey and green Fríkirkjan (Free Church; http://frikirkjan.is)), is yet another historical building which has had its ups and downs. It was originally built as a cold store in

which to keep ice cut from the lake which was then used for preserving fish. Later it served as a fish-freezing plant and a hot dance spot – so hot, in fact, that it once caught fire. Now renovated, the small gallery has a fine permanent collection of work by Icelandic artists, including the country's first professional painter Ásgrímur Jónsson (1876–1958, a museum is at Bergstaðastræti 74), supplemented by changing exhibitions. There is a café and a shop on the first floor.

## Around Tjörnin lake

On a clear day, it is worth taking some time to stroll around **Tjörnin lake** ⓮, which regularly attracts over 40 species of birds – most noticeably ducks. There are seats and a pleasant walkway along its eastern side (below Fríkirkjuvegur), giving views of a splendid row of houses on the opposite bank.

The **City Hall** ⓯ (Ráðhús Reykjavíkur) was built on the edge of the lake in the 1980s – an impressive postmodern edifice in its own right, but disliked by many Reykjavík residents for clashing with its serene environs.

There is a huge relief map of Iceland just beyond the entrance hall which is well worth a look, and at times this is the venue for free concerts and exhibitions. There is also a pleasant coffee shop with internet access and a lovely view of the lake.

On the north bank of Tjörnin, at the end of the City Hall walking bridge, is a corrugated-metal clad structure, which is fondly known as **Iðnó** (www.idno.is). It was originally constructed to house a craftsmen's guild but is best known for being the home of the Reykjavík City Theatre Company from 1897 to 1987. Iðnó reopened in 1999 after painstaking renovation transformed it back into one of Reykjavík's historical gems; it now serves as an occasional venue for music, dance and theatrical performances.

## South of Tjörnin lake

A bridge across Tjörnin leads to some grassy park areas with a series of public sculptures, followed by the **University of Iceland** (Háskóli Íslands; www.hi.is), which was founded in 1911 – although its ponderous Third

Reich-style main building dates from the 1930s.

Situated just southeast of the university is the **Nordic House** (Norræna Húsið; Sturlugata; www.nordichouse.is; exhibition space daily 11am–5pm), designed by the highly respected Finnish architect Alvar Aalto. Its purpose is to cultivate and strengthen ties between the Nordic countries. To that end, it has the Aalto Bistro l whose "New Nordic" menu by acclaimed chef Sveinn Kjartansson gives Scandinavian staples a contemporary spin, a library, a design shop and an ongoing programme of Scandinavian cultural events – many of which are free of charge.

On the edge of the university campus at Suðurgata 41 is the **National Museum** ⓰ (Þjóðminjasafn Íslands; www.thjodminjasafn.is; May–mid-Sept daily 10am–5pm, mid-Sept–April Tue–Sun 10am–5pm), which is essential viewing for anyone interested in Icelandic history and contemporary society. The museum's main exhibition, *The Making of a Nation*, is gripping stuff, tracing Iceland's history

*Completed in 1974, Hallgrímskirkja is designed to resemble columns of Iceland's basaltic lava. The tower, at 74.5 metres (244ft), is the second-tallest building in Iceland, after the Smáratorg office block in Kópavogur.*

*Waterfowl on the Tjörnin Lake in front of the City Hall.*

# Embracing the Night

**On weekend nights, those out on the town gravitate from bar to bar, bumping into old friends – it's this largely good-natured intimacy that sets Reykjavík's nightlife apart.**

Something curious happened to Reykjavík nightlife at some point in the early 1990s – it became very hip, especially for foreigners with money. One of these was a British pop star who was so taken with the scene that he returned again and again before finally purchasing a share in his favourite pub – and a flat nearby.

The initial rush of recognition may have subsided a little in the years since, but that isn't to say that the scene has diminished. Clearly, Reykjavík nightlife is still something to write home about and international media still send their people over to chronicle the festivities and wind up with colourful exposés. Quite a change from the old days when tourists wearing hiking boots and cameras around their necks barely awarded the capital a second glance.

*Reykjavík nightlife.*

And what is it that's so appealing? Perhaps it's the rip-roaring, spine-tingling Viking intensity with which the Icelanders approach their merriment: Icelanders tend to work hard yet drinking mid-week is seen as verging on the alcoholic – which means that there is a real feeling of letting off steam at the weekend. Or all those Beautiful People, packed like sardines into the small trendy cafés or lined up in queues outside the baking night spots, shivering in the latest fashions; never mind that it's s a mere 5°C (40°F) outside – that slip dress and those strappy sandals will stay on!

Inside, bartenders have their work cut out. A steady stream of alcoholic beverages leaves the bar, cocktail waiters and waitresses moving with amazing agility through the crowd. The loudness of the music makes regular conversation impossible. Bodies bop up and down and should there be a shortage of space the tabletops will do just fine, thanks. Actors and actresses rub shoulders with upstart politicians who rub shoulders with inebriated bohemians who claim to have solved the riddle of life.

## Lækjartorg Square

At closing time, typically 5, 6 or 7am at weekends (clubs and bars generally close at around 1am on weekdays, if they open at all), the lights go on, but the action continues out in the street. Everyone heads down to Lækjartorg Square to gather together sociably for a natter and maybe a smoke; if it's summer and the weather is good there will most certainly be a 5,000-strong crowd there, on the lines of a big outdoor house party. The crowd will be only slightly smaller if it's winter with a blizzard blowing.

Navigate your way through the throng and behold anything from ecstasy to wretched misery. For all this celebration does come at a price: a dark side exists, in the form of drunken minors passed out in doorways or the occasional random act of thuggishness. Reykjavík nightlife may not be as simple or as benign as it once was; but considering that this is a capital city packed from end to end with drunks at the weekend, it's amazing how little violence and vandalism are perpetrated.

For the most part, capital revellers can enjoy the absence of serious crimes and misdemeanours: Reykjavík is still a relatively safe place to embrace the night. And that, too, might be something to write home about.

from the Settlement down to the present day. The section on the use of DNA testing is particularly interesting, detailing research work on the teeth of the first settlers in order to determine their origins. Contemporary sections relate key periods in the country's development, such as the restrictive trade monopoly and the founding of the republic. Most of the archaeological finds around Iceland over the past few hundred years have ended up in the National Museum – including the impressive medieval wooden church door from Valþjófsstaður, carved in the 13th century with the story of a knight who slays a dragon.

Across from the National Museum, on the other side of Suðurgata, is the **National and University Library** ⓱ (Þjóðarbókhlaðan; Arngrímsgata 3; https://landsbokasafn.is; mid-May–Aug Mon–Fri 9am–5pm, May and Aug Sat 10am–2pm; Sept–mid-May Mon–Thu 8.15am–10pm, Fri 8.15am–7pm, Sat 10am–5pm, Sun 11am–5pm), housed in an airy, modern structure which opened in 1994 after a prolonged construction operation that lasted almost two decades. The library houses a manuscript collection (Mon–Fri 9am–5pm) and there are excellent research facilities for scholars, students and the general public.

## Hallgrímskirkja

East from the lake, the roads slope uphill towards the imposing **Hallgrímskirkja church** ⓲ (www.hallgrims kirkja.is; daily June–Sep 9am–9pm, Oct–May 9am–5pm; free except for tower), a modern concrete structure, built in nationalistic style to resemble volcanic basalt columns. Take the tiny lift, then continue up the stairs to the top of the 73-metre (240ft)-high tower and you are rewarded with the best views of Reykjavík and the deceptively close Snæfellsnes peninsula. On a clear day, as they say, you can see forever. In front of the church is a huge and impressive statue of Leifur Eiríksson, "Discoverer of America", a gift from the US on the 1,000th anniversary of the founding of the Alþingi in 1930.

Next to Hallgrímskirkja is the studio home of Einar Jónsson, now the **Einar Jónsson Museum** ⓳ (Safn

*Hop on a harbour tour.*

*The map inside City Hall.*

*Man-made geyser at Perlan.*

*Exhibit at the National Museum.*

Einars Jónssonar; www.lej.is; Tue–Sun 10am–5pm), which houses a collection of works by one of Iceland's great sculptors. Jónsson was a master of symbolism and epic, and many of his works combine a classical human form with symbols drawn from Norse, Greek and Oriental mythology. You can get a free taster in the little sculpture garden at the back of the museum.

## Perlan and Öskjuhlíð

The literally outstanding feature of the Reykjavík skyline these days is the glass-domed "Pearl" ⑳ (Perlan; www.perlan.is) – a revolving restaurant that sits on top of the glistening silver hot-water tanks on **Öskjuhlíð** hill, offering a breathtaking view of the city on clear days from its panoramic viewing deck and café. The tanks can take 24 million litres (more than 5 million gallons) of hot water and cater for almost half of Reykjavík's water consumption. Öskjuhlíð itself is a pleasantly leafy area thanks to tree-planting schemes and the creation of walking and cycling paths.

The "Pearl" is also the location of Reykjavík's **Saga Museum** (Sögusafnið; www.sagamuseum.is; daily 10am–6pm), an absorbing collection of lifelike silicon models of characters from Iceland's medieval literature. If you're keen to get to grips with the sagas, and have children in tow, the dramatic tableaux here are a fun option (however be warned that young children might be quite frightened by the pore-and-hair realism of the Viking models!). Beyond the Pearl lies another little jewel – Reykjavík's purpose-built geothermal beach, **Nauthólsvík** ㉑ (www.nautholsvik.is; mid-May–mid-Aug daily 10am–7pm, mid Aug–mid-May Tue, Thu and Fri 11am–1pm, Mon and Wed also 5–7.30, Sat 11am–3pm; free). This crescent of golden sand is a tiny slice of happiness on a sunny day, when people flock here to catch the rays and bathe outdoors in the heated saltwater of the bay.

North of Öskjuhlíð, cocooned in the suburban Miklatún park, a little off the beaten track, is **Kjarvalsstaðir** ㉒ (Flókagata; http://artmuseum.is/kjarvalsstadir; daily 10am–5pm), another part of the Reykjavík Art Museum. This gallery is dedicated to Iceland's most famous modern artist, Jóhannes Kjarval (1885–1972). Kjarval worked on a fishing trawler until his artistically minded fellow workers ran a lottery to raise money for him to study in Copenhagen. The museum offers changing displays of his work drawn from their collection; much of the gallery space is used for temporary exhibitions by international artists.

## Along the northern shore

Wandering (or better still, cycling) east along the shore from the Harpa concert hall, the first landmark that you will reach is by Jón Gunnar Árnason's **Suncraft sculpture** ㉓. Familiar from a thousand books and brochures, this shining silver boat nevertheless makes a striking photostop.

On a slight detour up Snorrabraut, opposite Hlemmur bus

station, is the **Icelandic Phallological Museum** (www.phallus.is; daily 10am–6pm), the world's only penis museum, with more than 215 specimens in its collection.

Located back down near the shoreline is what is probably Reykjavík's best-known building internationally, the **Höfði House** ㉔. This is the municipal reception hall behind whose clapboard exterior former presidents Ronald Reagan and Mikhail Gorbachev met in October 1986 to take their first bows before the *pas de deux* towards global disarmament. Now it is used for official city social functions, but is closed to the general public. At the time of its completion in 1909 to house the French consulate, Höfði was on the outskirts of the capital. It was sold to the poet and businessman Einar Benediktsson (1864–1940), who brought to the house not only his family but also a ghost. Reportedly, the ghost stayed on rent-free when the poet's family sold it to the British consulate, which in turn grew so tired of being haunted that the

building was eventually sold to the city. An electrical fault, rather than the troublesome spectre, was blamed for the fire that damaged the building on its 100th birthday, on 25 September 2009.

A little further east is the **Sigurjón Ólafsson Museum** ㉕ (Safn Sigurjóns Ólafssonar, Laugarnestangi 70; http://lso.is; June–Aug Tue–Sun 2–5pm, Sept–Nov, Feb–May Sat–Sun 2–5pm; closed Dec and Jan), dedicated to an Icelandic painter who lived from 1908 to 1982. In addition to the art collection there is a small family-run café with a lovely sea view and weekly music recitals in the summer.

If you've made it this far along the shore, you may as well hop aboard a boat and take a trip to **Viðey** ㉖. This peaceful little island was given to the Reykjavík authorities as a birthday present in 1987 when the capital celebrated the 200th anniversary of its municipal charter. Today it provides a haven for Reykjavík's inhabitants to "get away from it all". In summer there are daily ferry trips from Skarfabakki wharf at Sundahöfn, Harpa

*The exterior of the Perlan revolving restaurant.*

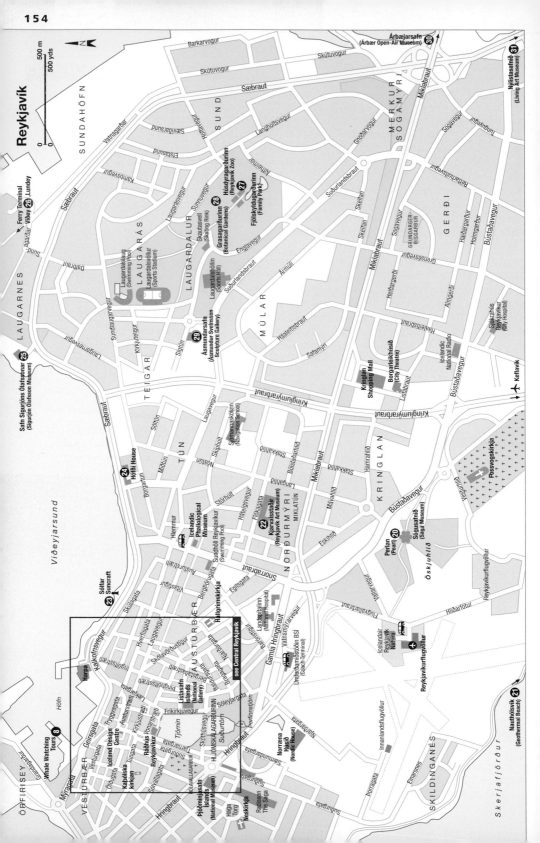

# Reykjavík

500 m

500 yds

N

ÖPFIRISEY

Whale Watching Tours **8**

VESTURBÆR

Harpa

Iceland Design Centre

Ráðhús Reykjavíkur

Kápólska kirkjan

Þjóðminjasafn Íslands (National Museum)

Listasafn Íslands (National Gallery)

Fríkirkjuvegur

Tjörnin

Norræna Húsið (Nordic House)

Neskirkja

Háa Torg

Radisson The Saga

SKILDINGANES

Skerjafjörður

Innanlandsflugvöllur

Reykjavíkurflugvöllur

Icelandair Reykjavík Natúra

Nauthólsvík (Geothermal Beach) **21**

Hlíðarfótur

ÖSKJUHLÍÐ

Perlan (Pearl)

Sögusafnið (Saga Museum) **20**

Perlvogskirkja

KRINGLAN

BÚSTAÐIR

Icelandic National Radio

Sílakaffis Reykjavíkur (City Hospital)

GERÐI

Keflavík

Kringlan Shopping Mall

Borgarleikhúsið (City Theatre)

NORÐURMÝRI

MIKLATÚN

Kjarvalsstaðir (Reykjavík Art Museum) **22**

Icelandic Phallological Museum

Sundhöll Reykjavíkur (Swimming Pool)

Hallgrímskirkja

Landspítalinn (National Hospital)

Gamla Hringbraut

Umferðamiðstöðin BSÍ (Coach Terminal)

Sólfar Suncraft **23**

Höfði House **24**

TÚN

TEIGAR

Safn Sigurjóns Ólafssonar (Sigurjón Ólafsson Museum) **25**

LAUGARNES

Ferry Terminal
Viðey **26** Lundey

LAUGARÁS

Laugardalslaug (Swimming Pool)

Laugardalsvöllur (Sports Stadium)

LAUGARDALUR

Skautasvell (Skating Rink)

Laugardalshöllin (Sports Hall)

Ásmundarsafn (Ásmundur Sveinsson Sculpture Gallery) **29**

Grasagarðurinn (Botanical Gardens) **28**

Húsdýragarðurinn (Reykjavik Zoo) **27**

Fjölskyldugarðurinn (Family Park)

MÚLAR

SUND

SUNDAHÖFN

SUNDAHÖFN

MERKUR

SOGAMÝRI

Árbæjarsafn (Árbær Open-Air Museum) **30**

Nýlistasafnið (Living Art Museum) **31**

Viðeyjarsund

see Central Reykjavík

AUSTURBÆR

and Ægisgarður pier (15 May–Sep from 10.15am, last trip from the island at 6.30pm). Outside the summer season, there is a limited weekend-only timetable from Skarfabakki (from 1.30pm, last trip from the island at 4.30pm).

High Sheriff Skúli Magnússon moved to Viðey in 1751 and had a fine residence – Iceland's first stone building – constructed there. After falling into disrepair, Skúli's former home was restored in 1988 and now houses a summer café. The church on the island dates from 1774 and is also one of the oldest in the country; before the Reformation, Viðey housed the richest monastery in Iceland, which owned a good part of Reykjavík and the land beyond, until it was torn down by Lutheran zealots. An ambitious scheme for a fisheries operation was launched in the early 20th century but eventually went bankrupt; remains of the "ghost town" can be visited on a pleasant walk around the eastern part of the island, which takes about an hour. A more modern construction, near to the café, is Yoko Ono's **Imagine Peace Tower** (http://imagine-peacetower.com), lit on the equinoxes, John and Yoko's birthdays and on New Year's Eve.

## Nature and high art

For all Reykjavík's modern expansion, the city's natural treasures remain as precious as ever. The **Laugardalur** area, a green belt situated northeast of the old city centre, has been largely preserved from development. It serves as the capital's main sports area, with a soccer stadium, sports hall and ice-skating rink. It also contains one of the most popular swimming pools in Iceland, the large open-air, geothermally heated **Laugardalslaug** (tel: 411 5100; Mon–Fri 6.30am–10pm, Sat–Sun 8am–10pm), with a 50-metre (165ft) main pool, kids' pool with curly slide, hot-pots and sauna. There is also the

Viking-themed mini-rides of the **Family Park** (Fjölskyldugaðurinn) and adjoining **Reykjavík Zoo ㉗** (Húsdyragarðurinn; www.mu.is; both daily mid-May–Aug 10am–6pm, Sept–mid-May 10am–5pm), which contains domestic farm animals, animals native to Iceland and a small coldwater aquarium, rather than lions and tigers. The nearby **Botanical Gardens ㉘** (Grasagarðurinn; http://grasagardur.is; open daily May–Sep 10am–10pm, Oct–Apr 10am–3pm; free) have an impressive collection of 5,000 plants and nearly the entire Icelandic flora.

Over the road from the soccer stadium is the sculpture gallery **Ásmundarsafn ㉙** (Sigtún; http://artmuseum.is/asmundarsafn; daily May–Sept 10am–5pm, Oct–Apr 1–5pm), a third part of the Reykjavík Art Museum dedicated to the sculptor Ásmundur Sveinsson (1893–1982). His works, inspired by saga events, folklore and everyday life, are set in and around his bizarre dome and pyramid studio/home. The outdoor sculpture garden is impressive, and open at all hours – many tourists

*Saga Museum mannequins.*

*Whale-watching tours depart from the Old Harbour (Höfn) in the city centre from April to October.*

*Reykjavík's beach, Nauthólsvík.*

pass it regularly, as several hotels are situated nearby.

## The New Reykjavík

Since World War II the capital has been expanding to the east, leaving its past behind. In the 1980s, as it approached a six-digit population, more modern and grandiose architecture appeared on its skyline. A new commercial and cultural centre was built entirely from scratch some 4km (2.5 miles) east of the old centre, including not only the large indoor shopping mall, **Kringlan** (www.kringlan.is), but also a complex to house the Reykjavík City Theatre company (www.borgarleikhus.is).

As new residential suburbs sprang up – tasteless "concrete lava fields" such as Breiðholt and Árbær, each many times more populous than the largest of rural Icelandic towns – so this new part of Reykjavík has become the geographical as well as the business and commercial centre. This expansion is perhaps the most instantly visible result of Iceland's rapid shift from a traditional, rural country to a modern technological society.

Located on the edge of the Árbær suburb is the **Árbær Open-Air Museum** ❸⓪ (Árbæjarsafn; http://borgarsogusafn.is; daily June–Aug 10am–5pm, Sept–May tours at 1pm, no booking needed), a living history museum that in the summer offers a schedule of events at weekends. A number of historical houses have been moved here from various locations in Reykjavík and around Iceland, and the past is re-created as accurately as possible. Household items and furnishings used throughout the centuries are on permanent display, and there is also an old turf church which is a popular spot for wedding services. The atmosphere is compromised by the busy road that runs next to it, however.

Another must-see for art enthusiasts is the **Living Art Museum** ❸① (Nýlistasafnið; Völvufell 13-21; www.nylo.is; Tue–Fri noon–5pm, only during exhibitions Sat–Sun 1–5pm; free), which relocated in 2014 to a new building with an area of 400 square meters. It was originally founded as a cooperative in the 1970s by a group

of artists who opposed what they saw as the National Gallery's shunning of experimental art. The museum stages ongoing exhibitions by both Icelandic and foreign artists and has become a permanent fixture on the artistic landscape.

Between the suburbs of Breiðholt and Árbær, and well within the city limits, runs the idyllic **Elliðaár** river, which pays handsome tribute to the lack of pollution in Reykjavík as one of the best salmon rivers in Iceland, with annual catches of around 1,600 fish. By tradition the city's mayor opens the fishing season on 1 May every year. Angling permits, being carefully shared out, are difficult for visitors to come by, but there is no problem in buying permits during the summer season for nearby **Lake Elliðavatn**, where there is good local trout in wonderfully calm and picturesque surroundings.

Elliðavatn borders the capital's **Heiðmörk** nature reserve to the south of the city, a popular spot for picnics and strolls, where wild patches merge harmoniously with areas reclaimed from wind erosion by the planting of trees.

## Greater Reykjavík

Reykjavík and the towns surrounding it grew so fast during the late 20th- and early 21st-century boom years that they now form an almost continuous conurbation, known as the **Greater Reykjavík Area**. The recent economic crisis has caused a rise in emigration, but the area is still home to over 200,000 people – almost two-thirds of Iceland's total population. The urban area extends some 11km (7 miles) to the east of the old city centre. Most of these towns are new and quite colourless, including Kópavogur, which has swollen in recent years to accommodate 33,000 people and is thus the second-largest community in Iceland. One of Kópavogur's claims to fame is that it is home to the country's biggest shopping mall, Smáralind (www.smaralind.is), opened in October 2001. Sightseeing tours from Reykjavík take in some of the more interesting and historic places, such as Hafnarfjörður and Bessastaðir (see pages 158 and 159).

*A capital city on a very human scale.*

# THE REYKJANES PENINSULA

Situated just south of the capital, the Reykjanes peninsula is a compact area to visit. The undisputed highlight is the stunning Blue Lagoon, but there are also excellent bird-watching sites and nature reserves.

**Main Attractions**
Hafnarfjörður
Blue Lagoon
Reykjavegur Trail
Krisuvikurbjarg cliffs

*Expanses of volcanic rock are typical of the Reykjanes Peninsula.*

The Reykjanes peninsula is easy to ignore – a smallish promontory southwest of **Reykjavík ❶**, it is undeniably overshadowed by the capital's greater pulling power. Yet most people's first glimpse of Iceland is actually of Reykjanes – Keflavík international airport is situated right in its heart.

Almost all arriving tourists simply jump aboard a bus or hire a car, and head for the mountains or the city without a backward glance. But one really should give the region a little time: the principal sights can be seen on a day tour, but hikers, whale-watchers, birdwatchers and devotees of the Blue Lagoon may find it harder to tear themselves away.

## Lashed by the Atlantic

Situated in Iceland's far southwest, the peninsula bears the full force of the violent storms that regularly pile in from the Atlantic. Small, nondescript fishing villages dot the coastline, while much of the inland area consists of lava fields, some of which flowed as recently as the 14th century. In fact the peninsula is a continuation of the Mid-Atlantic Ridge, which pushes apart two immense plates of the earth's crust at the rate of around 2cm (0.75ins) each year. Pillow lava and tufa formations from Ice Age eruptions give some indication of what the submarine ridge looks like. While the broad expanses of volcanic rock may seem grey and barren at first glance, in fact they have donned a coat of Iceland's typical grey-green moss, soft and springy underfoot. The tenacious moss has paved the way for higher plants, which thrive in the more sheltered areas. Two hundred species of grasses, mosses and flowering plants have been identified, with the occasional birch or other tree.

## Hafnarfjörður

The gateway to Reykjanes, only 15 minutes by bus south of central

Reykjavík, is the old town of **Hafnarfjörður ❷**. This was one of Iceland's most important ports long before Reykjavík had even grown into a village: in the 15th century it was run by English traders and in the 16th century by Germans, before the Danes imposed their trade monopoly of 1602.

Situated within the craggy Búrfell lava field which covers most of the peninsula, Hafnarfjörður has a population of 28,000. It is a part of the Greater Reykjavík area but is by no means a satellite town of the capital, with its own thriving port and fishing industry, and a broadly based local economy. The cool, white **Hafnarborg Arts Centre** (www.hafnarborg.is; Wed–Mon noon–5pm; free) by the harbour-side is a genuine highlight of the town, offering art shows and musical events, as well as a peaceful coffee shop. A pleasant public park, **Hellisgerði**, is situated in the middle of the town, in among the lava. **Hafnarfjörður Museum** (http://museum.hafnar fjordur.is) is based across four separate buildings: at Vesturgata 8, **Pakkhúsið** contains an interesting canter through the town's history and a little toy museum; next door is **Sívertens-Hús**, once the home of local bigwig, Bjarni Sívertsen, dating from 1803 and the oldest building in town (both June–Aug daily 11am–5pm; Pakkhúsið also the rest of the year Sat–Sun 11am–5pm); at the opposite end of the social scale is **Siggubær**, a tiny house belonging to a former fisherman (June–Aug Sat–Sun 11am–5pm); while the latest acquisition is **Bookless Bungalow** (Vesturgata 32; June–Aug daily 11am–5pm), which contains an exhibition on foreign fishermen at the turn of the 20th century.

Hafnarfjörður is also well known for its "hidden population". For as long as can be remembered, people have believed that elves, dwarfs and other supernatural creatures live in its lava cliffs in peaceful coexistence with other town residents. There is even a map available at the local tourist information centre, showing hidden sites where these mysterious beings live (see page 250).

In addition, Hafnarfjörður has become the "Viking centre" of Iceland. The nation's only Viking restaurant, Fjörukráin (http://fjorukrain.is), is located at the harbour, where traditional food is served with lively song and celebration. During the ancient Viking month of Þorri (late Jan–late Feb), this is one of the best places to sample the pickled, smoked, dried and salted foods, such as rams' testicles, cured sharkmeat and blood pudding, that once sustained people through the long winter months. In summer, over a long weekend in mid-June, fighting displays and feasting are staples of the town's annual Viking Festival.

## Bessastaðir

Bessastaðir ❸, north of Hafnarfjörður and just across the Skerjafjörður inlet from Reykjavík, has been the presidential residence since 1941, but the site has a much older history. Bessastaðir is first mentioned in the *Íslendinga Saga (Saga of the Icelanders)* by Sturla

*A typical Icelandic souvenir.*

*The Blue Lagoon.*

**FACT**

The creeping thistle (*Cirsium arvense*), otherwise rare in Iceland, grows in Grindavík. Local tradition claims that it grew up on the spot where both Christian and heathen blood was spilt.

Þórðarson, and archaeological excavations have yielded a range of artefacts dating back to the Middle Ages, when the place belonged to the famous Edda (Old Norse poetry) author Snorri Sturluson (see page 43). After Snorri's death, the farm was confiscated by the king of Norway and remained a royal estate right up until the late 18th century (the present-day building and the adjacent church date from this period). From 1805 Bessastaðir was the site of the highest educational institution in Iceland, the Lærði skólinn, for some 40 years.

Unless you are a foreign VIP being given a formal presidential reception at Bessastaðir, the interior of the house is off limits. However, visitors can take a peek inside the church, which was consecrated in 1796. Considerable repairs were carried out in 1946–8: the original stone floor disappeared under concrete, but can still be seen in the vestibule and tower. The windows illustrate themes from Icelandic ecclesiastical history. The altarpiece, by the Icelandic artist Muggur, is a triptych, painted in 1921.

## Along the peninsula

Route 41 along the north coast of Reykjanes leads to the twin towns of **Njarðvík** and **Keflavík** ❹ (combined population over 15,000), both trading centres since the Middle Ages. The two towns have virtually joined together in recent years (they are often referred to by the single name "Reykjanesbær"), with a shared economy based on fishing and other commercial enterprises. In 2006, the speedy and controversial closure of the American air base at Keflavík, where around one in 17 of the local population was employed, had an unsettling effect on the area, although it is slowly regenerating. The old base has since been reinvented as a data centre, taking advantage of Iceland's cool breezes and geothermal power to host servers for international companies. There are plans to re-establish an American military presence in Keflavik due to a rising threat from Russia In Njarðvík, the **Viking World** (Víkingaheimar; www.vikingaheimar.is; daily 7am–6pm, advance booking advised) exhibition investigates Viking life and New World exploration, and is based

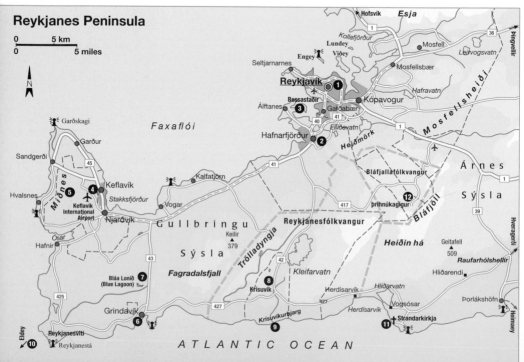

Reykjanes Peninsula

around a reconstructed Viking ship. In summer there is also a small Zoo.

Beyond Keflavík is the outcrop known as **Miðnes** ⑤, whose biggest settlements are the tiny fishing outposts of **Garður** and **Sandgerði**. Garðskagi, the headland just northwest of Garður, makes an interestingly windswept place for bird- and whale-spotting, while just south of Sandgerði is the small **Hvalsnes** church, built in 1887. The church's most treasured possession is a gravestone handcut by the poet Reverend Hallgrímur Pétursson in 1649. The stone came to light during excavations in 1964. The ruins of the village **Bátsendar** are nearby, destroyed by a freak tide at the end of the 18th century.

Route 425 follows the coast to the peninsula's southwestern tip, passing bleak lava fields, a low-key bubbling-mud geothermal area, and a hands-on energy exhibition based inside the **Reykjanesvirkjun power plant**; June–Aug daily 9am–4pm). Nearby is Iceland's oldest lighthouse, Reykjanesviti.

**Grindavík** ⑥, now a typical fishing community of about 3,000 people, can look back on a long and eventful history. It was a major trading centre during the Middle Ages, and in 1532 a business rivalry between English and Hanseatic merchants led to the murder of an Englishman, John "the Broad". Barbary pirates raided Grindavík in 1627, capturing a number of Danes and Icelanders, plus two merchant ships. Today Grindavík is a quiet and unassuming town, with a statue to the families of local fishermen lost at sea and the **Kvikan House of Culture & Natural Resources** (Hafnargata 12a; www.grindavik.is/kvikan; summer daily 10am–5pm, winter Sat–Sun 11am–5pm), with exhibitions dedicated to two of the keystones of Iceland's survival – saltfish and geothermal energy.

## Surreal spa

Iceland's most famous tourist attraction is located just outside Grindavík, only 15km (10 miles) from the airport. The **Blue Lagoon** ⑦ (Bláa Lonið;

www.bluelagoon.com; daily June–21 Aug 8am–midnight, 17–31 May and 22–31 Aug 8am–10pm, 2–16 May Mon, Tue, Wed, Thu 9am–8pm, Fri, Sat, Sun 8am–9pm, Sep–Oct Mon, Tue, Wed 8am–8pm, Thu, Fri, Sat, Sun 8am–10pm, daily Nov–Apr 8am–8pm; pre-booking is required) is a dreamy, steamy spa complex that epitomises the country's faintly unearthly reputation. Little wooden bridges criss-cross the lagoon's blue-white waters and hot-pots; a cave-like sauna is carved into the lava; and a thundering waterfall delivers a pounding massage. The complex also contains a spa treatment area, restaurant, snack bar, shop, conference facilities, and, should you care to spend the night, there is a guesthouse just over the lava field. All summer long (June–August), however, the changing rooms get crowded and it may be worth getting up early – or staying late – to beat the crowds. Also note that the mineral-rich water has adverse effects on your hair, so bring plenty of hair conditioner. For those who want to try the rejuvenating powers of the Blue Lagoon's silica, the new Silica Mud Bar

**FACT**

The **Reykjavegur trail** extends over 114km (71 miles) from the lighthouse at the southwestern tip of the peninsula to the Nesjavellir power plant east of Reykjavík. You can reach most of the trail's seven stage points by car, and walk from one to the next in a day. This region is one of the few places on earth where you can observe continental drift from marked-out and accessible areas.

*Saltfish exhibition in Grindavík.*

*Walking by the Seltun geothermal springs, Krisuvik.*

opened in 2016. If you're impressed by the Blue Lagoon's healing properties, a range of eponymous skin and bathing products are on sale across the island (see margin).

In spite of its evocative name, the lagoon is not a natural phenomenon but a fortuitous by-product of Iceland's geothermal energy usage. The nearby Svartsengi power plant pumps mineral-laden water from up to 2km (1.2 miles) beneath the earth's surface, at a temperature of 240°C (470°F). The superheated water passes through a dual process, on the one hand to generate electricity, and on the other to heat fresh water. This run-off water, now close to body temperature at 38°C (100°F) rich in silica, salt and other elements, once flowed out into a pool a few hundred metres from the present lagoon's site. Psoriasis and eczema sufferers noticed that bathing in the water seemed to ease their symptoms. Once the word was out, the lagoon was moved to its current location, and state-of-the-art facilities, carefully designed to complement the surrounding landscape, were built around it.

## Hot spot

Geothermal power in a more natural setting can be seen east of Grindavík at **Krísuvík** ❽, within the Reykjanesfólkvangur nature reserve. Here *solfataras* and boiling mud springs surround the world's largest blowing steam vent. The intention has always been to harness the geothermal energy at Krísuvík for heating purposes: an energy bill currently before the Icelandic parliament proposes seven new power plants on the Reykjanes peninsula, including four around Krísuvík. The whole area seethes with subterranean heat, so tread carefully and keep to the paths to avoid being scalded.

Near Krísuvík is the dramatic and somewhat spooky **Lake Kleifarvatn**, reputed to be the home of an aquatic monster. If you are not put off by this, you can also fish for trout here. Permits are available in Reykjavík, Hafnarfjörður and Keflavík. On the coast beyond Krísuvík is **Krísuvíkurbjarg** ❾, one of Iceland's best-known birdcliffs: the most numerous inhabitants are kittiwakes, while fulmar, razorbill, common guillemot and Brunnich's guillemot are also plentiful. Less common sightings are puffin, shag, herring gull and black guillemot, while seals can often be seen basking on the shore. Further offshore, one may occasionally glimpse groups of whales.

About 14km (9 miles) off the Reykjanes shore lies the island of **Eldey** ❿, a high rocky pillar towering 77 metres (250ft) out of the sea. Eldey is home to one of the North Atlantic's largest gannet colonies – around 16,000 birds nest on the island each year. The island is a fiercely protected nature reserve, with access forbidden to casual visitors. On a less positive note, the island is also the place where the last of the great auks was clubbed to death in 1844.

## Church of miracles

The little **Strandarkirkja** ⓫ (http://kirkjan.is/strandarkirkja) church on the south coast between Krísuvík and Þorlákshöfn has a bizarre history. Tradition says that

a ship on its way to Iceland ran into a storm; the crew prayed for deliverance, and promised to build a church if they were saved. An angel appeared on the shore and guided them to safety; they landed at the spot where Strandarkirkja stands today. A tradition arose that the church could work miracles: through the centuries seamen in peril have prayed and promised donations to Strandarkirkja, and they still do: this little church, which no longer has any parish to serve, is reputed to be one of the wealthiest in Iceland.

Near Strandarkirkja, at the small lake Hlíðarvatn, is the farm **Vogsósar**. Formerly a parsonage, the farm was the home of the Reverend Eiríkur (1638–1716), who added a dash of magic to his pastoral duties. A famous folktale tells how one wintry day, travellers passing by the farm helped themselves to hay from Eiríkur's haystack without asking. After feeding their horses on the stolen fodder, they continued down to the river; but when they got there, the horses began to drink and drink, and couldn't be made to walk on. Eventually Reverend Eiríkur himself appeared at the ford, and after observing the scene, he remarked "The hay of Vogsós is thirsty hay. You shouldn't give it to your horses again."

A little further to the west is the abandoned farm **Herdísarvík**. Above the farm is a big crag from which impressive lava streams have flowed. This was the home of the great Icelandic poet Einar Benediktsson, who died here in 1940. Herdísarvík bay may have inspired some of Benediktsson's lines from *Surf*: "I hear in thy short-lived waves wearingly rolled / The footfall of time that e'er onward must hold / And my blood surges on with the bruit of the main...."

North of Strandarkirkja, in the Bláfjöll mountains, lies an ancient wonder only recently opened to tourists. The **Príhnúkagígur volcano** 12 is the only one in the world with an empty, intact, multicoloured magma chamber into which visitors can descend. The chamber is big enough to fit the Statue of Liberty, with room to spare. Visitors go down through the crater's opening in an open elevator, which takes travels 120 metres in six minutes. To arrange a tour, see www.insidethevolcano.com.

**FACT**

There is an array of unusual health-giving salts, sprays and lotions on sale at the Blue Lagoon, containing a blend of minerals, silica mud and algae found in the lagoon's geothermal seawater. The active ingredients revitalise and protect human skin, and are particularly effective in treating chronic conditions such as psoriasis. Prices are high, though; buy at the duty-free shop at Keflavík airport instead.

*Inside Príhnúkagígur volcano.*

*The impressive Strokkur geyser.*

# THE SOUTHWEST

This area is full of historical sites from the time of the sagas, plus a wealth of natural wonders, all within comparatively easy reach of the capital and the Ring Road.

The rich farming land of south-west Iceland is one of the most heavily visited regions: some of Iceland's most famous attractions are within striking distance of Reykjavík, tied together under the label of "the Golden Circle". Every day, coaches whizz hundreds of travellers from one natural marvel to another: the waterfall Gullfoss; the spouting hot springs at Geysir; the Unesco-listed rift valley Þingvellir that housed the Viking's parliament; and many curiosities in between. But it's worth taking your time here, stopping to appreciate Iceland's mellow rural atmosphere, investigate Saga Age ruins, wander in the enchanting Þórsmörk nature reserve, and hike up to the Fimmvörðuháls pass to view the 2010 eruption craters.

## East of Reykjavík

The Ring Road east of Reykjavík quickly ascends to a volcanically scarred mountain pass. The moss-covered scoria lava field here, known as **Kristnitökuhraun**, was spewed up from the earth around AD 1000. The **Hellisheiði** area is a good walking destination en route from Reykjavík, with a well signposted trail network and detailed maps available.

There are panoramic views as the road descends towards the southwestern plain, with steaming crevasses and

yellow sulphur markings on the slopes above **Hveragerði ❶**, a town of 2,300 people that has made a living from harnessing geothermal activity. Its greenhouses provide the country with much of its home-grown produce, including tropical fruits like bananas. A small geothermal area sits in the centre of town, while the Naturopathic Health Association of Iceland operates a clinic here for spa and mud cures. The town was shaken by an earthquake measuring 6 on the Richter scale in 2008 – an exhibition in Sunnumörk shopping

**Main Attractions**

Stokkseyri and Eyrarbakki
Þingvellir
Geysir
Gullfoss
Þórsmörk
Skógar Folk Museum
Vík

*At Þjóðveldisbær, a re-creation of times past.*

*The Ghost Centre at Stokkseyri.*

centre shows the experience through local eyes. Lying 4km (2.5 miles) north of town is a stretch of geothermal river where it's possible to bathe; en route is a bubbling hot spring area activated by earthquakes in 2008. Hveragerði's neat little modern-art gallery **Listasafn Árnesinga** (Austurmörk 21; www.lista safnarnesinga.is; May–Sept daily noon–6pm, Oct–Apr Thu–Sun noon–6pm; free) provides a non-geothermal treat.

While Hveragerði itself is unlikely to hold travellers' attention for more than a couple of hours, it can be a base for hikes into the surrounding countryside. The whole area is enlivened by the Hengill volcano, and hiking trails run through the steaming landscape right the way to Nesjavellir and Þingvellir.

The next town along the Ring Road is **Selfoss** ❷ (population 6,500), the centre of Iceland's thriving dairy industry and a major road intersection.

## Stokkseyri and Eyrarbakki

To the south of Selfoss lie two tiny fishing villages which, between them, hold several unusual visitor attractions and two highly rated restaurants: the seafood Rauða húsið in **Eyrarbakki** (http://raudahusid.is) and the lobster restaurant Við Fjöruborðið in **Stokkseyri** (www.fjorubordid.is). In **Stokkseyri** ❸,

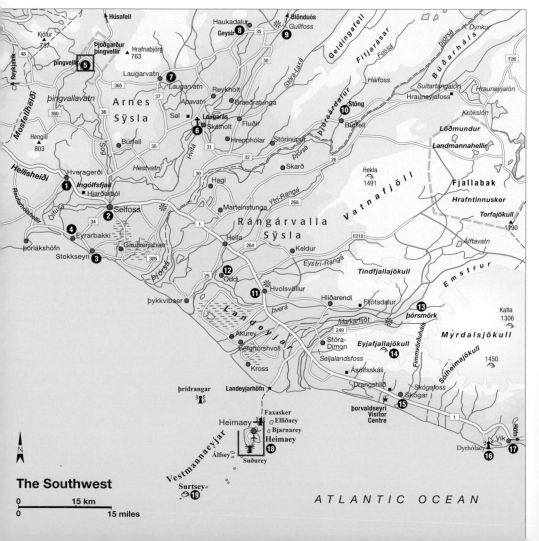

The Southwest

ATLANTIC OCEAN

0   15 km
0   15 miles

the **Ghost Centre** (Draugasétrið; tel: 895-0020; www.icelandicwonders.com; June–Aug daily 1–6pm, Sept–Apr upon request) sets out to spook its customers with a dark audioguided walk through Iceland's supernatural stories. In similar vein, **Icelandic Wonders** (June–Aug Mon–Fri 10am–6pm, Sat–Sun noon–6pm, Sept–May upon request) next door explores local superstitions about trolls, elves and the Northern Lights (see page 203).

More serious-minded is the village of **Eyrarbakki ❹**, set by the shores of a driftwood-strewn black sand beach. This was one of Iceland's main fishing ports from the 12th to the 19th centuries, and has several 18th-century buildings still intact. The oldest, simply called "Húsið" ("The House"), contains an interesting little **Árnessýsla Heritage Museum** (tel: 483 1504; www.husid.com; May–Sept daily 11am–6pm; Oct–Apr upon request). The **Maritime Museum** (same opening hours) is in an adjacent building. West of the villages lies the wide Ölfusá estuary and the Fuglafriðland reserve, a prime location for bird-watching.

## Þingvellir

Route 35 turns off north of Selfoss at the hillock of **Ingólfsfjall**, where the First Settler, Ingólfur Arnarson, is said to be buried. Among a group of smaller craters is the 55-metre (180ft)-deep Kerið, blasted out 6,500 years ago and now containing a lake. Continuing north it is possible to reach **Þingvellir National Park ❺** (also accessible directly from Reykjavík), the historical heartland of Iceland, and a Unesco World Heritage Site thanks to its marvellous natural setting and unique glimpse of medieval Norse culture.

When Iceland's unruly early settlers decided to form a commonwealth in AD 930, the site they chose for their new national assembly, the Alþingi, was the natural amphitheatre of Þingvellir ("parliament plains"). It was a grand experiment in republicanism at a time when the rest of Europe wallowed in rigid feudal monarchies, and it lasted, despite the odd lapses into chaos, for over three centuries.

Today Þingvellir is still regarded with reverence by Icelanders, its historical weight reinforced by a serene

*The view northeast across the Þingvellir plain, with the historic farmhouse and church in the foreground.*

natural beauty. Declared part of a national park in 1928, the historical section is set along the north of **Ping-vallavatn** – at 84 sq km (30 sq miles), Iceland's largest lake – and by the banks of the **River Öxará** ("axe river"). On the horizon in every direction lie low mountains, snowcapped for much of the year: to the north lies the volcano of Skjaldbreiður ("broad-shield") – whose lavas created Þingvellir – flanked by the mountains Botnssúlur, Hrafnabjörg and Ármannsfell. The latter is home, it's said, to Ármann, a spirit who is the guardian of Þingvellir. To the south lies the geothermally active Hengill.

The lava plain of Þingvellir itself is covered with wildflowers in summer and sumptuous shades of red in the autumn. This is also a spot where the two halves of Iceland – the Eurasian and North American tectonic plates – are tearing apart. Aerial photographs show that the great crack of **Almannagjá** ("everyman's chasm"), on whose flanks the Alþingi was held, is just one fissure in a huge series running northeast like an ancient wound through the plains. Occasional earthquakes have reshaped the site: a quake in 1789 caused the plain to drop about 1 metre (3ft). The plates are drifting apart at a rate of around 2cm (0.75ins) each year.

## Journey into the past

The **visitor centre** (tel: 482 2660; www.thingvellir.is; daily Nov–Mar 9am–5pm, Apr–Oct until 6pm) is located on the eastern side of the Öxará River, to the north of the historic sites. From here a track heads south to the church and farmhouse, while a path veers off southwest to the Lögberg, viewpoint and educational centre on the other side of the river. The point where the latter crosses the Öxará is **Drek-kingarhylur**, the famed "drowning pool" that came into use in the 16th century. Men condemned to death were beheaded, but women who committed adultery, infanticide or perjury were tied up in a sack and flung into the pool, which was then deeper and more turbulent than it is today. A short distance upstream is the Öxarár-foss waterfall.

*Þingvellir National Park.*

The path continues to what was the focal point of every Viking Alþingi: **Lögberg Ⓐ**, the "Law Rock", today marked by a stone and a flapping Icelandic flag, right by the Almannagjá fissure. On the smoother ground below, the Lögrétta (Legislature) took place, attended by the 36 (later increased to 39) goðar or chieftains who would debate new laws. All free men were welcome to listen or comment, but only the goðar could vote. It was also the site of the Quarter Courts, one for each section of the country. The proceedings were considered so important that farmer-warriors rode in from every corner of Iceland, some taking as long as 17 days to arrive from the East Fjords.

The whole business was run by the Law-speaker, who was elected from among the chieftains. His was a difficult job: apart from keeping the proceedings orderly, he had to recite from memory all of the Icelandic laws, one third every year, from the Lögberg. The acoustics here are still excellent.

Scattered amongst the grass and lava on either side of the Lögberg are the few remains of various **búðir Ⓑ**, or booths. Every chieftain set up his own personal booth for the two weeks that the Alþingi lasted (usually from the Thursday after 18 June each year), a canvas-covered place to sleep, eat, drink and meet. The stones that can be seen today all probably belong to booths from the 18th century. The remains of Hotel Valhöll, which burned to the ground in July 2009, are on the site of Snorri Sturluson's booth, **Valhöll Ⓒ**.

The path continues up to the **Interpretive Centre** (daily 9am–5pm, summer until 8pm) and lookout point at the top of the Almannagjá fissure, with great views across to the church and the Pingvellir plains.

## Religious centre

On the east bank of the river is the glistening white **Pingvallabær farmhouse Ⓓ** and **Pingvallakirkja church Ⓔ**, from where free guided tours depart (at 10am and 3pm in summer). The older part of the farmhouse, built in 1930, is today occupied by the park warden; the newer section,

*Eyrarbakki's oldest building, dating from 1765, houses the Folk Museum.*

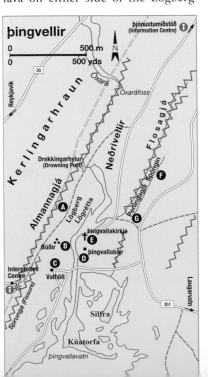

# Laying Down the Law

**Icelanders have always been rather quarrelsome – aptly, the law of the land covers every possible contingency.**

Much of Icelandic history does seem to concern aggrieved characters making a choice between taking up the sword or going to court. The annual Alþingi set up in AD 930 offered the best of both worlds: legal proceedings with an adjournment while the litigants fought pitched battles. They could then apologise to the court, sit down and allow the proceedings to continue.

"Icelanders", wrote an 18th-century English commentator, "have surpassed all other nations in legal chicanery. Jurisprudence was the favourite study of the rich. A wealthy Icelander was always ambitious to plead a cause before the Alþingi, and the greater skill he showed in the art of prolonging... the greater was his celebrity. A man gained as much reputation for defeating his adversary in a lawsuit as for killing him in a duel."

Law covered every contingency imaginable. Thus: "If a man holds his weapons in a peaceable

*Vikings in discussion.*

manner, as a person ordinarily does when he is not going to use them, and when they are in this position another man runs against them and wounds himself, he who held the weapons is liable to the punishment of banishment if competent witnesses can prove that he held them in this apparently quiet manner, in order that the other might run against them and be wounded thereby."

## Categorising the crime

This law reflected the fine calculation that made the punishment fit the crime. The case of a man who seduced a girl and was then wounded by the girl's father was considered all square. Punishment, when required, fell into three categories: death and two types of "banishment", exile or house arrest. The last normally carried the option of a fine; just as well, because it was almost impossible not to break laws and most people would have spent much of their life indoors.

The crimes of witchcraft and theft commonly carried the death penalty, but those of murder or manslaughter rarely so. Thieves were beheaded; those convicted of witchcraft, usually men, were burnt or drowned to reduce the risk of trouble with their ghosts. Killing was shameful only if it was done in an underhand manner, like killing someone asleep. In other circumstances, which drew no distinction between self-defence and mindless butchery, it could be sorted out by the payment of a fixed penalty determined by the victim's social status.

In retaliation for effrontery or insult, killing was absolutely honourable, merely requiring a public announcement of the deed, which had to be made on the same day. After the event, care had to be taken not to conceal the body beyond a covering to protect it from scavengers. If insults were not immediately dealt with by the offended party, offenders were liable to exile. Indictable insults included throwing sand at someone, a punch, and attempting to throw a man into a mire "though he may actually not fall therein". Exile lasted 20 years and in practice was not far short of the death penalty, since an exile had a price on his head and could be killed with impunity.

In today's Iceland the rule of law and order is no less important. In line with the other Nordic countries, Iceland operates one of the toughest drink-driving laws in Europe and is far stricter than in the UK, for example. The possession of even small quantities of soft drugs can lead to heavy fines or even imprisonment.

dating from 1974, is the summer residence of the Prime Minister.

A church at Þingvellir was the first in Iceland to be consecrated, probably soon after the conversion of 1000, although not at this location. The present version dates from 1859. Inside, there is a pulpit from 1683 and a treasured altarpiece, painted by Ófeigur Jónsson of Heiðarbær in 1834, that had been taken from Iceland and wound up in a church on the Isle of Wight in southern England. It was rediscovered only in 1974, and returned to Iceland in time for the 1,100th anniversary of the Settlement, which was celebrated at Þingvellir. There are three bells in the church steeple: one dating from the Middle Ages, one from 1698, and the third called Íslandsklukkan ("Iceland's bell") that was cast to ring out for Iceland's independence in 1944.

There are two cemeteries at the church, the higher one a circular plot of ground with only two graves in it: both of poets, the illustrious nationalists Jónas Hallgrímsson (1807–45) and Einar Benediktsson (1864–1940). Just

to the north of the church is **Biskupabúð**, the "Bishops' booth", which is the largest ruined booth in Þingvellir and one that dates back to its earliest Viking times.

Walk back to the visitor centre from here, with a short detour to a strip of land, **Spöngin** ⓕ, caught between two fissures. Some historians believe that the Lögrétta was initially held on the flat land near here, but had to be moved closer to the Lögberg when the Öxará was diverted. On the opposite side of the bridge is **Peningagjá** ⓖ ("coin rift"), a fissure whose bottom glitters with shining silver: the Danish king Frederick VIII instigated the coin-throwing tradition on a visit here in 1907.

## Around Þingvellir

It is possible to take day hikes into the surrounding countryside. Almost all paths lead to the old sheep farm of **Skógarkot**, abandoned in 1936, to the west of Þingvellir. About one kilometre (0.5 miles) south is **Skógarkotshellir**, a long cave that has never been fully explored. The less

*A bishop is consecrated in 14th-century Iceland.*

### KEY PLACE IN HISTORY

Almost every important moment in Icelandic history has taken place at Þingvellir. When the Alþingi was first held here, the land was owned by the descendents of the First Settler, Ingólfur Arnarson. Here the decision was made for Iceland to convert to Christianity in AD 1000. This was the place for legal cases to be argued and voted on, although they were often finally resolved by the Viking recourse to arms and the field of Þingvellir would be soaked in blood. In time, this violence grew out of control, and at Þingvellir in 1271 Icelanders voted away their independence.

The Alþingi at Þingvellir kept operating as a court until the 1760s, although with less and less relevance as first Norway and then Denmark asserted colonial control.

energetic can enjoy a drive on the narrow dirt roads around Lake Þingvallavatn, lined with luxurious summer houses for Reykjavík inhabitants.

From Þingvallavatn, roads cut off in every direction – west to Reykjavík, north to the deserts, east to Geysir and south to Selfoss – following the ancient routes that were once ridden by Viking farmers, every June, to their unique, quixotic assembly. The road (550) north is the **Kaldidalur** route between Þingvellir and Húsafell. This rocky track usually opens during July when the snows melt around the Langjökull icecap, and will give a small taste of the interior (although it's not strictly an 'F' road – check whether your car rental agreement permits you to travel it). Shield volcanoes dominate the skyline, the most impressive being the evenly shaped Skjaldbreiður (1,060 metres/3,500ft), while, on the ground, colourful tundra flowers stud ancient lava flows. River crossings are straightforward and the track runs very close to the hanging glaciers of the icecap.

*Visiting Gullfoss waterfall is a dramatic experience, with the huge volume of water producing a deafening roar audible from miles away.*

## Skálholt

Returning to Route 35, heading northwards, the road now enters an area that is known as Biskupstungur, between the Brúará and Hvítá rivers. There's not much to see there now, but **Skálholt** ❻ – Iceland's first Christian bishopric and a theological powerhouse for over 700 years – is a site of immense historical importance. Skálholt's dominance was built up by an influential dynasty of chieftain-priests. First it was the farm of Gissur the White, the brow-beating holy man who had led the pro-Christian faction at the AD 1000 Alþingi. His talented son, Ísleifur, was educated in Germany to become the first properly trained Icelandic priest and, in 1056, Iceland's first bishop. Finally, Ísleifur's eldest son, Gissur, took up where his father had left off, making Skálholt the undisputed Church centre of Iceland, its many schools financed by the first tithe to be imposed in northern Europe.

In 1953 the foundations were laid for the current church. In the process, archaeologists found the

remains of Iceland's largest wooden church, which had burned down in 1309. Even more unexpected was the discovery of the carved stone coffin of Páll Jónsson, another of the learned, tough early bishops. According to *Páls Saga*, the bishop's death in 1211 was greeted by an earth tremor and deluge. When excavators opened his coffin– revealing the skeleton and walrus-bone bishop's crook – there was one of the biggest downpours that Skálholt had seen in years. From the crypt, a medieval underground passage leads outside, to where the archaeological digs continue.

Within sight of Skálholt, 3km (2 miles) away, the idyllic working farm of **Sel** (meaning "summer farm") offers accommodation among sheep-filled fields. Just further on is the village of **Reykholt**, which has a geyser that erupts several times an hour and a pleasant, thermally heated swimming pool (Snorralaug). Lying south of Skálholt is **Laugarás**, a verdant, geothermally active area with a camping ground.

The paved Route 37 turns off directly north of Route 35 to the spa village of **Laugarvatn ❼** by the shores of the lake of the same name. Summer brings hundreds from Reykjavík to enjoy its gentle pleasures, including **Fontana** (www.fontana.is; daily 11am–10pm), a beautifully designed collection of steam baths, saunas and geothermal pools sitting alongside the lake. Laugarvatn is also the site of the historical hot spring **Vígðalaug**, used as an all-weather baptism spot by the first bishops of Skálholt.

## The land of boiling waters

Both Routes 35 and 37 finally lead to **Geysir ❽**, which has given its name to all such water spouts around the world. Sadly, the Great Geysir, which started erupting in 1294 and used to reach heights of around 60 metres (200ft), hasn't performed well for decades. In the 20th century, eager tourists tipped gravel and bits of rubbish into its mouth in an effort to force an explosion, and soap powder was used to break the surface tension on special occasions such as Independence Day;

**FACT**

The English poet W.H. Auden noted in the 1930s that Icelanders were already using liquid Sunlight soap to encourage Geysir to explode. The soap had to be imported, since the thinner local type did not work.

*The hot spring at Vígðalaug.*

*Kitted out for safe sailing on Laugarvatn lake.*

*Archaeological remains at Stöng.*

but the geyser continued its slump into a state of near-dormancy. Many people were therefore stunned when Geysir suddenly sprang back into life in June 2000, seemingly quite out of the blue. Water spouted up to 40 metres (130ft) into the air, and the activity continued periodically over several weeks. Earthquakes in Southern Iceland had briefly changed the subterranean pressure, giving the great Geysir a short spell of renewed vitality; since then, however, it has settled back into a slumberous state once again.

Luckily, the Great Geysir's ever-reliable neighbour, **Strokkur** ("the churn"), bursts upwards every five minutes or so to a height of around 20 metres (66ft). Meanwhile, the whole Geysir area is geothermically active, with walking trails marked out among steaming vents, turquoise pools and glistening, multicoloured mud formations. Don't stand downwind of Strokkur unless you want to get soaked; keep behind the roped-off areas; and definitely refrain from putting your hands in water pools to test their temperatures – it may sound

silly, but it's surprising how many people do it.

## The greatest waterfall

Nine kilometres (6 miles) further along Route 35 is perhaps Iceland's best-known natural wonder: the waterfall **Gullfoss** ❾ ("golden falls"; http://gullfoss.is). A path from the main upper parking area leads down to the deafening double falls, where the River Hvítá tumbles 32 metres (105ft) into a 2.5km (1.5-mile) ravine. Trails climb past the waterfall's northern face, allowing you to get within an arm's length of the awesome flow. Wear a waterproof, or the clouds of spray that create photogenic rainbows on sunny days will douse you from head to foot.

By the café, a small exhibition space adorned with a plaque remembers Sigríður Tómasdóttir, a farmer's daughter who lived on the nearby farm Bratholt. In the 1920s, private plans had been drawn up to dam the Hvítá river at Gullfoss for a hydroelectric project, but Sigríður walked to Reykjavík to protest to the government and even

announced that she would fling her-self into the waterfalls if construction went ahead. The government instead bought the falls and made them a national monument in 1975.

From Gullfoss, the road stretches ahead into the uninhabited deserts of central Iceland, and on a clear day you can see the icecap **Langjökull** ("long glacier") in the distance.

## Viking relics

For anyone even vaguely interested in Saga Age history, it is worth mak-ing the dusty, bumpy trip to the exca-vated Viking longhouse of **Stöng** ⑩, and to its re-created twin, **Pjóðveld-isbær** ("the Commonwealth farm"; www.thjodveldisbaer.is; June–Aug daily 10am–5pm), which lies close to Búr-fell hydroelectricity station.

Both are situated in **Pjórsárdalur** ("bull river valley"), off Route 32, formed 8,000 years ago by the biggest lava outpouring since the Ice Age. The valley is overshadowed by the snow-capped form of **Mount Hekla**. Instead of a classic volcano cone, Hekla is part of a rather squat series of ridges,

becoming progressively squatter with each eruption; however, even this is usually hidden behind the thick bank of clouds that earned Hekla its men-acing name, which means "hooded." The seafaring Irish monk St Brendan might have been the first to see Hekla's volcanic pyrotechnics as he sailed past Iceland in the 6th century, and soon after settlement Hekla showed that it was a presence to be feared. The vol-cano's notoriety grew such that, in medieval Europe, Hekla was widely known to be one of the twin mouths of hell. Being the most active and dan-gerous volcano of the island, it has erupted every decade since 1979: in 1970, 1980, 1991, with the last eruption taking place in February 2000. Another eruption is expected imminently, but they are notoriously hard to predict: the volcano only usually gives 30 to 80 minutes warning, in the form of mini earthquakes, before she blows.

Stöng was the farm of the warrior-farmer Gaukur Trándilsson, whose saga, sadly, has been lost. He moved there at the end of the 11th century, but in 1104 Mount Hekla erupted,

*Gullfoss waterfall on the Hvítá River, which is fed by Langjökull glacier.*

soon covering the once-lush valley with a thick layer of white ash. Stöng and 20 other nearby farms had to be abandoned, and Þjórsárdalur was never resettled. In 1939, archaeologists uncovered Gaukur's house: it was in the form of two long rooms built end to end, with two annexes for the dairy and lavatory. As Iceland's best example of an early medieval home, it became the model for the nearby reconstruction of Þjóðveldisbær, begun in 1974 to mark the 1,100th anniversary of Iceland's settlement.

It's worth visiting the turf-covered reconstruction first, designed by architect Hörður Ágústsson using the Stöng floorplan and built by traditional methods (note the irregular-shaped planks of wood for the roof, fitted together so as not to waste an inch of the precious building material, and the marks of axes used to plane them).

The original Stöng is hidden away several kilometres further along a very poor dirt road. A large wooden shed has been built over the ruins to protect them from the elements, but it is never locked. Although only the stone foundations remain, this damp, slightly overgrown set of stones is the best place in Iceland to get the historical imagination working. On a fine day, those with spare time might want to take the two-hour walk beyond Stöng to Iceland's third-highest waterfall, **Háifoss**.

## Following the south coast

Back on the Ring Road, the unassuming towns of **Hella** and **Hvolsvöllur** ⓫, with around 800 and 900 inhabitants respectively, mark the beginning of the countryside where perhaps the most famous of the Icelandic Sagas, *Njáls Saga*, took place. The **Saga Centre** (mid-May–mid-Sept daily 9am–6pm, mid-Sept–mid-May Sat–Sun 10am–5pm) in Hvolsvöllur has a simple exhibition that tells the story of *Njáls Saga* (see page 92; www.sagatrail.is) in an easy yet comprehensive way. The centre is signposted from the main road. However, if you're interested in Iceland's rich literary history, make sure to visit the Culture House (where the ornately written sagas themselves are on display) and the National Museum before leaving

*The magical Þórsmörk nature reserve.*

Reykjavík (see pages 147 and 149), as these two museums provide the visitor with the clearest understanding of Viking life in Medieval Iceland.

Between the two towns, Route 266 heads south to **Oddi ⑫** which has been home to some of Iceland's most crafty inhabitants, including the lawyer and saga writer Snorri Sturluson; and Oddi's first inhabitant, Sæmundur the Learned. Sæmundur was well known to be a wizard: the man had no shadow, since it had been stolen by the devil while he was studying at the "Black School" for satanists in Paris. Sæmundur offered his soul if Satan could take him back to Iceland without getting him wet. In the shape of a giant seal, the devil swam the North Atlantic with Sæmundur on his back, but as soon as they got near the coast, Sæmundur whacked him on the head with a prayer book. The wily wizard swam the rest of the way and, since he was soaked, kept his soul.

The church at Oddi today was built in the 1920s, but has a number of curious artefacts on display, including a silver chalice dating from the 14th century.

## Thunder god's forest

By the crashing waters of **Seljalandsfoss** waterfall is the turnoff to Route F249, which leads to **Þórsmörk ⑬** – literally, "Thor's forest" – one of Iceland's most spectacular but inaccessible wilderness areas. Sealed off by three glaciers, two deep rivers and a string of mountains, the valley has received added protection since 1929, when it became a nature reserve. The single dirt road into the park is impassable to everything but the specially designed high-carriage mountain buses – and some of the "Super Jeep" oversized Icelandic four-wheel drives, which can make it in when the glacial rivers are low, usually in the early morning. In 2010, glacial flows (*jökulhlaups*) from the Eyjafjallajökull eruption washed away part of the road (now repaired), and visitors to Þórsmörk were recommended to bring sunglasses, closed shoes and plenty of water as a precaution against suffering from the effects of volcanic dust.

Despite the difficulties, Þórsmörk often attracts well over 1,000 Icelandic campers every summer weekend and a growing number of foreigners

*Puffins in Dyrhólaey.*

*Four-wheel drives are popular in Iceland.*

*Black-sand beach and Reynisdrangur sea stacks.*

on day trips (there are no hotels or guesthouses here, but there are three mountain huts and a clutch of summerhouses – see www.volcanohuts.com for details). Visitors are rewarded with spectacular glacier views, fields of wildflowers, pure glacial streams and forests of birch and willow full of birds – particularly blackbirds, ravens and wagtails.

The Ring Road continues south along a narrow plain of farmland between the black sand coast and rugged cliffs that lead to the icecap **Eyjafjallajökull** ⑭. This placid-looking glacier was brought to the world's attention in the spring of 2010 when its underlying volcano erupted, throwing a black ash plume up to 11km (7 miles) into the atmosphere, and closing down European airspace for six consecutive days. Farms and settlements south of the glacier such as Skógar and Vík were evacuated during the eruption – the **Þorvaldseyri Visitor Centre** (www.icelanderupts.is; June–Aug daily 9am–6pm, May, Sept daily 10am–4pm, Oct–Apr Mon–Fri 11am–4pm), based at one such working

family farm 10km west of Skógar, runs a touching 20-minute film about the volcano's effect. Many bus tours from Reykjavík take visitors up to the Fimmvörðuháls pass, and then on an hour's walk to see the fresh craters **Magni** and **Móði** (named after Thor's sons), which are still steaming. South Coast Adventure (www.southadventure. is), based at Hamragarðar campsite along the F249, also offers guided hikes and volcano tours in the area.

Ruins of indeterminate age crop up at intervals along this section of the Ring Road, giving the area considerable atmosphere. Beside the driveway to the farm **Drangshlíð** are some collapsed turf houses built into caves. Three kilometres (2 miles) further east, **Skógar** ⑮ is home to a meticulously managed **Folk Museum** (www. skogasafn.is; daily June–Aug 9am–6pm, May–Sept 10am–5pm), the most visited of its kind in Iceland, and run since 1949 by a local character, Þórður Tómasson. His incredible collection began life in the school basement, but soon had to move into its own premises due to lack of space: it's

now divided into sections on fishing, farming, handicrafts and transport, and also features 13 old Icelandic buildings, including a turf-roofed farmhouse and a pretty little church. There is a summer-only Edda Hotel at Skógar (www.hoteledda.is), as well as the splendid waterfall **Skógafoss**, whose sheer fall offers one of south Iceland's best photo opportunities.

The trek from Skógar to Þórsmörk, passing between the icecaps of Eyjafjallajökull and Mýrdalsjökull over the **Fimmvörðuháls** pass, is very popular with the hardy between June and September, and the trail can become quite crowded in July. The 2010 eruptions began at Fimmvörðuháls, disrupting a section of the trail; a new path has since been marked out that skirts the fresh lava flow.

Six kilometres (4 miles) east of Skógar, **Fúlilækur** ("foul river") announces itself with the overpowering rotten-egg stench of sulphur. The river emerges from beneath the **Sólheimajökull** glacier, which can be seen from the road, and originates near the volcano Katla, whose subterranean activities beneath the Mýrdalsjökull icecap have often sent glacial tides to devastate this area – and may again, as eruptions of Eyjafjallajökull have often been a precursor to Katla's outbursts.

Further on, Route 218 cuts south to **Dyrhólaey** ⑯, a protected nature area with a steep cliff and a much-photographed natural rock arch out to sea; this is one of the best places to photograph puffins in south Iceland. Saga hero Njáll's son-in-law Kári had his farm here.

**Vík** ⑰ (sometimes referred to as Vík í Mýrdal to distinguish it from other Víks) is a small town of around 270 people set along a dramatic stretch of coastline: here the North Atlantic swell hits the land, its waves crashing dramatically on a long beach of black sand. At the end of the beach are the **Reynisdrangur**, towering fingers of black rock standing out to sea and inhabited by colonies of Arctic terns. The relentless, battering wind adds to the Gothic scene – helping to make this the only non-tropical beach to be rated by *Islands*, a US magazine, as one of the world's top 10 beaches.

**TIP**

As evidenced by the volcanic eruptions at Eyjafjallajökull and Grímsvötn, Iceland's landscape is prone to the occasional lively outburst. The Department of Civil Protection and Emergency Management (www.almannavarnir.is) issues the latest status reports on volcanic activity, evacuation procedure, restricted zones and road closures.

*Skógafoss, south Iceland's dramatic waterfall.*

The Westman Islands, where human landscaping and natural grandeur sit side-by-side.

# VESTMANNAEYJAR (THE WESTMAN ISLANDS)

The comparatively recent volcanic origins of this small and scattered group of islands off the southwest coast are clearly visible in their rugged appearance.

**Main Attractions**

Folk Museum
Surtsey Visitor Centre
Eldfell
Skansinn
Clifftop walks

*Heimaey beneath the erupting Eldfell volcano.*

The Vestmannaeyjar (pronounced, roughly, *vestman-air*) combine a seductive serenity with raw natural beauty. Comprising 16 small islands and some 30 rocks or skerries, the archipelago rises, tiny, rugged and inhospitable, from the cold sea. It is one of the world's newer volcanic creations – one of its islands, Surtsey, only emerged from the ocean in 1963. In contrast to its harsh surroundings, Heimaey, the only inhabited island, is one of the friendliest places in Iceland, its sense of community no doubt forged by isolation and fickle nature. Heimaey's precarious position on top of a volcano was brought into sharp focus in 1973, when an eruption nearly caused the island to be permanently abandoned.

## Violent birth

Although this area off Iceland's southern coast had been the scene of underwater volcanic activity for hundreds of thousands of years, scientists estimate that the first land did not emerge from the sea here until 10,000 years ago, and most islands were not formed until 5,000 years ago – the blink of an eye, in geological terms. Footage of Surtsey's fiery birth gives an idea of how the archipelago must have formed, with molten lava boiling away the sea, ash clouds filling the sky, fountains of scoria, and rocks being hurled kilometres away by the force of the explosions.

The first human settlement here was also steeped in violence. In the earliest years of Iceland's settlement, five Irish slaves ambushed and butchered their master, Hjörleifur Hróðmarsson, blood brother of the first successful settler, Ingólfur Arnarson. Dragging along a handful of slave women, they commandeered a rowing boat and – according to the ancient *Landnáma-bók (Book of Settlements)* – escaped from their farm near Vík to one of the small green islands visible from the country's south coast.

Not surprisingly, the slaves' new-found freedom was short-lived. Two weeks later, the other Viking settlers tracked them down, stormed their camp and mercilessly put the escapees to death. The whole archipelago is named after this incident: the Vestmannaeyjar (in English, the Westman Islands) is literally translated as "islands of the western men".

Today, visitors stay on/in **Heimaey**  (pronounced *"hay-may"*), the name of both the largest island and its township. Heimaey can be reached by a 25-minute flight from Reykjavík or a 40-minute ferry trip from Bakki, south of Hvolsvöllur, which is a two-hour drive from Reykjavík (see page 188). Heimaey's nearly 5000 inhabitants are a hardy and independent breed, steeled by generations of isolation, brutal living conditions and an extensive history of disasters. After the Irish slaves' abortive attempt to hide out here, the island was first occupied by a certain Herjólfur Barðursson, a reclusive farmer who had become tired of the constant strife on the mainland. Life was relatively peaceful – if not particularly easy – on the island for several centuries, until it became a target for pirate raids.

As if to repay the islanders for the depredations of their Viking ancestors, a series of cut-throats descended on the Vestmannaeyjar: British pirates ruled the islands for almost a century, and then, in 1627, Barbary corsairs (erroneously identified as 'Turks' by the beleaguered Icelanders) arrived from north Africa. Well into the 20th century, island children were terrified by the tale of the blood-thirsty heathens who put 36 men and women to the sword and carried off more than 200 as slaves. Those who tried to hide in the cliffs were shot down like birds.

Epidemics wracked Heimaey for the next couple of centuries, while the 1783 eruption of Laki on the mainland killed off the fish around the islands, reducing its inhabitants to living on sea birds and an edible root called *hvönn* (with plenty falling to their deaths from cliffs in pursuit of both).

Later, fishing accidents would take a dreadful toll: twice, when the island's population was less than 350, storms sent more than 50 men to the bottom of the sea on a single day; and in the 19th century, some 100 fishermen from Heimaey drowned. Being accustomed to life in a hostile environment may have accounted for the population's famous sangfroid in the face of the 1973 volcanic eruption, when at about 2.30am one January morning, the islanders awoke to find that their island home had transformed into an eruption zone (see page 188).

## Fishing capital

Today Heimaey is one of the most important fishing centres in the whole of Iceland, with the efforts of just 1 percent of the country's population producing some 15 percent of its exports. After Reykjavík and Grindavík, Heimaey is the home port of more fishing

*Signpost with a puffin theme.*

*Heimaey church.*

*House graveyard.*

*House graveyard – markers in Heimaey town indicate the location and the history of the buildings entombed deep beneath the lava flow of 1973.*

vessels than any other town in Iceland. A large part of the catch is processed on the island, giving locals a healthy slice of the country's prosperity.

**Heimaey town** Ⓐ is spread out around the harbour, where over 100 colourful trawlers can dock in the natural windbreak of the lava wall created by the 1973 eruption. The setting is spectacular, with rugged brown bluffs on one side and the two volcanic peaks, Eldfell and Helgafell, on the other. Keep an eye out for the colourful mural painted by school children on the side of a building near the harbour, depicting the fateful morning of the eruption.

East of the harbour, the street Kirkjuvegur runs along the edge of the **1973 lava flow**. Buried beneath this dry, dusky-red mass are 400 of Heimaey's homes and buildings – around one-third of the town was swallowed in the eruption. Steps and pathways have been built onto the convoluted lava fields, here covered with a thin film of green moss, through which the wind whistles eerily. At the edge of the lava, the rather curious **Pompei**

**of the North** project has excavated the ruins of several houses along Suðurvegur, and aims to dig out between seven and ten in total as a reminder of the destruction. You can learn all about the fatal eruption at the **Eldheimar Museum** (http://eldheimar.is; Wed–Sun mid-Oct–Apr 1–7pm, daily May–mid-Oct 10.30am–6pm), which features a house that was buried under a sea of lava, only to be carefully excavated 40 years later. The museum also has a Surtsey Visitor Centre and a special exhibition dedicated to the 1963 eruption, which brought four islands, including Surtsey, into existence.

With few cars in Heimaey, the streets are empty and peaceful – in fact, their utter desolation on Sundays gives them the haunting feel of a Bergman film. Points of interest include the picturesque white **church**, with a statue commemorating the island's fishermen lost at sea, and the **Sagnheimar Folk Museum** (www.sagnheimar.is; daily May–Sept 10am–5pm) above the library, which has a well-organised set of relics, model ships and photographs of the 1973 eruption. To see a small

display of live Icelandic fish (and sometimes puffin chicks in season), visit the **Sæheimar Aquarium** (http://sae-heimar.is; daily May–Sept 10am–5pm, Oct–Apr Sat 1–4pm and by previous arrangement). Particularly odd are the Icelandic cod, which appear to be made of white plastic, and the horrifying Icelandic catfish, a fish that boasts piranha teeth and a bad-tempered, strangely human expression.

## Exploring the island

Unless you have brought a car over by ferry from the mainland, or have the time and energy to walk, the easiest way to visit Heimaey's attractions is on one of the bus tours run by Viking Tours (tel: 488 4884; www.vikingtours.is).

A rough dirt road has been cut to **Eldfell Ⓑ**, the 221-metre (725ft)-high peak formed during the 1973 eruption. The spectacular view from the base clearly shows how one sixth of the island is now fresh lava flow. The vista stretches across brightly painted corrugated iron roofs to the harbour and, on a clear day, to the mainland. A short, marked path leads up the barren, steaming tephra slopes.

If the ground seems warm to the touch, carefully dig a few inches down – it's hot enough to bake bread, a quirk sometimes demonstrated by Heimaey's tour guides. Roads have also been cut into **Kirkjubæjarhraun Ⓒ**, the 3 sq km (7.5-acre) lava field spat up in 1973, but little else disturbs the dark lava's contorted expanse besides geothermal units, heating the town's water and houses.

On the very northwestern edge of the lava flow is Heimaey's most picturesque area, **Skansinn**, where a 15th-century fortress once defended the harbour. Next to nothing remains of the structure, but the view is pretty, looking down onto **Landlyst**, once the island's maternity hospital; and **Stafkirkjan**, a stave church presented to Heimaey in 2000 by the Norwegian government to celebrate 1,000 years of Christianity.

On the other side of town, a road leads past a surreal monument in the shape of giant football, to the lush natural amphitheatre of **Herjólfsdalur Ⓓ**. This grassy crater was once thought to be the home of the island's first settler, Herjólfur Barðursson, but archaeologists recently unearthed the

*The close-knit community on Heimaey – the only one of the Vestmannaeyjar archipelago's 16 islands (plus a further 30 tiny islets) to be permanently inhabited.*

*Boat in Heimaey.*

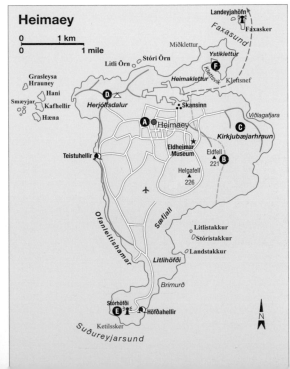

**Heimaey**

0        1 km
0            1 mile

Landeyjahöfn
Faxasker
Faxasund
Miðklettur
Litli Örn  Stóri Örn   Ystiklettur Ⓕ
Grasleysa                Heimaklettur   Klettsnef
Hrauney                       Klettsvík
Hani
Smæyjar  Kafhellir   **Herjólfsdalur** Ⓓ
Hæna                            •Skansinn
                    Ⓐ●Heimaey          Viðlagafjara
                        Eldheimar       **Kirkjubæjarhraun** Ⓒ
Teistuhellir Ⓔ          Museum    Eldfell
                               Helgafell  221 Ⓑ
                                226
                              ✈
                        Sæfjall
                                  Litlistakkur
            Ofanleitishamar          Stóristakkur
                                  Landstakkur
                        **Litlihöfði**
                            Brimurð
           Stórhöfði Ⓔ
                    Höfðahellir
           Ketilssker
      Suðureyjarsund           ↑N

**TIP**

The Landeyjarhöfn harbour, 30km southeast of Hvolsvöllur, shortens the distance between the mainland and Heimaey from 40 nautical miles to 7. From Landeyjarhöfn, there are a minimum of four ferries daily in each direction, taking around 35 minutes (for details, see page 318).

*Stafkirkjan, the stave church.*

foundations of Herjólfur's house next to the golf club. These days, Herjólfsdalur is famous as the camping ground where thousands of Icelanders gather around a giant bonfire for three days to celebrate the Þjóðhátíð festival in early August. Prodigious feats of drinking make this long weekend a must for many Icelanders, but most foreigners find it a good time to avoid the island.

## Puffin cliffs

There are splendid views of several block-shaped islands, including **Hæna**, **Kafhellir** and **Hani**, from the path across the nearby golf course. The cliffs here house the island's most accessible puffin colony. Although the islanders have traditionally hunted puffins (see page 190), their attitude towards these ungainly birds is not entirely mercenary. Late in August every year, baby puffins leave their nests as darkness falls. Instead of being guided out to sea by the moon, however, some of the fledglings become disorientated by the town's lights and accidentally waddle into the township of Heimaey. To save the pufflings from cats, dogs and cars, Heimaey's children

collect them in cardboard boxes and, come daylight, ritualistically fling the birds out to sea – and, hopefully, a successful puffin career. At least they will not end up on island dinner tables until they reach adulthood, since an unwritten law holds that the young puffins should not be eaten.

From Herjólfsdalur, precarious trails requiring mountain equipment lead along the cliffs to the northern promontory of **Ystiklettur**, above the harbour. An easier cliff-side walking path runs parallel to the road south to **Stórhöfði** Ⓔ, where a lighthouse looks out over the exposed coastline. This is officially the windiest place in Iceland: gales of 250kph (150mph) and waves of 23 metres (75ft) have been recorded here during storms.

## Boat cruises

A visit to Heimaey would not be complete without an excursion on the waves. A small boat, run by the same company as the bus tours, leaves twice daily from the harbour, bouncing its way around the whole island and finishing with a saxophone solo from the

## CRISIS ON HEIMAEY

Early on 23 January 1973, a mile-long fissure cracked open without warning on the eastern side of Heimaey, and a wall of molten lava poured out towards the town. Islanders were told to abandon their houses immediately. By great good fortune, the entire Heimaey fishing fleet was in dock that night: some 5,300 people left the island on trawlers and not one life was lost.

Over the next five months, some 33 million tons of lava spewed from the fissure, threatening to devastate the island. Hundreds of tonnes of tephra (volcanic debris) hailed down on the town, smashing windows and igniting houses. By early February the greatest danger was from the 165-metre (500ft) wall of lava moving towards the harbour – the lifeline of the local community. In an attempt to avert disaster, two commercial dredging ships equipped with water cannons pumped over 43 million litres (11.5 million gallons) of water a day to cool the lava. Heimaey was covered in a blanket of steam, and the lava flow was stopped before it blocked the harbour entrance. More pumps worked around the clock for the next three months to help cool over 5 million cubic metres (176 million cubic ft) of lava. Scientists pronounced the eruption over in July, and the residents were able to begin returning home.

captain inside the echoing Klettshellur sea cave. The trip gives views of Heimaey's steep cliffs crowded with sea birds (gannets, shearwaters, storm petrels, and five species of auk including guillemots and puffins) and usually several sure-footed sheep perched on what appear to be almost vertical green fields. If you're lucky, orcas (killer whales) can be spotted among the smaller islands, their glistening black and white flanks clearly visible as they leap from the waves. You also get good views of the other jagged outcrops in the island chain, visited on treacherous sailings by the islanders to collect birds' eggs and hunt puffins in spring and summer. Their seasonal huts can be seen on the clifftops.

**Klettsvík Bay ⑥** was briefly the home of Keikó, the world-famous killer whale, star of the film *Free Willy*. Captured off the coast of Iceland in 1979, Keikó spent three years in an Icelandic aquarium before being airlifted to Marineland in Niagara Falls, Ontario, where he was trained to perform. After spending seven years as an amusement-park attraction in Mexico, Keikó made his film appearance, which drew public attention to the poor conditions in which he was being kept. Once he had been nursed back to health, in September 1998 the 6.5-metre (21ft)-long animal, weighing about 4,500kg (10,000lb), was airlifted to a special pen in Klettsvík bay, the next stage on the road to releasing him back into the wild. Keikó did manage to swim to Norway in 2002, but sadly died the following year.

## Half man, half seal

One night in March 1984, a fishing vessel capsized 5km (3 miles) off Heimaey's coast. All of the crew quickly perished in the freezing winter seas, except for a fisherman named Guðlaugur Friðþórsson. He staved off the confusion of hypothermia by talking to hovering sea birds, and set off swimming for shore. It took him six hours – about five hours longer than anyone else has ever survived in water that temperature.

As if that weren't enough, Guðlaugur swam ashore onto some of the sharpest lava on the island, cutting his feet and losing blood as he stumbled to the town. Doctors could not

**TIP**

Since Surtsey is off-limits to all but a small number of research scientists, the only way to get close to the island is on a boat trip organised by Viking Tours (tel: 488 4884; www. vikingtours.is). Departures are on request and require a minimum number of passengers. There's a good chance you'll spot whales on the journey, too.

*The verdant landscape at Herjólfsdalur.*

find his pulse, but the fisherman survived. Later, when the London Hospital Medical College performed tests, Guðlaugur's body fat proved to closely resemble that of a seal. It's a story that islanders recount fondly, as if to steel themselves for the next skirmish with the sea, the winds or the volcanic peaks that threaten them every day.

## The birth of an island

The youngest island, **Surtsey** ⑲, burst from the North Atlantic in a dramatic eruption in 1963. Captured on film by airborne camera crews, highlights of its fiery, four-year-long birth were seen around the world, providing a fascinating glimpse of how volcanic islands are formed. It is still giving scientists unique and invaluable data on how virgin habitats are colonised by plant and animal life.

The eruption began below the waves in the Mid-Atlantic Ridge, the submarine mountain chain that runs into the south coast of Iceland. Island fishermen were the first to notice smoke rising from the sea in November 1963. Molten lava spewing onto the sea floor was cooling on contact with the icy waters, but soon a pile of volcanic debris had risen the 130 metres (430ft) to the surface to create a burning mass above sea level. A pillar of black ash, intertwined with a stream of steam, was sent 10km (6 miles) into the air – looking menacing from nearby Heimaey and visible from as far away as Reykjavík. The first flights over the site confirmed that a 16th member of the Vestmannaeyjar was forming: fluid lava was piling up over the mound of tephra and solidifying, turning it from a giant volcanic refuse heap into a permanent presence.

## A scientific laboratory

The new island was named after the fiery Norse giant Surtur, who sets the world alight at Ragnarök, the end of the world. For the next four years, until June 1967, Surtsey provided the world's scientific community with the spectacle of its ongoing formation, before finally settling down to an area of 1.57 sq km (0.5 sq miles) and 155 metres (510ft) in height. During the same period, two smaller islands emerged from the

*A puffin hunter with his catch.*

---

### HUNTING FOR PUFFINS

The Vestmannaeyjar islanders' affection for the puffin as Iceland's national emblem does not discourage them from seeing it as a source of food. Until a few years ago, puffin-catchers were a common sight on Heimaey, swinging their long nets on the cliff tops by the golf course, scooping the flittering birds from the air. Catchers were careful to avoid catching immature birds so that the colony's numbers were not endangered.

However, other forces have had a devastating effect on puffin numbers. An increase in sea temperature around the islands has driven sandeels, the puffins' main food source, further out to sea. Until recently, tens of thousands of chicks would leave their nests in August, but numbers reached an all-time low in 2010, when the island's children found just ten pufflings. A complete hunting ban was imposed on the island, and numbers recovered a little, but biologists are watching the nests with great concern, particularly as the issue is affecting other nesting seabirds too.

Puffin and guillemot, usually under the name of *svartifugl*, appear on adventurous restaurant menus. The dark, gamey meat, with a slightly fishy taste, is often served fried or boiled, often with a distinctly exotic curry sauce, or it may be smoked. Plummeting numbers of these birds raise serious ethical questions about their consumption by humans.

eruption but have since eroded away and disappeared below the waves. Indeed, other islands in the archipelago, which formed in the same way as Surtsey several thousand years ago, have been substantially eroded by the heavy seas and the wind since their creation. Surtsey too has been reduced in size by half since its formation, but will probably continue to exist for several centuries before it loses the war against wind and waves and vanishes for good.

Fascinating as Surtsey's formation had been, its greatest scientific value started after the eruption had ended. Its 1,000°C (1,830°F) surface temperatures during the eruption had left it completely free of any living organism: the island became a sort of natural laboratory approximating how Iceland itself must have been when its first segments emerged from the sea some 20 million years ago. In line with its unique scientific status, in 2008 Surtsey was added to the Unesco World Heritage List as an example of a pristine volcanic island and its newly evolving ecosystem.

Seeds arrived on the island in its first summer, carried by the wind, sea and passing sea birds. The first sprouting plants were noticed during the following year, 1965, even before the island's eruption had completely finished. By the end of 1967, no fewer than four species of plants had established themselves around the coastline.

Midges and flies were the first animals to settle the island, with seals making an appearance after the surrounding seas became restocked with fish. In 1970, black-backed gulls became the first birds to nest on Surtsey. Since that time, scientists have observed 91 bird species on the island – some are just stopping off on their migration to other shores, while 15 have built nests and raised their chicks here.

Surtsey is still a scientific station and remains off-limits to unauthorised visitors. Any uncontrolled intrusion might upset the island's natural development, either by damaging fragile plant life or accidentally bringing in new presences (a seed caught on a visitor's shoe, for example, might sprout into a plant). Fly-overs in light aircraft, taking about two hours, however, can be organised in Reykjavík.

*The striking volcanic coast at Surtsey Island.*

*Jökulsárlón glacial lagoon.*

# THE SOUTHEAST

In this region overshadowed by the vast Vatnajökull icecap and precariously situated on expanses of glacial debris, the highlight is the rugged and popular Skaftafell area of the Vatnajökull National Park.

Icelanders often say that their country was unfairly named, since it is, after all, strikingly green for much of the year. But anyone paying a visit to the southeast of the country will have ice on their minds, no matter what the season. The whole area is dominated by Europe's largest icecap, Vatnajökull, whose enormous glaciers pour through every crack in the coastal mountains. Indeed, such is the size of Vatnajökull – as large as the entire English county of North Yorkshire – that driving along its southern flank can take several hours and is one of the most memorable trips this part of the country has to offer. It may even feel strangely familiar from films and TV: the most recent series to utilise this dramatic backdrop was the HBO fantasy *Game of Thrones*.

Volcanoes regularly erupt beneath Vatnajökull, devastating farmland with sudden explosive flows of melted ice and debris (known as *jökulhlaups*) as large in volume as the Amazon River. Little wonder then if the Viking explorers – including the First Settler, Ingólfur Arnarson, who spent three years in the southeast – thought the name "Iceland" appropriate.

The damage caused by Vatnajökull's glacial flows made much of the coast next to impassable for centuries. Until the Ring Road was finally driven through in 1974, parts of the southeast

were among the remotest in Iceland. To reach Skaftafell or Höfn by land, for example, one had to drive the entire 1,100km (680 miles) around the north of the country.

Today the highway from Reykjavík to the southeast is fully paved, and the glacier-riddled Skaftafell area of the Vatnajökull National Park has become the most popular wilderness area in the country. (In fact, on June and July weekends, it becomes so crowded that it is probably best avoided by travellers seeking solitude in nature.) Meanwhile,

**Main Attractions**
Laki and Lakagígar Craters
Skaftafell
Vatnajökull icecap
Jökulsárlón glacial lagoon

*Stunning effect created by light shining on an ice block.*

*Camping in the southeast.*

the drive along the coast passes a luxuriant, haunting landscape dotted with tiny farms and historic settlements.

## Curse of the Irish monks

The gateway to the southeast is the town of **Kirkjubæjarklaustur** ❶ (call it "cloister" and you will be understood). This is a green oasis in the volcanic desert formed by the eruptions of the Lakagígar craters in 1783 – an event that devastated Iceland and is still considered to be one of the worst natural disasters in recorded history.

Kirkjubæjarklaustur was first settled by Irish monks, who fled the Vikings but left a curse that no pagan would ever live here. A Christian Norseman named Ketill the Foolish (so named by his peers for converting from the worship of Thor) lived on the site quite happily for many years. But when another Viking, Hildir Eysteinsson, decided to move in, he no sooner clapped eyes on his future farm than he dropped down dead. Perhaps, reasoned the Norsemen, Ketill had not been so foolish after all.

Religion plays a big part in the rest of Kirkjubæjarklaustur's history. In 1186,

Benedictine nuns set up a convent here (*klaustur* means cloister), which was closed in the 16th-century Reformation. It can't have been a model institution, since two of the nuns were burned at the stake: one for sleeping with the devil, the other for maligning the Pope.

Contemporaneous with the nuns' convent at Kirkjubær was the monastery at Þykkvibær, a short distance away. It is said that the abbot and the monks of Þykkvibær often went up to Kirkjubær to see the mother superior and the sisters. On one such occasion the abbot and some of the monks spent the night at Kirkjubær. The story goes that in the middle of the night the mother superior went with a light to check on the propriety of the sisters' conduct. In one cell, she came upon a monk and a nun sleeping together. The mother superior was about to reprimand the nun when the latter noticed her superior's headgear and said: "What is that you have on your head, dear mother?" Then the mother superior realised that she had taken the abbot's underpants by mistake and put them on instead of her bonnet. As a

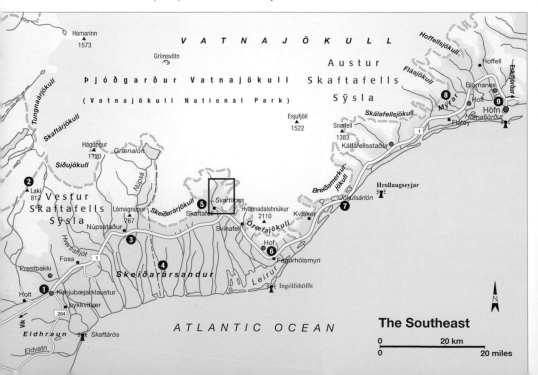

result, she softened her voice, saying as she retreated: "We are all sinners, sister".

During the 1783 Laki eruptions, a wall of lava looked like wiping out the settlement when the local curate, Jón Steingrímsson, herded everyone into the wooden church. There he delivered the ultimate fire-and-brimstone sermon whose effect, with great chunks of ash smashing down just outside the window, can only be imagined. When the sermon had finished, the congregation stumbled outside to find that the lava had been diverted and the church saved. The modern **Steingrímsson memorial chapel** has been built on the old church's site to commemorate this neat piece of divine intervention.

Today Kirkjubæjarklaustur is a pretty but somnolent outpost of 120 people, with the waterfall **Systrafoss** spraying down from steep cliffs as its backdrop. A national park visitor centre is located on the left as you drive through the village (www.visitklaustur. is; daily mid-Apr–Aug 9am–6pm). There are several exhibition rooms – in one you can see a documentary on the Laki eruptions – a bookstore and a bicycle rental. The 1783 lava fields, dotted with pseudo-craters, can still be seen just south of town, en route to the curious **Kirkjugólf** – the name means "church floor", since Viking settlers assumed it was part of a stone floor built by the curse-happy Irish monks. It is, however, a natural formation, with the tops of hexagonal basalt columns fitting together as perfectly as tiles.

Many people stay in Kirkjubæjarklaustur as a jumping-off point to the infamous 2.5km (1.5-mile) -long **Lakagígar crater row ❷**, responsible for the 1783 eruptions (commonly referred to as "Laki", after the mountain around which the fissures opened). Over a period of 10 months, 30 billion tons of lava and three times as much sulphuric acid belched forth from the so-called "Skaftá fires". Houses and farms were wiped out by the flow, but far worse was to come. The line of 130 craters sent up a cloud of noxious gas that began the

"Haze Famine", killing half of Iceland's livestock and a fifth of its population – a toll so dramatic that plans were made to evacuate the island completely. There are some fantastic views to be had from the peak of Mt Laki. The mountain and its unearthly craters, a surprisingly fragile environment in spite of their devastating history, nestle within the protective boundaries of Vatnajökull National Park.

The Ring Road east of Kirkjubæjarklaustur runs to the attractive farm of **Foss**, named for the thin waterfall flowing from the cliffs on the property, followed by the basalt columns of **Dverghamrar**. A sunken plain of moss-covered lava – once again created by the Laki eruptions – must be crossed before finding the farm of **Núpsstaður ❸**, at the base of the imposing 770-metre (2,500ft) cliff called **Lómagnúpur** ("loon peak"). Núpsstaður has one of Iceland's most charming 17th-century churches and a still-working antique harmonium.

At this point begins **Skeiðarársandur ❹**, the biggest of the southern *sandurs* – great wastelands of black sand and

**TIP**

Laki can be reached only by four-wheel-drive vehicles. Tours run there daily in summer (www.re.is), collecting passengers from the Skaftafell service centre and the N1 petrol station in Kirkjubæjarklaustur; visitors have around four hours to explore the craters. Take refreshments with you.

*Foss waterfall gives its name to Foss Farm.*

glacial debris carried out by volcanic eruptions from underneath Vatnajökull. Before the Ring Road was built, the only way across here was on horseback, accompanied by one of the farmers from Núpsstaður who had spent their lives learning to navigate the treacherous terrain. Today, cyclists dread this stretch of road most in Iceland: it is completely monotonous, and regular sandstorms make any open-air activity a misery.

One of the worst culprits is **Grímsvötn**. Located under Vatnajökull, it is the most active of Iceland's many volcanic craters, and capable of inflicting impressive damage through its *jökulhlaups* (glacial bursts). The last eruption under the ice began on 21 May 2011, with a plume of volcanic ash rising to over 20km (65,000ft) in altitude. Some European air traffic was disrupted, and the whole of Kirkjubæjarklaustur was coated in a thick grey dust, but the eruption had fizzled out by 28 May.

The area got off lightly compared to the chaos caused by the September 1996 eruption of a nearby fissure, Gjálp, which filled the Grímsvötn caldera with meltwater over the course of two months. On the morning of 5 November, the long-awaited glacial burst began. Large parts of Skeiðarársandur disappeared under black and muddy floodwater, electric cables across the sands were destroyed, as was a 12km (7-mile) stretch of the Ring Road itself. The bridges over the Sæluhúsakvísl and Gígja rivers were swept away, and the 906-metre (2,980ft)-long bridge over the River Skeiðará was badly damaged. South of the road the flood carried immense amounts of sediment to the sea and the beach stretched 800 metres (2,600ft) further out into the ocean than it had before the flood. Two days later, when the burst came to an end, a million tons of ice had broken away from the margin of Skeiðarárjökull glacier, which dominates the view on the north side of the road. Damage to the road, bridges and power lines was estimated at 25 million euros.

## Skaftafell

Approached from the west, **Skaftafell** ❺, the most popular area of Vatnajökull National Park, is announced by views over its rugged peaks and the three glaciers that have worked their way between them: from the left, **Morsárjökull**, **Skaftafellsjökull** and **Svínafellsjökull**. The twin glaciers of **Kvíárjökull** and **Fjallsjökull** can be seen further on. These are all dwarfed by **Öræfajökull**, a glacier whose peak, **Hvannadalshnúkur**, is the highest in Iceland at 2,110 metres (6,700ft). All are fingers of the icecap **Vatnajökull**, which, like other icecaps in Iceland, is believed to have been formed not during the Ice Age but in another cold period just 2,500 years ago.

Skaftafell National Park was established in 1967 and expanded in 1984 to take up some 1,600 sq km (580 sq miles). In June 2008, this protected area became part of the newly created Vatnajökull National Park – at a mighty 13,600 sq km (5,300 sq miles), covering 13 percent of Iceland's total area, Vatnajökull is now Europe's largest national park.

### VATNAJÖKULL ICECAP

Vatnajökull, 1,000 metres (3,300ft) thick in parts, is the largest icecap in the world outside of those countries which are designated as polar regions.

At first sight Vatnajökull displays a general resemblance to the main polar ice sheets, but its nature is quite different. This is a so-called temperate glacier. Its temperature is at melting point, or very close to it, at any given depth. The exception is in the top layers, where frost may remain until far into the summer, although the timing for that is subject to variations.

During the first centuries after settlement the glaciers of Vatnajökull were smaller than they are now, but towards the end of the 12th century the climate began to cool and the ice started to expand. Vatnajökull's glaciers reached their greatest extent during the 18th and 19th centuries.

Since 1890 however, they have withdrawn and thinned, especially during the period from 1920 to 1960. Between 1960 and into the 1990s, Vatnajökull thickened and the recession of its glaciers slowed, although global warming is now starting to reverse this trend at alarming speed – a recent report by Iceland's climate change committee forecasts that all of Iceland's glaciers will have vanished by 2150.

Settlers first came to Skaftafell in the Saga Age, and there are still two farms here. The park service operates an **Information Centre**  (www.vatna jokulsthjodgardur.is; Dec 11am–5pm, Jan 10am–4pm, Feb–Apr and Oct–Nov 10am–5pm, May–Sept 9am–7pm) and café next to a parking area and large camping ground. On summer weekends, this becomes a cross between a particularly raucous Reykjavík pub and a refugee camp, so anyone interested in communing with nature should come on a weekday.

All walks into the park depart from this point. The easiest is to the snout of the glacier **Skaftafellsjökull** 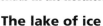, less than half an hour away. Covered in volcanic refuse, the ice is actually a shiny grey, like graphite. You can climb onto the edge of the glacier, but be careful. It's slippery – and a fall would dunk you straight into a near-freezing meltwater stream that soon disappears underground. If you want to get up onto the glaciers, it's best to book a guided walk: in summer, several companies operate staffed huts in the parking area, offering guided walks with crampons and ice axes, as well as mountain-biking and guided hikes, making it a convenient one-stop shop for activities and adventure.

The most photographed attraction in Skaftafell is **Svartifoss** 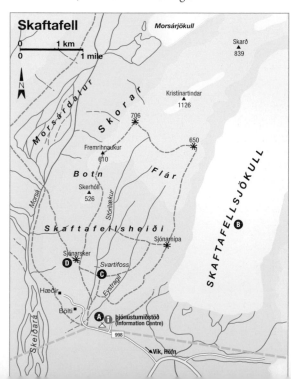, a short walk into the park. The waterfall is surrounded on both sides by black basalt columns, giving it a grand organ-pipe effect and its name ("Black Waterfall"). The path continues on to the peak of **Sjónarsker** and then further into the mountains: the more energetic can make a day-trip to include views of Morsárjökull and Skaftafellsjökull, which look like twin seas of ice.

In the **Morsárdalur** valley, surrounded by high mountains and huge icecaps, you will also find one of the most impressive woods of the country, with birches reaching a height of 10 metres (33ft). It's in this area, too, that you'll find one of Iceland's many natural hot pools: across the Morsá River and a

short hike up the hillside behind, a trail leads to a sublime geothermal source which has been dammed to create a small round pond where weary hikers can cast off their clothes and steam to their heart's content while enjoying an unsurpassed view of the unsullied expanses of the national park – a quintessentially Icelandic experience.

The Information Centre can give instructions for other day trips into the park. Nature lovers can spot over 200 species of plants around Skaftafell as well as Iceland's usual plethora of birds. The surrounding Skeiðarársandur wasteland is also one of the most important breeding areas for great skuas in the northern hemisphere.

## The lake of ice

East of Skaftafell along the Ring Road is the farm **Svínafell**, which was the home of Flosi Þórðarson, the murderer of Njáll and his family in *Njáls Saga*, followed by **Hof**, which offers picturesque farmhouse accommodation and has a small turf church. It is near here that the First Settler, Ingólfur Arnarson, lived before moving to

*Exploring glaciers calls for special equipment.*

Reykjavík – the promontory of **Ingólf-shöfði** marks the site. It was here that Ingólfur spent his first winter in Iceland before setting off in search of his high seat pillars, which he had tossed in the water as he approached the Icelandic coast. (The posts, an important symbol of power, were later discovered where Reykjavík is located today.) The headland is now a **nature reserve**, perfect for birdwatchers, and is accessed by the most unusual method – by guided haycart tour across the black-sand estuary. Bird-watching is at its best during the breeding season in May and June, although trips depart from the farm **Hofsnes** until August.

Immediately after a suspension bridge over the Jökulsá River is one of Iceland's most photographed sights: the iceberg-filled lake of **Jökulsárlón** ❼. The ice has calved from the glacier Breiðamerkurjökull, which runs into the lake, burying its snout underwater. The lake was formed only when the passage to the sea was blocked by land movements in the 20th century, but climate change has seen the glacier melt so quickly that Jökulsárlón,

with a depth of 250 metres (820ft), is now the deepest lake in Iceland. There are around 40 boat trips per day on Jökulsárlón in July and August (fewer at other times). It's exciting to be afloat among the glistening ice formations, but you can see the icebergs just as well from the shoreline. If you can reach a small piece of the 1000-year-old ice easily, pick it up for a closer look – it's astonishingly dense and clear.

James Bond fans may get a sense of déjà vu at Jökulsárlón – the opening scenes of the film *A View to a Kill* were shot here, as well as part of *Die Another Day*.

## Excursions on the icecap

East of Jökulsárlón, a turn-off to the left advertises trips to **Jöklasel** at the top of Vatnajökull. Road F985 itself is passable only by four-wheel-drive vehicles, but those without such transport can meet the Glacier Jeeps (www.glacierjeeps. is) tour bus from Höfn at the car park here, at 9.30am and 2pm from May to early September for the ride up. A small chalet has been built at the edge of the icecap, and hire of snowmobiles

*The expansive Skaftafellsjökull glacier.*

can be arranged. It's not entirely environmentally sound – bringing much noise and the first touches of air pollution on the pristine icecap. On a clear day, you can see for miles across the white sea of Vatnajökull.

The river valleys along this part of the Ring Road are beautiful but thinly populated, and the flatlands of **Mýrar** ❽ are excellent for bird-watching. On one farm here, **Bjarnanes**, a troll woman named Ketillaug is said to have been seen taking a kettle of gold up into the multicoloured alluvial mountain **Ketillaugarfjall**. There is one day of the year when humans can try and take the kettle from her, but those that attempt it are subject to hallucinations – typically of the farm below catching fire – and always run back to give the alarm.

## Höfn

The southeast's administrative centre, with a population of about 1,700, is **Höfn** ❾. The name means "harbour" and indeed it has one of the few in the southeast. The town's fortunes improved rapidly with the completion of the Ring Road in the 1970s, turning it from a one-horse town to its present, ungainly concrete self. But what it lacks in aesthetic appeal is made up for by its beautiful setting on **Hornafjörður** fjord, which is almost completely cut off from the sea by spits to form a tranquil lake. The spits can be explored by organised boat and quad-bike tours from town.

In 2013, Höfn gained a shiny new **National Park Visitor Centre** (www.vatnajokulsthjodgardur.is; daily June–Aug 8am–8pm, May and Sept 9am–5pm, rest of the year 9am–1pm), set in an elegantly restored 150-year-old wooden building by the harbour. The display space was still under construction at the time of writing, but will include exhibits from the former folk museum and glacier exhibition.

Höfn is an important fishing centre where high-value species such as Norway and Icelandic lobsters are caught. A lobster festival is held in town every year at the end of June.

From Höfn it's also possible to arrange a "glacier tour" of Vatnajökull which includes snowmobiling or snowcatting and a visit to the glacial lagoon in a single, easy trip.

*Tourists can journey around Iceland's glaciers with the help of a guide.*

# NATURAL WONDERS

**From volcanoes to glaciers, Iceland is home to a concentration of nature's wonders, both hot and cold, greater than in any other place on earth.**

In 1963, the island of Surtsey exploded out of the sea off Iceland in a great arch of flame and lava. It was only the latest natural wonder in Iceland's long, turbulent life. The Mid-Atlantic Ridge, which runs through the middle of the country from southwest to northeast, is the cause of the geothermal activity that has shaped much of Iceland's geology and unique landscape. Equally responsible are the thousands of years of glaciation, and the glacial meltwater, which together have modified the land.

The area close to the Mid-Atlantic Ridge has the greatest number of volcanoes: all around, smoke and steam rise constantly. Here can be found spouting geysers, hot springs and craters – both active, like those near Mývatn, and inactive, solidified into fantastic lava shapes or filled with calm lakes. In some areas the ground is still very warm, and Icelanders may even use a small covered pit as an oven to bake a delicious speciality – lava bread.

At the other end of the scale are glaciers, many of which pour like frozen torrents from the icecap Vatnajökull. One of these glaciers, Breiðamerkurjökull, creates a particularly photogenic scene: when it calves (when a mass of ice breaks off), it fills the nearby Jökulsárlón lake with icebergs. The glaciers are bleak and dramatic moonscapes of peaks, crevasses and a surprising range of colours from dirty black to pure icy blue. Meltwater feeds many of the powerful waterfalls that are also a feature of this dramatic land.

*Grjótagjá underground hot spring, Lake Mývatn.*

*Dimmuborgir volcanic pillars, Lake Mývatn.*

*Visitors are fascinated by the burst of water and steam that spouts to a height of around 20 metres (66ft) from the Strokkur geyser, roughly every 5 to 10 minutes.*

*The aurora borealis over Jökulsárlón.*

## THE NORTHERN LIGHTS

The bewitching aurora borealis, commonly known as the northern lights, flashes, flickers and pulses across the winter sky like silent fireworks. This eerie green lightshow, sometimes tinged with purples, pinks and reds, has been the source of many a high-latitude superstition: the Vikings, for example, believed it was the Valkyries riding across the sky. The scientific explanation is no less astonishing. The lights are actually caused by streams of charged particles – "solar wind" – that flare into space from our sun. When the wind comes into contact with the Earth's magnetic field, it is drawn towards the Poles, where its electrical charge agitates particles of oxygen and nitrogen in the atmosphere, making them glow.

Solar activity follows an 11-year cycle, which reached its peak or "solar max" between 2012 and 2013. In Iceland, the lights can be seen between September/October and March/April, with midnight being the most likely time to see them...but as with all natural phenomena, there's no timetable and sightings are not guaranteed. Choose a cold, clear, moonless night, and a place with minimal light pollution; then look heavenwards and hope.

*Jökulsárlón glacial lagoon.*

*Leirhnjúkur crater, Lake Mývatn.*

*Dynjandi waterfall,
West Fjords.*

# SNÆFELLSNES AND THE WEST

This large area between Reykjavík and the West Fjords is easy to explore and has a variety of places to visit, from sites associated with the sagas to remote fishing villages.

celanders, in their more lyrical moments, are apt to dub their homeland the Saga Isle. This description is particularly appropriate for the Snæfellsnes peninsula and the west, where some of the most dramatic events of the sagas took place, including the terrifying hauntings of *Eyrbyggja Saga* and the tragic romance of *Laxdæla Saga*. The region is packed with historic and literary associations, but the jewel in its crown is the work of nature alone. The Snæfellsjökull icecap, at the western end of the Snæfellsnes peninsula, can be seen glinting in the sunlight from as far away as Reykjavík, 100km (60 miles) to the south across Faxaflói bay.

## North from Reykjavík

The glacier-bound traveller setting out from the capital can choose from two routes for the first leg of the journey to the north: either to follow the scenic coast road as it stretches 20km (12 miles) east and then the same distance west again along the sides of Hvalfjörður fjord; or to take the shortcut through the 6km (3.5-mile) toll tunnel under Hvalfjörður.

Taking Route 1, the Ring Road north out of Reykjavík, a detour east on Route 36 leads to two famous farms: **Laxnes** where the writer Halldór Laxness was born; and **Mosfell**,

where saga figure Egill Skallagrímsson died – supposedly after ordering his slaves to bury his treasure, and then slaughtering them to ensure secrecy. Close to Laxnes, the author's later home **Gljúfrasteinn** (tel: 586 8066; www.gljufrasteinn.is; June–Aug daily 9am–5pm, Sept–May Tue–Sun 10am–4pm) is just as he left it: book ahead for a fascinating tour.

The Ring Road leads along the roots of **Esja**, 918 metres (3,011ft) high, before turning into **Hvalfjörður**. In the mountains at the head of the

**Main Attractions**
Settlement Centre of Iceland
Reykholt
Snæfellsjökull
Stykkishólmur
Flatey

*Sightseeing at Breiðafjörður bay.*

fjord, about an hour's walk above the road, is **Glymur** , which used to be Iceland's highest waterfall at 198 metres (650ft). (Its number one spot was taken in 2011 by a previously unknown waterfall, near Morsárjökull glacier in southeast Iceland, which is 228 metres/748ft high.) The modern church at **Saurbær** ❷ on the northern coast of Hvalfjörður is dedicated to the memory of Iceland's greatest devotional poet, Reverend Hallgrímur Pétursson, who served this parish in the 1600s.

On the peninsula at the northern side of the fjord lies the town of **Akranes** ❸ (population 6,600),

offering hotels, guesthouse accommodation and restaurants. About one kilometre to the east in Garðar is the **Akranes Museum Centre** (www. museum.is; daily mid-May–mid-Sept 10am–5pm, rest of the year by previous arrangement), whose emphasis is on maritime history and a good collection of boats, but also has a mineral collection, farm equipment and sporting paraphernalia. The town's Irish Days festival, held on the first weekend in July, celebrates the arrival of the first settlers in AD 880 – two Irish brothers (of Norwegian descent) named Þormóður and Ketill Bresason.

*Bringing Iceland's early history to life at the Settlement Centre of Iceland, in Borgarnes.*

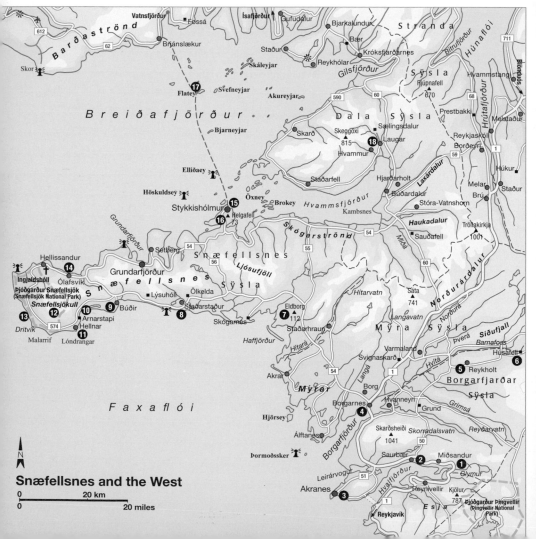

## Snæfellsnes and the West

| 0 | | 20 km |
|---|---|---|
| 0 | | 20 miles |

Continuing north, the town of **Borgarnes** ❹, near the mouth of **Borgarfjörður**, has grown up close to the very spot, **Borg**, where Egill Skallagrímsson lived in the 10th century. The son of one of the first Norse settlers, Egill was a paradoxical figure: a fierce and often cruel Viking warrior, he was also a great poet in the *skaldic* tradition of intricate word-play and metaphor. A striking multimedia exhibition at Borgarnes, the **Settlement Centre of Iceland** (www.landnam.is; daily 10am–9pm) uses the sagas to explore the country's early history. Half of the centre is dedicated to Egill, and uses rough-hewn sculptures and dramatic sound and lighting to depict key moments in his violent life.

These vignettes are taken, of course, from one of the country's best-loved sagas, *Egils Saga*, which preserves the warrior's poetry for posterity, and was probably written by one of his descendants, Snorri Sturluson (see page 43). In 1241, Snorri was ambushed and murdered by his enemies on the orders of the King of Norway at his home at **Reykholt** ❺ – today a tiny hamlet some 36km (22 miles) east of Borgarnes on Route 30.

Snorri's farmstead is long gone, but a hot pool remains where the scholar and chieftain once bathed (see page 88). A tunnel (now partly restored) led from the pool to the farmhouse. A modern statue commemorates Snorri's masterly *Heimskringla (History of the Norwegian Kings)*, which saved centuries of Norwegian history from oblivion, and a research centre in the village gives a detailed insight into Snorri's life and turbulent times.

## Lava caves and waterfalls

The green, rolling country of Borgarfjörður is at its most beautiful up beyond Reykholt. **Hraunfossar** is a multitude of tiny cascades tumbling into the Hvítá river along a 1km (0.5-mile) stretch. A footbridge crosses the river at the churning **Barnafoss** waterfall, where the Hvítá flows through a rugged chasm. At nearby **Húsafell** ❻, summerhouses cluster

*Early exploration of the Surtshellir lava cave, c.1860.*

in one of Iceland's largest woods. Húsafell farm is first mentioned in *Laxdæla Saga*. Its most famous occupant was Snorri Björnsson, who lived here at the end of the 18th century. Besides being a well-known sorcerer, he was said to have tried his strength on the 180kg (400lb) boulder **Kvía-hella**, which still can be seen close to the pens that he built.

The area is full of geothermal water. In Húsafell alone you will find two swimming pools, three hot pools, a water slide and a steam bath. Also look out for the sculptures of local artist Páll Guðmundsson, whose work reveals enigmatic faces from inside the boulders that he collects from nearby river gorges. As of 2015, Húsafell has become a starting point (buses leave at 10am, noon and 2.30pm May–mid-Oct) for an amazing trip into the heart of Iceland's second largest glacier, Langjökull. Into the Glacier operates tours to this unique, man-made labyrinth of 500m-long, artificially lit corridors and caves dug into the glacier's cap. Visitors can admire the extraordinary

*The view over Snæfellsjökull.*

shades of blue which change as the tunnels descend through the layers of time, an ice chapel, and even a magnificent glacial crevasse. The trips vary in length from 2 to 11 hours and can also be organised from Reykjavik. See https://intotheglacier.is for details.

Hidden beneath **Hallmunda-rhraun** lava field lies Iceland's longest lava cave, **Surtshellir**, 1.5km (1 mile) in length. Signposted from the road, the cave is found by following a marked trail. Good shoes and torches are essential for exploring. Surtshellir was already known in the Saga Age, when a band of outlaws lived in the cave. It took some time for the farmers to overcome them, and place names refer to this time in history – for example Vopnalág ("weapons hollow") and Eiríksgnípa ("Erik's pike"). Ancient traces of human habitation can still be seen today. Close to Surtshellir is another cave, **Stefán-shellir**, which also makes an interesting tour. A third cave in the area, **Víðgelmir**, is the largest known in Iceland, and is filled year-round with sparkling ice formations. Fljótstunga

farm (www.thecave.is) arranges guided tours, complete with hard hats and torches.

## West to the peninsula

To the west along paved Route 54 from Borgarnes lies the Snæfellsnes peninsula and its mysterious glacier. The first landmark is **Eldborg** ➐, a perfectly symmetrical scoria crater 60 metres (200ft) high, formed in a volcanic eruption 5–8,000 years ago. The crater, which commands magnificent views, is about 40 minutes' walk from the farm Snorrastaðir.

The **Kerlingarskarð** pass along Route 55, which reaches 311 metres (1,020ft) above sea level, was once a hazardous trail that claimed many lives in bad weather. Tales of ghostly apparitions have long been attributed to it, and even today stories are told of travellers who sense the presence of an "extra passenger" in the car as they cross the pass.

A peculiarity of the Snæfellsnes peninsula is its mineral springs, producing naturally fizzy water – a rarity elsewhere in the country. Probably the most famous is on **Ölkelda** farm (literally "ale spring", the Icelandic name for a mineral spring) near **Staðarstaður** ➑ on the south side of the peninsula. Staðarstaður is believed to have been the residence of Ari the Learned (1068–1148), author of the *Book of Icelanders*, one of the most important sources on the nation's early history.

At the horse farm **Lýsuhóll**, mineral water is found in a geothermal area: it produces hot, bubbly water, which is used to heat a swimming pool. **Búðir** ➒, once an important fishing centre, is now better known for its isolated, romantic hotel of the same name. **Arnarstapi** ➓ and **Hellnar** ⑪, small fishing villages beneath the Snæfellsjökull glacier, are famed for their strange rock formations and their birdlife. Close to Hellnar is a sea cave, **Baðstofa** ("farmhouse loft"), where bizarre effects of light and colour are seen. Opposite the cave, on the beach, a small coffee-shop is run in the summer by the locals. Hellnar is the birthplace of Guðríður Þorbjarnardóttir, one of

**TIP**

You can travel to the top of Snæfellsjökull by snowcat or snow mobile, starting from Arnarstapi tourist centre.

*Snæfellsjökull looms large over the western end of the peninsula.*

the heroines of the Norse discovery of Greenland around AD 1000. She emigrated to Greenland as a young girl, then later settled with her husband, Karlsefni, in Vínland, the Norse colony in North America, where she gave birth to her son Snorri, the first white child to be born in North America. Natural wonders at Arnarstapi include **Sönghellir** ("song cave"), with remarkable acoustics, and a huge stone arch. Sea birds nest on the cliffs in their thousands.

The focus of the peninsula, the **Snæfellsjökull glacier** ⓬, sits inside the crater of a brooding and little-studied volcano – at 1,446 metres (4,743ft), the glacier dominates the surrounding countryside. It can be approached from Arnarstapi to the south or Ólafsvík to the north, although the former is easiest. The summit is four to five hours' walk; or you could drive part way along the F570 (if you have your own car: hire cars are not usually insured for F-roads) and then walk; or join a snowmobile tour run by the Arnarstapi-based company Snjófell

*The Volcano Museum in Stykkishólmur.*

(www.snjofell.is). The rutted stretch of road from Ólafsvík really requires a 4WD vehicle. The walk up to the glacier itself is fairly easy, but in summer a guided walk is recommended for the glacier itself, as crevasses start to open up in the ice; global warming means that increasingly glacier walks only run until around July, depending on the weather. The highest of the three mountain peaks is difficult to scale without special climbing gear. A ski lift goes partway up the mountain in winter.

## Test your strength

Further down the coast from Hellnar, by **Malarrif**, stand two lofty pillars of rock, **Lóndrangar**. The taller, 75 metres (248ft) high, is called "Christian pillar", and the lower is "heathen pillar". While fishing remains the livelihood of the peninsula, some communities have now disappeared, leaving only traces of the centuries of fishing seasons: 60 boats used to row out from **Dritvík** ⓭, for example, where today there is nothing left but spectacular wilderness – including

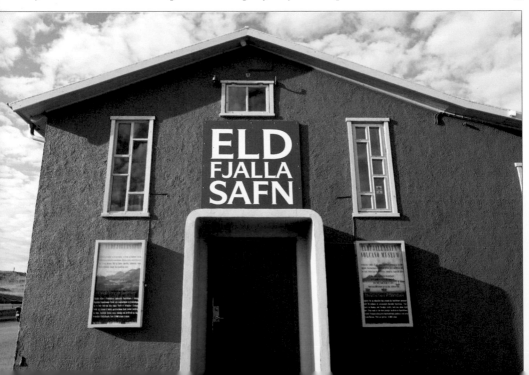

the great rock formation called **Tröllakirkja** ("church of the trolls").

Those who wish to try out their muscle power in true Icelandic tradition should stroll along the shore from Dritvík to Djúpalón, where four boulders present an age-old test of strength. The aim is to lift them up onto a ledge of rock at about hip height. The largest, *Fullsterkur* ("full strength") is 155kg (341lbs), the second, *Hálfsterkur* ("half strength"), 140kg (308lbs), the third, *Hálfdraettingur* ("half as poor"), 49kg (108lbs) and the last, *Amlóði* ("weakling") 23kg (50lbs). Lifting at least *Hálfsterkur* was a requirement for joining the crew of a boat from Dritvík.

## Ólafsvík and Stykkishólmur

Now a deserted farm and church just inland from Rif, **Ingjaldshóll** was once a major manor and regional centre. Just to the east, **Ólafsvík** ⓮ is one of the larger communities on the peninsula, with a population of 1,100. Ólafsvík still earns its living as a fishing town – making it one of the more recession-proof places in

Iceland – and its maritime history is explored at the **marine museum** (Sjávarsafn; June–Aug daily 11am–5pm), with live fish and a collection of old boats. **Stykkishólmur** ⓯ the biggest town on Snæfellsnes peninsula; is also the starting point for those who are going to the West Fjords by ferry. Nearby is **Helgafell** ⓰ ("holy mountain"), a 73-metre (240ft) hill. According to local folklore, those who climb Helgafell for the first time will have three wishes come true, provided a few conditions are observed: you must not look back or speak on the way; you must make your wishes facing east; you must not tell anyone what they are; and only benevolent wishes are allowed. Even if your wishes are not fulfilled, Helgafell is worth climbing for the spectacular views of **Breiðafjörður** bay.

Helgafell has, in fact, always been considered supernaturally charged. The first settler here, Þórólfur Mostraskegg, built a wooden temple to Thor at its summit. His son, the curiously named Þorstein Cod-Biter,

**TIP**

Breiðafjörður bay, off the north coast of the Snæfellsnes peninsula, is one of the best places in Iceland for seeing rare white-tailed sea eagles and other birdlife. Boat trips run from Stykkishólmur from mid-May to mid-September. Book through Seatours, tel: 433 2254, www.seatours.is.

*The start of the descent at Snæfellsjökull in Jules Verne's Journey to the Centre of the Earth.*

## JOURNEY TO THE CENTRE OF THE EARTH

During the late 19th century, the book *Journey to the Centre of the Earth* by French writer and pioneer of science fiction, Jules Verne, became essential reading. Published in 1864, it tells the story of the German geologist, Professor Lidenbrock of Hamburg, and his nephew Axel (called Harry in some English translations), who discover a coded message about a path into the centre of the earth which descends from Snæfellsjökull in Iceland. With their Danish-speaking guide (Iceland was part of Denmark at this time), the three intrepid explorers descend into the bowels of the earth and embark on a remarkable adventure. Their subterranean world is filled by an immense ocean and after encounters with unsavoury monsters, a prehistoric human and a powerful maelstrom, the book's heroes are finally swept upwards to the earth's surface, emerging on the volcanic island of Stromboli off southern Italy.

Snæfellsjökull is an active volcano, with its last eruption (a major one) taking place around 1,800 years ago. The mountain's explosive past has riddled its surface with lava formations, craters and a large number of caves – the likely inspiration for it as Verne's choice as the portal into the earth's interior. The distinctive shape, and impressive bulk, of the mountain has also imbued it with a natural mystique bound to stimulate a novelist's imagination.

claimed that on Helgafell he was able to see Valhalla, where dead Norse warriors drank with the gods.

In the 10th century, Helgafell became a Christian holy mountain with its own church built by Snorri the Priest. According to the *Eyrbyggja Saga*, a long blood-feud was sparked off when a certain family group, unmindful of Helgafell's religious significance, used it as a toilet. Helgafell is supposedly also where Guðrún Ósvífursdóttir, heroine of *Laxdæla Saga*, lived out her last years as a hermit.

Stykkishólmur offers three hotels and some excellent guesthouses. Bird-watching or sea-angling trips out onto the fjord from Stykkishólmur harbour are a highlight of a visit here. The local **Regional Museum** (www.stykkisholmur. is; June–Aug daily 11am–6pm, winter Tue–Thu 2–5pm) is housed in the beautiful timber **Norwegian House**, imported in kit form from Norway in 1828. The 19th-century interior must look very much as it did when William Morris was a guest here.

Stykkishólmur's modern church overlooks the town. Also worth investigating is the **Library of Water** (www.libraryofwater.is; June–Aug daily 1–5pm, Sept–Mar Tue–Sat 1–5pm): once the town library, the building now contains an installation by the American artist Roni Horn, combining "water, words and weather reports". Newer still is the **Volcano Museum** (Eldfjallasafn; www.eldfjallasafn.is; May–Sept daily 11am–5pm; winter Tue–Sat 11am–5pm), set up by a local volcanologist to give visitors an insight into Iceland's explosive character.

## Subarctic archipelagos

The car/passenger ferry *Baldur* plies Breiðafjörður between Stykkishólmur and Brjánslækur in the West Fjords, calling at the island of **Flatey** (see page 318 for details). Breiðafjörður is dotted with about 2,700 islands, which once supported a large population thanks to the abundant fisheries. Flatey was the site of a 12th-century monastery and a major cultural centre until the 1800s. One of the greatest treasures of Icelandic literature, *Flateyjarbók* (the Flatey Book), was preserved here for

*A hot spring feeds this picturesque outdoor pool.*

centuries before being presented to the Danish king in the 16th century. In 1971 it returned to Iceland.

The islanders gradually deserted their remote homes during the early part of the 20th century, and few remain. Flatey, though, is a delight, a perfectly preserved example of what an Icelandic village used to be. While the island is all but uninhabited in winter, many families spend their summers there renovating the lovely old timber houses of their ancestors. A triumph of painstaking restoration is Iceland's oldest, and smallest, library (4.75 metres by 3.43 metres, or 15ft 6in by 11ft 3in), built in 1864 to house the collection of the Flatey Progress Society.

## Viking romance

North of the Snæfellsnes peninsula is **Hvammsfjörður** fjord, with the village of **Búðardalur** at its head. Route 59 runs along **Laxárdalur** (Salmon River Valley). This is saga country, and almost every place name strikes a chord for Icelanders. In the **Haukadalur** valley (Route 586) is the site of the farm **Eiríksstaðir**, the home

of Erik the Red, discoverer of Greenland. A replica **longhouse** (June–Aug daily 9am–6pm) at the site – a turf lodge built using traditional tools and materials, with central fireplace and a seating ledge set into the 1.5-metre (5ft)-thick walls – gives visitors a sense of how this adventurous Viking family lived. Erik's son Leifur, who later travelled to America sometime around AD 1000, is thought to have been born here. Just east of Stykkishólmur, the uninhabited island of **Oxney** also once played home to Erik and Leifur.

The farm **Hjarðarholt**, just outside Búðardalur, is the birthplace of Kjartan Ólafsson, whose ill-starred love for Guðrún Ósvífursdóttir from **Sælingsdalur**, 30km (18 miles) to the north, is the central theme of *Laxdæla Saga*. Geothermal springs made Sælingsdalur an important centre in Guðrún's day: a hot bathing pool can still be seen at the farm of **Laugar** ⓲. A modern swimming pool now uses the natural hot water, while a summer Edda hotel and a small **Folk Museum** (summer daily 10am–4pm) operate in the school.

*Most houses on the island of Flatey are only occupied during the summer months.*

# THE WEST FJORDS

This remote, inaccessible region has whole areas that are deserted, creating natural reserves of a beauty and fertility unknown elsewhere in Iceland.

Shaped like an outstretched paw, the westernmost point of Iceland is characterised by tiny communities, threaded together by dirt roads lost among the brooding mountains. Many people scurry around the Ring Road, omitting this region altogether – the West Fjords receive only a third of the visitors who make it into the inhospitable highland deserts. Yet this is one of the most scenic parts of Iceland: dizzying views greet you around every hairpin turn. And the region's friendly capital Ísafjörður has its own odd folklore and festivals, including the musical bonanza Aldrei fór ég suður ("I never went south").

The West Fjords have a raw and jagged beauty that moves the soul; but there's no denying that historically this has been one of the harshest of Iceland's harsh environments. With no fertile lowlands, the inhabitants have had to look to the sea for their livelihood ever since the days of Settlement. Land travel has always been difficult and dangerous: waves batter every shoreline, and the steep mountain slopes constantly threaten the villages and hamlets at their feet with snow avalanches or mud slides.

The mechanisation of the fishing industry in the 20th century made things somewhat more comfortable, but young people in particular were attracted by the city lights of Reykjavík, leaving behind an ageing population and many small, abandoned farms. Between 1920 and 2013, the population of the region has almost halved – from 13,397 people to just 7,129 – and the decline is continuing.

Travellers in the West Fjords face a string of serious obstacles, including some of the worst roads in the country. Yet the region offers Iceland's most dramatic fjords and some of its best hiking, in the uninhabited Hornstrandir peninsula, home only to curious Arctic

*Flowers in the West Fjords.*

foxes, while soaring cliffs host literally millions of breeding sea birds. Under the rough and rocky mountains, an independent, and in many ways strange, local culture has developed, rich with tales of monsters, ghosts and evil spirits. And, once the proverbial ice is broken, its self-reliant people prove to be among the most hospitable in the land. (See page 226.)

## A base for exploring

Most visitors make **Ísafjörður ❶**, the focal point of the region, their base. With a population of 3,000, it is the only town of any size, with a choice of accommodation and some good restaurants. The site of a 9th-century farmstead, **Eyri**, is the oldest part of town, with one of Iceland's best natural harbours. On a fine summer evening, a stroll through the Old Town is an unforgettable walk through the past. The oldest buildings at the end of the sandspit are four restored timber buildings dating from the 18th century. More by accident than design, these ancient (by Icelandic standards) houses were left standing as fish factories and warehouses sprang up around them.

Oldest of the four is **Tjöruhús**, built in 1733–42, followed by the adjoining **Krambúð**, dating from 1761 and originally a shop. The meticulously restored

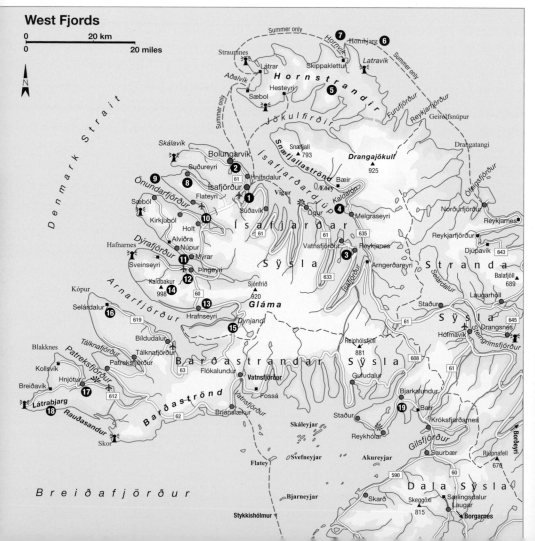

**West Fjords**

Turnhús (Tower House) was built in 1744. It once housed a salt-fish plant and now contains the **West Fjords Heritage Museum** (also known as the Maritime Museum; www.nedsti.is; mid-May–mid-Sept daily 9am–6pm). Exhibits trace the development of the town and its fishing industry, with all sorts of unusual nautical paraphernalia and a rather fine accordion collection. Ísafjörður is a calling port for many cruise ships, and passengers are often greeted at the museum by traditional dancing displays.

In March, the **Aldrei fór ég suður** music festival coincides with the town's Easter **Skiing Week**: the Seljalandsdalur valley above town has cross-country trails, while Tungudalur is for downhill skiers. Ísafjörður hosts the **European swamp soccer championships** in early August. In summer, kayaking sessions and **boat trips** depart from the town's busy harbour.

## Around Ísafjörður

The broad fjord of Ísafjarðardjúp, on which Ísafjörður sits, almost severs the West Fjords in two. Near its mouth to the northwest of Ísafjörður is **Bolungarvík ②**, the second largest town in the region. Between here and **Hnífsdalur** is the steep mountainside Óshlíð, where avalanches and landslides have often occurred – these affected the old road so badly that in 2010 a 5.4km (3.3-mile) tunnel was bored straight through the mountainside. In Bolungarvík is Ósvör, an old fishing hut from rowboat times, which has been restored and turned into an interesting **Maritime Museum** (http://www.osvor.is; June–Aug daily 10am–5pm; winter by appointment). There is also a **Natural History Museum** (www.nabo.is; June–Aug daily 10am–5pm; winter weekdays 9am–4pm and by appointment). A jeep track continues to **Skálavík** where those seeking solitude will find plenty at a remote, uninhabited bay facing the Greenland Sea.

Route 61, which hugs the southern shore of Ísafjarðardjúp, southeast from

Ísafjörður, was completed in 1975. Súðavík is the only village in these parts, developing from a Norwegian whaling-station c.1900. Of the 70 houses in Súðavík, 23 were completely destroyed by the 1995 avalanche; the village was afterwards rebuilt in a safer area. Its community-run **Arctic Fox Center** (www.melrakki.is; May and Sept daily 10am–6pm, June–Aug until 8pm, Oct–Apr weekdays 10am–2pm) contains a permanent exhibition on one of Iceland's few mammals, the elusive Arctic fox. Once hunted for its fur, the creature is still culled around the country to protect livestock, but is a protected species in the West Fjords region.

Further along, close to the tip of the Ögurnes peninsula is **Ögur**, an impressive farmstead. Built in the 19th century, it was at the time one of the largest in Iceland; today it houses the Ögur Travel company (tel: 857 1840; www.ogurtravel.com), who can arrange hiking and kayaking trips for those wishing to get out into the wilds. Another ancient farm site is at **Vatnsfjörður**, in its heyday a wealthy estate that produced several pastors of note.

*Fish drying.*

*West Fjords Heritage Museum.*

*Cheery bollard.*

The former school of **Reykjanes** ❸, at the head of Ísafjarðardjúp, is one of several places in the West Fjords with geothermal water. The complex contains basic accommodation and a huge 50-metre (165ft) swimming pool.

The road continues as Route 635 along Ísafjarðardjúp's northern shore to **Kaldalón** ❹, a sheltered beauty spot. A small glacier here tumbles down from Drangajökull, the only large ice-field in the north of Iceland. At the head of the valley there are some grassy islets, then moraine brought by the descending glacier tongue.

Beyond Kaldalón, the road comes to an abrupt halt at Unaðsdalur valley, where the uninviting Snæfjallaströnd ("snow mountain coast") begins. The snow line is lower here than anywhere else in the country – even in mid-summer, some snow lies at sea level.

## Islands and wilderness

Two of Ísafjarðardjúp's islands are inhabited (although barely: each has just one tenanted farm!): **Vigur** and **Æðey** ("eider island"). There are regular boat tours from Ísafjörður in the summer. A

walk around Vigur gives the visitor an opportunity to enjoy the rich birdlife in its natural environment. Thousands of eider ducks, Arctic terns, puffins and other sea birds can be found on the island. There is also a small and homely coffee-shop in the mid-19th-century farmer's house, as well as a mini post office, where guests can mail their cards and letters. Æðey is the biggest island in Ísafjarðardjúp and, as its name suggests, also has an impressive bird population.

Ísafjörður is also the jumping-off point for trips to the uninhabited nature reserve of **Hornstrandir** ❺ to the north. The Reserve includes the whole area north of Skorarheiði from the end of Hrafnfjörður to the end of Furufjörður. Abandoned by its farming community during the first decades of the 20th century and free from the destructive grazing of sheep, plants and wildlife alike thrive on a scale unknown elsewhere in the country. Here you can wade knee-deep in meadows of wild flowers, fertilised by the guano of countless breeding sea birds, and listen at sundown for the haunting bark of the arctic fox, unpersecuted and tamer here than anywhere else in Iceland. The Nature Reserve is off limits to all motor traffic, making the only way to explore it by boat or on foot. There is no accommodation – just 16 camping places where you can put up your tent – and little evidence of the once-flourishing farming community. Traces of bridle paths crisscross the mountain passes, linking the fjords and inlets.

In summer, a ferry sails daily from Ísafjörður to a number of destinations in Hornstrandir, bringing day-trippers, hikers and descendants of the original landowners who now use the remaining old farmsteads as summer cottages. As long as there are enough people to make the trip worthwhile, another ferry also sails south from Hornvík along the Strandir coast to Norðurfjörður (see page 227), making it possible to travel south from Hornstrandir without first backtracking to Ísafjörður in order to continue your journey. Ferry

## THE EMPTYING LAND

Rural depopulation is known throughout Iceland. However, in the West Fjords it has been a particularly serious problem for decades, threatening the continued existence of many remote communities and totally claiming the lives of others. Human settlement of the Hornstrandir peninsula of the West Fjords, for instance, was always marginal at best: winters came earlier, snow lasted longer and temperatures were always lower than elsewhere in the region. Surprisingly life here, although tough, was prosperous, at least for a while. At Hesteyri in Hornstrandir, abandoned houses and a church suggest a once flourishing settlement. A trading place since 1881, Hesteyri was the base for a Norwegian whaling station until 1912, ruins of which are still clear to see. In the 1920s a herring processing factory was built in the village, where about 80 people lived. This closed in 1940 and in 1952 the last inhabitants moved away. Not only was the harsh climate of Hornstrandir an added challenge but the only source of geothermal water in the peninsula is Reykjafjörður, several days' hike away. Elsewhere in the region, poor communications have been to blame for rural depopulation. Even today, travel around the region can be exasperating due to the highly indented nature of the coastline and the fjord system at its heart. Stony mountain plateaux between the fjords only add to the difficulties.

times and tickets are available from the West Tours booking service (tel: 456 5111; www.westtours.is) inside the tourist office in Ísafjörður (Aðalstræti 7; tel: 450 8060; www.isafjordur.is; June–Aug Mon–Fri 8am–6pm, Sat 8.30am–2pm, Sun 10am–2pm, winter weekdays only 8am–4pm). Scheduled stops include Aðalvík and Hesteyri in the northwest, Hornvík in the north, Hrafnfjörður in the southwest and Veiðileysufjörður in the west. The return voyage itself is an adventure as a day trip, but most people choose to disembark at either Aðalvík or Hesteyri and hike east across to Hornvík. Another option is to take the ferry to Hrafnfjörður and then hike north to Hornvík. Check the times and sailing schedule of the ferry carefully before setting out because these destinations are not served on a daily basis and Hornstrandir is a pretty remote location – it's not somewhere to get stranded.

## Sea birds and driftwood

Not far from the Hornbjargsviti lighthouse rise the majestic bird-cliffs at **Hornbjarg** ❻, the nesting ground for tens of thousands of pairs of noisy guillemots, Brunnich's guillemots, razorbills, puffins, kittiwakes and fulmars. Not for the fainthearted, **Kálfatindur** peak, the highest point along the cliffs, is a 534-metre (1,760ft) vertical drop to the Greenland Sea. From its lofty summit, the noise is deafening and the view simply breathtaking – some claim to have seen the distant Greenland icecap from here.

In view of Kálfatindur is attractive **Hornvík Bay** ❼. It has a long sandy beach, some impressive waterfalls, a plentiful supply of driftwood and is a pleasant camping spot. In a rare bout of clear weather (for some reason, more likely in late summer), the place is nothing short of idyllic and makes an ideal base from which to explore the area. Across the bay is **Hælavíkurbjarg**, another impressive bird-cliff. Spring still draws daring Icelanders to lower themselves on ropes down the cliff-face and collect the prized guillemots' eggs.

Besides seal-hunting, coastal farmers of the West Fjords have always harvested something else from the sea: driftwood. These benefits are unevenly distributed as some farms have better

*Stuffed exhibits at the Arctic Fox Center, Súðavík.*

*A sweeping West Fjords beach.*

**TIP**

Given the circuitous nature of many roads in the West Fjords, one of the best ways to get to and around the region is by air. Indeed, there are no fewer than three airports in the area, a sure sign of the difficult terrain: Ísafjörður, Bíldudalur and Gjögur on the Strandir coast. The aerial views of the West Fjords' flat-topped mountains can be breathtaking.

*Rocky slopes flank Arnarfjörður.*

driftwood-beaches than others. There has always been a lot of driftwood on Hornstrandir and it was extensively used in the past, as little timber was imported. Dealing in wood was profitable for local inhabitants, and many of them were also known as skilled craftsmen, making useful items such as tubs and barrels, and selling them in the West Fjords and other parts of the country. Driftwood is still collected in Hornstrandir, now mainly used for fenceposts, which are sold all over Iceland.

## South of Ísafjörður

Route 60 winds over several high passes to link the fjords south of Ísafjörður. A tunnel has been made through the basalt rocks of Breiðadalsheiði, which at 610 metres (2,013ft) is the highest pass in the area; it was often blocked in the past, cutting off villages for days, sometimes weeks, at a time.

The village of **Suðureyri** ❽, 17km (10 miles) off the main road, is buried in the shadow of the extremely steep **Súgandafjörður** fjord. The village's main claim to fame is that it lives

without direct sunlight throughout the four winter months, longer than any other village in Iceland. The sun's rays first peek over the high mountains and strike the village on 22 February each year, an occasion celebrated, as everywhere else in the West Fjords, with "sunshine coffee".

**Önundarfjörður** ❾, a fjord between the Barði and Sauðanes headlands, is unmistakable because of its sandy beach, which almost straddles the fjord in a golden arc. On rare sunny days the shallow waters heat up and locals from nearby **Flateyri** throng to bathe in the Greenland Sea. The headland, on which the 237 inhabitants of Flateyri live, was probably left there when a large part of a mountain cleaved into the sea. In 1792 Flateyri became an authorised trading place, and fish and fish-processing are still the main industries. There is said to have been a pagan temple on the hill Goðahóll above the village. Flateyri suffered an avalanche in 1995 that killed 20 people, after which a 20-metre (66ft)-high avalanche dam was built to protect the settlement from further such catastrophes. Today, it is a popular base for kayakers and sea anglers. Culture buffs may also visit the local museum located in the old bookshop, which tells the story of the town, or have a peek at the **International Doll Museum** (www.westfjords.is) or **Nonsense Museum**.

Across the fjord, the historical parsonage of **Holt** ❿ was the birthplace of the 17th-century bishop, Brynjólfur Sveinsson. The attractive timber church here dates from 1869 and contains artefacts from the time of Bishop Brynjólfur. The town is also known for its beautiful golden-sand beach and dunes, which curl out into the fjord.

**Dýrafjörður**, the next fjord south, ranks among the most scenic in Iceland – sheer mountains seem to rise straight from the shore, leaving little or no lowland for farming. The inhabitants have made do with other resources and the village of **Mýrar** ⓫ has Iceland's largest eider duck colony of 7,000 pairs. The

first settler at the nearby farm Alviðra was none other than a son of King Harald Fairhair of Norway.

## National saints and sinners

Across the fjord, **Þingeyri ⑫** (population 262) was the first trading post in the West Fjords. It takes its name from an ancient assembly whose sacred site was said to be enclosed by walls at either end of the mountain **Sandfell**, rising above the village. The old residents still remember the walls and in the town there are ruins of an ancient booth, used by visitors to the assembly, which are a historical monument.

From the top of Sandfell (accessible by 4WD or on a gentle one-hour walk from Þingeyri), there is a beautiful view of the mountains separating Dýrafjörður from Arnarfjörður. This mountain ridge is often called the "West Fjord Alps". In the 19th century the French wanted to establish a colony in Þingeyri to support their fishing fleet, but were turned down. In nearby **Haukadalur** valley there is a French seamen's cemetery. This valley is also the setting for the tragic events of the saga of Gísli Súrsson. Outlawed for a suspected vengeance killing, Gísli spent a gruelling 13 years on the run, but was eventually tracked down and slain. Saga Age ruins in the valley are thought to be Gísli's farm Hóll and his brother-in-law's neighbouring farm Sæból (8km/5 miles along the fjord from Þingeyri).

The village of **Hrafnseyri ⑬**, in Arnarfjörður fjord, was the birthplace of nationalist Jón Sigurðsson (see page 56). There is a small **museum** (www. hrafnseyri.is; June–Aug daily 11am–6pm) and a **chapel** to his memory.

Further along the fjord, an indistinct route leads up Fossdalur valley to **Mount Kaldbakur ⑭**, the highest peak in the region. It is officially 998 metres (3,273ft) high, but locals have added a cairn to credit the region with its only 1,000-metre peak. In clear weather the full-day hike is well worth the effort, with views as far away as the Snæfellsnes icecap.

**Dynjandi waterfall ⑮** is a collection of cascades located at the head of the northern arm of Arnarfjörður. Fjallfoss ("mountain falls"), the main cascade, literally drops 100 metres (330ft) off the edge of the mountain, fanning out to a width of 60 metres (200ft) at its base. Dynjandi continues falling in a series of individually named cascades: Hundafoss, Strokkur, Göngumannafoss, Hrísvaðsfoss and Sjóarfoss.

## The most westerly point in Europe

Some kilometres beyond here the road splits. If you head west, Route 63 passes the fishing villages of **Bílduda-lur** and **Tálknafjörður** (5km/3 miles off the main road). Cryptozoologists may want to stop off at Bíldudalur's **Sea-Monster Centre** (Skrímslasetrið; www.skrimsli.is; mid-May–mid-Sept daily 10am–6pm), whose odd films and first-person scare-stories will have you eyeing the waters of Arnarfjörður with deep unease.

From Bíldudalur, the difficult but impressive Route 619 passes the opening of several valleys, before it ends at

*Road sign.*

*The picturesque cascades of Dynjandi waterfall.*

**FACT**

Traditionally the difficulty of a high pass was measured by the number of fish-skin shoes that were worn through to cross it. In the passes south of Ísafjörður a nine-skin pass was not unusual. Nowadays these routes are more of a test of the nerves of the driver and the suspension of the car.

Selárdalur ⑯ farm, where the pastor Páll Björnsson (1621–1706) lived, famous for witch-burning. According to a legend, a black-sailed pirate schooner was once seen off Selárdalur. The pastor (an unusually good linguist) went out to the vessel, spoke to them in an eastern language and told them the area was full of witches. As a result the pirates exchanged gifts with him and sailed away. Another famous inhabitant of the farm was the outsider artist Samúel Jónsson (1884–1969). Samúel spent his old-age pension money on plaster of Paris to create the weather-beaten sculptures (of lions, a seal and Leif the Lucky), currently being renovated outside the farm.

Also on Route 63 is the larger town of **Patreksfjörður**, with the Fosshótel (opened in 2013) and a cosy café containing an exhibition about pirates, although little else of real interest to the visitor. Across the fjord, **Hnjótur** ⑰ has the **Egill Ólafsson Museum** (www. hnjotur.is; May–Sept daily 10am–6pm), featuring diverse objects relating to fishing, farming, aviation, rescue missions and local West Fjords characters.

*Látrabjarg, marking Europe's western boundary.*

Exhibits are neatly presented and original drawings show how the old tools and equipment were used.

The real lure of the area is the bird-cliffs at **Látrabjarg** ⑱, at the western-most point of Iceland and accessed by an appallingly narrow and rutted dirt track. Extending for 14km (9 miles) and rising to 444 metres (1,465ft) at their highest point, the cliffs are home to one of Iceland's greatest concentrations of sea birds. During the breeding season, puffins here often allow visitors to approach to within a few feet of them as they stand above their cliff-top burrows. On Monday, Wednesday and Saturday in high season, a bus service stops at the cliffs on the journey between Ísafjörður and the Breiðafjörður ferry (if booked in advance – tel: 893 6356), allowing around two hours' exploration time. The bird-cliffs have also been the scene of human dramas. When the British trawler *Dhoon* ran aground below the cliffs in the winter of 1947, a remarkable rescue operation by the local farmers saved all 12 crew members. Lowering themselves by ropes as if they were collecting eggs, they hauled the exhausted men up the 200-metre (650ft) cliff-face to safety. Southeast of Látrabjarg is Iceland's most magnificent stretch of golden sand, **Rauðasandur**.

## Another first settler

At the head of Patreksfjörður fjord, Route 62 crosses over to the southern coast of the West Fjords – **Barðaströnd** – a region that gets more than its share of foul weather. This entire stretch of coast has fewer than 500 inhabitants – the unforgiving elements might have something to do with it. This was where the Viking Hrafna-Flóki made one of the first settlements in Iceland, long before Ingólfur Arnarson arrived. The *Landnámabók (Book of Settlements)* relates that the fishing was so good that Flóki neglected to make hay for his livestock, and they perished over the winter. In spring he climbed a high mountain and, looking north, saw

ice-filled fjords. It was this drift ice, and not the glaciers, that prompted him to name the land "Iceland" on his eventual return to Norway. However, it is said that he came back some years later and spent the rest of his life in Iceland.

Brjánslækur, at the entrance to Vatnsfjörður, is the terminal for the Breiðafjörður ferry, which connects twice daily (no Saturday service outside high season; www.seatours.is/ferry-baldur/schedule) with Stykkishólmur on the Snæfellsnes peninsula.

Route 60 continues south around the fjords, a long and winding drive. There is a chance of spotting the rare white-tailed sea eagle here, though only around 70 pairs (with 40 living around Breiðafjörður) of this now protected species remain after centuries of hunting. The main settlement here is **Bjarkalundur** ⑲, the unofficial gateway to the West Fjords, with a hotel and camping facilities within sight of the twin peaks of Vaðalfjöll.

## The Strandir coast

The rugged eastern flank of the West Fjords is one of the least visited parts of Iceland. The population of the area has been steadily declining, and now the only town of any size is **Hólmavík**, which has basic facilities. It draws in visitors with its unusual **Museum of Icelandic Sorcery and Witchcraft** (www.galdrasyning.is; daily June–mid-Sept 9am–7pm), which brings to life some of the darker aspects of living in such small and isolated communities. Farming in the region is hard, and good harbours are few: **Djúpavík**, for example, a once-bustling herring station, is now virtually abandoned, but has a wonderfully situated hotel. The museum also has a small restaurant that serves a local delicacy – blue mussels.

The village of **Norðurfjörður** is the end of the road. Beyond here, a hiking trail follows the coast to Hornstrandir. Allow between 10 and 14 days, expect all kinds of weather, take double the normal rations – and don't count on meeting another soul.

From Norðurfjörður, there's also a summer ferry connection to Hornvík in Hornstrandir which sails twice a week from late June to mid-August.

**TIP**

If you're a fan of beautiful golden beaches, you're in luck. The West Fjords have two of Iceland's most enchanting sandy strands: Breiðavík and Rauðasandur, both within easy reach of each other. Regrettably though, sunbathing is unlikely to be an option even on the sunniest of days since the air remains stubbornly chilly. Breiðavík is also accessible by public transport from Ísafjörður.

*Driving through an isolated expanse of beautiful Icelandic scenery.*

# OBSERVING ICELAND'S SEA BIRDS

**One of the most unforgettable sights in Iceland is that of a huge, cliff-side sea bird colony – a common and noisy occurrence in breeding season.**

Sea birds can be seen and heard everywhere in Iceland – circling overhead or offshore but, most often, stacked in vast, raucous colonies on steep cliffs and island coastlines. They live here in their millions, and many more birds arrive in late spring to breed – some 25 species in all, plus a few more on passage north or south. No wonder the great aim for many human visitors to Iceland is to watch these birds, sometimes by walking and climbing long distances to see the colonies. Watching sea birds is easiest by boat or from a nearby cliff, where the gap between birds and observers gives the birds a sense of security.

The northernmost island of Grímsey, on the Arctic Circle, is home to about 90 shepherds and fisherfolk. But great breeding colonies of birds outnumber them by their thousands – fulmars, including the rare blue fulmar, guillemots, including the Brunnich's sub-species, gannets and many others.

Even Reykjavík, with 120,000 inhabitants, also has its own colonies of auks, gulls such as kittiwake – easily distinguished by the cry that gives it its name – eiders and many other ducks. Near the golf course, a colony of Arctic terns use the golfers for diving practice.

In Iceland's great peninsulas, the West Fjords, Snæfellsnes and islands such as the Vestmannaeyjar, pointing the binoculars at the ever-changing sea or the steadfast cliffs, you do not have to be an expert to feel the thrill of finding a species that, to you at least, is new.

*The razorbill's chunky beak, with its vertical white stripe, can be part of the mating ritual – a bird attracts a mate by using its beak to make a castanet-like rattle.*

*Photographing birdlife from a rocky outcrop.*

*Seagulls descending on a freshly landed catch, Siglufjörður.*

*Arctic terns on a glacial lagoon. These birds migrate long distances.*

## THE LAST OF THE GREAT AUKS

The great auk was once the king of the auk species – black and white seabirds with short, stubby necks, including guillemots, razorbills, little auks and puffins. At one time, there were great auk colonies in Iceland, North America, Greenland and the Faroes.

But the great auk had one major disadvantage. It was flightless. Sitting stolidly on a rock, the great auk was easy prey for hunters in remote areas. The colonies grew smaller until, by the start of the 19th century, few remained except on St Kilda and on Iceland's islands. Still they were hunted. In 1844, two hunters visiting Eldey island, southwest of the Reykjanes peninsula, strangled the last pair of great auks, and stamped on the egg that the two birds were tending.

*The great auk lost its battle for survival in 1844, primarily due to over-hunting.*

*The modestly sized puffin, with its distinctive curved red, blue and yellow beak in summer, is everyone's favourite. Pairs of puffins breed and raise their young in burrows on clifftops.*

*Pair of fulmars.*

# HÚNAFLÓI AND SKAGAFJÖRÐUR

**This rugged region of mountains, waterfalls, cliffs and islands has been largely bypassed by tourism – few turn off the Ring Road to find the coast's more remote attractions.**

Reykjavík

Jutting into the icy Arctic Ocean, the Skagi peninsula divides the northern coast of Iceland into the Húnaflói bight and Skagafjörður fjord. It may not have the breathtaking glaciers of the south, or the drama of the wiggling west fjords, but it will reward the patient. It is well worth following the narrow dirt roads into a windswept wilderness of basalt cliffs, nesting sea birds, black volcanic sand spits and beaches frequented only by seals. In places, the past seems a single heartbeat away: it feels as though the workers have just stepped out of the Herring Era museum in Siglufjörður; or that saga hero Grettir is about to return to his stony hideout on Drangey.

## Rural backwater

The Ring Road runs through rich agricultural land here, its alluvial soil weathered from some of Iceland's oldest rocks. The entry point to the area is **Brú ❶** ("bridge") – a tiny hamlet which is really little more than a petrol station. It is dominated by the huge bulk of **Tröllakirkja**, a hill that stands over 1,000 metres (3,300ft) from the flat surrounding farmland. Brú is at the head of narrow **Hrútafjörður** fjord, formed by the extensive glacial moraines (deposits) which dominate the area. The land in this region is rich in minerals and this, coupled with high rainfall,

encourages many rare alpine and arctic plants, particularly gentians.

The farmstead/youth hostel of **Ósar** lies 18km (12 miles) north along Route 711 on the **Vatnsnes** promontory, from where there are superb views across the **Húnafjörður bay** to Blönduós. In the foreground is the moraine-dammed inlet of **Sigríðarstaðavatn**, with the Hóp lagoon beyond. Grey seals bask on sand spits at low tide while eider duck and terns nest among the lyme grass. A short distance along the shore is the distinctive basalt sea-stack

Map on page 236

**Main Attractions**

Skagaströnd
Króksbjarg and Bakkar cliffs
White-water rafting (Varmahlíð)
Hólar church
Herring Era Museum (Siglufjörður)

*Inside Hólar church.*

**Hvítserkur**, with three holes through its base and white guano flecking its ledges like icing. According to folklore, this 15-metre (49ft)-high stack was a troll turned to stone by the sun.

**Hóp ❷** is the largest saltwater lagoon in Iceland, virtually cut in half by a narrow sand spit and almost isolated from the sea by **Þingeyrasandur**, a low-lying, black sand dune with great swards of lyme grass on its seaward side. This was used in the past as a seed crop to mill for flour. Over the centuries, the dune has expanded seaward as more sand has been deposited by the ocean. Tundra plants have colonised the older dunes to provide great flashes of colour: purple thyme, yellow lady's bedstraw, white northern orchid, deep blue gentians, and parnassus grass and silverweed. Overhead, Arctic skuas wheel about attacking Arctic terns; below, running free across the sands, are Icelandic horses, which are particularly common in this area.

On the way to the dunes, the dirt track (Route 721) passes one of Iceland's greatest historical sites, **Þingeyrar ❸**, whose name reflects the site's original function as a þing (district assembly). The local bishop Jón Ögmundarson built one of Iceland's first Benedictine monasteries here in 1133. It quickly became a literary hotspot, with monks working full-time transcribing the Bible and the sagas. Today nothing remains of these two early sites. The estate is a horse farm, guarded by a solitary and rather splendid basalt church, completed in 1877, which is open to visitors in the summer months.

Near to where Route 721 meets the Ring Road is **Þrístapar**, the hilly site of Iceland's last execution, which occurred on 12 January 1830, when the murderers Agnes and Friðrik were beheaded. Across the road is the **Vatnsdalur valley ❹**, a geologist's dream dotted with steep mounds of ground moraine. Just as striking is evidence of Iceland's largest known landslip, which occurred here in October 1720. The side of the huge ridge, **Vatnsdalsfjall** (800 metres/2,600ft high), collapsed and dammed the river below to create a new lake – **Flóðið**.

The town of **Blönduós ❺**, with 881 inhabitants, has plenty of services but makes a rather uninspiring base. That matters little if you're an angler – the town sits on the **River Blanda**, which is the longest salmon river in Iceland; a permit to fish it can cost a small fortune. The Ring Road crosses a bridge over the river, and there is a turn-off to the heart of Blönduós, with its fine swimming pool, hotel, hospital, garage and three small museums (of Icelandic costume; salmon; and sea-ice and polar bears, which commonly drift over from Greenland).

In the middle of the river, to the east of Blönduós, is the island of **Hrútey**, reached via a small footbridge from the north bank. There is a circular path through the tundra scrubland and it is a good place for birdwatching. The river torrent slows as it passes into the tidal stretches of Blönduós, where rare ducks and divers congregate. From Blönduós, the Ring Road runs directly to Akureyri, passing eventually through the **Öxnadalur** valley, considered the finest scenery

*Hvítserkur arch visible above the water.*

on the highway from Reykjavík. Alternatively, Akureyri can be reached following the rougher roads along the wild northern coast.

The **Skagi** peninsula lies northeast of Blönduós. The dirt highway that hugs its western edge passes through a narrow band of agricultural land overshadowed by the mountains behind. **Skagaströnd ⑥**, with a population of barely 480, was an important trading port in the 16th century, but today it is a quiet fishing centre built on a rocky outcrop. It is most famous today for its eccentric inhabitant Hallbjörn Hjartarson, a country-and-western fanatic who set up his own C&W bar (Kántrýbær) and radio station in town. Brightly coloured wooden houses edge a sweeping bay with the snow-splashed mountain peaks of **Spákonufell** as the towering backdrop.

North of Skagaströnd, sand dunes and shingle bays give way to cliffs. The ever-deteriorating road climbs upwards and across the top of the **Króksbjarg** and **Bakkar** cliffs – home to a large number of sea birds. Rows of sandstone outcrops contrast with the black basalt lava, usually hexagonal in section. Thousands of kittiwakes vie for nesting space on ledges whilst fulmars nest on the tops of the columns. Near to where the River Fossá cascades over the cliff is a small grassy headland undermined by the sea – a great place from which to observe the sea birds. North is **Vogurviti**, an unusual outcrop of basalt rock.

## Sauðárkrókur

**Sauðárkrókur ⑦** is the region's administrative centre at the head of the fjord. First settled by Scotsmen from the Hebrides, today Sauðárkrókur has a population of about 2,500, making it second in size to Akureyri on Iceland's north coast. Its many amenities include a swimming pool, cinema and even a gliding club. And if you've been surprised and intrigued by the wolf-fish clothing and salmon handbags for sale around Iceland, the world's only **fish-leather tannery** (www.sutarinn.is;

visitor centre June–mid-Sept Mon–Fri 9am–6pm, Sat 11am–3pm) is also based in Sauðárkrókur, with guided tours at 10am and 2pm Monday to Friday.

Thermal springs supply the town's hot water, and a natural hot pool, Grettislaug, can be visited just to the north at **Reykir ⑧**. From here, there are daily boat trips in summer to the small island of **Drangey**, rich in birdlife, where the outlawed hero of *Grettis Saga* hid out for the last three years of his life.

In Glerhallavík Bay, near the pool, thousands upon thousands of exquisitely beautiful quartz stones, polished by the pounding surf, have been washed up on the beach (though you should note it is forbidden to remove any of them). Access is only possible at low tide on foot from Reykir.

Another mountain track (Route 744) with superb views of the area runs over **Þverárfjall** into moorlands of cottongrass. South of Sauðárkrókur, at **Glaumbær ⑨**, is a finely maintained turf farmhouse **museum** (May daily 9am–5pm, June–late Sept daily 9am–6pm, Oct Mon–Fri 10am–4pm), whose wood-framed buildings are insulated

*Hardy Icelandic horses.*

*Hólar church and its surroundings.*

# North Central Iceland

0 ——— 20 km
0 ——— 20 miles

N

Myvatn

Myvatn

Laxá

Nes

Fosshóll

Goðafoss

Barðardalur

843

F26

Skjálfandafljót

85

842

Húsavík

Laxamýri

Björg

Ljósavatn

Háafell
918

Bakká

Myri

**Þingeyjar Sýsla**

Lundey

Flatey

Skjálfandi

Viknafjöll

Fnjóská

Svalbarðseyri

Reykir

Fnjóská

Skjólfell
1085

Flateyjarheiði

Laufás

Fnjóská

83

Munkaþverá

Grund

829

Skjálfandafljót

Gígurtá

Kaldbakur
1167

Grenivík

Hjalteyri

Akureyri

Kristnes

Hrafnagil

Grund

Hólar

821

F821

Grímsey

Hrísey

Mööruvellir

Súlur
1213

Saurbær

Torfufell

Torfufell
1240

Ólafsfjarðarmúli

Árskógssandur

Stærri-Árskógur

Sölur

Bægisá

**Sýsla**

**Öxnadalur**

Austari-Jökulsá

Hofsá

Siglunes

Dalvík

805

Urðir

Gljúfurá
1384

Reykir

Myrkárkoll
1387

Tungufjall
1293

Silfrastaðir

752

Goðdalir

Vestari-Jökulsá

F752

Siglufjörður

Ólafsfjörður

82

76

**Tröllskagi**

**Heljardalsheiði**

Hólar

**Eyjafjarðar**

Héraðsvötn

752

**Eyjafjarðardalir**

Miklavatn

Barð

Höfðavatn

Viðvík

76

Reykir

Mælifell

**Grímstaðaheiði**

Málmey

Drangey

Hofsós

76

Hóp

Glaumbær

Varmahlíð

Viðimýri

Svartá

Blanda

**Skagafjörður**

Reykir

Reynistaður

75

Bergstaðir

Blöndulón

Skagatá

Hraun

Reykir

Tindastóll
989

Glaumbær

Svínavatn

F35

Saurðárkrókur

Mikfavatn

Svínadalr

Vatnsdalsá

Hvanneyri

744

Holtastaðir

Fröðmundarvötn

Vatnsdalsá

Reynisnes

Frammes

745

Skagaströnd

74

Blönduós

**Vatnsdalsfjall**

Fitjá

Viðidalsá

**Skagaheiði**

Fossá

745

Húnafjörður

Þingeyrar

Hóp

**Vatnsdalur**

**Viðidalsfjall**

**Húnavatns Sýsla**

**Húnaflói**

Ósar

Vesturhópsvötn

Laugabakki

704

Erpmúpur

Reykjaness

Gjögur

Tjörn

Vatns

Miðfjörður

72

Melstaður

Reykjaskóli

Staður

Húkur

Balafjöll
689

Gjögur

711

Miðfjörður

68

Borðeyri

**Stranda Sýsla**

Laugarhóll

Drangsnes

Grímsey

Broddanes

Hrútafjörður

Prestbakki

Melar

Brú

**Borgarnes, Reykjavík**

Reykjarnes
643

Bitrufjörður

Bjarnarfjörður

by thick turf walls and roofs. **Áshús**, a house built in the 19th-century style that supplanted the turf house, contains a coffee-shop that also serves Icelandic pancakes.

South of Glaumbær, **Varmahlíð** is a small service village with a bank, two hotels, tourist office and swimming pool. The rivers south of town are Iceland's best for white-water rafting. **Vicking Rafting** (tel: 823 8300; http://vikingrafting.is), located 15km (9 miles) south of Varmahlíð on route 752, operate rafting trips on the beautiful glacial rivers Jökulsá Vestari and Jökulsá Austari.

## East of Skagafjörður

The eastern flank of Skagafjörður is lined with steep mountains. The 1,300-metre (4,265ft)-high interior beyond can only be penetrated by backpackers willing to brave the remnants of an ancient icecap. Accessible by car, however, is the ancient bishopric of **Hólar** ⑩, founded in 1106 and for over 600 years the religious centre of the North. The high-towered "cathedral", dating from 1763, is charming. The early 16th-century altarpiece, believed to be Dutch, was donated by Jón Arason, the last Catholic bishop of the area who was executed during the Reformation. A difficult hike, from Hólar to the Urðir valley and Dalvík, crosses the snow fields of Heljardalsheiði through some of north Iceland's finest scenery.

Further north is the little fishing village of **Hofsós** ⑪, containing the **Icelandic Emigration Centre** (www.hofsos. is; June–Aug daily 11am–6pm or by prior booking). The centre, on the seafront by the harbour, houses four fascinating exhibitions tracing the history of the 16,000–20,000 Icelanders who emigrated to America between 1850 and 1914; there is also an information service, library and souvenir shop. The centre's creation has gone hand-in-hand with restoration work on the village's most important historical buildings, including one of the oldest warehouses in Iceland, built in 1777 in the style of

a log cabin. A fabulous fjordside **swimming pool** (tel: 455 6070; www.facebook. com/sundlauginhofsosi; June–Aug daily 9am–9pm, Sept–May Mon–Fri 7am–1pm, 5.–8pm, Sat–Sun 11am–3pm), one of Iceland's finest.

Visitors driving north around Skagafjörður towards Siglufjörður will find their eyes drawn to the island of **Málmey** offshore. This concave-shaped outcrop of lava is 4km (2.5 miles) long and rises at either end into high cliffs. Until 2010, the attractive town of **Siglufjörður** ⑫ sat in splendid isolation at the end of its own road, but it is now linked to its neighbour Ólafsfjörður by two long mountain tunnels. Set amidst a range of glaciated mountains, the town's current population of 1,200 is its lowest in recent history, but a generation ago this was the centre of the herring industry and home, at least seasonally, to 10,000 workers. The award-winning **Herring Era Museum** (www.sild.is; daily June–Aug 10am–6pm, May and Sept 1–5pm) traces the town's glory days in five historical buildings by the harbour, including the old shipyard, boathouse and slipway..

*Lush Hólar landscape.*

*Enjoying a drink with friends on the marina at Skagafjörður.*

*Mighty Goðafoss.*

# AKUREYRI AND SURROUNDINGS

Akureyri is Iceland's second city, and makes an ideal
base for trips to the nearby fjords and some of the
country's most photographed attractions.

B y Icelandic standards, Akureyri
is a thriving metropolis: it is the
country's second "city", although
in reality, its 18,500-strong population
makes it more of a provincial town.
Akureyri's setting is spectacular: at
the base of Eyjafjörður fjord, with a
backdrop of sheer granite mountains
tipped with snow all year. Despite
being only 100km (60 miles) from
the Arctic Circle, it enjoys some of the
country's warmest weather, bringing
the flowers, the café tables and the
people out into the pedestrianised
streets in summer. Its gentle charms
include a landmark church, a cluster
of older wooden buildings, a handful of small museums and some good
restaurants, making it an excellent
base for exploring Eyjafjörður and a
launchpad for bus and boat trips further afield.

## Gateway to the north

The first settler to claim the Eyjafjörður region was the Norwegian
Helgi the Lean (named after a stint on
the Orkney Islands as a child, when he
was poorly fed by foster parents). Helgi
had indiscriminate religious habits: in
traditional pagan fashion, he tossed
the high-seat pillars from his longship
into the sea, allowing the god Thor to
choose the site of his new home. But
when they washed up 7km (4 miles)
south of modern-day Akureyri, Helgi

*Colourful Akureyri street signs.*

named his farm Kristnes (Christ's Peninsula), just in case.

The Viking farmers who ended up
around Eyjafjörður were relatively
peaceful, to judge from their low
profiles in the sagas. A notable exception was Víga-Glúmur. A morose and
gangly youth regarded as a buffoon
by his peers, Víga-Glúmur surprised
everyone on a journey to Norway by
slaughtering a berserk warrior in com-
bat. He became a worshipper of Odin
and returned to Iceland to make the
lives of his former tormentors a misery,

**Main Attractions**
Akureyrarkirkja
Akureyri Museum
Hrísey
Goðafoss Waterfall

becoming chieftain of the Eyjafjörður region by trickery and intimidation. However, he offended the goddess Freyja by butchering one of his in-laws in the goddess's sacred cornfield. After 40 years, Freyja had her revenge – in old age, Víga-Glúmur lost Odin's protection and had to abandon his estates. He died blind and alone.

## The profit motive

The town of **Akureyri** ⑬ grew from humble beginnings in the 16th century when Danish merchants built a couple of storehouses here. In the 1770s, the first permanent house was built, and the settlement became an authorised trading post in 1786, when it had a grand total of 12 inhabitants. The town failed to prosper, however, and lost its precious trading licence a mere 50 years later, before finally regaining it in 1862. An excellent harbour soon made this the centre of the new cooperative movement among Icelandic farmers (see page 116).

By the early 20th century, grandiose wooden mansions had filled the southern part of Akureyri. The spit at

*Akureyri Museum.*

the northern part of town, **Oddeyri**, became the port and warehouse area, and it remains so to this day (the name Akureyri is a blend of *Akur*, meaning field, and *eyri*, spit, after the land that projects into the fjord). Akureyri has a university and a modest local flourishing of the arts, with several theatre groups, plus a number of nightspots and cinemas.

The residents have a mixed reputation in the rest of Iceland. The town is seen as the bastion of middle-class values and, despite the good weather it enjoys, its people are considered closed, traditional and even somewhat dour. Icelanders say that you can't get to know the people of Akureyri unless you are born and raised there – being conceived in the town while your parents were on holiday doesn't count. Even being raised there may not be good enough: tales are told of Akureyri neighbours who accidentally meet in Reykjavík and have long, friendly conversations, only to act like virtual strangers once they return home. Whatever the truth of this, Icelanders have no qualms about

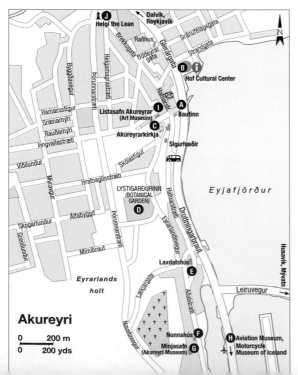

flocking to Akureyri, especially at weekends, when flights from Reykjavík are packed, and people from every corner of the North drive in to their figurative "big smoke" for a taste of the action.

## Exploring the town

Akureyri is compact enough to explore on foot, and the most logical place to start is the partly pedestrianised main shopping street **Hafnarstræti.** This is where the hustle and bustle (such as it is) of this small town's life takes place. An Akureyri institution, the **Bautinn restaurant** Ⓐ (www.bautinn.is) at No. 92 sits on a crossroads and is a good place to watch the world go by.

The fjord **waterfront** is only a short hop downhill from the restaurant, usually with a few picturesque trawlers or an impressive cruise ship sitting in port. Passengers are welcomed at the swish **Hof Cultural Centre** Ⓑ, which contains the town's **tourist office** (Strandgata 12; tel: 450 1050; www.mak.is/en; mid-June–mid-Sept daily 8am–6.30pm, May–mid-June weekdays 8am–5pm, weekends 9am–4pm, late Sept Mon–Fri 8am–5pm, Sat–Sun 9am–4pm, Oct–May Mon–Fri 8am–4pm). Uphill, the basalt **Akureyrarkirkja** Ⓒ has dominated the town since its construction in 1940. Designed by Guðjón Samúelsson (the architect of Reykjavík's Hallgrimskirkja), the church can look distressingly unattractive in some lights. Even so, it is Akureyri's pride and joy, and worth the five-minute walk up Kaupvangsstræti for a visit. Inside, the stained-glass windows show scenes from Icelandic history and the life of Christ in a style that can only be described as cartoon-book. There is an organ with 3,200 pipes, while the centre window in the chancel was donated by England's Coventry Cathedral – it was one of the only parts that survived the bombing during World War II. Most curious is the model ship hanging from the ceiling, a tradition in Iceland, Greenland and the Faroe

Islands to protect the parish's fishermen at sea.

A short climb up **Eyrarlandsvegur** leads to the **Botanical Garden** Ⓓ (Lystigarðurinn; www.lystigardur.akureyri.is; June–Sept Mon–Fri 8am–10pm, Sat–Sun 9am–10pm; free), famed for its 7,000 species of local and foreign flowers blooming outside in Akureyri's warm microclimate. The park was set up by a local women's association in 1912, then taken over by the town in the 1950s; two of the voluntary managers are commemorated by statues. The gardens are a perfect place to relax on a sunny afternoon, all the more so since lovely little Cafe Laut (daily 10am–10pm; summer) threw open its doors.

## Historical tour

From the main shopping street, walk to the foot of the church and follow the footpath up to Eyrarlandsvegur 3, to the building known as Sigurhæðir. Built in 1903, this was the home of one of Iceland's most revered poets and dramatists, Mattías Jochumsson. Jochumsson penned the lyrics for

*Typical Akureyri architecture.*

**TIP**

On the way back into town from the Botanical Garden on Eyrarlandsvegur, keep an eye out for Einar Jónsson's sculpture *The Outlaw*, depicting Fjalla-Eyvindur ("Mountain-Eyvind") and his wife Halla, who spent 20 years as outlaws, mainly in the interior of the country (see page 302).

*Akureyri's Botanical Garden is well tended.*

Iceland's national anthem, *Iceland's 1,000 Years*, in 1874.

Back downhill, head into Akureyri's old business district by taking a stroll south along Hafnarstræti, which leads you past the **bus station**. The area still has many fine mansions in the so-called Icelandic frame-house tradition – to the uninitiated, they look like Swiss chalets. The last one was built in 1911, when other styles came into vogue, including the use of metal sidings pressed into a brick pattern and painted over to look like stone and mortar. Near the intersection with Lækjargata is Akureyri's oldest house, **Laxdalshús ❺**. Built in 1795, this tiny restored wooden building was occupied until 1978, when it was home to some 30 people from three or four families.

South along the waterfront following Aðalstræti is **Nonnahús ❻** (June–Aug daily 10am–5pm). This is the restored home of Reverend Jón Sveinsson, nicknamed Nonni, author of a series of children's books that are still well loved in Iceland and continental Europe. The house, where Nonni spent some years of his childhood, was built in 1850 and has been maintained in its original form – even the kitchen still has its old implements – making this the most interesting of Akureyri's old homes.

The **Akureyri Museum ❼** (Minjasafn; www.minjasafnid.is; June–mid-Sept daily 9am–5pm) has an exhaustive collection of local memorabilia, from old farming tools to milk cartons, as well as some excellent 19th-century photographs. Outside, a small church, which was moved from Svalbard across the fjord, sits beside Iceland's first nursery.

At the end of this picturesque street is a small museum, detailing Akureyri's 20th-century industrial heritage; and a drab kilometre walk down road 821, by the airport, is the **Aviation Museum ❽** (www.flugsafn.is; June–Sept daily 1–5pm, winter Sat 1–5pm; also by arrangement outside usual hours) with a large hangar full of antique aircraft, some of which are wheeled out and flown around from time to time.

Anyone not yet sated by museums can head back into town to see the

**Motorcycle Museum of Iceland** (Krókeyri 2; www.motorhjolasafn.is; daily June–Aug noon–6pm, Sept–May Sat 3–7pm), which is located in a stunning new building and covers the 100-year-old history of motorcycles in Iceland, or go to the nearby **Akureyri Art Museum ❶** (Listasafn Akureyrar; www.listak.is; June–Aug daily 10am–5pm, Sept–May Tue–Sun noon–5pm; free), which offers visitors one of the best insights into the town's present-day cultural life.

At the northern edge of central Akureyri, on a rock between Glerárgata and Þórunnarstraeti, is a statue of **Helgi the Lean ❿** (see page 241), with an impressive view over Eyjafjörður.

## Short excursions

Pleasant as strolling around Akureyri can be, the real attraction is the surrounding area. A few short trips are very close to town. Only an hour on foot or 10 minutes' drive south is **Kjarnaskógar forest**, one of Iceland's few wooded areas, and a popular picnic place. Hikers can head for the symmetrical, Fuji-like **Mount Súlur ⓮**, visible on clear days from Akureyri. Drive west on Súluvegur (past the rubbish dump) to the small creek – look out for a wooden ladder over the barbed wire, then follow the yellow markers. You should allow several hours of hard (and not very inspiring) walking to reach the 1,213-metre (3,980ft) summit looking out over the **Glerá** valley. In winter, skiing fans head for **Hlíðarfjall** (www.hlidarfjall.is), offering the best slopes in the area only a 10-minute drive from town, with day passes costing ISK4,900. Many non-skiers also head there for the view of the **Vindheima-jökull** glacier.

## Exploring the fjord

Perhaps the most popular day trip from Akureyri – and one that can be driven alone or organised through the tourist office – is along the western flank of Eyjafjörður fjord. The well-paved Route 82 offers sweeping views over the rich farming land of the area, with glacier-scoured mountains to the west (their peaks are often buried behind a steady line of grey cloud) and steely blue waters to the east. The district here is known as **Árskógsströnd**. As in the rest of the North, the fields are dotted in summer with hundreds of gigantic white plastic rolls containing hay for the winter – a high-tech innovation that has quickly replaced the more poetic but inefficient methods of traditional hay-gathering. Cows, sheep and geese wander at will, and it is not unusual for traffic to be stopped while a farmer leads a line of cattle over the road to pasture.

Although Route 82 can be followed directly north, a turn-off at Route 816 leads to a ruined medieval port area, called **Gásir**; for many centuries it was the biggest port in northern Iceland. Its overgrown ruins can still be made out in the grass. Another short side road (Route 813) leads to the farm

*Pretty flowers in the Botanical Garden.*

*Fishing in Akureyri.*

**Möðruvellir**, birthplace of the children's writer Jón Sveinsson (better known as Nonni). There is a much-photographed farmhouse at **Stærri-Árskógur**, flush against a steep mountain backdrop.

**Dalvík** ⑮ (population about 2,000) is the dominant town on this side of the fjord. A prosperous fishing village today, Dalvík's claim to fame in Iceland is the 1934 earthquake measuring 6.3 on the Richter scale that brought rocks crashing down from the nearby mountainside and destroyed about half of the town's homes. Its unusual little museum **Byggðasafnið Hvoll** (www.dalvik urbyggd.is/byggdasafn; June–Aug daily 11am–6pm, Sept–May Sat 2–5pm and by previous arrangement) has a room dedicated to local personality Jóhann Pétursson (1913–84), Iceland's tallest man. Dalvík-based company Arctic Sea Tours (www.arcticseatours.is) is a more peaceful whale-watching alternative to the scrum of people and boats at Húsavík. The ferry over to Grímsey island (see page 255) also departs from Dalvík.

*A statue of much-loved children's author Jón Sveinsson.*

## Hrísey Island

**Hrísey island** ⑯ is the second largest island off Iceland's coast (after Heimaey), giving Eyjafjörður ("island fjord") its name. During World War II it was the billet for five British servicemen whose job it was to check up on all trawlers entering the fjord, with only a broken machine gun to back them up.

On a fine day, the 15-minute boat trip from Árskógssandur (just south of Dalvík) is a joy, and the sparsely inhabited island makes for pleasant wandering.

Hrísey is the location of Iceland's quarantine centre: when it opened in 1974, all animals on Hrísey had to be killed to minimise the risk of cross-infection. The result has been that the island now supports some of the lushest vegetation in the entire country. Much of it is private property and so off-limits to hikers, but there are still plenty of trails across the flat moorlands, covered in purple heather and full of birdlife. If you don't feel like walking, you can be pulled around the island on a **hay cart** towed by an elderly tractor.

## KEA

The people of Akureyri joke that virtually everything in their town is owned by kea. Whilst this wry comment may not reduce the average visitor to fits of laughter, it is certainly true that kea (incidentally, nothing to do with well-known Swedish furniture store, IKEA) is omnipresent in this small town of 18,500 people. kea, or the Kaupfélag Eyfirðinga, was founded in June 1886 by a group of farmers from around Eyjafjörður, to strengthen their hand in the negotiation of export prices for their sheep being sent to England. Ten years later kea opened its first store – one of the first cooperative shops in Iceland – and a slaughterhouse for cows soon followed. Throughout the 20th century things really boomed for the cooperative, which grew in size and became involved in numerous ventures. Indeed, a short stroll around Akureyri today reveals the kea logo emblazoned on everything from fishing boats to hotels. kea, proud of its northern roots, concentrated its business in and around the Akureyri region, although there were attempts to enter the Reykjavík market by building a shopping centre at the bsí bus station. In recent years, kea has narrowed its portfolio (selling off its hotel chain, for one); and like every Icelandic business, it was hit hard by the 2008 crash. But it's still going strong, with almost half of Akureyri's loyal inhabitants belonging to the cooperative.

The small village has 170 inhabitants and a few facilities, including a geothermal pool, an exhibition on Icelandic shark-fishing, and the restaurant Verbudin 66, where you should try the excellent catch of the day.

## North from Dalvík

A popular side trip from Dalvík is into **Svarfaðardalur** valley, a wetland nature reserve popular with birdwatchers, entering on Route 805 and returning along Route 807. From the end of Route 805, hikers and horseriders can head into the wilderness of **Heljardalsheiði** for camping trips in some of the finest mountain country in Iceland.

North of Dalvík, a nerve-wracking and treacherous gravel road winding along the steep coastline was made more bearable by the opening in 1991 of a 3.5km (2-mile) tunnel. This one-lane passage through the mountainside has become something of a tourist attraction in itself, although claustrophobes might prefer to risk the old road around the headland of **Olafsfjarðarmúli** – which,

incidentally, is a good place to see the midnight sun in July, with views on a clear day to Grímsey island, on the Arctic Circle.

**Ólafsfjörður ⑰** is a fishing village of 790 people nestled amongst a ring of snow-capped, 1,200-metre (3,900ft)-high peaks. Despite the setting, it has little more of interest than fishing boats and factories.

## Points south

Heading south from Akureyri, Route 821 runs along the Eyjafjarðará river valley. The pretty farm **Kristnes**, built on the site where Helgi the Lean first settled, is 7km (4 miles) along on a hill with a strategic view of the fjord. A few minutes further south is another farm, **Grund ⑱**, which has one of the most unusual churches in Iceland; with its several Romanesque spires, it looks as if it has been transplanted from St Petersburg. The farmer Magnús Sigurðsson built it to his own design in 1906 to serve the whole river valley. The church broke a nearly millennium-old tradition by being built on a north-south axis instead of east-west.

*Farm with Hrísey island in the background.*

A good example of a more traditional church, made of turf and stone, is at the farm of **Saurbær** ⑲, 27km (17 miles) south of Akureyri on Route 821. The quaint interior is open to visitors. At this point, the road continues to the farm of **Torfufell,** or across the river valley to return to Akureyri on Route 829. En route is the historic farm of **Munkaþverá**. Originally known as Þverá, this was the birthplace in the 10th century of the notorious Odinworshipping Viking Víga-Glúmur. In the 12th century, a Benedictine monastery was built on the site, although none of it remains. Finally, at **Ytri Hóll**, look out for a classic turf house that is still in use: the tiny chimney poking out from the grassy roof only makes it look even more like a hobbit's hole.

### Eyjafjördur's eastern shore

The Ring Road crosses the fjord and rises northwards, giving some of the best views of the town and passing the door of **Safnasafnið** ⑳ (www. safnasafnid.is; mid-May- Aug daily 10am–5pm), which contains a huge collection of folk and outsider artwork, plus all kinds of other bits and bobs.

About 10km (6 miles) north of the museum, turn off at Route 83 for **Laufás** ㉑, a beautifully situated farm looking out over Eyjafjörður with a small white church and 19th-century turf farmhouse **museum** (June–Aug daily 9am–5pm). Built in the 1860s, the dirt-floored building was a vicarage and upper-crust home, and is now crowded with antiques. A famous touch is the carved woman's face and duck placed over the middle segment of the farmhouse.

Just 22km (14 miles) from the Ring Road turn-off is the picturesque but somnolent fishing town of **Grenivík** ㉒ (population 278). Only founded in 1910, Grenivík is at the edge of the rugged Fjörður peninsula, which has been uninhabited since World War II.

The Ring Road continues east towards Lake Mývatn, but first passes the small lake **Ljósavatn** ("lightwater") and a turn-off to the farm of the same name. This was the Saga Age farm of the chieftain Þorgeir Þorkelsson, Law-speaker in the Alþingi in AD 1000, who was forced to decide whether Iceland should be pagan or Christian. As the *Kristni Saga* tells it, Þorgeir spent 24 hours under his cloak before deciding for the Christians. Riding back from Þingvellir to his home at Ljósavatn, he passed a giant waterfall and decided to toss all his carved images of pagan gods into its waters. This powerful waterfall, **Goðafoss** ㉓ ("fall of the gods"), is virtually beneath the Ring Road a few kilometres further on, and is one of the easiest of Iceland's major falls to visit. Most cars and buses en route to Mývatn stop here at the petrol station/souvenir shop at **Fosshóll**.

The surrounding area of the **Bárðardalur** valley is a 7,000-year-old lava flow, through which the Skjálfandafljót river has cut a path to form Goðafoss.

*Stunning Eyjafjörður fjord scenery.*

*Fish are hung up to dry on the outside of a house.*

# Icelandic Hauntings

**One in every 500 inhabitants of Iceland is a ghost according to *Vættatal*, the spiritual *Who's Who* of Iceland by folklore historian Árni Björnsson.**

*Vættatal* claims that more than 500 ghouls, trolls and paranormal beings haunt Iceland, making a substantial – or perhaps insubstantial – addition to its 320,000-strong human population. This high ghost quotient is not entirely unexpected, as the island is the perfect home for any spook, what with long periods of darkness in winter and an abundance of grotesque rock and lava formations providing perfect camouflage for monsters and ogres.

Flesh-and-blood Icelanders, it seems, enjoy excellent relations with their other-wordly neighbours. In a survey on the supernatural in Western Europe, Icelanders topped the league for ghostly experiences, with 41 percent claiming contact with the dead, compared to the European average of 20 percent.

*Meeting trolls in Akureyri.*

## Zombies, spirits and trolls

Traditionally, however, ghosts were not harmless visitations from the dear departed. They usually took the form of an *afturganga*, a dead man turned zombie, and were capable of killing people or (worse) taking them to hell. Only the spiritual powers of a priest or the physical prowess of a strongman could exorcise such a nightmarish spook.

A very uncomfortable characteristic of the *afturganga* is his tendency to walk again before anyone knows he has died. One such was the Deacon of Dark River, who in the 18th century drowned on his way to his girlfriend's to take her to a dance. He nonetheless turned up, a little late, and the unsuspecting girl got on the back of his horse. As they rode through the night, she overheard him muttering:

*The moon hides, as death rides,*
*Do you not see the white mark*
*On my brow, Garun, Garun.*

Fortunately, this ditty held two clues to his true nature: firstly, ghosts always repeat things, and secondly they cannot say "God". The girl's name was Guðrún, and Guð is "God" in Icelandic. The terrified Guðrún managed to jump off seconds before the ghostly rider and horse vanished into an open grave leading straight to hell. She was never the same again, and some say she lost her mind completely.

Other forms of ghost are the *fylgja* or familiar spirit, and its close relations the *móri* and the *skotta*. These are shadowy, malevolent spirits, and when they are ill-wished onto a man, it is said that they will follow him and his descendants unto the ninth generation.

Then there are the trolls – elemental beings who, fortunately, turn into stone if they are caught outside in daylight. All of Iceland is dotted with trolls who stayed out just that little bit too long – including the great stone troll-cow, Hvítserkur, caught having a drink of sea water just off the northwest coast.

## The hidden people

All things considered, Icelanders probably prefer their more attractive neighbours from the other world, the elves. Like Hollywood filmstars, they look like humans – but are richer, more glamorous and usually completely amoral. According to one legend, the elves were the children that Eve hadn't finished washing when God came to visit; they were not fit to be seen, so she had to hide them. Thus, they are also known as the Hidden People, and with good reason: only 5 percent of Icelanders have actually met one. Nevertheless, elves are held in the highest regard.

In legend, those who visit the elves and survive the experience return to the human world laden with riches but often strangely changed. In nearly all cases, the elves decide when and where they will be seen by humans. Usually, this is when they need assistance. Human women, it is said, are sometimes fetched by distraught elfen husbands to act as midwives to elf-mothers having difficulties in childbirth.

One 20th-century figure to have had an encounter with the Hidden People was trade-union leader Tryggvi Emilsson, who, as a young man, was saved from death by an elf-maiden after he had fallen down a gully. Her beauty, he said, haunted him for the rest of his life. Elf-women have been known to have even more intimate physical relations with human men, and are obviously more liberated than their human counterparts, often leaving their lovers holding the baby, as it were. (It is of some consolation that these semi-supernatural offspring are usually highly talented and handsome.) Elf-men, on the other hand, make conscientious and kind lovers, according to legend.

The elves of Iceland are treated with great respect. The rocks and hills in which they make their homes are diligently preserved: great harm traditionally comes to those who tamper with these elusive neighbours. Roads skirt round well-known elf-hills. One such is the road that runs from Reykjavík to the suburb of Kópavogur, which is actually called Álfhólsvegur, or Elf-Hill Road. On a street in the town of Grundarfjördur, a rock stands between the houses numbered 82 and 86 – the elves live at number 84.

Despite these superstitious gestures, Dr Árni Björnsson says that true believers in elves and ghosts comprise a tiny minority in Iceland. "Most of us do not actively believe in these things, but on the other hand we are reluctant to deny their existence," he says. "It is really a form of scepticism. We live in a land which is highly unpredictable. So we have learnt not to rely too much on the factual evidence of our senses." And, of course, the existence of elves in our modern world is such a nice idea. "People think it would be fun if they did exist, so they pretend to believe in them. Unlike other nations, we aren't in the least ashamed of it. In fact, we are rather proud of our elves." He adds: "Iceland is a big country. We've plenty of room for neighbours of all kinds."

Indeed, this laissez-faire attitude is ensconced in folk tradition and the sagas. The medieval bishop, Guðmundur the Good, once set off to consecrate Drangey, to drive away the multitude of ghouls, fiends and devils that haunted this island. As he went about his holy work, a voice rang out from the rocks. "Consecrate no more, Guðmundur," it cried. "The wicked need some place to be." The bishop sensibly took the point and quickly returned to shore.

*House graveyard in the Westman Islands.*

*A lighthouse in the midst of the isolation.*

# GRÍMSEY

Situated on the Arctic Circle, the island of Grímsey is a remote outpost, home to huge colonies of sea birds and just 90 islanders.

The folk on the remote, weather-beaten island of **Grímsey** ㉔ tell the tale of a local minister who discovered that the Arctic Circle ran right through his house. He decided that it not only bisected his bedroom, it bisected his bed: the minister slept on one side of the Arctic Circle, his wife on the other, and rarely did either cross the great divide.

The apocryphal story is told and retold in various forms (sometimes it's a minister, sometimes an old magistrate), but it sums up the tongue-in-cheek attitude the Grímsey islanders have to the Arctic Circle – an imaginary line which, to the outside world, puts Grímsey on the map. They can only regard with some bemusement anyone who makes the pilgrimage all the way to their remote polar outpost just to say that they've walked across a geographical abstraction. "How did it feel?" someone might ask with good-natured concern. "Have your feet turned blue yet?"

But, although its location on latitude 66°30' N may still be Grímsey's claim to fame, a steady stream of travellers are finding out that the island has more concrete attractions to offer. The sheer isolation of this tiny piece of land, with a population of only 90 souls, has its own peculiarly Icelandic appeal: the scenery is wild and beautiful, the birdlife extraordinary, while the people remain beguilingly eccentric. And Grímsey has

one of the strangest histories in Iceland, settled by chess-playing Vikings and supported by a 19th-century American millionaire. (And, frankly, it is quite fun to know that you're standing on the Arctic Circle.)

## Island of chess players

Grímsey was first settled in the 10th century by a Viking named Grímur (hence the name "Grím's island"), whose descendants took the Icelandic obsession with chess to new extremes. Tradition has it that long summers and

**Main Attractions**
Sandvík
Clifftop Walks
Standing in the Arctic Circle

*The coastline of wild Grímsey.*

*Chess has a rich history in Iceland.*

*A place of worship.*

longer winters were spent devoted to the game, with some players spending weeks confined to their beds devising new stratagems. Chess was more important than life itself: it was not unknown for a player to fling himself into the sea rather than bear the shame of defeat.

Perhaps not surprisingly, Grímsey did not prosper as a fishing port. On one occasion in the 18th century, the entire male population except for the minister was lost in a single fishing accident (perhaps they were exhausted from playing chess). According to folklore, the minister took responsibility for repopulating the island himself.

Then, in the late 19th century, the island's eccentric reputation was brought to the attention of a wealthy North American named Daniel Willard Fiske – prominent journalist, Old Icelandic scholar, friend of both the Icelandic independence hero Jón Sigurðsson and the writer Mark Twain, and, in 1857, chess champion of the US. Although Willard Fiske only glimpsed the shores of Grímsey as he passed it in a steamship, the island fired his vivid imagination and he decided to take its local population under his wing.

First Fiske sent the essentials: a gift of marble chess sets to each of the farms on the island. These were followed by masses of firewood and a bequest to finance the island's first school and library. Finally, on his death in 1904, Fiske left the inhabitants of Grímsey $12,000 – at that time the most money anyone had ever given to Iceland. Today, Fiske is still revered on Grímsey as a sort of secular saint. His birthday on 11 November is celebrated with a cake buffet in the community hall. Fiske's portrait still watches over the islanders from the library wall, but unfortunately, Grímsey hasn't kept up the love of chess. Hardly anybody plays it – these days, the favourite game is surfing the internet.

## Last stop before the Pole

Until the 1930s, the only way to reach Grímsey was on the mail ship that left Akureyri once every six months (you could return six months later, provided bad weather didn't prevent the ship from running).

## A NATION OF CHESS PLAYERS

Probably introduced by the first settlers in the 9th century, chess was a common pastime in Iceland through the Middle Ages, as shown by numerous old expressions from the game which have been preserved in everyday speech. When Willard Fiske visited in 1879, he found eager players all over the country. Fiske published Iceland's first chess magazine, providing a theoretical training ground that guided the game into the realms of organised sport. In 1958, Friðrik Ólafsson became the nation's first grandmaster. The next generation was inspired by the "Match of the Century", which took place in Reykjavík in 1972, when Bobby Fischer wrested the world championship from Boris Spassky. Among the enthusiasts were Helgi Ólafsson and Margeir Pétursson, then in their teens and now both international grandmasters. In their wake came a further eight Icelandic grandmasters, bringing the country's total to 11.

Bobby Fischer became a fugitive from the US in 1992, after breaking sanctions by playing chess in the former Yugoslavia. In 2005, Iceland controversially gave Fischer Icelandic citizenship so that he could avoid facing criminal charges in the US. And so one of the greatest chess-players of all time lived out his last three years in a Reykjavík suburb, and was buried in Icelandic soil in a quiet country cemetery just outside Selfoss.

Today, there is a year-round ship service three days a week (Mon, Wed, and Fri), taking about three hours each way from Dalvík. Light aircraft flights from Akureyri (daily in summer, three days a week the rest of the year) take only 25 minutes to cover the 41km (25 miles). Arriving by plane in Grímsey is a truly memorable experience since, more often than not, the plane flies low over the runway before attempting to land, in an effort to chase away the hundreds of birds which gather here to feed (see page 258).

Both the plane and the ferry allow same day return trips – which, until 1991, when a new guesthouse opened, was just as well, since the only accommodation previously had been on the floor of the community centre. (Camping is permitted if you site your tent discreetly.)

Getting acquainted with the island is not difficult. There are 10 old farms on the island, but most of the inhabitants live in the "village" of **Sandvík** – the name for the 15 houses lined up along the harbour.

After World War II, Grímsey still didn't have electricity, there was little fresh water and the occasional case of scurvy was reported among the islanders. Modern fishing techniques have brought affluence here – the township may have a rather scruffy look, thanks to the relentless beating it takes from the weather, but the houses are modern, there are satellite dishes to pick up television, greenhouses to grow vegetables and a large indoor swimming pool. Although there is only one road on Grímsey – 3km (2 miles) long – the island boasts a handful of private cars and several tractors.

The Grímsey **community centre** can be identified by the mural on its walls. Built on the site of the old school financed by Fiske, it still contains the library, original photographs of the benefactor and the only one of the 11 marble chess sets still in existence. Nobody seems to know where the rest have gone.

A short walk west of the village is the whitewashed, late-19th-century wooden **church**. Above the altar is a replica of Leonardo da Vinci's *Last Supper*, painted by a mainland artist, Arngrímur

**TIP**

The island is only 4km (2.5 miles) by 2km (1.2 miles) in size, and can be circumambulated in about 5 hours. A hiking trail begins from the airport and strikes out across towards the island's west coast and several sheer bird-cliffs before gradually descending towards the harbour, where it joins the main road. It's now a straightforward stroll past the church and the village store back towards the airstrip.

*The last propeller plane in the run-up to Christmas arrives.*

Gíslason. The nearby **parsonage**, which was built in 1909, is now maintained by a layman – Grímsey pays for a minister to come every three months from Akureyri (the doctor turns up more frequently – every three weeks). It's long been rumoured on the island that the Arctic Circle runs right through the middle of the priest's bed, putting an icy division between him and his wife. However, in reality, this is extremely unlikely since the Arctic Circle is not constant but is currently creeping northwards, due to the earth's uneven orbit, at a rate of 15 metres (50ft) or so every year. It won't be for another 10,000–20,000 years that the northward movement will stop, by which time the Circle will have reached 68 degrees north, well to the north of Grímsey's geographical position, and will then start moving slowly south again.

Along the coast are the traditional fish-drying racks.

## Dive-bombers of the Arctic Circle

Heading back to the eastern end of the island, the road runs straight into the bitumen runway of the airport (where the Básar guesthouse, one of two places for formal accommodation, is also to be found). The runway is carpeted by resting sea birds – before some landings or take-offs, a car or tractor is driven up and down in an attempt to shoo away these potential hazards to aircraft. (On departure from Grímsey, it's not uncommon for birds to strike the aircraft's wings as they and it take off at the same time).

Usually that's the end of the matter. Should you be visiting in June or July, however, the scene is more like something from Alfred Hitchcock's *The Birds*. That's when the Arctic terns are nesting all over the island, and anyone coming near a bird's young is fair game for a dive-bomb attack. The screeching call *kría! kría! kría!* (which is actually the bird's name in Icelandic) is the prelude to a possible peck on the back of the head – which is why, in this season, everyone wears a thick hat (a leather glove under a beany or beret is recommended) and carries a big stick (the Básar Guesthouse will lend out plastic rods to guests for self-defence).

*Midwinter aurora.*

On the northern side of the runway is the Grímsey road sign, theoretically marking the location of the Arctic Circle. Arrows point to various major world cities (including New York: 4,445km/2,763 miles; Sydney: 16,317km/10,027 miles; London: 1,949km/1,225 miles).

A path leads away from the airport towards 100-metre (330ft) cliff faces, which can be followed completely around the island. Soon the trail disappears beneath a bed of thick, matted grass, which seems to glow green against the blue of the sea. The polka-dot of yellow weeds finishes off the colourful effect (there are a total of some 100 species of flowering plant on Grímsey).

The cliffs on the north and east sides of the island are where the most spectacular birdlife can be found, the large sea-bird colonies creating a din that is little short of cacophonous. Around 60 species of bird have visited the island, with 36 choosing to nest there. There is a large puffin community, and it is quite possible to come within a few metres of these birds (but don't walk too close to the edge of the cliffs, since underground puffin nests can be accidentally crushed). There are fulmars, kittiwakes, gulls and Arctic terns, and Grímsey was one of the last places in Iceland where the little auk, which usually nests closer to the Pole, came to breed (although they haven't been seen for the last few years).

Although it is located on the Arctic Circle, Grímsey's summers and winters are never as extreme as one would imagine: the June midnight is bright but never blinding, and there are about four hours of vague light in December (provided the weather isn't very cloudy, that is, in which case it stays dark).

Even so, life on the island is still tough. In the recent past, schoolchildren, who study on the mainland from the age of 14, almost always returned to Grímsey. However, as in many remote places in Iceland, the population is steadily decreasing and is almost half what it was in the 1980s. Fishing and fish-processing bring in plenty of money; and the wealth stays, since there's nothing to spend your money on here; but it takes a certain kind of gritty, eccentric, indomitable spirit to stick life out on the edge of the world.

**EAT**

There are only a couple of places to eat on Grímsey. **Básar Guesthouse** (tel: 467 3103; www.gistiheimilid basar.is) makes simple but tasty home-cooked meals for its guests, if requested in advance. **Krían** (tel: 467 3112; open daily in summer, otherwise upon request) is a café down by the harbour serving something-and-chips and other fry-ups.

*Arctic terns in flight.*

*The Hverir geothermal field looks almost extra-terrestrial.*

Lake Mývatn.

# LAKE MÝVATN

This outstandingly beautiful area has the twin
attractions of the serene lake at Mývatn, one of
Iceland's major breeding grounds for birds, and
spectacular volcanic activity.

**S**itting just to the west of the Mid-Atlantic Ridge that is slowly tearing Iceland apart, the Lake Mývatn district (www.visitmyvatn.is) is one of the most volcanically active regions on earth. Created by a powerful basaltic lava eruption 2,300 years ago, the lake and its surrounding landscapes are dominated by curiously shaped volcanic landforms such as pillars of lava. The surrounding wetlands are a favourite breeding and feeding spot for many varieties of waterfowl, especially ducks, attracted here by a plentiful supply of food in the form of the countless insects which congregate here in the summer months. In this respect, Mývatn is unusual: Iceland's relatively low summer temperatures and strong winds do not provide a ready habitat for insects.

In the mid-1970s, earthquakes centred here were felt in the entire north of the country, with lava erupting from nearby Mount Krafla over several years to spectacular effect. Activity continued through the early 1980s and today there are almost daily subterranean rumblings (although they are mostly too small to be noticed except by scientific instruments). Nowhere else in Iceland can you see the same combination of craters, fresh lava fields, hot springs, geysers and bubbling mud pools.

Meanwhile, the lake's natural beauty and role as a wildlife breeding ground led to it being set aside as a national conservation area in 1974 – a status that actually gives it more protection than a National Park. The lake is a veritable oasis on the fringes of Iceland's bleak northern deserts, supporting, among other things, the world's largest population of breeding ducks. As a result, Mývatn has established itself as one of Iceland's most visited tourist attractions outside of Reykjavík and the "Golden Circle", and is a place

**Main Attractions**

Birdwatching and Sigurgeir
   Bird Museum
Skútustaðagígar
   Pseudocraters
Höfði
Hverfell
Mývatn Nature Baths
   (Jarðböðin)
Hverir Geothermal Field
Leirhnjúkur Crater

*Steaming rocks at Hverir.*

*Captivating landscape at Leihrhnjúkur.*

that has been known to keep nature lovers occupied for weeks. And while offering plenty to explore in its own right, it also makes a good base for trips to the Northeast and to Askja in the interior.

## In search of sulphur

Although the winters are long and cold, covering the lake with ice for seven months of the year, Mývatn enjoys more sunshine and receives less rain than almost anywhere else in the country. As a result, it has been popular with settlers from the Saga Age onwards: in 1908, archaeologists dug up a Norse longhouse whose wall was over 40 metres (130ft) in length, and may have contained a temple of Thor.

Dating their ancestry back to those days are the Reykjahlíð family, whose farm covers the whole surrounding area – at some 6,000 sq km (2,300 sq miles) in size, it is the biggest farm in Iceland and more than twice the size of Luxembourg. The family's days of glory were in the 14th century, when sulphur was mined from Námaskarð on their land and sent to Europe to be made into gunpowder. This remote corner of Iceland helped keep the world's wars rolling until the 19th century, when other sulphur sources were found.

Farming in the area also prospered despite the devastating eruption of the Leirhnjúkur crater (10km/6 miles northeast of Reykjahlíð). The "Mývatn-fires" lasted for five years, from 1724 to 1729, wiped out three farms and wrecked Reykjahlíð's buildings – but created some of the bizarre lava formations that now make the area so fascinating.

Today the farm is still working, although the owners have invested in the tourist business and allow visitors access to almost every part of the property. Travellers started arriving in numbers to see Mývatn and its surroundings in the early 20th century, and the family built the first hotel, the **Hotel Reykjahlíð**, in the 1940s – it has since housed everyone from Prince Harald of Norway to a steady stream of backpackers. In 1968, a diatomite plant was opened at Bjarnarflag near Mývatn, and a small village, also known as **Reykjahlíð ❶** sprang up around the hotel northeast of the lake to become the service centre of the area.

With hotels, camping grounds, a supermarket and a bar-restaurant, Reykjahlíð is a functional base for travellers. It also has a **church**; although it was rebuilt in 1972, it is on the site of the original church that was in the path of the lava flow in 1729 and seemed certain to be destroyed. Miraculously, the lava parted literally at the church door and flowed on either side of the wooden building, an event that the devout ascribed to divine intervention.

Next to the Samkaup supermarket and petrol station, the **visitors' centre**, run by the Icelandic Nature Conservation Agency, has information on routes around the area and its natural history, with some excellent lava exhibits.

## Circuit around the lake

A narrow road circles Lake Mývatn, connecting the various points of interest. The lake itself is 37 sq km (14 sq miles) in area, making it the fourth largest in Iceland, but unusually shallow – the average depth is only 2 metres (7ft), with the deepest point only 4.5 metres (15ft). This shallowness allows the sun's rays to reach the bottom, so creating a thriving growth of algae and plankton, including rare marimo balls – globes of green algae (*Aegagropila linnaei*) that occur in only four places in the world. The lake contains 50 islets.

The name Mývatn actually means "midge lake" and, for long stretches of the summer, clouds of these tiny flying insects can make any visit a misery. Billions usually emerge in June and August to dive into eyes, noses and ears with relentless energy. They are often joined by biting blackflies, so make sure you bring some insect repellent. (Head nets are, not surprisingly, sold in most shops.) It is cold comfort to learn that the midges are crucial to the lake's ecosystem: their corpses fertilise the lakeside and the larvae are a staple for birds and fish.

The surfeit of midges as fodder has made the River Laxá, which flows through Mývatn, the source of Iceland's biggest salmon (they spawn in the lower part of the lake). Mývatn also offers the best trout fishing in the country.

## The fields of fire

Heading north from Reykjahlíð, Route 87 crosses the lava flow from the 1720s that dominates the topography of the village and the northern landscape of the lake. Called **Eldhraun** ("fire lava"), this barren landscape gives a glimpse of the desert that Route 87 runs into – so devoid of life that NASA sent its Apollo 11 crew for training missions here in the late 1960s. Keep an eye out on the left-hand side for a giant bubble of dried lava, where the surface layer has been cracked like a huge egg.

Turning left onto Route 848, the landscape becomes much greener and quickly reaches the marshes of the **conservation area**. This is the

**TIP**

A great way to get to grips with the landscapes around the lake is to take a sightseeing flight from the airstrip at Reykjahlíð with the Mýflug airline (www.myflug.is). Flights operate during the summer and require a minimum of two passengers. Tours vary in duration from twenty minutes to two hours, with the longer flights also taking in Krafla, Dettifoss, Ásbyrgi and the Jökulsárgljúfur canyon.

*Bird-watching devotees swear that the bridge on the Ring Road over the Laxá River is Iceland's premier location for spotting birds.*

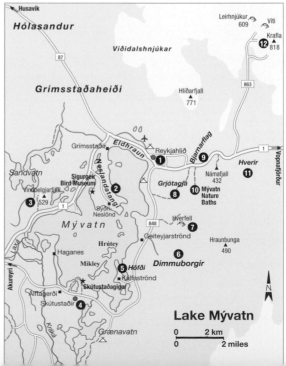

Lake Mývatn

*Höfði reserve.*

*There are easy walking routes in the area.*

main breeding ground for the lake's birds, and during the nesting season (15 May–20 July) its shoreline is off-limits. Around 115 species of birds have been recorded around the lake, including 28 species of duck, with 15 breeding here regularly. Most of the birds are summer migrants, arriving from late April onwards. The tufted duck and the greater scaup are the most prolific species, but the beautiful Barrow's goldeneye, red-breasted merganser and the teal are also common. The Barrow's goldeneye is one of the few birds to spend the winter at Mývatn, carefully choosing ice-free areas of the lake which are kept open by warm currents. Virtually the entire European population of the species breeds here. In addition to ducks, the unusual red-necked phalarope, Slavonian grebe and whooper swan are common visitors, as are the great northern diver and red-throated diver. Incidentally, there is a long tradition in the Mývatn area of collecting birds' eggs for private consumption, though local people are sure to follow the age-old tradition of always leaving at least

four eggs in the nest for incubation. For more information, ornithologists should head for the **Sigurgeir Bird Museum** (www.fuglasafn.is; daily mid-May noon–7pm, daily June–Aug 9am–6pm, daily Sept–Oct noon–5pm, daily Nov–mid-May 2–4pm) on the **Neslandatangi peninsula ②**, which almost cuts the lake in two. The low-lying museum houses the private collection of avid bird- and egg-collector Sigurgeir, and also acts as his memorial: he died in 1999 at the age of 37. The museum contains an example of every species of Icelandic bird, except for the grey phalarope. There's a calm café with huge windows overlooking the lake – particularly serene at dusk – and bird hides nearby.

South of the conservation area, the 529-metre (1,735ft) peak of **Vindbelgjarfjall ③**, seen to the right, can be climbed in a couple of hours for views of the lake. Beyond that, another smaller lake, **Sandvatn**, is probably the best place in the area to see gyrfalcons.

South of here, the road now runs into the Ring Road. On the southern shore of the lake is Mývatn's secondary service centre of **Skútustaðir ④**, with a petrol station, hotel, church and café-restaurant.

From here, there is an easy hour-long path around the **Skútustaðagígar pseudocraters**. These were formed when water was trapped beneath flowing lava, boiled and burst up through the surface, creating what looks like volcanic cones. Some were formed so recently that their sides are still charred.

## Picnic promontory

One of the most sheltered and relaxing spots on the lakeside is **Höfði ⑤**, a forested promontory that has been turned into a reserve, with a small admission fee. There is a vaguely fairy-tale atmosphere to the place, with paths running through flower-covered lava outcrops and forests of birch trees. Large rocks by the lakeside rocks also provide ideal picnic hideaways.

It is also an excellent spot for bird watching.

A turn-off to the right leads to **Dimmuborgir** ❻ ("black castles"), a vast, 2,000-year-old field of contorted volcanic pillars, some extending as high as 20 metres (65ft). There is a helpful visitor centre and café (June–Aug daily 9am–10pm) here, offering guided walks in the area. A viewing platform looks out over the expanse, and visitors can wander about among the haunting arches, caves and natural tunnels. The most famous formation is **Kirkjan** (the Church), a cave that looks like the doorway of a Gothic cathedral, and a 3-metre (10ft) hole that provides an amusing photo opportunity.

Further along the same road is the looming 1,000-metre (3,280ft)-wide crater of **Hverfell** ❼, formed in an eruption 2,500 years ago and these days likened to a giant football stadium. A steep path runs up the side of the crater, which is made entirely of loose volcanic rubble, or tephra. Hverfell's rim provides one of the most sweeping views of the Mývatn area.

En route back to Reykjahlíð, a track to the right leads to **Grjótagjá** ❽, an underground hot spring made by a buckle in the earth, about 1km (0.5 miles) from the main road. The green waters may feel tepid to the touch, but below the surface they can be scalding, so swimming is forbidden.

A popular tourist attraction and guesthouse, the unique **Cowshed Café** (Vogafjós; www.vogafjos.is; June–Aug daily 7.30am–11pm) backs onto a milking shed, so you can watch the working life of the farm while you sample Icelandic ice-cream.

## Volcanologists' paradise

The Ring Road running east of Reykjahlíð immediately leads to a completely different landscape, a desolate, sandy plain of mixed orange and brown hues known as **Bjarnarflag** ❾. Further on is the site of Mývatn's former diatomite plant, which once processed microscopic fossils (diatoms) from the lake floor into a porous material used in filtering systems, amongst other applications; on the right is a brick factory, putting the local excess of

*The Mývatn Nature Baths.*

*The way down to Grjótagjá, an underground hot spring.*

*Walking is a great way to explore the area.*

tephra to good use. However, of more interest to visitors, the **Mývatn Nature Baths** ❿ (Jarðbóðin við Mývatn; www. myvatnnaturebaths.is; daily June–Aug 9am–midnight, Sept–May noon–10pm) are the north's answer to the Blue Lagoon. This sublime open-air geothermal pool lies just off the Ring Road and is an altogether more agreeable experience than its more famous cousin on the Reykjanes peninsula. There are far fewer bathers here, giving you the opportunity to loll undisturbed in the aquamarine waters as long as you like. The water comes from a local geothermal source and is cooled to around 38–40°C (100–104°F) to make it pleasant for bathing. In addition to the main pool, there are two steam saunas and (of course) hot-pots.

An overwhelming stench of sulphur greets travellers as the road climbs over the ridge of **Námafjall**, whose series of cracks – the largest appeared as recently as 1975 – betray its location plumb on the Mid-Atlantic Ridge. The Námafjall geothermal field has had 14 boreholes sunk into it over the past 50 years, the highest recorded

temperature being 320°C (608°F) at a depth of 1.8km (1 mile). Steam and mud craters formed in this field during the Mývatn-fires of 1724, and new fissures spread south into the area in April 1728. At the pass is a parking area with views over the lake, and stretching out on the other side is the famous geothermal field of **Hverir** ⓫ – perhaps one of Iceland's most infernal and fascinating sights. Walkways run across the multicoloured clay of the area, through dozens of bubbling mud pits and steaming vents. The surface here is particularly thin, and at some places likely to crumble, so to avoid being boiled alive in a mud pot, keep well within the marked paths.

## Man-made disaster

A rough dirt road leads 7km (4 miles) north to the **Krafla area** ⓬, named after one of the mountains at the centre of the region. Pipes from the Krafla geothermal power plant form a metal doorway to the area, which is strangely appropriate: the construction of the plant in 1973, with its many bore holes into the earth's crust, is considered by

some scientists to be responsible for triggering the eruptions that began here in 1975 – the first since the 1700s. Between 3 and 8km (2–5 miles) beneath the Krafla field lies a magma reservoir which is the source of local volcanic activity in the area. Magma builds up in the reservoir, causing the earth to rise, until it is released as rock intrusions or volcanic eruptions, resulting in the earth's surface sinking again.

The activity in the early 1970s, known as the "Krafla-fires" began with a dramatic spurt of molten lava that lit up Reykjahlíð by night. Some 17 eruptions followed in the next decade, but luckily the lava all flowed away from the small village and no major damage was done. However, volcanologists are expecting Krafla to blow again any time.

A stern warning sign (volcanic hazard zone – do not enter) at the first parking area here was put up during the 1984 eruptions to keep tourists away, but had the opposite effect: hundreds gathered here to watch the fireworks. The warning sign has now been removed, and during the summer there is still a stream of visitors who go out to the black, partly warm lava field of the Krafla caldera that was spat up from the earth during the 1970s and 1980s, and the colourful crater of **Leirhnjúkur** (formed during the explosions of the 1720s). If you can forget the disconcerting possibility of being blown to kingdom come, this whole lifeless, primeval area gives as good a glimpse of the freshly formed earth as anyone is likely to get.

Further on, a second parking area sits at the base of **Víti** ("hell"), a dingy-brown explosion crater – now thought to be inactive. Its 320-metre (1,050ft)-wide bowl contains a pool of cold blue-green water (not to be confused with the other Víti crater further south, whose turquoise waters are warm and full of bathers – see page 311). It is close to Mount Krafla itself, which, far from being a classic volcanic cone, is the rim of a larger caldera that has been worn and exploded almost beyond recognition. A walking trail leads around the crater rim. Víti was the initial source of the 1724 volcanic eruptions which blighted crop production for years afterwards.

*Hverfell crater,*
*1 kilometre across.*

# OUTDOOR PURSUITS

**The vast open spaces and wild landscapes of Iceland offer a wealth of opportunities for all who love the great outdoors.**

Iceland is an adventure holiday destination *par excellence*. Mountains, glaciers, lakes and thundering waterfalls are all here in abundance, and with its expansive wilderness areas and clear air, ever increasing numbers of visitors want to get out and experience all that wild nature for themselves. And there is a great deal on offer, from gentle hikes and horse-riding excursions to more demanding pursuits such as ice-climbing, white-water rafting and enough wilderness adventures to satisfy the most demanding free spirit.

One of the advantages of a rugged, sparsely populated country (about three people per sq km) is that you can really get away from it all. If you want peace and solitude, this is where you can be sure of finding it. Trekking holidays – usually undertaken as an organised group through a specialist agency – are the classic way to experience remote and roadless regions. Iceland's glaciers and icecaps are another major draw for those in search of a different kind of experience, be it skidooing, ice-climbing, cross-country skiing or simply walking in the pristine environment.

A great way to reach places where no vehicle (even a 4x4) can easily take you is on horseback. Riding all day among deserted valleys and mountains, fording rivers, leading your second mount which carries supplies and bedroll, you will gain real insight into the way Icelanders used to live.

For more details on what's available and a list of tour operators, see page 327.

*Boy diving in the East Fjords.*

*Lighthouse on the Reykjanes Peninsula.*

*Don't tackle the glaciers without walking boots.*

*Bathing in the Blue Lagoon.*

## GETTING INTO HOT WATER

Thanks to Iceland's lively geology, the country has an abundance of naturally heated geothermal water...and Icelanders take every opportunity to channel this water into their beloved swimming pools. Legally, every child must be taught how to swim, and students cannot graduate unless they have mastered this basic skill.

There are over 120 (mostly outdoor) municipal swimming baths in Iceland, each with its own character and quirks, and most of them filled with volcanically heated water. And then, of course, there are the naturally occurring hot springs, rivers and mountain pools known only to the initiated, plus mineral-rich seawater spas, such as the Blue Lagoon, whose waters are the by-product of a geothermal power plant.

A particularly Icelandic curiosity and one found in most municipal baths is the "hot-pot", a small circular pool whose water steams at a deliciously high temperature (between 37°C and 42°C). These are the buzzing social centres of Icelandic life, where people gather for conversation, gossip and even business meetings. As Icelandic pools are filled with constantly flowing water, chemical cleaners are rarely used. In order to keep the water as clean as possible, all swimmers must take a shower in the nude before entering – which can come as something of a shock to the more bashful tourist.

*Mountain-biking at Hverir.*

*Camping is a delight in Iceland.*

*Walking in the East Fjords.*

# THE NORTHEAST

In this remote and little-visited region you can see sea birds and whales in their natural, unspoilt environment, and visit the unexpectedly lush Jökulsárgljúfur area, the northern section of Vatnajökull National Park.

**Main Attractions**
Húsavík whale-watching tours
Jökulsárgljúfur
Ásbyrgi Canyon
Dettifoss
Vopnafjörður

*The interior of Húsavík Church.*

**B**ypassed by the Ring Road, the northeast is one of Iceland's most isolated areas. Only two places usually pull in the crowds: the town of Húsavík, Iceland's "whale-watching capital"; and the Jökulsárgljúfur section of Vatnajökull National Park, whose canyons and waterfalls feature on a thousand postcards. Very few people continue on to explore the rugged coastline. It's true that tourist attractions as such are few and far between; but if you're looking to explore off-the-beaten-track Iceland, this is it. Here, you're guaranteed a rare insight into what it's like to live on the very edge of the Arctic, in a part of Iceland as obscure to most Reykjavíkers as it is to foreigners.

Transport services are poor, roads can be bad, and there are few good hotels; yet the coastal route has a number of attractions for those with their own vehicle and an interest in finding out what lies around the next lonely headland. Dozens of atmospheric fishing villages cling precariously to this shore just south of the Arctic Circle. Exploring these quiet, conservative outposts and the craggy cliffs and wilderness areas around them reveals the harsh seafaring world that is in many ways Iceland's backbone.

## Gateway to the northeast

The transport artery of the region, following the whole coastline, is Route 85. Approaching from Akureyri or Lake Mývatn, this road runs through the Aðaldalur valley right down to the shoreline of Skjálfandi ("shivering fjord"), an expanse of sand dotted by small lakes with an impressive wall of mountains as a backdrop.

Rows of picturesque fish-drying racks by the roadside fittingly announce the main town in the region, **Húsavík ❶** (population 2,200). The name "house bay" was given by the Swedish Viking Garðar Svavarsson, who journeyed to Iceland in the late 860s after his mother had seen it in a dream.

Long before the official First Settler, Ingólfur Arnarson, set foot on the island, Garðar spent a winter at Húsavík. When he sailed away, his slave Náttfari and two others were left behind, settling down across the bay from Húsavík (the site can be seen from town). The *Landnámabók* mentions the incident, but we can only speculate as to why the book does not consider them to be Iceland's first settlers – perhaps because Náttfari was a slave; or perhaps because he did not stake his land-claim correctly.

Húsavík today is a tidy and agreeable town set above the first-rate harbour that provides for its existence: fishing and fish-processing are still major industries. The view of the colourful trawlers, murky black waters and snow-spattered granite mountains across the bay is particularly impressive. However, it is another harbour-reliant activity that draws busloads of tourists to this trim little town: Húsavík is Iceland's "whale-watching capital" thanks to its location on Skjálfandi Bay, a plankton- and fish-rich feeding ground. The two local companies who operate **whale-watching tours** claim a 98 percent success rate for cetacean sightings. There are a huge variety off the coast, with the most commonly sighted species being minke, humpback, white-beaked dolphins and harbour porpoises; luckier travellers might glimpse sei whales, northern bottlenose whales, fin whales, killer whales, pilot whales or even blue whales.

Before your whale-watching trip, it's well worth a visit to the excellent harbourside **Húsavík Whale Museum** (www.whalemuseum.is; May–Sept daily 8.30am–6.30pm, Oct–Apr weekdays 9am–2pm), which has exhibits on the history of whales and whaling in Iceland, and on whale species and biology; plus there's a gallery of whale skeletons.

Dominating the town is an unusual cross-shaped **church**, with a 26-metre (85ft) spire and modern sculptures in the garden. The church, built in 1907, was designed by the Icelandic architect Rögnvaldur Ólafsson and made from Norwegian timber. It is among Iceland's most attractive churches and seats about 450 people. When it was built there were only 500 people living in the parish. The

*Learn about these colossal mammals at Húsavík's Whale Museum.*

impressive altarpiece, depicting Lazarus raised from the dead, was painted in 1931 by Sveinn Þórarinsson from the neighbouring county of Kelduhverfi.

Húsavík's other museum, **Safna-húsið** (www.husmus.is; June–Sept daily 10am–6pm, mid-Sept–May Mon–Fri 10am–4pm) is the best in the northeast: prize exhibits include a replica of the 1584 Guðbrandur's Bible (the first translation of the Old and New Testaments into Icelandic, still considered the most ambitious publishing project ever undertaken in Iceland); and the polar bear that floated from Greenland to Grímsey island in 1973, only to be greeted by a bullet in the skull. Centrally located, the Exploration Museum (www.explorationmuseum.com; 2-7pm) celebrates human exploration, from the prehistoric times to the space age. The exposition includes photographs and artefacts from the Apollo Training Centre, near Húsavík, where US astronauts trained for their trip to the moon.

## Arctic vista

For a panoramic view over the whole Húsavík area, drive 1km (0.5 miles) north of town to the unmarked yellow gate on the right, then continue as far as your car can take you (only a four-wheel drive should attempt the full distance on this dangerously slippery road). There is a viewfinder at the top, from which you can spot two small islands in the bay: **Flatey** had over 100 inhabitants 50 years ago but has now been abandoned, while **Lundey** is crowded only with puffins. In puffin season (mid-April to mid-August) the two Húsavík whale-watching companies also offer tours that swing by to see these distinctive little birds.

From this point, the roads become dustier and road signs fewer. Lying north along Route 85 is the squat peninsula of **Tjörnes ❷**, whose 60-metre (200ft) cliff faces are renowned among geologists for their ancient fossils and easily visible geological strata (note that it is strictly forbidden to remove any fossils from this area). This well-known but difficult-to-find seashore site is reached by a slippery dirt road located just before **Hallbjarnarstaðir** farm, once the home of farmer Kári Sigurjónsson, who helped scientists

*Rubbery slices of preserved shark – hákarl.*

*Ásbyrgi canyon.*

to research shells. For further details, ask at the tourist desk in the Húsavík Whale Museum.

The road reaches the coast, then steeply descends the alarming cliff face at **Hallbjarnarstaðakambur Crest**, a dip on either side of the river where the layers of geological deposits are obvious to the naked eye and fossils of molluscs lie scattered across the ground. At the shore, look out for a large greenish slab of rock, not native to Iceland, thought to have arrived from Greenland on sea-ice.

East of Tjörnes, the plain of **Kelduhverfi** is made up of sandy glacial wash (similar to the larger *sandur* in the south –see page 197), and is at the northern point of the great rift zone where Iceland pulls itself in two. Volcanic activity in the 1970s was related to the eruptions at Krafla near Lake Mývatn. The whole area is at the mouth of the **Öxarfjörður** fjord. To the north of the highway is **Lake Víkingavatn** ③, an important nesting site for Slavonian grebes. The nearby farm of the same name has been occupied by descendants of the same family since the 1600s.

## Giant hoof print

The great attraction of the Northeast is **Jökulsárgljúfur** ④, the country's longest river canyon at 25km (16 miles). Its full name, meaning "glacial river canyon", is difficult for non-Icelanders to pronounce but can be referred to as Jökulsá Canyon – pronounced *yerkool-sow* (where "sow" rhymes with "cow"). Once private property within the huge Ás estate, the ravine and 150 sq km (58 sq miles) of the surrounding wilderness became the Jökulsárgljúfur National Park in 1973. In 2008, Jökulsárgljúfur became a part of the newly formed Vatnajökull National Park, which covers approximately 13,600 sq km of the country.

One of the area's gems is the great horseshoe-shaped canyon of **Ásbyrgi**, located almost immediately at the turn-off from Route 85. It's not hard to see why the first Viking settlers decided that the canyon had been formed by Sleipnir, the god Odin's flying horse, crashing a giant hoof into the earth. A 100-metre (330ft) cliff face makes a smooth, 1km (0.5-mile)-wide ring around a profuse carpet

### TIP

If you are planning to camp in the National Park, stock up at the Ásbyrgi petrol station and supermarket at the Ásbyrgi farm outside the park. This is the only place selling supplies within about 25km (15 miles).

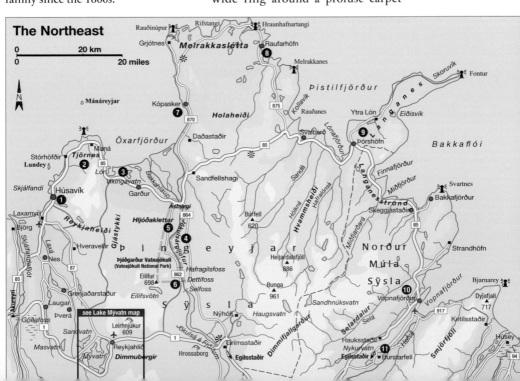

of greenery, while a smaller outcropping of cliffs (suitably called Eyjan or "island") rises in the middle.

Geologists believe that the canyon was formed relatively recently by a gigantic *jökulhlaup* or glacial flow from an eruption under the faraway icecap of Vatnajökull. The best view is from the furthest part of the canyon, which can be reached by walking 100 metres (330ft) west from the parking area. Turning east from the car park leads to a natural spring for drinking water, while taking the trail straight ahead ends up at a small lake full of ducks – their quacks echo around the natural amphitheatre.

Camping is permitted near the canyon's entrance, where an **information office** sells brochures detailing the park's main hiking routes. From here, a path leads to the top of the cliffs, climbing the canyon at its easiest point (although a rope is provided to help in the ascent). Once up, walkers can follow the cliffs, with excellent views over the whole canyon, or even take the trail as far south as Dettifoss – two days' walk away.

*Dettifoss waterfall, Europe's largest.*

No matter whether you walk for an hour or a day, this is one of the most pleasant hikes in Iceland, and if you get tired, just lie on the heather and eat some of the wild bilberries that grow abundantly in the canyon's summery climate.

## Towards Dettifoss

The rest of the park follows the powerful **Jökulsá á Fjöllum**, Iceland's second-longest river. Two roads run down the length of the park, one on either side of the river: the western road runs across some classic highland heather to **Vesturdalur** walking trails and the mysterious natural columns of **Hljóðaklettar** ❺ ("echoing rocks"), which form a ghostly stone forest that can be explored for hours. Further on, the road heads to **Hólmatungur**, a lush stretch along the river canyon, before crossing a suddenly barren desert landscape to Dettifoss.

The western road is deeply corrugated. While it is no longer classified as an F-road, two-wheel drives will need to crawl along at a gruelling 15kph (10mph); those with hire cars

should check with their hire company to see if travel along it is permitted. The eastern road is better, but after Dettifoss it becomes a jeep track.

**Dettifoss** ⑥ is Europe's largest waterfall, and the effort needed to reach it only seems to add to the excitement. There is nothing contained or artificial here, no wooden boardwalks or viewing balconies installed to detract from Nature. Clouds of spray can first be seen several kilometres away; from the car parks, visitors scramble over square blocks of grey lava, hearing the thunderous drumming before getting a glimpse of the falls. Some 500 cubic metres (17,700 cubic ft) of water spill over its ledges every second: although it is just 44 metres (145ft) tall, the sheer hypnotic volume of the flow makes this arguably Iceland's most awesome waterfall; Dettifoss featured in the opening scene of the 2012 Hollywood blockbuster *Prometheus*.

For those who want to see more falls, **Hafragilsfoss** is 2km (1 mile) downstream, and **Selfoss** about the same distance upstream.

## Cod coast

Heading north from Ásbyrgi leads to the northeast coast, Iceland's least visited area.

The first village, **Kópasker** ⑦, with a population of 122, can seem like a ghost town on most days. Like the other villages of the area, Kópasker thrived on the herring boom until the late 1960s, when herring migration patterns changed. Today its biggest employer is the farmers' co-operative Fjallalamb, a lamb-processing factory. The **Earthquake Centre** (Jun–Aug 1–7pm; free), in Kópasker, features installations and photographs concerning seismic activity from around the world and provides detailed information on the region's geography. In 1976, the town was struck by a powerful earthquake measuring 6.3 on the Richter scale, which caused extensive damage to several buildings and created two nearby lakes.

Beyond Kópasker is the flat, exposed peninsula of **Melrakkaslétta** ("fox plain"), where winds howl straight from the North Pole in winter and, on a bad day, summer can seem almost as dismal. The cliffs at **Rauðinúpur** are the only place in the world where it is possible to watch gannets nesting on land from below and the side rather than just from above. The northernmost part of mainland Iceland, **Hraunhafnartangi**, is marked by a lighthouse – the Arctic Circle lies just 2.5km (1.5 miles) offshore.

Even so, the remoteness of the barren plain, which can support very little agriculture, is perversely appealing. The coastline is covered with driftwood from as far away as Siberia and supports a good deal of birdlife.

Although **Raufarhöfn** ⑧ made the transition from herring to cod fishing in the 1970s, it never recaptured the great days when thousands of seasonal workers came to its factories. Today there are many more buildings and jetties than the population of 250 can use, and Raufarhöfn is losing more young people to the cities. In an attempt

*Northeast teens.*

*Café with a gorgeous view.*

to keep people in this economically important area, the Icelandic government built an airstrip, though it is no longer profitable to fly here (during long winters, the town had been completely cut off except by sea). Even so, the isolation of this town – which over long periods has not even had a local doctor – is extreme. In an attempt to attract tourists and boost the flagging economy, local hoteliers are building an Arctic version of Britain's famous Stonehenge on top of the hill which overlooks the village. The "Arctichenge" (www.arctichenge.com), based loosely on mythology from the Eddic poem *Völuspá*, and with its arches aligned to frame the midnight sun, is around 50 metres (160ft) in diameter. There are also six, 1 metre (3-ft) -high gates, each one facing different side of the world, to admire.

Southeast of Raufarhöfn is **Þórshöfn 9**, a pretty fishing village with a regular air link to Akureyri where it's worth breaking your coastal journey. Although there's little in the way of specific sights, the busy harbour provides a focus to the village. One of

*The Northern Lights glimmer above the Atlantic Ocean.*

the best hiking trails in the Northeast is now within easy reach.

From Þórshöfn, a dirt road heads northeast past the airstrip, into the windswept **Langanes** peninsula, whose marshy, cliff-bound expanses are the last word in Icelandic remoteness (it can only be visited by four-wheel drive or on foot). From the youth hostel and farm, **Ytra Lón**, the hike along the peninsula's edge passes a monument to some shipwrecked English sailors who managed to climb the 100-metre (330ft) cliffs only to die of exposure. There's a good chance you'll spot gyrfalcons on the way to the peninsula's tip, Fontur, marked by a lighthouse.

Back on the main road heading south, Bakkafjörður is an uneventful and very small fishing village that is typical of the area, which most visitors bypass en route for the more rewarding **Vopnafjörður 10**, set in a picturesque location at the head of its eponymous fjord. The snow-capped mountains behind the town trail downwards into the sea, complemented by the granite range across the fjord. Here the weather is better and the atmosphere more optimistic – the feeling is closer to the East Fjords than the northeast. Vopnafjörður has a poignant history as an emigration point – in the 19th century, around 2,000 Icelanders left for Canada from its harbour. The highlands around the village were also the inspiration for Halldor Laxness's best-known work, *Independent People*. A glitzier sort of fame was bestowed on Vopnafjörður in 1988, when local girl Linda Pétursdóttir became Miss World.

From Vopnafjörður, the highway runs away from the coast, passing **Bustarfell 11**, an excellent **Folk Museum** (http://safnabokin.is/museum/bustarfell-museum/; mid-June–mid-Sept weekdays 10am–5pm) in a 19th-century farmhouse. The road now climbs into the northeastern desert, passing a viewing platform over **Lake Nykurvatn**, before rejoining the Ring Road in some of Iceland's most barren landscape.

# Icelandic Horses

**One of the incidental advantages of Iceland's near total isolation over the centuries is that the Icelandic horse has survived almost completely unchanged for over 1,000 years.**

The Icelandic horse, the stocky breed introduced by the first Nordic settlers, is today protected by strict regulations which forbid the import of horses into Iceland, and which state that an Icelandic horse sent out of the country can never return to Iceland, for fear of importing diseases to which the local breed would have no immunity.

"Elegant" is not an adjective which springs to mind to describe the Icelandic horse. These chunky, thick-set, muscular animals bear little resemblance to their leggier European relatives, though they can put on a fine turn of speed. They have adapted to the cool climate by growing a thick, shaggy overcoat for winter, which is shed in the spring. In summer, their coats can be groomed to shining smoothness.

In spite of their relatively small stature (13 hands on average), Icelandic horses are famed for their strength and stamina. They have played a vital role in Iceland's history, for centuries a roadless, bridgeless land. Known affectionately as Þarfasti Þjónninn ("most useful servant"), the horse was the sole form of overland transport in Iceland until the arrival of the first car in 1904 (which was unsuccessful on Iceland's bad roads, and was returned to Denmark in 1908). Even today, the horse has a vital role during the autumn round-up, when sheep are herded from remote mountainsides.

Surefooted, intelligent, affectionate, home-loving and sometimes headstrong, the Icelandic horse is also known for its five gaits. In addition to the conventional walk, trot and canter/gallop, it has two additional steps in its repertoire: the *tölt*, or running walk, and the *skeið*, or flying pace. The *tölt*, almost unknown in other breeds of horse, is a smooth run, which (unlike the trot) does not shake the rider excessively in the saddle, and therefore provides a more comfortable and popular alternative when it comes to long-distance overland travel.

## Horses for fun

Horses are not just important as a working animal; horse-riding is now Iceland's number-one leisure activity. Riding clubs flourish all over the country (it's estimated that a tenth of Icelanders are active riders), and various competitions and shows are held throughout the summer. Iceland's equine population numbers in the region of 80,000: horse breeding and trading is becoming an important business.

Nineteen national organisations in Europe, North America and New Zealand are affiliated to the International Federation of Icelandic Horse Associations (FEIF), and numerous international Iceland-horse championships are held annually. Iceland always sends a team of horses and riders to compete in the world championships, and invariably finishes with many prizes – although by law horses taken overseas are not re-admitted to the country, so riders must leave their beloved animal behind. The biggest horse show in Iceland is the bi-annual Landsmót (www.landsmot.is), which is held in late June/early July at changing locations: at the Hella showgrounds in 2014, and at Hólar University in 2016. The next show will take place in 2018, and is currently due to be held at Víðidalur in Reykjavik.

*Sturdy Icelandic horse.*

Blue sky over the East Fjords.

# THE EAST FJORDS

This region of Iceland, often overlooked by tourists, offers peace and tranquillity – from the long, thin lake Lögurinn, surrounded by forest, to remote farms and small fishing village.

F or travellers arriving from mainland Europe and the Faroe Islands by ferry, the jagged, snow-capped mountains lining Seyðisfjörður are a breathtaking welcome to Iceland. But most visitors pass through the east quickly, en route to somewhere else – a pity, because there are charms here to be winkled out. The rugged coastline is dotted with fishing villages that, like Borgarfjörður-Eystri, have hung on to an attractively slow-paced way of life. Inland, Lögurinn lake, bordered by the country's largest forest, is a popular holiday spot for Icelanders. The dry interior contains some starkly beautiful wilderness areas, populated by immense flocks of pink-footed geese, herds of roaming reindeer and a handful of people, still making a living on their remote farms.

## Hub of the east

Whether arriving by ferry, car or bus, travellers use as an orientation point the East's most important urban crossroad, **Egilsstaðir ①** (population 2,300). The town was established less than 70 years ago, and Egilsstaðir still has an unfortunate prefabricated feel. There's no town centre to speak of: instead a small number of suburban streets seemingly strike off in different directions from the Ring Road, which slices through the settlement. As a result it's unlikely you'll want to

linger and Egilsstaðir is best used as a staging post. Like many smaller towns in this part of Iceland, its social and economic life seems to hinge on the N1 petrol station. Flanking the station are the camping ground, tourist information office and a big supermarket.

Egilsstaðir also has some good-quality hotels which make a convenient base. Its sister-settlement, **Fellabær ②** (population 400), lies across a long bridge – at 301 metres (990ft) this was the longest bridge in Iceland for many years – and enjoys a more picturesque

**Main Attractions**
Seyðisfjörður
Borgarfjörður-Eystri
Lögurinn lake
Petra's Stone Collection
(Stöðvarfjörður)
Papey Island

*Lögurinn lake.*

*Taking a dip in the North Atlantic.*

*Houses at Seyðisfjörður.*

setting. Try for lakeside accommodation in huts on the Skipalækur farm; advance booking is advised.

The port of **Seyðisfjörður** , where the ferry from mainland Europe docks, lies directly east along Route 93, and is surrounded by sheer mountains. The journey is worth making even for those not taking the boat: in complete contrast to Egilsstaðir, Seyðisfjörður is full of character, thanks to its colourful wooden houses (shipped to Iceland from Norway in ready-made kit form in the 1930s) and its friendly inhabitants. Today its huge harbour accommodates the *Norröna* ferry owned by Smyril Line, which operates throughout the year and links Seyðisfjörður with the Faroe Islands and Denmark. The terminal building contains a café and tourist office.

Most of Seyðisfjörður's 658 inhabitants are involved in fishing in some way, and the arrival every autumn of herring schools in the shallow waters of the nearby fjords is still a cause for mass mobilisation at the fish factories. The ferry also brings Seyðisfjörður to life when it docks each week, on Thursdays in high summer and Tuesdays in the shoulder season. Classical music and light jazz concerts are held in Seyðisfjörður church every Wednesday evening from mid-July to mid-August.

A 20-minute walk up the mountainside is *Tvísöngur*, a site-specific sound sculpture by German artist Lukas Kühne, inspired by the ancient *fimmundarsöngur* or *tvísöngur* two-part singing style, said to date back to the Vikings.

Nineteen kilometres (12 miles) out of town, at the tip of the southern headland, the remote nature reserve **Skálanes** (www.skalanes.com) offers basic accommodation to bird-watchers visiting its bird-cliffs; the reserve is accessible only by four-wheel drive or a hike.

There are fine views of the town and fjord from the highway, which winds up past small waterfalls into the **Fjarðarheiði** mountains. The best spot for taking photos is a columnar basalt monument to the first postman of the region, who regularly made this journey on horseback

when it was decidedly more dangerous than it is today.

## Haunted highway

Another spectacular excursion from Egilsstaðir is to Borgarfjörður-Eystri, following Route 94 north. The highway passes **Eiðar**, once a boarding school, before entering an expanse of marshland bordered to the north by the Jökulsá á Dal river. The whole area is crowded with birdlife.

Over a high pass, **Dyrfjöll**, one of Iceland's most dramatic mountain ranges, comes into view. Watch out on the left for the bridge of a fishing trawler sitting in a field – it was dragged there on the back of a truck by a local, Fitzcarraldo, who wanted to piece together a boat in Borgarfjörður. He gave up half way, leaving a surreal vision for passers-by. This is an unnerving stretch of highway, with dramatic drops down into the sea and graphic evidence of recent landslides. To make matters worse, a monstrous creature named Naddi once lurked in a ravine here, attacking passers-by. In the early 1300s, locals erected a cross for protection. It has been replaced innumerable times, but each bears the Latin inscription, *"Effigiem Christi: qui transis pronus honora"* – "You who are hurrying past should honour the image of Christ."

**TIP**

Without your own transport, the only way to reach Borgarfjörður-Eystri is by hitching a ride with the postman. The mail van leaves Egilsstaðir every weekday at noon for the switchback ride over the mountains to the village. The truck also serves as the local post office once it arrives.

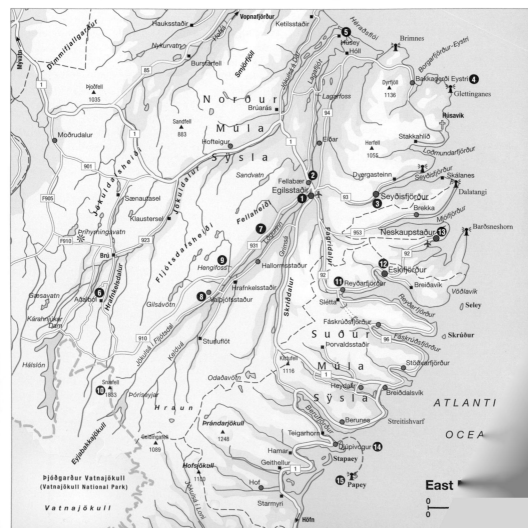

*Children can engage with the animals at Húsey farm.*

*Sporting event in Borgarfjörður-Eystri.*

The town **of Borgarfjörður-Eystri** ❹ (East Borgarfjörður, to distinguish it from the bigger Borgarfjörður in western Iceland) is also known as **Bakkagerði**. It is ringed by dramatic mountains: the ochre range to the east, past the black sand beach, is made from an acidic form of lava called rhyolite. Along with pieces of jasper and agate, the rock is polished into shiny trinkets for sale at the **Álfacafé** (May–late-Sept daily 10am–8pm), at the north end of the village.

The renowned artist Jóhannes Kjarval was born in Borgarfjörður and made the area famous in his paintings. He was said by one critic to have "taught the Icelanders to experience the beauty of their own landscape". A monument to the artist can be seen by the main road, just outside the village, and there is a small exhibition dedicated to him in the village community centre. However, a more fitting memorial can be found in the local **church**, which contains an altarpiece painted by Kjarval. It depicts a very Icelandic "Sermon on the Mount", with Jesus preaching in front of the Dyrfjöll mountains. Across the street from the church is a colourful turf house that is still inhabited and, towards the beach, a stone hillock called **Álfaborg** ("elf hill"), held to be inhabited by the hidden people (see page 250).

## Eastern isolation

A second road north of Egilsstaðir (Route 925, via the Ring Road) leads to **Húsey** ❺, a farm that has earned a measure of fame for its remoteness and serenity. Lying in the flatlands just south of the Jökulsá á Dal river, in the shadow of the Dyrfjöll mountains, Húsey's gaily painted corrugated-iron buildings date from the 1930s. Horses are still bred here – visitors can get to know the animals better on short and long treks into the surrounding wilderness. Across the heather, down by the black sand beach, Iceland's two species of raptor – gyrfalcons and merlins – can often be seen hovering overhead. Húsey's utter peacefulness is seductive, and many visitors stay much longer than planned. The old-style hostel accommodation offered is simple but comfortable (bring your own food), and lying in bed at night listening to the howling wind, one gets a vivid idea of just how isolated Icelandic farmers have been through the centuries.

Inland from Húsey, the Ring Road follows the **Jökulsá á Dal** river, which flows 150km (93 miles) from the Vatnajökull icecap before hitting the central deserts en route to Lake Mývatn. Until recently, this was east Iceland's most powerful river. Today, it's a trickle of its former self following the completion of the contentious Kárahnjúkar project in 2009, which stemmed the flow with three huge dams upstream.

West of the farm **Hofteigur**, look out for the rise of Goðanes overlooking the river south of the highway: this was supposedly once a temple of Thor, and sacrifices were held nearby. Today there are ruins below the hill, of indeterminate age.

The rough Route 923, which turns south off the Ring Road along the

Jökulsá á Brú, first passes the farm **Klaustursel**, which sells handicrafts and keeps a small herd of reindeer for summer visitors to pet. The unusual-looking bridge here is the country's oldest, a former American railway bridge rebuilt over this glacial river in 1908. Around 16km (10 miles) further along the road, turn left onto the even rougher Route 910 and drive another 12km (7.5 miles) to reach the farm **Aðalból** ⑥, one of Iceland's most remote highland farms, set in country related to the much-beloved *Hrafnkels Saga*.

The story tells of Hrafnkell Hall-freðarson, a power-hungry chieftain who lived at Aðalból and worshipped Freyr, the Norse god of fertility and fruitfulness. Hrafnkell dedicated his favourite horse, Freyfaxi, to the god, swearing that he would kill anyone who rode him without permission. When one of his shepherds innocently did so, Hrafnkell stood by his sacred oath, hunting him down and chopping open the poor fellow's skull. A blood feud resulted in Hrafnkell being outlawed at the Alþingi and ambushed by the victim's cousin, Sámur – who,

rather than killing Hrafnkell, maimed him horribly by stringing him up with a rope through the Achilles tendon. Sámur then seized his lands, flinging the horse that had caused all the trouble into a pond to drown.

At this stage, Hrafnkell decided that Freyr was little practical use as a deity and abandoned his worship. Appearing to turn over a new leaf, he took over a nearby farm and slowly began to rebuild his fortune. Of course, Hrafnkell was only biding his time: six years later, he took his revenge, descending on Sámur with a band of warriors and driving him from the East. According to the Saga, Hrafnkell then lived happily ever after. Some ruins from Viking times have been found at the farm Aðalból, but saga fans will mostly have to use their imaginations.

Also south off the Ring Road, Route 901 and then Route 907 lead to **Sænautasel** (daily 10am–6.30pm). This picturesque turf farmhouse was abandoned after a volcanic eruption in 1875, but is now lovingly restored and serves pancakes (*flatkokur*) to passersby. This area partly inspired

*Húsey offers space to roam.*

*Delicate flora at Hallormsstaðarskógur.*

*Picturesque stream at Hallormsstaðarskógur.*

Halldór Laxness's masterwork, *Independent People*.

## The great Icelandic forest

South of Egilsstaðir stretches the pencil-shaped lake of **Lögurinn ❼**. Over 100 metres (330ft) deep, the lake is said to be home to the Lagarfljót serpent. Sightings of this strange creature have been recorded since the 14th century. It appears on the lake, according to written documents and eyewitnesses, in different forms – as a snake, dragon, seal, horse or even in the shape of a house.

On the eastern shore is the country's largest forest, **Hallormsstaðarskógur**, a place revered by Icelanders, for whom trees are a rarity. Nearly all of the woods were protected from grazing animals between 1905 and 1927, and now cover an area of 740 hectares (1,830 acres). In 1903 a nursery was established to grow different kinds of native and foreign trees. Since then it has distributed some 12 million plants. An arboretum was formally opened in 1993, and now contains around 70 tree species from around the world. The

reforestation programme (using tough plants from Alaska and Siberia among others) has created optimism that other parts of Iceland might return to their pre-Viking state of being "covered by woods from mountain to shore". Shaded by the surrounding trees, **Hallormsstaður** is a popular spot for Icelandic holidaymakers (there is a camping ground and a cluster of accommodation options run by Hótel Hallormsstaður (www.hotel701.is).

A little further towards the end of the Fljótsdalur valley is the farm Hrafnkelsstaðir, where the hero of *Hrafnkels Saga* lived after he had been maimed. At the southern end of the lake, **Valþjófsstaður ❽** farm is where the beautiful carved wooden church door, dating back to AD 1200 and on display in the National Museum in Reykjavík, used to hang. The modern 1960s church now on the site sports a shiny new replica.

Nearby **Skriðuklaustur** (www.skriduklaustur.is; daily June–Aug 10am–6pm, May and Sept noon–5pm) was the site of a monastery from 1493 until the Reformation; finds from an ongoing archaeological dig are displayed inside

the quirky black-and-white house that now stands on the site. This was designed in 1939 for the author Gunnar Gunnarsson, well known for his novels in Denmark and Germany. Gunnar later presented the house to the Icelandic state for use as a cultural centre and writers' retreat. The first-floor café features local produce, with a daily lunch and cake buffet.

Skriðuklaustur's next-door neighbour **Snæfellsstofa** (tel: 470 0840; www. vatnajokulsthjodgardur.is; June–Aug 9am–5pm, May and Sept 10am–5pm, mid-Apr and Oct 10am–4pm) is one of four visitor centres for Vatnajökull National Park, with some excellent exhibitions on east Iceland's flora and fauna.

North of Lögurinn, a steep hour-long walk leads to the "hanging falls" of **Hengifoss** ❾, the fourth-highest of Iceland's waterfalls at 110 metres (360ft).

## Hiking country

A rough four-wheel-drive road runs south of Lögurinn to **Mount Snæfell** ❿, the 1,833-metre (6,013ft) peak that dominates the valley. Further on are the **Kverkfjöll** mountains at the northern edge of the icecap. Special buses run from Egilsstaðir to the hut at the base of Snæfell in summer. The mountain is an ancient primary volcano, surrounded by colourful rhyolite. If you are in good shape, the hike from the hut up to the peak, which stands about 800m (2,600ft) above sea-level, takes about 4–6 hours. The hut warden can provide all the necessary information.

For those who want to spend more time exploring the area, a popular long-distance walk is between Snæfell and Lónsöræfi – taking from three to seven days, depending on how long is spent at each stop. This is a spectacular hike in an uninhabited wilderness. Multicoloured rhyolite rocks can be found in many places, while impressive canyons and ravines cut through the land. There are plenty of flowers in early summer, and reindeer herds can sometimes be seen along the way. It is essential to have a good, up-to-date hiking map and to

contact the Snæfellstofa national park office to obtain all necessary information about the route, including a weather forecast and the state of rivers and streams. Do not attempt the walk alone – much of it is remote and mist and ice are common hazards.

Starting from Snæfell hut it is best to organise a lift in a four-wheel-drive towards Vatnajökull glacier. From here it is possible to walk over the **Eyjabakkajökull** glacier, a tongue of Vatnajökull (you will need crampons) towards the hut at **Geldingafell**. From there the next hut to head for is at **Kollumúli**. The hut is run by the local Travellers' Association and situated by the tranquil lake **Kollumúlavatn**. It is a good idea to spend two nights here and use a whole day for exploring the surroundings, perhaps hiking down into the **Víðidalur** valley. The next stage of the walk is through the haunting rock formations of **Tröllakrókar**, down the steep slopes of **Leiðartungur**, and towards the Múlaskáli hut. The last day's hike takes you to the crest of **Illikambur**, from where most people arrange in advance to be picked up.

*Throwing stones at Lögurinn lake.*

**TIP**

Boat trips (tel: 478 8119 /862 4399) to Papey island run from Djúpivogur (June–Aug daily 1pm). Papey is about 30 minutes away, and the whole trip, including a guided walk on the island, usually takes about 4 hours. This undulating island of tussocky grassland and marshes is a favourite breeding spot for many species of bird, especially puffins. An old wooden church on the island is said to be the oldest in Iceland.

*An isolated beacon on Papey Island.*

## Following the fjords

The Ring Road runs directly south of Egilsstaðir, although many prefer to take the slower but better-paved and more scenic route hugging the coast. The start of the coast road runs through a steep river valley lined by pencil waterfalls at regular intervals – each would be a marvel in other countries, but in Iceland they are just part of the backdrop. **Reyðarfjörður** ⓫ is the first of many quiet fishing villages along this part of the coast, magnificently situated at the base of the steepest fjord in the East. The town itself only came into being in the 20th century and was the centre of Iceland's biggest environmental row (see page 106) when a huge aluminium smelter was built here in 2004–8. Of interest to visitors is the **Icelandic Wartime Museum** (June–Aug daily 1–5pm), which documents the billeting of 3,000 Allied soldiers on the village in World War II.

From Reyðarfjörður, Route 92 runs north along the coast to **Eskifjörður** ⓬ (population 1,100). Its **Maritime Museum** (tel: 470 9063; www.sjominjar.is;

June–Aug daily 1–5pm, by appointment rest of the year) is housed in the village's oldest building, dating from 1816, and contains exhibits on the fishing and whaling industries in the East Fjords. Nearby, **Randulffssjóhús** is a 19th-century herring-salting shed where you can taste dried shark and hire rowing boats.

Further along Route 92, **Neskaupstaður** ⓭, with a population of around 1,500, enjoys a remote position on the far side of Iceland's highest mountain pass: it's literally at the end of the road. The beautifully renovated **Museum House** (May–Aug Mon–Sat 1–9pm and Sun 1–5pm) is home to the Museum of Natural History, Tryggvi Ólafsson's Art Collection and Jósafat Hinriksson's Seafaring and Smithy Collection. From May to mid-September, boat trips sail from Neskaupstaður around the headland into near-deserted **Mjóifjörður**, past the highest sea-cliff in Iceland.

Heading south along the fjords from Reyðarfjörður, the road is squeezed between the choppy North Atlantic and steep mountains – their twisted peaks are usually shrouded in a haunting mist, making this look like troll country. The

small villages of **Fáskrúðsfjörður**, **Stöð-varfjörður**, **Breiðdalsvík** and **Djúpiv-ogur** ⑭ all pass in quick succession. It is worth making a stop in **Stöðvarfjörður** to visit the sparkling **Petra's Stone and Mineral Collection** (www.steinapetra.is; May–Sept daily 9am–6pm) amassed by Petra Sveinsdóttir over a long lifetime; and those wanting to visit the nature reserve of Papey Island will need to catch the boat from Djúpivogur.

On the Ring Road southwest of Djúpivogur, heading towards Höfn, is the farm of **Stafafell** (www.stafafell.is), which offers accommodation to travellers and has become a popular base for hikers making day trips into the surrounding river valleys. It has a small church with some interesting artefacts. Nearby is the large and peaceful **Lón** lagoon.

The surrounding area of **Lónsöræfi** is renowned for its wild and dramatic landscape, where deep valleys and chasms have been carved among the mountains by the glacial river Jökulsá. There are plenty of fine hiking trails throughout the area. Using Stafafell as a base, there is a relatively easy day hike,

taking about four to six hours. It starts by taking the path up the mountain above the farm, and from there through the **Selárdalur** valley down to the colourful Hvannagil gorge. The trail carries on along the stream at the bottom of the gorge, towards the river Jökulsá, and ends on a track, passing a few summer cottages, before returning to Stafafell.

## Papey Island

The uninhabited island of **Papey** ⑮, just 2 sq km (0.75 sq miles) in size, is clearly visible from Djúpivogur, the departure point for summer boat trips (see page 292). Named after Irish monks *("papar")*, who are said to have lived here before the Settlement, the island was occupied from the 10th century until 1966, when the last farmers moved to the mainland. The remaining buildings are retained as summer houses, along with their tiny wooden church, which is chained to the ground to prevent it from blowing away in the fierce winds. Today the island is a nature reserve, home to sea birds (including 30,000 puffin pairs) and a large breeding colony of eider ducks.

*Taking advantage of Iceland's short summer.*

*The stone and mineral collection at Stöðvarfjörður.*

The turquoise water of Bláhver, a
geothermal spring at Hveravellir.

The Vatnajökull glacier.

# THE INTERIOR

Home to Iceland's wildest, most extreme scenery, the vast, empty interior can be accessed by a number of routes suitable only for four-wheel-drive vehicles.

Reykjavík

During the Age of Settlement few Viking colonists braved the desolation of the interior. Only outlaws, banished from their society – and thus from the fertile coast – took refuge in its chilly expanses. By the 13th century, however, some paths had been created through the Central Highlands as short cuts to reduce the journey time when travelling from north to south. Today, 800 years later, the vast region of the interior is still almost totally uninhabited.

This large, empty region is Iceland's premier attraction for adventurous travellers. Nowhere else in Europe is so remote from civilisation, or offers such a range of scenery, the most dramatic Iceland has to offer: broad icecaps which split their sides into great glacial tongues; volcanoes of every size with extensive fields of block lava and pumice; freezing deserts and endless outwash plains of black sand. There are two main routes that go right across the interior: the Kjölur and the Sprengisandur. Other routes offer further opportunities for exploring this unique area.

In the southeast of the interior in the pristine land immediately to the north of Vatnajökull icecap, the dam at Kárahnjúkar has divided public opinion and led to the biggest debate Iceland has ever seen on environmental protection (see page 106).

*The Kjölur highland road.*

## Challenge of the wild

There are serious logistical problems to be overcome before visiting the interior. Roads are reduced to mere tracks, most passable only in four-wheel-drive vehicles. The interior routes are open only in the middle of summer and even then snowfalls and blizzards can still occur. There are years when some tracks never open due to severe weather.

The weather is unpredictable and camping is the main form of accommodation, although there are a few

**Main Attractions**
Hveravellir
Aldeyjarfoss
Landmannalaugar
Herðubreið
Víti crater
Kverkfjöll Mountains

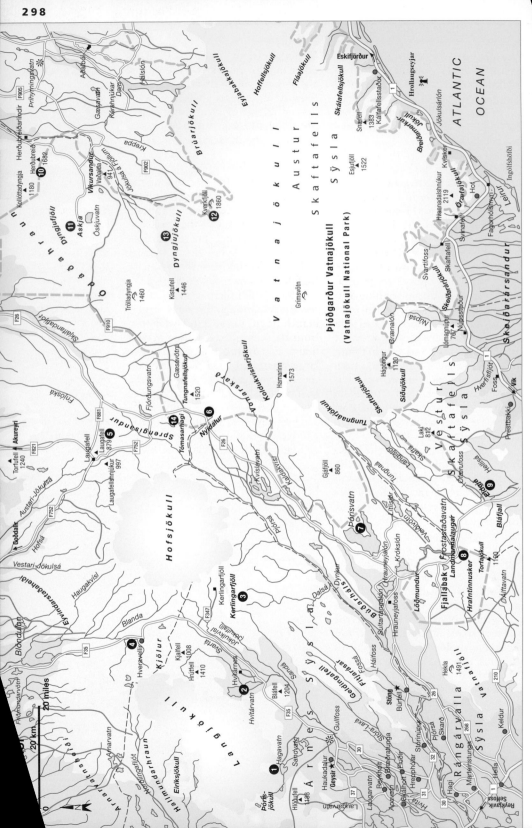

huts operated by the walking-tour groups Icelandic Touring Club (Ferðafélag Íslands) and Útivist. Located in key areas, like the Sprengisandur and Kjölur, facilities are very basic but feel luxurious after several nights in a gale-battered tent.

Modes of transport through the interior vary from the buses that operate between Reykjavík and Akureyri via the Kjölur route in summer (see page 302, see page 311 and see page 317 for details) to the latest high-tech 4x4 or beaten-up Land-Rover, to mountain bikes and walking. If you are bringing your own transport, extreme care is required in preparation. You must take everything you will need with you, including all food and water, and in some cases fuel, and to be aware of how to deal with the punishing terrain and weather conditions (see pages 103 and 319). Because of the dangers, many travellers opt to embark with one of the adventure-tour operators based in Reykjavík. These use short-wheelbase, four-wheel-drive coaches for tours ranging from day excursions to longer-term camping trips. For the latter, the vehicles are heavily modified, often to include a kitchen and a full complement of picnic tables and chairs. An alternative form of adventure tour is traversing the interior on horseback.

## The Kjölur route

The Kjölur route (F35), based on an ancient byway used in Saga times, is one of the main links across the interior, passing between the Langjökull and Hofsjökull icecaps. A four-wheel drive is advisable but other vehicles are sometimes seen on the southern part of the main track, which begins at the majestic **Gullfoss** waterfall in the southwest (see page 176) and runs northwards to the **Blöndudalur** valley. The first part of the journey, to the hot springs of Hveravellir, is on a road of gravel, stones and rock. Beyond Hveravellir, the route deteriorates as the track becomes muddy.

Nonetheless, in comparison with other interior routes, the Kjölur has always been relatively well travelled (historically, its grassy stretches were important grazing areas for travellers on horseback), and today all of the main rivers on the F35 are bridged.

## Into the interior

Leaving Gullfoss, the grassland on the plain above the falls soon changes to lichen-dotted stones. There is a steady drop in temperature as the landscape becomes increasingly bleak and uninviting. On the skyline the only relief is the snow-sprinkled mass of **Mount Bláfell** (1,204 metres/3,950ft).

Before Bláfell there is a ford across the **River Sandá** and a track (F335) branching off to the left. This detour from the main route, taking several hours as a round trip, goes to the large glacial lake **Hagavatn ❶** and the icecap of **Langjökull**. As the track bumps its way towards the edge of the ice, it crosses a once volcanically active fissure several miles in length. All that remains today is a high ridge of black rock with a narrow break

*A weather station sits on the distinctly alien landscape. Fittingly, NASA scientists have found a plausible model for Martian conditions beneath the barren surface. The existence of microbes, surviving in extreme conditions at Grímsvötn, bolsters the theory of life on the red planet.*

*A hiker admires a glacial cave at Langjökull.*

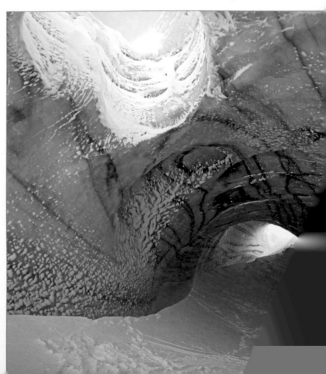

that allows access through to the edge of the glaciers. The final approaches to the icecap are very steep due to huge deposits of glacial moraine, and vehicles should be left below. Water gushes out from the top of the moraine where lake Hagavatn has formed. Standing on the edge of the moraine, buffeted by the cold wind, travellers have a view of the lake, edged in ice, and, way below, the sweeping plains of black sand that are blown southward and enrich the agricultural land beyond Gullfoss.

Back on the main Kjölur route you head towards a second, even larger glacial lake, **Hvítárvatn ❷**. Skirting around the bulk of Mount Bláfell to the east, the track descends to the **River Hvítá**, crossing four or five tributary streams and small rivers. A spectacular view opens up across desolate dark tundra towards the distant blue glaciers of Langjökull icecap and Hvítárvatn lake.

On the horizon lies another icecap, **Hofsjökull**: the conflicting winds from the two icecaps create swirling dust clouds in between.

From the bridge over the Hvítá, there is a clear view to the lake. Small icebergs can usually be seen in the water, and on the far shore towers the outlet glacier from which they originated. A good base for a more extended exploration of the area is the Touring Club hut at **Hvítárnes**. Beyond, the brown dusty plain turns to gravel and then a great black stretch of volcanic clinker, with mountains and glaciers always on the horizon.

The track soon crosses the southern stony slopes of the small mountain **Innri-Skúti**. As well as affording a panoramic view over the **Jökulfall** river valley to the Hofsjökull icecap and Kerlingarfjöll mountains, the slopes are particularly rich in tundra plants. Most are no more than tiny specks that eke out an existence sheltered between the rocks. Small pink cushions of moss campion compete with white mountain avens and other alpines for space. Long, severe winters, followed by short, relatively warm summers mean that the growth of these tundra plants is very

*Tourists crossing cracks in the glacier at Langjökull.*

stunted. Dwarf willows grow barely centimetres above the ground; as soon as they grow above this height, they become bent over by the constant wind.

The track detour (F347) to **Kerlingarfjöll** ❸ (www.kerlingarfjoll.is) is well signposted as it dips down into the Jökulfall river valley. The first stream you reach is easy to cross; for the second, Blákvísl, a slow, steady drive across the water is recommended. Nearby is a small airstrip. These are dotted throughout the interior for emergency use but this one also allows access to the former ski school – the warming climate has led to its redevelopment as a mountain resort/hiking area. Facilities here are uncommonly good for the highlands, with made-up beds, sleeping-bag accommodation, a campsite, café-restaurant, electricity, a mobile-phone signal and hot tubs.

The Kerlingarfjöll region itself is an excellent climbing area with superb views of Hofsjökull, many deep ravines and well-vegetated slopes. The mountain peaks, rising to 1,400 metres (4,600ft), are made of rhyolite, making a stark contrast to the dark plains of Kjölur. In a succession of small gorges, sulphur and boiling water vent to the surface – particularly eerie when there is a mild drizzle in the air and great clouds of steam rise out of the myriad small fissures in the ground. Boiling pools have splashed mineral-laden waters across rocks, colouring them green, red and yellow. These mountains can be a very cold place to camp and there are occasional snowfalls even in August.

Returning to the main Kjölur route, you will see the table-mountain **Kjalfell** (1,008 metres/3,307ft). To the northeast of it, on a low lava ridge, is **Beinahóll** ("hill of bones"). In 1780 four men from Reynistaður farm in Skagafjörður perished here in bad weather with a flock of sheep. Because of this incident, most travellers over Kjölur for the next hundred years chose to pass on the west of Kjalfell, instead of using the main track to the east of the mountain.

## A warm oasis

**Hveravellir** ❹ (www.hveravellir.is), 100km (60 miles) from Gullfoss, is an oasis within the cold desert. The hot springs here are very different from those at Kerlingarfjöll. Deep pools of brilliant, near-boiling blue water are lined with white silica; all around are small mud pools of black, brown and red minerals. Hissing jets of steam emerge from tall rocky cones, while a number of springs run gently down the slopes. The deposits of silica and sulphur cover the ground like great sheets of glass with fine traces of yellow.

Hveravellir is another relatively comfortable highland hub, due to the presence of two touring huts with ever-available hot water, a campsite, summer café, small shop and petrol station. Some of the blue pools are as near as the natural world comes to a jacuzzi. With the air temperature near freezing, bathing is possible in one of the outlet pools located by

**FACT**

The Icelandic playwright Jóhann Sigurjónsson (1880–1919), a resident of Copenhagen, wrote a very successful play about the lives of the outlaw Eyvindur and his wife Halla, who lived at Hveravellir. In 1917 the play was turned into a film.

*Hiking at Landmannalaugar.*

---

**TIP**

Scheduled buses run
between Reykjavík and
Akureyri via the Kjölur
route daily between
mid-June and early
September. Departure
from both cities is at
8am. From Reykjavík,
buses arrive at
Hveravellir at 2.15pm,
and then on to Akureyri
for 6.30pm. Heading
south from Akureyri,
Hveravellir is reached by
11.15am. All buses stop
at Gullfoss and Geysir.
See www.sba.is for more
information.

---

*A photographer
enjoying the rising sun
at Hveravellir.*

the car park. Among the peculiar hot springs in the area are **Bláhver** and **Öskurshólshver**, the latter being so noisy in earlier times that it reminded 18th-century travellers in Hveravellir of a screaming lion. Another is **Eyvindarhver**, named after the 18th-century outlaw Fjalla-Eyvindur, who is said to have boiled his meat in the spring. Ruins of the outlaw's shelter can be found nearby on the edge of the lava. Born in 1714, Eyvindur became a thief. In his early thirties, he went into self-imposed exile in the mountains for over 20 years. He met and married Halla Jónsdóttir, and the couple set up home at Hveravellir, where they were gradually joined by a gang of thieves. On one occasion, though, Halla was captured and taken away. One night, as the kidnappers camped in Borgarfjörður in West Iceland, the exhausted guards fell asleep. Next morning Halla was gone. The swiftest horse was also missing and so were the provisions. Clear footprints of two horses led to the mountains – Eyvindur had come in the night to free his wife.

From Hveravellir a rough track runs north, meeting up with the hard road at the Blöndudalur valley 110km (68 miles) away. En route, the shallower parts of the winding **River Seyðisá** attract water birds, such as phalaropes, which churn up the bottom by walking in circles to dislodge small animals for food. Much of the water comes from the two icecaps and on a clear day the views are magnificent.

## Sprengisandur route

The route through the Sprengisandur area can be reached in several ways from the north of Iceland. Although it is easier to reach than the Kjölur route, a four-wheel drive is still necessary. There are three main ways to reach the start of the route proper, all of which converge at or near Laugafell at the edge of the Sprengisandur. After making the crossing through the interior, the main route reaches the beautiful and remote area around Landmannalaugar, where it is well worth taking the time to go hiking, before continuing down to the south coast.

## Reaching the Sprengisandur

The most easterly way into the interior takes Route 842 then F26 through the Bárðardalur valley via Goðafoss. A scraped road soon degrades into a rough track, which climbs past the beautiful waterfall of **Aldeyjarfoss** with its tall basalt columns. On clear days there are spectacular views across the Ódáðahraun towards Askja. The shield volcano of Trölladyngja, part of the Gæsavatnaleið route, is clear on the horizon to the south.

The more central F821 goes from the end of the Eyjafjörður valley. Passing the abandoned farm of Nýibær, where there used to be a weather station, the road continues to Laugafell.

The third, most westerly, route to the Sprengisandur is via Route F752 through the Vesturdalur valley, which starts in Skagafjörður. The jeep track begins by the farm of **Þorljótsstaðir**, which was abandoned in 1944. The track crosses **Orravatnsrústir**, wet grasslands covered with cottongrass and sedge, around the two lakes of **Reyðarvatn** and **Orravatn**. The area is extremely marshy, with large hillocks covered with low-growing bushes. In the centre of the area is a small hill, **Orrahaugar**, where there is a refuge hut. Shortly before this route joins Route F821 near Laugafell it crosses the **Austari Jökulsá**, a huge glacial river fed by several streams and rivers from the Hofsjökull glacier. The river used to be a great obstacle to those travelling this route, but there is now a bridge at **Austurbugur**.

### A cold desert

At **Laugafell** ⑤, on a ridge leading northwest from the mountain of the same name (879 metres/2,900ft) there are several warm springs, which reach 40–50°C (104–120°F), and a warm bathing pool. Various kinds of grass flourish around the springs. Close to the tourist hut there is a small trough, most likely man-made, containing warm water. According to an old story a woman named Þórunn, daughter of Jón Arason, Iceland's last Catholic bishop, brought her family to stay here in the 15th century during the Black Death, and made the pool with

*Four-wheel drive needed.*

*Aldeyjarfoss waterfall is spectacular.*

# Flowers among the Lava

**Mosses and lichens are in their element on Iceland's "barren" volcanic landscape, and flowering plants add splashes of vivid colour in high summer.**

Well over half of Iceland's area is wasteland. Visitors arriving at Keflavík Airport often think they could be on the moon when they look out on the treeless lava fields and the dark mountain slopes beyond. This impression is, however, misleading. While Iceland has next to no trees and the ones that exist are usually restricted in height (a waggish visitor once remarked, "if you're lost in an Icelandic forest, stand up"), there is plenty of compensation. Mosses, lichens and flowering plants flourish all over the country. And even in the barest highland sections, an occasional bloom takes root.

Birch, Iceland's most widespread tree, generally takes the form of a relatively low-growing shrub, often in dense copses and thickets. In the rare locations where it can grow straight and tall,

*An unlikely splash of colour.*

the birch may reach 10–12 metres (30–35ft). Reforestation efforts have introduced many foreign tree species, particularly evergreens, so mixed glades and woods are now seen in many parts. Iceland's largest forest is at Hallormsstaður (see page 290) in the east.

Botanists believe that half of Iceland's plant species are survivors of the Ice Age, while around 20 percent have been introduced, deliberately or by chance, since humankind's arrival in the 9th century.

The local vegetation has been characterised as oceanic subarctic in character. About one-third of the plant species are of the arctic-alpine type. Many species of sedges and rushes are found in marshes and bogs; cottongrass (common and Scheuchzer's), which flourishes in wetlands all over the country, was formerly used to provide wicks for fish-oil lamps, which were the main form of lighting.

In addition to its 490 vascular plants (31 of them rare enough to be protected by law), Iceland is home to no fewer than 600 different species of mosses and liverworts. Mosses are generally the first plants to take root on lava fields, preparing the ground for subsequent colonisation by grasses, ferns and, later, trees. One of the most interesting species among Iceland's flora is the misnamed *Bryoxiphium norvegicum*, sword moss. Though named "norvegicum," sword moss has never actually been found in Norway, and was first identified at Lake Kleifarvatn in 1928. Sword moss has also been found in the US, Mexico and parts of Asia. However, it is unknown anywhere else in Europe, apart from in northeast Greenland.

## Food for the table

About 755 lichens and 550 forms of higher fungi are known in Iceland (a lack of local lichenologists and mycologists mean that true numbers are unknown). Very few of Iceland's mushroom species are harmful to eat, and none is deadly poisonous, so mushroom-picking is a popular autumn pastime. Courses in mushroom identification are held from time to time, generally culminating in field trips to gather mushrooms under expert supervision.

Berry-bearing plants such as the crowberry, blueberry and bog whortleberry are common on heathlands. In the autumn families often travel out into the country in search of the biggest, juiciest berries.

her own hands. Near Laugafell the gravel expanse of the **Sprengisandur** truly begins, with magnificent vistas eastwards to **Vatnajökull** and the smaller icecap of **Tungnafellsjökull** and westwards to Hofsjökull. A number of river crossings later, the blue tongues of glaciers come into view. A track forking to the east leads off the gravel plain to **Gæsavötn**, a small yellow-green oasis and crystal-clear lake amid the dark dramatic landscape. Beyond lie the Gæsavatnaleið and Askja routes.

At **Nýidalur** ❻, close to the geographical centre of Iceland, stand several huts – invariably a welcome sight. Wardened during the summer months, they have occasionally been cut off for a few hours by snow and bad weather. But, whatever the climate outside, the atmosphere inside is always congenial, with travellers habitually swapping tales and sharing food. There is a small campsite on the only patch of green in the area, but even in the middle of summer high winds and near-freezing temperatures make camping a desperate option.

The dusty track south crosses the mountain of **Kistualda** (790 metres/ 2,600ft), with panoramic views, before continuing to **Þórisvatn** ❼ (Iceland's second largest lake) through a landscape of glaciers and black gravel plains. Just beyond the lake and on the main track is a veritable metropolis in this desolation: the **Hrauneyjar Highland Centre** (www.hrauneyjar. is) at Hrauneyjafoss, where there is a petrol station, a café-restaurant and a guesthouse (its summer-only neighbour **Hotel Highland**, 1.5km (1 mile) down the road, is the interior's only hotel). With the development of new hydroelectric schemes, several lakes (not shown on all maps) can be seen close to the fork in the main track southeastwards to Landmannalaugar.

## On to Landmannalaugar

There is a steady increase in traffic south of Hrauneyjafoss en route to Landmannalaugar. The greatest change here is in the colour of the scenery. Instead of the dark Sprengisandur gravel, gaudy green mosses now coat the ancient rhyolitic rocks.

*Camping ground at Landmannalaugar.*

The hills are bright yellow, green and red, dotted with deep blue lakes, creamy brown outwash plains and snow patches lying on grey Rhacometrium mosses. Shortly before Landmannalaugar a side road to the east leads to the edge of **Ljótipollur** (the "ugly puddle"), a picturesque explosion crater which has colourful sides and some greenish water at the bottom.

## Exploring Landmannalaugar

Hot springs form the nucleus of **Landmannalaugar** ⑧, and steam rises from every corner of the valley. Volcanic activity in the last 10,000 years has been restricted to a few northeast to southwest fissures. The youngest, the **Veiðivötn** fissure, created lava formations and other craters, including Ljótipollur, extending about 30km (21 miles) to the north.

This is a highly popular centre for tourists and there are several camping areas, but in midsummer the main site near to the hot pools, used for swimming, tends to become crowded. Landmannalaugar lies near the outskirts of the **Torfajökull** volcanic district. Warm and cold springs at the foot of the lava flows make it a true "paradise in the desert". **Laugahraun**, the lava above the tourist hut, was deposited in a relatively recent eruption, probably at the end of the 15th century. The streams of geothermal and spring water, coming from under the lava-wall, mix to make streams and pools of an ideal temperature for bathing.

Landmannalaugar is part of the **Fjallabak Nature Reserve** and forms a good base for the many walks in the area. The bedrock of Fjallabak dates back about 8–10 million years. The varying and delicate colours of the mountain peaks that predominate here are due to their composition of rhyolitic rock. With the cold climate and frequent sandstorms, vegetation is scarce, although willow grows on the dry lava sands, and cottongrass in the marshes. Interglacial rhyolite lava can be found in **Brandsgil**, which is only about an hour's walk from the hut at Landmannalaugar.

*Rocky Herðubreið.*

Other popular hikes are to the summit of **Bláhnúkur** (940 metres/3,100ft), formed by sub-glacial rhyolites, and to the fumaroles of **Brennisteinsalda** – these walks take between one and two hours each. Sub-glacial activity has also produced some hyaloclastite (*"móberg"*) mountains such as **Loðmundur** and **Mógilshöfðar**.

There are trout in most of the lakes around Landmannalaugar, including Ljótipollur and Frostastaðavatn. Arctic char have also been added to some lakes in the area.

Slightly longer walks in the area include a five- or six-hour hike to the summit of **Háalda** (1,090 metres/3,600ft) and a walk around Frostastaðavatn taking two to three hours. The major trek in this area is the 53km (33-mile) Laugavegur Way to Þórsmörk in the southwest, which takes four or five days if you are reasonably fit. It is best attempted only between mid-July and early September. The scenery encompasses lava flows, rhyolite hills and spectacular views over glaciers. Along the way

there are overnight huts at Hrafntinnusker, Álftavatn and Emstrur. Many people extend the walk to finish in Skógar on the coast, passing by the still-smoking ground at Fimmvörðuháls created by the 2010 Eyjafjallajökull eruption .

## Returning to the coast

Travellers are faced with several routes from Landmannalaugar. It is possible to take a track southwestwards on routes 26 or 32 to join up eventually with the Ring Road near the south coast. Perhaps the most dramatic, however, is southeast to **Bláfjall** and eventually the coast. Although improved, the track here still provides adventure in the form of numerous river crossings, many of which require long periods of wading down the rivers to check their depth. Again only four-wheel drives should attempt these crossings due to deep water and possible quicksand.

Before Bláfjall there is a track off to the gorge and waterfall of **Eldgjá** ❾ (the "Fire Fissure"). Eldgjá is the most extensive explosion fissure in

*Off-road biking.*

*A field of cotton grass, surrounded by rhyolite mountains at Landmannalaugar.*

The *Landnámabók (Book of Settlements)*, compiled probably in the 12th and 13th centuries, tells of a number of settlers from the British Isles, some of whom may themselves have been descendants of Norwegians. Significantly, however, there are virtually no words of Celtic origin in the language apart from a few place names, such as Papey and Dímon, and personal names such as Kjartan and Njáll.

*Öskjuvatn lake sits in a volcanic crater.*

the world. It is a 40km (25-mile)-long volcanic rift, reaching from the Mýrdalsjökull glacier to the mountain **Gjátindur** (950 metres/3,100ft). The most impressive part is the northern end, where it measures 600 metres (2,000ft) wide and 200 metres (660ft) deep. A part of it is supposed to have been formed in a violent basalt eruption around AD 934. There are indications that the fissure is related to the volcano Katla, which is under the ice of Mýrdalsjökull glacier (see page 181).

Cascading into the rift is the famous waterfall of **Ófærufoss**. It used to have a much-photographed natural arch of basaltic rock that formed a footpath over the lower cascades. The arch, which featured in the Icelandic film *In the Shadow of the Raven*, collapsed in 1993 due to heavy snow and flooding. The hilly region around Bláfjall is a popular walking area. Ancient lava flows are carpeted with mosses and lichens, while innumerable streams and small waterfalls pour out of rocky fissures, only to disappear again under broken lava and cushions of moss.

## The Askja route

This track through the interior is more difficult than the Sprengisandur and Kjölur routes, and even four-wheel drives are sorely put to the test. Most tracks are marked by yellow poles or cairns of stones and, with reference to good maps, navigation is fairly straightforward.

The track (F88) that leads off Route 1 (the Ring Road) to the east of Lake Mývatn is marked by several makeshift signs warning against two-wheel drive vehicles attempting to go any further. It travels for some 64km (39 miles), following close to the glacial river Jökulsá á Fjöllum, before reaching the mountain of Herðubreið. To begin with, the view west across the Ódáðahraun plain is quite intimidating. A flat expanse of black gravel and pebbles *(grjot)*, which is made up from the country's largest lava flow, stretches almost to the horizon.

The going is hard due to the severe corrugations in the track. A small range of black hills has to be negotiated, whose summit offers a

spectacular view of the Jökulsá – a vast, braided glacial river. Patches of black sand become more frequent with pockets of stabilising lyme grass and ancient, twisted frames of dwarf willow are testimony to the harshness of the environment. Among the dark gravel lie balls of primordial-looking grey lichens; under stones protected from the wind sit small brown moths, barely moving, the only visible sign of animal life.

The track twists and turns eventually towards the edge of the River Lindaá, a tributary of the Jökulsá, and the first major river crossing. Along the river banks are great carpets of the pink-flowered arctic river beauty, contrasted against the black sand.

## A black landscape

The track undulates considerably for the next 20km (12 miles) as it climbs and descends an extensive lava field. The bare rock is covered at times with patches of sand and pumice. The mountain of **Herðubreið** ⑩, 1,682 metres (5,518ft) high, gradually comes to dominate the view as it rises above the surrounding plain. On a cloudy day the upper reaches of Herðubreið are often hidden from view, which only adds to the mountain's gloomy splendour.

For centuries Herðubreið was held to be impossible to climb. The first attempt was made by the English traveller Richard F. Burton in 1872. Accompanied by a local farmer from the Mývatn area, Burton had to turn around, because of rockfalls, shortly before they reached the top. First to get to the top of the mountain were the German geologist Hans Reck and the Icelander Sigurður Sumarliðason in 1908.

For safety's sake, those who intend to climb the mountain should check in and out with the warden in the hut at **Herðubreiðarlindir**, who can also supply in-depth information about the route (allow around 12 hours to get from the hut to the summit and

back). A helmet is recommended due to falling rocks and scree.

Herðubreiðarlindir is a wonderful oasis in the middle of black sands and lava fields. It is rich in vegetation and water springs, which appear from under the lava. Ruins of an ingeniously fashioned shelter made by the 18th-century outlaw Fjalla-Eyvindur can be found here. He spent one winter here, which he claimed was the worst time of his long exile, since he had no warm water and was forced to live on raw horse-meat all winter long. The Jökulsá á Fjöllum nearby becomes a violent glacial torrent, creamy brown with rock flour and running between banks of dark lava.

The journey from Herðubreið to Askja is another 35km (21 miles), much of which is across the yellow pumice fields of **Vikursandur**. The soft honeycombed segments of pumice, originally produced by the eruption of Víti in 1875, have been blown by the wind into small yellow dunes, contrasting with the dark block lava beneath. Storms in this area can make travelling very hazardous.

**TIP**

At both Herðubreið and Askja there are basic tourist huts (sleeping-bag space about ISK6,000) and campsites (tent site about ISK1,500), managed by the Akureyri Touring Club (Ferðafélag Akureyrar; www.ffa.is). Tents have to be pegged into the pumice and the only flattened area doubles as an airstrip. Wardens are present in the middle of summer.

*A waterfall negotiates the tortuous volcanic landscape.*

*Crossing a river in a four-wheel-drive.*

*Speleologist Johnny Martinez supervises the course of sulforhoda-mine in the upper river of Kverkfjöll.*

To the north of Askja lies the centre of the vast **Ódáðahraun** ("ill deeds lava field") which, at over 3,000 sq km (1,080 sq miles), is the world's largest lava flow. This vast area remained unexplored for centuries and was thus seen as mysterious, giving rise to tales of extensive outlaw settlements. Organised travel and exploration did not begin until the early 19th century.

## A forbidding caldera

Mount Askja ⑪ is not the neat cone that it appears on the horizon. Seen from closer up, it is a 45 sq km (16 sq mile) caldera of black lava, cream pumice screes and white snow. Low cloud often clings around the summit, which is located amid the sprawling **Dyngjufjöll** massif. A narrow track winds around the base of Askja, through the **Öskjuop** pass to a small parking area. A walk leads through the outer walls of Askja into the huge crater, where the great jagged **Vikrabor-gir** lava field was created as recently as 1961. A deep inner crater is partially flooded with steaming water and marks the site of the 1875 eruption.

**Öskjuvatn**, a lake several kilometres across, is the deepest in Iceland at 220 metres (721ft). Its water has collected in a deep depression that developed following a tremendous volcanic explosion in the Askja caldera in 1875. This eruption was the first in the Dyngjufjöll mountains to be scientifically researched. At the beginning of 1875 powerful and consistent earthquake shocks were felt in the surrounding area. At the same time, an increasing volcanic cloud was seen over the mountains. Four men from the Mývatn district took it upon themselves to venture in the middle of the winter south to Dyngjufjöll, where they discovered craters in the southeastern corner of Askja. They found three slag cones, two of them active, little or no new lava, but the ground had subsided a good deal, and deep cracks had developed in the vicinity of the craters. After the men returned, the eruptions continued and came to a climax at Easter. Then there was an enormous volcanic explosion that spread a thick layer of grey pumice over a great part of the

eastern countryside, devastating many farmsteads and damaging others. This explosion has been traced to the **Víti crater**, but others in the area were probably also active at the same time.

First to arrive at Askja on 16 July (after trekking across the Vatnajökull icecap) was an Englishman, W.L. Watts, accompanied by two guides. He discovered a deep depression with a circumference of about 8km (5 miles), filled with gaping fissures and seething hot springs, spewing steam and water high into the air. A black column of smoke was rising out of the Víti crater, scattering clay dust in all directions. Because of the tremendous volume of smoke, it was difficult for Watts and his guides to get a clear view of the crater. Throughout the summer of 1875 there were considerable outbursts in Askja, causing volcanic ash to fall in the closest rural districts.

In 1907, a small team of German scientists, the ill-fated Knebel expedition, came to study the area. One of its members, Hans Spethmann, who was collecting samples in the mountains, returned to camp to find that his companions Walter von Knebel and Max Rudloff had vanished. The next year, Knebel's fiancée, Ina von Grumbkow, travelled to Askja with the geologist Hans Reck. Their attempts to throw light upon the disappearance of Knebel and Rudloff proved fruitless, although it is thought that the men probably drowned in the lake.

The last eruption of Askja began at the end of October 1961 and lasted for just over three months. The lava flowed from five craters, now named Vikraborgir, covering a great part of Öskjuop, the entrance to the caldera. When in Askja, be sure to visit the nearby Holuhraun lava field. Formed during an eruption of the Bardarbunga volcano that lasted from August 2014 to February 2015, the Holuhraun lava field covers a huge area of 85 sq km (33 sq miles).

## Onward from Askja

From the route between Herðubreiðarlindir and Askja there is a signposted side track (F910, then the F902) to the magnificent **Kverkfjöll** ⑫ ("Nook Mountains") at

*Bubbling hot pool at the main entrance to the Kverkfjöll ice cave network.*

**FACT**

The old 120km (72-mile) Gæsavatnaleið route from Askja to Tómasarhagi was immortalised in Desmond Bagley's thriller *Running Blind*. The way that the book's hero Alan Stewart drove in his Land Rover has changed little since then except for the bridging of the River Tungnaá at the end. It may be difficult, but at least you're unlikely to have a hail of bullets at your back, as Stewart had.

*Snowy terrain on the Gæsavatnaleið route.*

the northern edge of Vatnajökull. Close to the centre of the range is the second-highest volcano in Iceland, rising to 1,860 metres (6,102ft). It is split from north to south by a steep and rugged glacier named **Kverkjökull**, which has burrowed out a deep valley, leading to an almost entirely ice-filled caldera. Kverkfjöll has erupted several times in recorded history, although it is less notable for its volcanic activity than for its geothermal nature. A valley named **Hveradalur** ("hot spring valley") cuts southwestwards into the mountains at a height of 1,600 metres (5,250ft). The traveller who hikes into the valley will be rewarded with the entire spectrum of yellow, red and green nuances that characterise *solfatara* areas. Vapours rise everywhere from fumaroles and bubbling mud pits, and in the northeast where the valley is at its narrowest, it is almost blocked off by vapours from the largest vent. The valley is more than half-way surrounded by a brilliant white névé glacier, and at its southwest end there is an oval lake

with greenish-blue ice walls. On a clear day, there is a magnificent view over Ódáðahraun wasteland to the mountains rising up above the high plateau. Beautiful **ice caves** have been discovered in the area above the Sigurðaskáli hut – ask the warden there for directions; however, the caves are dangerous to enter due to frequent ice falls.

## The Gæsavatnaleið route

Running southwest from Askja, two tracks connect the Askja route with the more westerly one that runs through the Sprengisandur.

The original Gæsavatnaleið route (an unnumbered track) skirts the southern edge of the volcano **Trölladyngja**, very close to the Vatnajökull icecap. It is exceptionally hard going in places, but is the more interesting of the two. It is essential to have a tough four-wheel-drive vehicle and experience of fording rivers. Count on an average speed of no more than 10kmph (6mph). The second route (F910) is the easier route, although again you will need a suitable vehicle

and 4WD experience, plus patience and respect. It takes a longer journey around the northern edge of Trölladyngja.

The first obstacle is common to both routes, although it applies to a longer section of the old track, after the newer road veers northwards. Spring meltwater floods from the Vatnajökull icecap, bringing with it black volcanic sand. This outwash plain runs for many kilometres towards Askja. Late on warm summer days and after heavy rain, meltwater comes roaring out of Dyngjujökull glacier, creating wide rivers that flow all over the sands east of Urðarháls, an old glaciated volcano. These rivers are called Síðdegisflæður ("Evening morasses") and their sinking sands can be dangerous for all motor vehicles – avoid them at times when water levels are likely to be high.

The old track, marked at intervals with yellow poles, reaches the icecap at the forbidding black glacier of Dyngjujökull ⑬. Close inspection reveals that the ice is covered in black volcanic ash. Up above is the tufa mountain Kistufell (1,446 metres/4,750ft). In September 1950 the Icelandic aircraft *Geysir* crash-landed on Bárðarbunga in Vatnajökull. The successful rescue operation had its headquarters on Kistufell.

Navigation becomes more treacherous on both routes when they cross the difficult boulder-strewn sides of **Trölladyngja**, the greatest shield volcano in Iceland, measuring 10km (6 miles) in diameter and rising to about 600 metres (2,000ft) above the surrounding area. The weather here can be cold and wretched, and blizzards are commonplace in summer, but the solitude of the wilderness is awe-inspiring.

After hours of slow driving across block lava spewed out by a succession of volcanic craters, the two tracks rejoin on the edge of the Mid-Atlantic Ridge, above the Sprengisandur plain. This is also where the meltwater from the icecaps collects in a succession of rivers, giving you more experience of four-wheel-drive fording before you reach the small oasis of **Tómasarhagi** ⑭, with a junction of braided rivers, beneath the glacier Tungnafellsjökull.

*Intricate rock detail.*

# TRAVEL TIPS
# ICELAND

# TRANSPORT

# GETTING THERE AND GETTING AROUND

## GETTING THERE

### By Air

All international flights arrive at Keflavík airport, 50km (31 miles) from Reykjavík. After every flight arrival a bus (no.55) transports passengers to the BSÍ bus station about 1.5km (1 mile) from the centre of Reykjavík. The journey takes about 45 minutes and costs ISK1,680 or ISK2,200. If you take Flybus, buy tickets from the ticket machine or ticket booth next to the airport exit. There is also the Airport Express bus (www.airportexpress.is), which connects the airport with Reykyavik and Akureyri which costs ISK2,100. If you require an onward minibus connection from the BSÍ bus station to your Reykjavík hotel, the extended journey costs about ISK2,500.

Icelandair is the main airline for Iceland, serving 35 gateways in Europe and North America. When booked in advance, a single ticket from the UK to Iceland costs from about £145. In summer it is essential to book

*Boat in Heimaey harbour.*

well in advance to secure the lowest fares. Icelandair regularly reviews its destinations and although the following list was correct at the time of publication, it is well worth checking that your airport is still served by the airline when planning your trip. In the UK, Icelandair serves London Gatwick, London Heathrow, Aberdeen and Glasgow; in mainland Europe, cities include Amsterdam, Barcelona, Copenhagen, Frankfurt, Helsinki, Oslo, Paris and Stockholm; and in North America, Boston, Chicago, Denver, Los Angeles, Minneapolis, New York, Orlando, San Francisco, Seattle, Toronto and Washington D.C. Book online at www.icelandair.co.uk or www.icelandair.com.

WOW Air is the main budget airline operating flights to Iceland, with daily year-round departures from London Gatwick and Copenhagen, as well as several flights weekly from Alicante, Barcelona, Berlin, Paris, Salzburg, Vilnius and Warsaw. The airline reviews its destinations every year: check the latest schedules and book online at www.wowiceland.co.uk. WOW

Air operates fluctuating pricing and fares are generally cheaper the earlier you buy.

EasyJet has recently opened a few routes to Iceland from Edinburgh, London Luton and Manchester, with a couple of flights a week from each airport.

### Icelandair

**Iceland**: Ticket office, Reykjavíkurflugvöllur, 101 Reykjavík, tel: 505 0100, email: sales@icelandair.is, www.icelandair.is
**UK**: Adam House, 2nd floor, 1 Fitzroy Square, London W1T 5HE. Reservations, tel: 44 (0) 20 7874 1000 , email: uk@icelandair.is, uk@icelandairholidays.com
**US**: 1900 Crown Colony Drive, Floor 1, Quincy, MA 02169. Reservations, tel: 1-800 223 5500, email: america@icelandair.is

### WOW Air

**Iceland**: Katrínartún 12, 105 Reykjavik, tel: 590 3000, email: wowair@wow.is, www.wowiceland.co.uk
**UK** call centre: tel: 0118 321 8384

### easyJet

UK call centre: tel: 0843 104 5000, www.easyjet.com
International call centre: tel: (+44) 843 104 5454

Air Iceland, the domestic airline (see page 317), also operates flights from the Faroe Islands and Greenland.

### Stopovers

Icelandair offers a free stopover in Iceland of up to 7 days for people travelling between Europe and North America. This may not always apply to the cheapest internet fares; if in doubt check with the airline.

## Domestic Air Routes and Prices

So-called "net offers" are available on most Air Iceland flights, which, when booked in advance, help to secure the best price for any particular flight. It is always worth checking with the airline before paying for a full-price ticket since they may be able to offer an alternative fare or departure.

The cheapest internet fares are as follows: **From Reykjavík to:** Akureyri,Egilsstaðir and Ísafjörður from ISK7,600; ; Grímsey ISK23,000; Vopnafjörður ISK19,800.

**From Akureyri to:** Grímsey Vopnafjörður from ISK11,600.

## By Sea

The Faroese shipping company, Smyril Line, operates a ferry service to Iceland between April and late October. The ship *Norröna* sails from Hirtshals in Denmark to Seyðisfjörður in eastern Iceland, calling in at Tórshavn (Faroe Islands). Routes and schedules are complicated and change according to the season. For the latest information see the Smyril Line website. Passenger and vehicle fares are expensive and it is almost always cheaper to fly to Iceland and then hire a car.

**Faroe Islands:** Yviri við Strond 1, PO Box 370, FO-110 Tórshavn, Faroe Islands, tel: (+298) 345900, email: office@smyrilline.com.

**Iceland:** Smyril Line Ísland, Stangarhylur 1, 110 Reykjavík, tel: 570 8600, email: office@smyrilline.com.

If you are planning to bring your own car to Iceland by ferry, see page 318.

## GETTING AROUND

Getting to Iceland, both by air and ferry, can prove to be a major expense, although for travellers from the UK, flights have become significantly cheaper in recent years, and domestic air travel is relatively inexpensive. Moreover, when you get there car hire is also relatively expensive – four-wheel drive is even more costly but a necessity for the highland routes.

Many independent travellers opt for a travel package. Tour operators offer a wide range of options from a simple fly-drive or flight and bus or air pass deal to a week in Reykjavík or a full-board hotel, farmhouse or camping tour. It is often cheaper to take a package of some sort.

### Arrival and Departure

Almost all travellers arrive in Iceland at Keflavík Airport. All Faroe Islands and Greenland flights land at Reykjavík Airport and the odd international flight lands at Akureyri, in the north of Iceland. Arriving by sea, Smyril Line's *Norröna* ferry docks at Seydisfjörður, in the east of the country, and cruise ships also call in at Reykjavík, Akureyri, Heimaey and Ísafjörður.

The "Flybus" transfer coach meets all incoming flights and takes about 45 minutes to cover the 50km (30 miles) by road from Keflavík to Reykjavík's BSÍ bus station. From here, an onward transfer service is provided to the major hotels. Buses 1, 3 and 6 run regularly from the BSÍ bus station to Lækjartorg bus station in the centre of town, and buses 1, 3, 6, 14, 15 and 18 run to Hlemmur bus station,throughout the day and evening.

For returning to the airport, the Flybus leaves the bus station two hours and fifteen minutes before flights leave Keflavík. Arrange pick up at your hotel reception desk; buses are provided from other major hotels to connect with the Flybus. Many people flying out of Iceland combine the journey to Keflavík with a visit to the Blue Lagoon. Most tours to the Reykjanes peninsula let you get off at the airport for afternoon flights.

### By Air

Most of Iceland's main towns are linked by air to Reykjavík. **Air Iceland** (Flugfélag Íslands) is Iceland's main domestic airline.It also operates flights from Iceland to Greenland and to Tórshavn in the Faroe Islands. Currently, it runs flights from Reykjavík to Akureyri, Ísafjörður and Egilsstaðir. From Akureyri flights operate to Grímsey, Þórshöfn and Vopnafjörður.

**Eagle Air** (Flugfélag Ernir) also operates internal flights from Reykjavík to Bíldudalur and Gjögur in the West Fjords, Húsavík, Höfn and the Vestmannaeyjar.

All domestic flights to and from Reykjavík use the central city airport, rather than the international airport at Keflavík. In winter, when many roads are blocked by snow, flying is simply the only way to get around. Icelandic pilots are reputed to be among the most experienced in the world because of the variety and frequency of extreme conditions that they fly in. Reservations are advisable on all routes, especially in the summer months:

**Air Iceland** (Flugfélag Íslands): Reykjavík Airport, tel: 570 3030, www.airiceland.is

**Eagle Air** (Flugfélag Ernir): Reykjavík Airport, tel: 562 2640, www.eagleair.is, www.ernir.is.

## By Bus

Bus travel in Iceland is efficient but not cheap. It can in fact work out more expensive than flying on most of the longer routes. From Reykjavík, long-distance buses depart from the **BSÍ Bus Terminal** at Vatnsmýrarvegur 10. In summer, buses depart daily for destinations around Route 1 (the Ring Road) and elsewhere. On some routes, brief stops are made at tourist attractions en route.

Because of road conditions and distances, some destinations, such as Egilsstaðir in the east, require an overnight stop in Akureyri or Höfn. On other routes, for example to the West Fjords, services are less frequent. In summer, scheduled bus tours also operate from the BSÍ Bus Terminal (with a pick-up from some hotels) to places of interest, including Þingvellir, Gullfoss and Geysir, Þórsmörk, Landmannalaugar and Eldgjá (all daily) and across the central

## Main Bus Routes

Below are the scheduled main bsí bus routes, frequency, journey times and approximate cost during summer months:

**Reykjavík–Akureyri:** daily (6 hours), ISK17,000.

**Akureyri–Mývatn–Egilsstaðir:** daily in summer (5 hours), ISK9,600.

**Egilsstaðir–Höfn:** daily June–mid-September only (4.30 hours), ISK9,400.

The BSÍ website, www.bsi.is, provides full details of many bus routes in English and is a good starting point for planning journeys by public transport.

For timetables and routes in Reykjavik contact Strætó (www.straeto.is).

highlands over the Kjölur (daily) and Sprengisandur routes (three weekly). Some have a human guide or a CD guide that the driver plays, but most are unguided.

Full details of bus operators, routes and schedules are available online and in the "Iceland On Your Own" booklet, published each year and available from the BSÍ bus station, tourist offices and tour operators.

Timetables and prices are available from **BSÍ Travel**, Vatnsmýrarvegur 10, 101 Reykjavík, tel: 562 1011, email: bsi@bsi.is, www.bsi.is.

### Bus Passes

For information on bus tickets and passes, contact BSÍ (see above).

There are an ever-expanding variety of bus passes that are well worth considering. The **Ring Road**

**Passport** (ISK42,000) allows one full circuit around the Ring Road following the same direction, with no time limit other than those set by road conditions. You can stop off as often as you like. Another useful pass is the **Highlights Passport,** which offers unlimited travel to some of Iceland's top attractions, including Gullfoss, Geysir, Þingvellir, the Laki craters, Landmannalaugar, Þórsmörk, Skaftafell, Jökulsárlón, Akureyri and Mývatn. It also includes transport across the interior by both the Sprengisandur and Kjölur routes. The price of this pass depends on the length of its validity; it is available from 7 days (ISK46,500) to 15 days (ISK80,000).

Combined bus and air travel tickets – **Air/Bus Rover tickets** – permit a round trip including some of the highland bus routes and offer a small discount. You can purchase them abroad through many of the tour operators.

## Scheduled Ferry Services and Prices

**Landeyjarhöfn–Heimaey: (Vestmannaeyjar):** Aferry service runs from Landeyjarhöfn harbour, 30km (19 miles) southeast of Hvolsvöllur, to Heimaey and back four times Tue and five times Wed–Mon mid-May to mid-Sept, and five, four or three times daily mid-Sept to mid-May. The journey takes 35 minutes. Price: one way, ferry only ISK1,320 for adults, ISK2,120 per vehicle up to 5 metres (15ft). Reservations are essential for vehicles, at least 30 minutes prior to departure. For information and bookings, contact **Eimskip**, tel: 481 2800; www.herjolfur.is. There are bus connections from Reykjavík to the harbour for three of the four/ five daily sailings, setting off from the city around 2.5 hours before each ferry departure: for details contact Strætó, tel: 540 2700, www. straeto.is.

**Þorlákshöfn–Heimaey (Vestmannaeyjar):** Twice daily in winter, and sometimes at other times in bad weather, the Vestmannaeyjar ferry sails to Þorlákshöfn harbour on the mainland, instead of to Landeyjarhöfn, with a sailing time of 2 hours 45 minutes – see the website www.herjolfur.is for details.

**Árskógssandur–Hrísey:** From Mar to Oct, the ferry Sævar sails daily every 2 hours each way (Mon– Fri 7.20am–9.30pm, Sat–Sun 9.30am–9.30pm) – outside those months there's a slightly reduced service. The journey takes 15 minutes and costs ISK1,500 round trip. A bus service is available from Akureyri on summer weekdays. For information and bookings contact tel: 695 5544 or see www.hrisey.net.

**Dalvík–Grímsey (via Hrísey):** The Sæfari sails Mon, Wed and Fri, leaving Dalvík at 9am, arriving in Grímsey 3 hours later and departing from there at 4pm. A bus service used to link Akureyri with Dalvík

to meet with the ferry – the route was recently taken over by Strætó (www.straeto.is) – contact them for the latest timetable. Price: one way, ferry only ISK4,830. Contact **Landflutningar-Samskip**, Ranarbraut 2b, 620 Dalvík, tel: 458 8970, 853 2211, email: samskip@ samskip.is. www.landflutningar.is/ saefari.

**Stykkishólmur–Flatey– Brjánslækur:** The car ferry Baldur sails twice daily from June to late Aug from Stykkishólmur at 9am and 3.45pm, returning from Brjánslækur at 12.15pm and 7pm. Once daily Sun–Fri in other months (plus Saturday sailings in late May/early Jun/late Aug/early Sept), departing from Stykkishólmur at 3pm (9am on Sat) and from Brjánslækur at 6pm (noon on Sat). The journey takes 2.5 hours, and all summer sailings call at Flatey Island (check with the ferry company if you wish to visit Flatey in other months). If you wish you can stop over in Flatey and catch a later sailing. Price: ISK5,460 for adults, ISK2,730 for 16–20-year-olds, under-16s free. Cars up to 5 metres (15ft) long cost ISK5,460 one way. Reservations must be made for cars. Connecting buses run from Brjánslækur to various places in the West Fjords in summer only. For information and bookings, contact **Sæferðir**, Smiðjustígur 3, 340 Stykkishólmur, tel: 433 2254, email: seatours@ seatours.is. www.seatours.is.

**Ísafjarðardjúp–Jökulfirðir– Hornstrandir:** from Ísafjörður there are regular scheduled ferry services to various locations in this part of the West Fjords in the summer. They vary in departure days and length, and each leg of the journey has a different price: for schedules and prices, call Vesturferðir, tel: 456 5111, email: westtours@westtours.is; www.vesturferdir.is.

## By Ferry

Iceland has a number of small offshore islands dotted around its highly indented coastline. A few are inhabited because in past centuries they offered easy defence against enemies as well as good fishing. Sea birds too were an important supplement to the diet and their droppings fertilised the grassy soil, making the land ideal for farming. Scheduled ferry services link these islands with towns on the mainland; services are less frequent from September to May (see box).

## Hitchhiking

If you have unlimited time and patience and are prepared to carry a tent and plenty of food, and walk where necessary, then hitchhiking will get you round the Ring Road and on some of the more travelled minor roads. However, bear in mind that the sparse traffic on Icelandic roads often consists of visitors and locals on holiday, with little space to spare in their vehicles. There is hardly any long-distance commercial traffic, and you may find that most rides are from locals on a trip to the nearest shop.

Hitchhiking is reasonably safe, and though quite reserved, most Icelanders do speak English. Once the ice is broken they may go out of their way to help and provide fascinating snippets of information about their country.

## Cycling

For the mountain-bike enthusiast, Iceland might seem an obvious choice. There are miles of empty rugged mountain tracks, and even the main roads can hardly be called busy. However, there are snags: accommodation and shops are far apart and virtually non-existent in the highlands, so carrying a heavy load is unavoidable; high winds, sandstorms and driving rain can make the cyclist's life a misery; if you damage your bike, you may have to resort to a bus to get you to a repair shop. It is fair to say that most Icelanders regard foreign cyclists as clinically insane.

Nonetheless Iceland is growing in popularity for cyclists, and a number of tour operators offer biking holidays with support vehicle back-up.

The international airlines charge a fee for carrying bicycles, of around US$50/100 for each leg of a European/North American flight. When booking, make sure you specify that you are taking a bike, double-check any weight restrictions, and preferably pack it in a specially designed bicycle box, available from bicycle shops. Around Iceland you can transport your bike on the buses for between ISK2,500 and ISK3,000, if there is space available, but you may be asked to remove pedals and wheels. Iceland does not have many specialist cycle shops, but for repairs most villages have a *verkstæði* (workshop).

### Useful Addresses

Icelandic Mountain Bike Association, PO Box 5193, 125 Reykjavík, tel: 562 0099, e-mail: ifhk@ fjallahjolaklubburinn (ensure subject line is "Cycling in Iceland"), www. fjallahjolaklubburinn.is

### Reykjavík City Card

The Reykjavík City Card is valid for unlimited travel on city buses, and admission to swimming pools and municipal museums (including the National Museum, Culture House and the Reykjavík 871+/-2 Settlement Exhibition). It is available for 24, 48 or 72 hours and costs ISK3,500, 4,700 and 5,500 respectively. The cards may be purchased at the Tourist Information Centre at Aðalstræti 2; hotels, guesthouses, hostels and the campsite; bus terminals and museums.

### Bike shops (and repairs) in Reykjavík:

GÁP, Faxafeni 7, 108 Reykjavík, tel: 520 0200, www.gap.is.
Hvellur, Smiðjuvegur 30, 200 Kópavogur, tel: 577 6400, http://hvellur.com.
Kría Cycles, Grandagarður 7, 101 Reykjavík, tel: 534 9164, www.kria cycles.com (also repairs and tours).
Markið, Ármúli 40, 108 Reykjavík, tel: 517 4600, www.markid.is (also repairs).
Örninn, Faxafen 8, 108 Reykjavík, tel: 588 9890, www.orninn.is (also repairs).
Útilif, Kringlan 4–10, tel: 545 1500, www.utilif.is.

### Bike hire in Reykjavík:

Borgarhjól, Hverfisgata 50, 101 Reykjavík, tel: 551 5653, www.borgarhjol.is
Reykjavík Bike Tours, 101 Reykjavík, tel: 694 8956, http://icelandbike.com (rental and tours)

Some places around Iceland hire out bikes; make enquiries at tourist offices, hotels and campsites. Cycling is popular around Lake Mývatn: Hike & Bike run tours and rent bicycles in the area, tel: 899 4845, email: info@ hikeandbike.is, www.hikeandbike.is.

### Reykjavík Transport

Reykjavík's city centre is tiny in comparison to its sprawling suburbs. You can easily wander through the narrow streets clustered around the harbour and lake on foot and cover most points of interest in a morning.

### By Bus

Many hotels and guesthouses, as well as the main youth hostel and camping site, are outside the centre, so it makes sense to use the excellent public bus system run by the Reykjavík bus company **Strætó**. Most services operate Mon–Fri 6.30am–midnight, Sat 7.30am– midnight, with a reduced service on Sunday. At peak times buses run at 10- to 20-minute intervals and at 30-minute or one-hour intervals in the evenings and at weekends. Bus stops are marked "Strætó" and a flat fare is charged with no change given. If you need to change buses, ask for a transfer ticket *(skiptimiði)*, which is usually valid for 75 minutes. If you plan to use the buses a lot, it is worth buying either a Reykjavík City Card (see page 319) or pre-paid tickets, which give a small discount, available along with a route map from the two terminals at Lækjargata and

Hlemmur. For bus information, tel: 540 2700.

### By Taxi

Hailing taxis on the street is a hit and miss affair. It is easier to go to one of the taxi ranks around town or ring the taxi firms directly:
**Airport Taxi**, tel: 520 1212; www.airporttaxi.is.
**Hreyfill-Bæjarleiðir**, tel: 588 5522 or 553 3500; www.hreyfill.is/en/
**Taxi Reykjavík**, tel: 561 0000; http://taxireykjavik.is/.
**Borgarbílastöðin**, tel: 552 2440; www.borgarbilastodin.is.

The majority of taxis seat four passengers but some larger vehicles seating up to seven people are available on request. If you have unusually large or long items of luggage, ring Sendibílastöðin, tel: 553 5050, and ask for a transit van *(sendibíll)*. These are often less expensive than a taxi but are only licensed to carry one or two passengers plus the luggage.

Tipping taxi drivers is not customary in Iceland. All taxis are metered and if you require a receipt ask for a *nóta*. Most drivers speak some English. The busiest time for taxis is after midnight on Friday and Saturday nights, when it can be virtually impossible to find one.

### Driving

### Rules of the Road

Iceland drives on the right. It is mandatory to drive with headlights on at all times; the use of seat belts, both front and rear, is also mandatory. Drink driving is a serious offence, with a zero-tolerance policy in operation – you cannot consume any alcohol and then drive a vehicle. Priority, unless otherwise indicated, is given to traffic from the right; when in doubt, give way.

Speed limits are 30kph (20mph) in residential areas, 50kph (30mph) in urban areas and often 60kph (37mph) on approaches to towns. On gravel roads outside urban areas the limit is 80kph (50mph), and 90kph (60mph) on paved roads.

From November to May, snow tyres or studded tyres are mandatory; all rental cars will be fitted with them.

By law, driving off marked roads and tracks is prohibited. The high latitude and cool climate means the growing season is very short: four months in the lowlands but only two months in the highlands. As a resul? damaged vegetation takes years, sometimes decades, to recover.

Particularly at risk are marshlands and mossy areas, where deep ruts caused by vehicles leave huge scars. The very fine, loose soil is vulnerable to erosion and damage is likely to accelerate the process.

### Driving Conditions

Though road conditions in general fall below the standard of their European and North American counterparts, Route 1, also known as the Ring Road, which goes around the island, together with minor roads in settled districts, present no major problem to the normal two-wheel-drive car in summer. Most of Route 1 is now paved, as are many of the minor country roads, particularly in the south and west of Iceland. A tunnel under the Hvalfjörður fjord, near Reykjavík, was opened in 1998 and markedly improved communications in the southwest of the country. The price for passing through is ISK1,000 one way for a normal family car.

Unpaved sections of road can become potholed and rutted, unpleasantly dusty in dry weather and muddy when it rains, but are still perfectly passable. Where the surface is loose gravel, it is vital for vehicles to slow down for oncoming traffic. In fact, you should always drive on gravel surfaces with great caution: fatal accidents are not uncommon. Throw in narrow roads, blind bends, single-lane bridges and wandering sheep, and it's best to take things steady!

For travelling around the coast, a two-wheel drive is perfectly adequate. Anyone contemplating a trip to the interior is entering a different league. Four-wheel drives are essential, and even then you should travel in teams of two or more cars (note that insurance companies will not cover hire cars driven on F-roads).

For the jeep enthusiast Iceland is a playground of unbounded delights,

its many rugged mountain tracks and unbridged rivers a challenge for even the most experienced. Travel through the uninhabited highlands also requires extreme caution; year after year unwary visitors (and Icelanders) undergo the unpleasant and sometimes fatal experience of their vehicle overturning in a seemingly innocuous river or the less serious but still frequent occurrence of getting stuck in sand. Fording rivers requires the utmost care.

Highland routes generally open the first week in July and close at the end of August, but this varies according to the weather. It is forbidden to attempt these routes before they are opened. The Ministry of Tourism publishes a brochure on travels in the Iceland highlands which is available free from many travel agencies and tourist information centres. However, the best place to find up-to-date information is from the **Icelandic Road Administration** (tel: 522 1100; www.vegagerdin.is): its website includes a route map showing weather conditions and road closures that is updated twice an hour between 7am and 10pm. They also operate a road conditions telephone line (tel: 1777).

### Motorcycling in Iceland

The weather is rarely perfect but, nonetheless, Iceland – in summer at least – is a magnificent destination to explore by motorbike. If you are staying on the main roads then a standard road bike is fine; however a trail or enduro machine will open up the interior and the numerous gravel or dirt roads elsewhere. It is important to realise, though, that there are no fuel stations away from the main settlements and the Ring Road: if you are venturing into the interior you will need to plan accordingly. The gravel and dirt roads can be treacherous, and fast-flowing rivers need to be forded. For this kind

of adventure, it is advisable to avoid travelling alone.

If you don't want to bring your own bike (on the ferry or by air), you can hire motorcycles from, or sign up for a tour with, the finely named **Biking Viking** (www.rmc.is, tel: 588 3220).

### Bringing your Vehicle

Given the high cost of hiring vehicles in Iceland, it may seem an obvious choice for Europeans to bring their own vehicle. However, remember that road conditions are not good, and unless you drive only at low speed, your suspension may suffer. Flying stones from passing vehicles are likely to damage your paintwork, whatever speed you drive. The constant vibrations from rutted and potholed roads may also damage your vehicle, not to mention the copious quantities of dust that will enter every nook and cranny. Nevertheless many visitors do bring their own car, year after year, without suffering major damage.

On arrival in Iceland your vehicle may be inspected to ensure that it is roadworthy. You will need to produce the following documentation: a passport, driving licence, car registration document and a green card or other proof of auto insurance while in Iceland. A temporary importation permit will then be issued for the duration of your stay, which may not exceed one year. Other conditions for temporary import of vehicles are that the vehicle must be imported by the owner only or anyone having legal possession of it (eg through hiring); the vehicle must be brought to the country when the owner arrives, or within one month of arrival the vehicle must be used by him, his spouse or a hired chauffeur; the vehicle must not be lent, sold or hired; and the vehicle must be re-exported within the stipulated time period. Fuel may only be imported in the vehicle's fuel tank. Full details can be obtained from the Icelandic Directorate of Customs (www.tollur.is).

Use of mudguards is compulsory to minimise stones being thrown onto oncoming vehicles on gravel roads. It is advisable to buy a grille for the front of the car to protect headlights from damage. Before leaving home try to make your vehicle completely dust-proof and ensure that any luggage stored on the roof is adequately protected against both dust and water.

### Hiring a Vehicle

You can hire anything from a small car to a 40-seater coach in Iceland, depending on your needs and group size, but prices are high (less so

*Motorbiking towards Vatnajökull.*

outside the peak tourist season). Four-wheel-drive vehicle hire is very expensive. It is almost always cheaper to arrange car hire online before you travel; try searching for cheap car hire through price-comparison websites such as www.travelsupermarket.com, www.kayak.co.uk or www.carrentals. co.uk. You could also consider arranging vehicle hire with one of the tour operators abroad who offer a package that includes flights and car hire.

When arranging your rental, check what the rates include. The majority of rates advertised are for up to 100km (65 miles) per day. Prices double for unlimited mileage, if that is available. Also check to see whether the hefty 24 percent VAT, a collision damage waiver or the highly recommended fully comprehensive insurance are included in the daily rental price.

If you wish to hire locally, the following companies offer a full range of vehicles:

**Átak Car Rental**, Smiðjuvegur 1, Kópavogur, and at Keflavík Airport, tel: 554 6040, email: atak@atak.is, www.atak.is

**Avis**, Knarrarvogur 2, Reykjavík, tel: 591 4000, and at Keflavík Airport, plus other sites around the country (see website), email: avis@avis.is, www.avis.is

**Budget**, Vatnsmyrarvegur 10, Reykjavík, tel: 562 6060, e-mail: budget@budget.is, www.budget.is

**Hertz**, Reykjavík Airport, 101 Reykjavík, tel: 522 4400, or at Keflavík Airport, plus other sites around the country (see website), email: hertz@hertz.is, www.hertz.is

**National/Europcar**, Reykjavík Airport, 101 Reykjavík, tel: (877) 222 9058; www.nationalcar.com

*Driving in the West Fjords.*

Many hire companies offer one-way rentals, allowing you to drive from Reykjavík to Akureyri, for example, and then return by air. Provided you stick to roads designated for the category of vehicle, assistance will be provided in the event of breakdown. Hire nothing but a four-wheel drive for a tour across the highlands. It is worthwhile going over your intended route with the rental company to check what roads are allowed for your type of vehicle.

### Petrol

Petrol is quite expensive in Iceland, and is roughly the same price everywhere across the island. Regular, super and unleaded petrol and diesel fuel are available in towns, villages and even in remote country districts, but not always at frequent intervals.

Before leaving a town or village it is always a good idea to check how far it is to the next petrol station. In uninhabited areas there is no petrol available and you will need to take spare fuel tanks with you. Remember that petrol consumption is particularly heavy on the rough interior routes.

Petrol stations also stock basic spare parts and most have toilets and either a cafeteria or a restaurant available.

Petrol stations usually open daily at 7.30, 8 or 9am and close any time from 7.30 to 11.30pm, with shorter opening hours on Sundays. Several petrol stations in Reykjavík and Akureyri are open 24 hours. After-hours petrol can be bought at station pumps – these are labelled *sjálfsali* (self-service) and they usually accept both cash and most major credit/debit cards, or the service station's own prepaid cards. Some pumps may not accept US cards.

### Driving in Reykjavík

Reykjavík is still small enough for drivers not to experience serious traffic jams, though the city centre – particularly Miklabraut – can often get congested during rush hour. Negotiating the inner city by car can also be tricky since there are a lot of narrow and one-way streets. The best compromise is to park in one of the numerous car parks on the fringe of the inner city, and then walk into the centre.

Most car parks close during the night; their hours are clearly stated on the ticket machine upon entering. Note that you must pay at the vending machine before returning to your car. Payment at street parking meters and in metered parking lots is mandatory from 9am–6pm on weekdays and 10am–4pm on Saturdays. Parking varies in price, with the more central P-1 zones costing the most – around ISK250 per hour. Parking fines are ISK2,500–10,000, depending on the violation.

### Driving in Akureyri

One of Akureyri's quirks is that city-centre parking lots require you to "set" a parking clock and leave it on the car dashboard. Pick up a parking clock at the tourist office, the bank or any pe station in Akureyri free of charge.

## Crossing Rivers by Four-wheel Drive

Many rivers, particularly if glacial, can vary enormously in flow. Heavy rainfall or a warm sunny day can treble their flow in hours. Generally, in warm weather, the flow is highest in late afternoon and lowest in early morning.

If the river looks deeper than knee height, stop before crossing and look for the best place to ford, checking the flow in several places. With sediment-laden glacial rivers it is difficult to judge the depth. Narrow crossings are the deepest, wider crossings will be shallower, especially on straight stretches. On bends, the deepest water is usually on the outside. Where there is an

obvious fording place, where the water enters a calm phase forming a pool, the water will be shallower on the downstream side.

Watch out for large boulders swept down into the fording place by strong flow, or sand – both should be avoided. If it is necessary, and safe to do so, wade first, using a safety rope. If in doubt, do not cross. Wait for another vehicle, get a second opinion, and help each other through. Keep in first gear, in low ratio if available, and drive slowly and steadily without stopping. If there is a strong current, try to cross by heading downstream to avoid fighting against the current.

# A – Z

# A HANDY SUMMARY
# OF PRACTICAL INFORMATION

## Accommodation

Accommodation is relatively expensive when compared to mainland Europe. Rooms are always clean, but guests, particularly those accustomed to US hotels, are sometimes heard to comment on the small size of hotel rooms. Reykjavík's high-end accommodation has all mod-cons, but elsewhere facilities and services can be simple; and almost all Icelandic buildings have thin walls. In spite of the long summer nights, thick curtains and black-out blinds are as rare as hens' teeth – bring an eyemask if light bothers you. Note, you can often find good discounts with early or online bookings. Rates can be 30 percent lower September–April. You should be able to find space to bed down at camp sites but even youth hostels are usually fully booked during the peak summer period.

Most forms of accommodation, except camp sites, can be booked through tour operators in your own country; better rates can often be found this way. Links can also be found on the website of the Icelandic Tourist Board (www.visiticeland.com).

There is no publication that covers accommodation for the country as a whole, but some organisations (eg Hostelling International, Icelandic Farm Holidays) publish annual brochures listing details of their accommodations; further information is given below under the relevant ▸ections. Hotels usually accept ▸yment by credit card, but payment ▸guesthouses, farms, hostels and ▸p sites is generally by cash only.

## Admission Charges

Although Iceland is not the cheapest country to visit as a tourist, admission charges for museums and galleries are generally quite reasonable. Expect to pay around ISK700–1,300 for entry into most museums around the country. Some attractions do not charge admission. In some instances, an entry ticket for one museum will give free entry or reduced entry to another (if they are operated by the same organisation – ask locally).

During the winter months, there is often a charge for checking in a coat when entering a bar or smart restaurant. This is not a strict admission charge but if you refuse to pay you will be denied access.

## Budgeting for Your Trip

Following the 2008 financial crisis and the devaluing of the króna, Iceland became much cheaper for foreign visitors, although the Icelandic currency has recovered nearly all its value since then. However, a small population and high import costs still conspire to make most items and services more expensive than you will be used to paying at home. Adding to the cost, VAT on accommodation (including camp sites) was increased from 7 percent to 11 percent in January 2015; the standard VAT rate is now 24 percent. Accommodation prices change significantly according to the season: they are up to one-third lower outside the main tourist summer season.

A sit-down lunch in a restaurant costs from ISK1,500 (but look out for cheap lunchtime buffet deals), and dinner from ISK3000. Alcohol is expensive: a small bottle of beer purchased from a Vín Búð liquor store costs around ISK350, and a mid-range bottle of imported wine from ISK2,500 – expect to pay almost triple in a bar or restaurant. It's a good idea to bring your maximum duty-free allowance with you from home.

Reykjavík's city bus service is good value, with bus tickets costing ISK420. Taxis are costly – the meter starts running as soon as the vehicle pulls up to your hotel, and a trip from Reykjavík to the international airport costs around ISK15,000 (compared to the Flybus ticket price of ISK2,200).

Generally, if you visit during the summer, stay in decent hotels, eat out in restaurants most nights and undertake a few activities, you should expect to pay upwards of ISK30,000 per person per day, based on two people sharing. However, it is possible to cut costs by staying in guesthouses or youth hostels and eating the odd meal in a restaurant – for this, you should reckon on about ISK20,000 per day. Camping and self-catering will cost around ISK10,000 per day.

## Climate

Iceland's temperate oceanic climate is surprisingly mild for the latitude (63–66°N), thanks to the Gulf Stream and prevailing southwesterly winds. However, these mild breezes frequently meet with icy Arctic air, creating extremely changeable weather fronts. The south and southwest of the country are more prone to storms and rain: for example, the south side of Vatnajökull, covered in thick spongy moss, receives 10 times the annual 400mm (16ins) of rain that falls on its barren northern side.

The Icelandic language allows for at least eight different degrees of wind, from *logn* (calm) to *rok* (strong gale), and you can expect to encounter most of them during your stay: Icelanders rarely bother with umbrellas, since they usually end up inside-out. Storms in the central highland deserts or glacial outwash plains can be unpleasant, whipping up soil and ash and covering the land in a brown haze.

### Summer (June to August)

The main tourist season runs from June to August, when (if you're lucky) you will experience Iceland's finest weather. Rather than blistering sunshine, this means an average daily high temperature of around 12°C (54°F); and even in the middle of summer, you should prepare for rain, as there is a 70 percent chance that a little will fall.

For haters of heat and hayfever, though, Iceland's climate in summer is delightfully refreshing. Combine this with White Nights during the first half June, when the sun stays above the horizon for almost 24 hours, and you are blessed with bright, mild days that seem to last forever.

High summer is also the time for hopping into a 4WD to explore the country's interior: most of the highland routes open in July, depending on the snow thaw.

### Spring (May) and autumn (September)

The first day of September signals the end of summer, and many sights and

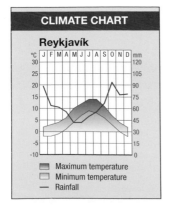

## CLIMATE CHART

### Reykjavík

Maximum temperature
Minimum temperature
Rainfall

accommodation options beyond the capital close their doors. However, for those seeking to escape the summer crush of visitors, May and September are good alternatives. May is a good month for birdlife, while the weather in September can be Indian-summer glorious, with many of the highland routes still passable with care – the added dimension of autumn colours and a dusting of snow on the mountain ranges can make this one of the most beautiful months. Many accommodation and flight prices fall outside high season.

### Winter (October to April)

Although winters in Iceland are not particularly cold (the average daily temperature is around 0.5°C/33°F), Arctic winds, frequent storms and long, dark days can make them feel bleak. The winter nights draw in quickly, with 12 hours of daylight in late September diminishing to just four in December. On the positive side, the dancing, billowing Northern Lights are visible between September and April.

Reykjavík is gaining in popularity as a winter-break destination, and a number of tour operators offer bargain packages out of season. Hotels, most museums and some excursions operate all year in the city. Some bus routes and most flights operate year-round but schedules can be disrupted by weather. If you plan to hire a vehicle in winter, a four-wheel drive is a must.

### What to Wear

"If you don't like the weather, wait five minutes and it will change" – so runs the local saying. Layers are the best option: besides normal summer clothing, invest in a quality wind- and rainproof outer layer and a good fleece or two. For footwear, bring a thick-soled pair of walking shoes or trainers. If you're camping, thermal underwear is also a bright idea.

If you plan to travel around the country, go walking or head into the uninhabited interior, you must dress accordingly. Even if you don't plan to do any serious hiking, a pair of lightweight hiking boots is worthwhile – many of Iceland's most visited sights are reached on foot via uneven paths.

Icelanders are clothes-conscious: if you plan to eat out at one of the city's better restaurants, you should dress up. Although most pubs are casual, people do get dressed up to go to smarter bars, and a few clubs maintain a policy of no jeans or trainers.

## Weather Information

The Icelandic Meteorological Office provides recorded weather bulletins in English, recorded daily; tel: 902 0600, then choose 1 on a touch-tone phone (this service is not available from all telephones). For a weather forecast on the internet, go to http://en.vedur.is.

For travel in Iceland between October and May, conditions can be severe. Although prolonged cold spells are rare, temperatures as low as -20°C (-6°F) can occur and, with the wind chill factor, it can feel very much colder than that. So, any visitor planning to travel outside the Reykjavík area in winter must be well kitted out.

Make sure you bring a swimsuit whatever the season, since Iceland has fabulous swimming pools.

## Crime and Safety

Iceland is one of the world's safest countries. Public places are well lit. Violent crime is virtually non-existent, bar the odd domestic dispute and drunken brawl. The latter is most likely on Friday and Saturday nights, when the city's youth takes to the streets of central Reykjavík on a (mostly good-humoured) drunken spree.

Pickpocketing and street crime are rare. Petty theft does occur in swimming-pool changing rooms (always leave valuables at the pay desk) and in bars and nightclubs – use common sense, as you would anywhere, and keep an eye on your bag or wallet. In the event of theft or loss, contact the nearest police station, where you will be required to fill in a statement. A copy is invariably required to claim on your travel insurance.

## Customs Regulations

Visitors aged 20 and over are allowed to bring in 1 litre of spirits (up to 47 percent alcohol content), 1 litre of wine (up to 21 percent alcohol content) and 6 litres of beer.

Visitors aged 18 and over may bring in 200 cigarettes or 250 grams of tobacco. As alcohol is expensive, it is worth bringing your full allowance. If you do not use it yourself, it will make a very welcome gift.

You may bring in 3kg (6lbs 9oz) of food up to the value of ISK25,000 free of duty, but the import of uncooked eggs, raw milk products and uncooked meat, including salami, bacon and uncooked ham, is prohibited.

On entering or leaving the country, if you are carrying more than €10,000-worth of Icelandic currency, you must declare it to a customs official.

Angling gear that has been used outside Iceland, including boots and waders, must be disinfected by a vet before being taken into the country. Bring a certificate from the vet stating that this has been done, otherwise your equipment will be disinfected by Icelandic customs at your own expense. It is also forbidden to introduce any animal into Iceland without permission from the Ministry of Agriculture. A lengthy quarantine period is required for all animals.

## D

### Disabled Travellers

Smaller hotels and guesthouses in Iceland rarely have elevators, and high curbs and the narrow doorways and small rooms of many buildings in Reykjavík's old town can make wheelchair access to restaurants and shops difficult. However, wheelchair access is available at most of the major purpose-built hotels, museums and larger department stores, as well as the Kringlan Mall.

Rough terrain and a lack of developed facilities mean wheelchair access to Iceland's natural wonders is rare. There are paved paths at Geysir, Gullfoss and Þingvellir National Park, and one leading to the glacier at Skógar.

The public bus system is adapted for wheelchair users. Hertz car hire have a minivan suitable for

*Icelandic currency.*

one wheelchair (tel: 522 4400). All Iceland Tours (tel: 781 2022, www. allicelandtours.is) arrange sightseeing, horse-riding and whale-watching trips for disabled visitors. The ferries Baldur and Herjólfur have good wheelchair facilities. All airlines serving Iceland can accommodate disabled passengers.

The campaigning organisation Sjálfsbjörg, the Association of the Disabled in the Capital Area, can help with queries: tel: 550 0360, email: sjalfsbjorg@sjalfsbjorg.is, www. sjalfsbjorg.is.

## E

### Electricity

The electric current in Iceland is 240V AC 50 Hz. To use North American and Japanese electrical devices in Iceland, you will require a voltage converter.

Icelandic electrical plugs are of the European two-pin type, so UK visitors and those from outside Europe will require a plug adapter for their electrical devices.

### Embassies

**Australia:** Australian Embassy in Copenhagen, Denmark, tel: (+45) 70 26 36 76, www.denmark.embassy. gov.au.
**Canada:** Túngata 14, tel: 575 6500, www.canada.is.
**Ireland:** Honorary Consul in Reykjavík, Mr David Thorsteinsson, tel: 554 2355, email: davidcsh@ islandia.is.
**UK:** Laufásvegur 31, tel: 550 5100, www.gov.uk/government/world/ organisations/british-embassy-reykjavik.
**US:** Laufásvegur 21, tel: 595 2200, http://iceland.usembassy.gov.

The Icelandic Foreign Ministry has a full list of diplomatic representatives on its website: www.mfa.is.

### Etiquette

Shyness towards visitors may be mistaken for coldness, but Icelanders are by nature hospitable, innately curious and great socialisers. Family ties are strong in this small, closeknit society, and Icelanders are quick to establish family connections when introduced by delving into each other's genealogies.

If you are invited to an Icelander's home, it will most likely be for coffee, often accompanied by copious quantities of cakes and biscuits. The younger generation may be more

### Emergencies

For police, ambulance, the fire brigade or other emergency situations, call 112.

likely to invite you for dinner; in this case a small gift – wine or flowers, for instance – is appropriate though not essential. It is customary to shake hands when greeting and leaving, and Icelanders always remove shoes before entering anyone's home.

Smoking is strictly prohibited in public buildings.

Icelanders always use first names and visitors will be expected to follow suit. The concept of titles, except for ministers of religion, is unknown. The exception to this is on formal letters, when Herra (or Hr.) Magnús Jónsson or Frú Kristín Jensdóttir would be a correct form of address on the envelope.

In the telephone directory, all entries are listed under first names. If the prospect of sifting through pages and pages of Jón Jónssons is daunting, many entries also give the person's profession (in Icelandic) as well as the address.

## G

### Gay Travellers

Iceland has a tolerant attitude towards gays and lesbians. It had the world's first openly gay prime minister from 2009 to 2013, and passed a gender-neutral marriage bill in 2010.

For information and advice contact: **The Gay and Lesbian Association/ Samtökin '78**, Suðurgata 3, 101 Reykjavík, tel: 552 7878, email: office@ samtokin78.is. Office open Mon–Fri 1–4pm; Thursday evenings are open house, with the library and coffee bar open 8–11pm. **Samtökin '78** also have a website: www.samtokin78.is.

There is more information about the gay scene in Iceland at www. gayice.is.

## H

### Health and Insurance

Iceland is a very healthy country. Nonetheless, all visitors should have adequate medical insurance, though an agreement exists between Iceland, the UK and Scandinavian countries for limited health insurance coverage of its residents. Travellers from those countries should obtain the European

Health Insurance Card (EHIC) before leaving home. No vaccinations are required for visitors, unless you are arriving from an infected area. Tap water is glacier-clean and delicious.

In Reykjavík, the **National Hospital** (Landspítali Háskólasjúkrahús; tel: 543 1000, Mon–Fri 8am–4pm) has a 24-hour casualty department in Fossvogur; tel: 543 2000, or phone an ambulance directly on the emergency number 112.

For non-emergency medical treatment outside normal hours the **Medical Centre** (Læknavaktin; Smáratorg 1, in Kópavogur; http://laeknavaktin.is) is open Mon–Fri 5–11.30pm and Sat–Sun and public holidays 9am–11.30pm. Their helpline (tel: 1770) is open Mon–Fri 5pm–8am and 24 hours at weekends. They can provide advice by telephone, direct you to the nearest place with after-hours care, or send a doctor to your accommodation.

Emergency *dental care* is available – tel: 575 0505 for information about dentists on duty.

Most pharmacies (*apótek*) are open normal business hours (Mon–Fri 9am–6pm, Sat 10am–4pm). However, Lyfja at Lágmúli (tel: 533 2300; daily 8am–midnight) has longer opening hours.

## I

### Internet

Virtually everyone in Iceland has internet access at home, hence there are very few internet cafés across the country. A free guest computer is often available in the lobby of hotels and guesthouses. Libraries generally have bookable internet access for a small fee (no more than ISK200–300 per hour). Tourist offices usually also have one or two terminals for internet use, with a nominal fee similar to that in libraries. Most cafés and bars in Reykjavík have Wi-fi, so if you are travelling with your own laptop, you can access the web for the price of a coffee. It is also possible to rent a portable mobile Wi-Fi hotspot.

## L

### Left and Lost Luggage

Hotels, guesthouses and hostels will often store luggage free of charge for guests; and the BSÍ bus station in Reykjavík has a left-luggage office (tel: 591 1000; 4am–midnight). If you lose

something while out and about, the lost and found office in Reykjavík is at the police station at Hverfisgata 113, tel: 444 1000; Mon–Fri 8.15am–3.30pm.

## M

### Maps

Visitors can obtain a useful (and free) tourist map of the country and city plan of Reykjavík, which is adequate for general planning purposes and orientation but not for actual touring, from tourist information centres, airports, bus terminals and accommodation throughout Reykjavík and the rest of the country.

More detailed maps can be bought from tourist offices and all larger bookshops in Iceland, as well as at many fuel stations, or before you travel from the Ferðakort website www.ferdakort.is. For general touring purposes the **Insight Fleximap** (1:910,000) has a laminated finish ideal for withstanding Iceland's wind and rain. The 1:500,000 touring map *Ferðakort Ísland* is excellent, as is the 1:200,000 *Ferðakort Ísland Vegaatlas (Road Atlas)*. There are five new touring maps available that cover the country at a scale of 1:250,000: **Northwest; Northeast; Southwest; Southeast; and the Highlands.**

Large-scale 1:100,000, 1:50,000 and 1:25,000 maps of areas of particular interest to visitors, such as Þórsmörk/Landmannalaugar, Akureyri/Mývatn/Húsavík/Ásbyrgi, Skaftafell, The Golden Circle, Vestmannaeyjar and Hornstrandir, are also available. But a word of warning: the accuracy of such maps, especially when marking footpaths and cliff faces, falls far short of maps in other countries. A general map series on the same scales also covers all areas of the country but some sheets are still under preparation or out of print.

### Media

#### Newspapers and Magazines

English-language newspapers and magazines are on sale in Reykjavík, one or two days after publication. They can also be found in public libraries (*bókasafn*).

The magazine *Iceland Review* (www.icelandreview.com) is published in English with informative articles and great photographs. The *Reykjavík Grapevine* (www.grapevine.is) is an irreverent, free English-language newspaper containing articles,

reviews and listings, which publishes around 18 issues per year and is available wherever there are tourists.

Of the Icelandic-language media, the daily newspaper *Fréttablaðið* has the largest circulation (about 90,000) – it is distributed free, and is relatively lightweight in both content and size. *Morgunblaðið*, the longest-established daily, has excellent coverage of foreign affairs, reflecting an isolated nation's desire to keep pace with the world. *DV*, the main tabloid, publishes on Monday, Wednesday and Friday.

The free monthly listings booklet *What's On in Reykjavík* (www.whatson. is) is available at the tourist office.

#### Television

The government-owned RÚV and the privately owned Stöð 2 are the two main TV channels in Iceland. Also broadcasting are several subscription-based pay-TV channels. Alongside homegrown programmes, you will find foreign films, serials and documentaries, mostly imported from the US. These are usually subtitled in Icelandic, save for children's programmes, which are dubbed. Satellite TV is available by subscription in Iceland, giving direct access to international news and entertainment channels including CNN and the BBC.

### Money

The monetary unit is the Icelandic króna (ISK; plural: krónur), divided into 100 aurar. Notes are in denominations of ISK 10,000, 5,000, 2,000, 1,000 and 500. Coins are in denominations of ISK100, 50, 10, 5 and 1.

In August 2016 the exchange rate was ISK153 to the pound sterling, ISK116 to the US dollar and ISK132 to the euro.

You can bring in unlimited foreign currency in the form of travellers' cheques or bank notes and up to €10,000-worth of Icelandic currency. However, it is rarely worth purchasing Icelandic króna abroad, as you usually get a poor exchange rate. Similarly, you should change back all unused króna before leaving Iceland (this can be done at the airport departure lounge) and you may need to produce receipts of exchange transactions from foreign currency or travellers' cheques to króna. Icelanders use cards much more readily than cash, even for very small purchases; visitors may as well do the same.

#### Exchange Facilities

The simplest way to obtain Icelandic króna is to find an ATM cash machine – plentiful in Reykjavík and other Icelandic towns. Banks will change foreign currency or travellers' cheques – US dollars, sterling and euros are all easily exchanged. Some tourist shops will accept payment in euros and US dollars, but usually at unfavourable rates.

Hotels usually exchange travellers' cheques and banknotes for guests, at a rate slightly below the bank rate, depending on the availability of cash in the till.

Outside normal banking hours 24-hour exchange facilities are available at Keflavík Airport: look for *Landsbankinn* in the arrival hall for arriving passengers; on the second level for departing passengers.

### Credit Cards

Credit cards are used everywhere in Iceland, with the most ubiquitous being Visa and MasterCard/EuroCard. American Express, JCB and Diners are far less common.

Cash advances are available on Visa and MasterCard/EuroCard from all banks, savings banks and automatic cash machines displaying the respective logos. Credit card companies usually apply a hefty charge for this, however.

### Debit Cards

Visa, Delta, Maestro/EDC and Electron debit cards are widely accepted. Cash may be obtained against these cards in all banks and automatic cash machines displaying the relevant logos.

### VAT refunds

Foreigners making purchases in excess of ISK6,000 are entitled to a partial VAT refund when they leave Iceland.

## Lost Credit Cards

Credit-card issuers strongly recommend that you take the emergency credit-card telephone number in your home country with you when going on holiday. However, if you lose your credit card, you can phone the following numbers for initial assistance:
**Visa.** Emergency number 525 2000/525 2200 (24 hours).
**MasterCard/EuroCard/Diners Club.** Emergency number (in Denmark): (+45) 3673 7373. (24 hours).
**American Express.** Emergency number: 800 8111.

## O

## Opening Hours

Banks are open Mon–Fri 9.15am–4pm, but rural branches may have more limited opening hours. All banks have a few branches with extended opening hours, particularly in shopping malls such as Kringlan. All offer foreign exchange services.

Offices open Mon–Fri 9am–5pm. Most post offices open Mon–Fri 9am–6pm (for details visit www.postur. is/en).

Museum opening times vary. They are usually open from 10am or 11am until 5pm or later in high season. Outside Reykjavík, many museums only open from June to August; so if you are travelling out of season but have set your heart on seeing a particular collection, ensure that the museum has not closed for winter.

Cafés throw open their doors between 10am and 6pm. In Reykjavík, many cafés become bars after 6pm, remaining open until 1am Sun–Thu and anywhere between 3am and 6am Fri–Sat. Restaurants have short, sedate hours: usually from 11.30am–2.30pm and 6–10pm or 11pm.

Off-licences (liquor stores) vary greatly, with many outside Reykjavík only opening for a couple of hours a day.

## P

## Photography

Crystal-clear air and long hours of daylight create ideal conditions for photography, and enthusiasts will probably take many more photos than they plan to. If your camera can be fitted with one, don't forget to use a UV/skylight filter when photographing outdoors. Memory cards for digital cameras are readily available, but all photographic equipment is expensive: bring your own or purchase it at the Duty Free Shop at the Keflavík airport. If you do have to buy film in Iceland, bear in mind that outside Reykjavík slide film, in particular, may be hard to get hold of.

## Postal Services

Post offices (*Íslandspóstur*; www. postur.is) are found in all major towns and villages and some

*Bright postbox.*

country districts. The postal system is efficient, with letters taking two to six days to reach Europe or North America. Letters are sent by either priority (A) or economy (B) service, but delivery time abroad is not noticeably different between the two services. Air-mail letters or postcards to Europe cost ISK180 (A) or ISK165 (B); to other areas they are ISK240 Aor ISK210B. You can buy stamps from post offices. Some shops that sell postcards also stock stamps. The Central Post Office has a philatelic section, and stamp collections are also sold at souvenir shops. Icelandic stamps often show native birds and natural phenomena, making an unusual and affordable gift to take home. Poste restante is available at post offices throughout the country. Mark letters clearly with the surname in capitals or underlined.

Post offices are generally open Mon–Fri 9am–4.30pm. The **Central Post Office** on Posthússtræti 5 (near Austurvöllur) in Reykjavík is open Mon–Fri 9am–6pm, and in June, July and August also Sat 10am–2pm.

## Public Holidays

**January** New Year's Day/ *Nýársdagurinn* (1st).
**March/April** Maundy Thursday, Good Friday, Easter Monday; First Day of Summer/*Sumardagurinn fyrsti* (first Thursday after April 18th).
**May** Labour Day (1st); Ascension (sixth Thursday after Easter); Whitsun (eighth Monday after Easter).
**June** Independence Day (17th).
**August** *Verslunnarmannahelgi* (first Monday).
**December** Christmas Day (25th), Boxing Day (26th). Christmas Eve and New Year's Eve are half-day holidays.

TRANSPORT

# R

## Religious Services

Around 75 percent of Icelanders belong to the Evangelical Lutheran Church, 6 percent to other Lutheran churches, about 3 percent are Roman Catholics, 5 percent are atheists, and various denominations account for the remaining 11 percent of the population.

Reykjavík has a number of churches that hold regular services on Sundays and in the week. Churches in central Reykjavík include: **Hallgrímskirkja**, Skólavörðuholt, tel: 510 1000; **Dómkirkjan** (the cathedral), Kirkjustræti 16, tel: 520 9700; **Landakotskirkja** (Catholic cathedral), Hávallagata, tel: 552 5388 (celebrates Holy Mass in English on Sundays at 6pm); **Fríkirkjan** (Free Church), Fríkirkjuvegur 5, tel: 552 7270.

Outside Reykjavík there are Lutheran churches in all towns and villages and on many farms as well, though services may not be held every Sunday in rural districts. Apart from the main **Akureyrarkirkja** (tel: 462 7700), Akureyri also has a Catholic church at Eyrarlandsvegur 26.

# S

## Student Travellers

Student discounts are rarely, if ever, advertised, but it is worth asking at museums to see what is available.

# T

## Telecommunications

The Icelandic word for telephone is *sími*. Public telephone kiosks are something of a rarity in Iceland: restaurants, roadside service stations, swimming pools and hotels sometimes have coin-box telephones, taking ISK10, 50 and, usually, 100 coins. Most call boxes will also accept phonecards – available from post offices and petrol stations. Call costs vary according to the time and day of the week, and the distance that you are telephoning. Try to avoid calling from your hotel room – hotels often charge three times the official rate.

For European visitors, the cheapest way to make local calls is usually to buy an Icelandic SIM card, available from kiosks, book shops, petrol stations and post offices, to use in

your own mobile phone. (Visitors from outside Europe should check with their service provider whether their phone will work on the GSM 900/1800 network – many US phones, for example, will not). GSM phones can also be rented from Iceland Telecom, Ármúli 27, Reykjavík.

Direct dialling is available to most countries – to call internationally from Iceland, first dial 00 followed by the country code. Country codes and international dialling procedure in English are listed in the telephone directory. For international directory enquiries dial 1811 (local 118).

All Icelandic telephone numbers have seven digits, with no area codes. The international code for calling Iceland from abroad is 354.

The main tourist information office in Reykjavík has telephone and fax facilities, available to visitors.

## Time Zone

Iceland is on Greenwich Mean Time (GMT)/Coordinated Universal Time (UTC), but no daylight saving time is applied. This means that in summer it is one hour behind London, four hours ahead of New York and seven hours ahead of California. In winter, it is on the same time as London, five hours ahead of New York and eight hours ahead of California.

## Tipping

Tipping is not customary in Iceland and is not expected.

## Toilets

Public toilets are a rarity. It is better to make use of the facilities at your accommodation or at a bar or café.

## Tour Operators

A wide range of travel packages are offered by tour operators in Iceland and abroad. Itineraries range from short coach-based sightseeing tours to longer camping tours and activity holidays – including horse-riding, whale-watching, hiking, river rafting, snowmobiling and mountain biking. Those who prefer a roof over their head but do not mind roughing it a little could try sleeping-bag accommodation holidays. Winter packages offer cross-country skiing, snowmobiling and jeep touring.

Outside main towns with tourist offices, it is worth asking at your hotel for details of local tours. Some operators offer a special

service for schools and universities. Local tourist offices usually offer sightseeing tours ranging from one morning to several days.

For more detailed information contact the Icelandic Tourist Board (www.ferdamalastofa.is/en) or tourist information offices.

### Tour Operators in Iceland

**Arinbjörn Jóhannsson,** Brekkulækur Farm, 531 Hvammstangi, tel: 451 2938, email: info@abbi-island.is, www. abbi-island.is. A company offering unique holidays in northwest Iceland. Especially notable are a 10-day Icelandic-style Christmas/New Year celebration and a spring hiking tour in May to observe nature's awakening. Also does horse-riding (see page 328).
**Guðmundur Jónasson Travel,** Vesturvör 34, 200 Kópavogur, tel: 511 1515, www.gjtravel.is. A diverse range of tours including horse-riding and river rafting.
**Iceland Excursions** (Gray Line), Klettagarðar 4, 104 Reykjavík, tel: 540 1313, email: iceland@grayline. is, www.icelandexcursions.is. Day tours from Reykjavík to the west and southwest of the country, including whale-watching, the Blue Lagoon and glacier tours.
**Iceland Travel,** Skógarhlíð 12, 105 Reykjavík, tel: 585 4300, 585 4210, email: info@icelandtravel.is, www. icelandtravel.is. Part of the Icelandair group, this company seemingly offers every kind of tour imaginable: with trips to all parts of Iceland and a variety of adventure tours.
**Icelandic Farm Holidays,** Síðumúli 2, Reykjavík, tel: 570 2700, email: ifh@farmholidays.is, www.farmholidays. is. Specialising in farm holidays and farmhouse accommodation, including self-drive packages.
**Nonni Travel,** Brekkugata 5, Akureyri, tel: 461 1841, email: nonni@ nonnitravel.is, www.nonnitravel.is. This travel agent can arrange trips around Akureyri and nearby areas including Mývatn and Grímsey, plus jaunts to Greenland and the Faroe Islands.
**Reykjavík Excursions,** BSÍ Bus Terminal, 101 Reykjavík, tel: 580 5400, email: main@re.is, www.re.is. This bus company is one of the oldest and largest organisers of day trips around the west and the southwest, with the possibility of incorporating activities such as horse-riding.
**Snæland Grímsson,** Langholtsvegur 109, 104 Reykjavík, tel: 588 8660, email: snaeland@snaeland.is; www. snaeland.is. Hiking tours, group tours, day excursions, winter excursions, jeep safaris and more.

A – Z

LANGUAGE

## Adventure Tours

A number of tour operators specialise in adventure tourism, such as river rafting, glacier tours, kayaking, winter excursions and mountain climbing. Many larger tour operators (see page 327) may also offer such trips as part of their regular programme.

**Hesta Sport,** Vegamót, 560 Varmahlíð, tel: 453 8383, email: info@riding.is, www.riding.is. Offering horse-riding tours through the highlands, mountains and the outback of Skagafjörður.

**Dive.is,** Hólmaslóð 2,101 Reykjavík, tel: 578 6200, email: dive@dive. is, www.dive.is. Daily diving and snorkelling tours to the Silfra rift in Þingvellir National Park, plus diving tours to other sites around Iceland.

**Glacier Jeeps Glacier Tours,** Vagnsstaðir, 781 Suðursveit, tel: 478 1000, 894 3133, email: glacierjeeps@simnet.is, www.glacierjeeps.is. Snowmobiling onto the Vatnajökull icecap, sailing on Jökulsárlón glacial lagoon and ice-walking on a glacier. Protective gear provided.

**Hike & Bike,** Reykjahlíð, 660 Mývatn, tel: 899 4845, email: info@hikeandbike.is, www.hikeandbike.is. Day trips and overnight bicycle-based tours around the Lake Mývatn area; also cross-country skiing and snowshoeing in winter.

**Into the Glacier,** Húsafell, tel: 578 2550, email: info@intotheglacier. is, https://intotheglacier.is. Trips on Langjökull glacier by 8x8, snowmobile and super-jeep.

**Iceland Excursions** (Gray Line; see page 327). In addition to a plethora of bus tours, this large tour operator arranges jeep and ATV trips, snowmobiling, glacier hikes, ice climbing and more.

**Icelandic Mountain Guides** (Íslenskir Fjallaleiðsögumenn),

(see page 327)

## Tourist Offices

**Reykjavík:** Tourist Information, Aðalstræti 2, 101 Reykjavík, tel: 590 1550, email: info@visitreykjavik.is, www.visitreykjavik.is; daily 8am–8pm..

Icelandic Travel Market, Bankastræti 2, tel: 522 4979, www.icelandtravelmarket.is; daily 9am–7pm, until 9pm in summer.

**Akureyri:** Tourist Information Centre, Hof Cultural Centre, Strandgata 12, 600 Akureyri, tel: 450 1050, email: akureyrarstofa@akureyri.is; www.visitakureyri.is; weekdays 8am–4pm.

Stórhöfði 33, 110 Reykjavík, tel: 587 9999, email: info@mountainguides.is, www. mountainguides.is. An association of mountain and trekking guides with years of experience, which offers the usual day-long activity tours (glacier walks, horse-riding etc), plus a range of rugged multi-day hikes and treks for experienced walkers and/or climbers. Can also custom-design tours for individuals and groups.

**Mountaineers of Iceland,** Köllunarklettsvegur 2, 104 Reykjavik, tel: 580 9900, email: ice@mountaineers.is, www.mountaineers. is. Offers super-jeep and snowmobile tours off the beaten track.

**Öræfaferðir,** Hofsnes-Öræfi, 785 Fagurhólsmýri, tel: 894 1317, email: info@localguide.is, www.localguide.is. Located in south Iceland, the people on this farm specialise in tours of the Öræfi region: from gentle coastal trips and bird-watching walks, to ascents of Hvanndalshnúkur (Iceland's highest mountain) and ski mountaineering expeditions.

## Hiking Tours

Two local outdoor organisations – the Iceland Touring Association (Ferðafélag Íslands) and Útivist – offer guided backpacking tours and day walks.

The backpacking tours are graded according to level of difficulty and accommodation is usually in mountain huts. Participants must bring their own food and equipment.

Both organisations are practically national institutions and are extremely popular with Icelanders. Consequently, these tours provide an excellent way to meet the natives. The downsides are that tours book out extremely quickly; and they are guided in Icelandic, though the majority of guides do speak English as well.

**Iceland Touring Association** (Ferðafélag Íslands), Mörkinn 6, 108 Reykjavík, tel: 568 2533, email: fi@fi.is, www.fi.is. Founded in 1927 and offers various hiking and cross-country skiing tours with mountain hut accommodation. Trips usually depart from the ITA's Reykjavík office, but check when booking.

**Útivist,** Laugavegur 178, 105 Reykjavík, tel: 562 1000, email: utivist@utivist.is, www.utivist.is. Hiking tours to Þórsmörk and other south Iceland locations, with camping and mountain hut accommodation. Trips usually depart from the BSÍ bus terminal in Reykjavík, but check when booking.

## Visit Iceland

The official Icelandic tourist board is **Visit Iceland** (Sundagarðar 2, 104 Reykjavík; tel: (+354) 511 4000, www.visiticeland.com). Their website, with links to the main tourist offices and main tour operators across Iceland, is a good place to start your research.

## Horse-riding Tours

The Icelandic horse is a delightful creature: small, sturdy, sure-footed and good-natured. It has five different gaits, including the *tölt*, a fast, smooth trot. Since the 1980s the Icelandic horse has become increasingly popular worldwide, and many foreign Icelandic-horse lovers come to Iceland especially to ride the horse in its natural environment. Besides, experiencing Iceland on horseback is utterly exhilarating. A number of tour operators specialise in horse-riding tours of long or short duration.

**Arinbjörn Jóhannsson,** Brekkulækur Farm, 531 Hvammstangi, tel: 451 2938, email: info@abbi-island.is, www. abbi-island.is. Based in the northwest of Iceland. A variety of longer and shorter horse-riding tours, including winter excursions to observe the northern lights and starry night sky.

**Eldhestar** (Volcano Horses), Völlum, 810 Hveragerði, tel: 480 4800, email: info@eldhestar.is, www.eldhestar.is. Offers short and long riding tours, riding camps, lessons and special holidays including tours to the National Equestrian Meets.

**Íshestar** (Icelandic Riding Tours), Sörlaskeið 26, 220 Hafnarfjörður, tel: 555 7000, email: info@ishestar. is, www.ishestar.is. Organises diverse riding tours of various lengths, including visits to the annual sheep round-up, driving herds of horses and historical trekking routes across the beautiful Icelandic interior.

**Polar Horses,** Grýtubakki 2, 601 Akureyri, tel: 463 3179, email: polarhestar@polarhestar.is, www. polarhestar.is. A family-run outfit offering tours with such intriguing names as "Riding with the Elves". Also organises tours to the National Equestrian Meet and farm holidays with daily riding tours incorporated.

## Sightseeing Air Tours

**Norlandair,** Norlandair Akureyri Airport, tel: 414 6960www.norlandair. is. Flights across the Arctic Circle to Grímsey.

**Eagle Air (Flugfélagið Ernir),** Skaftafell Airport, Skaftafell

(Vatnajökull National Park), tel: 562 4200/562 2640, email: info@eagleair. is, www.eagleair.is. Scheduled flights from Reykjavík to five destinations around Iceland; plus sightseeing flights along the south coast, including over Landmannalaugar, Hekla, the Vestmannaeyjar and the 2010 Eyjafjallajökull eruption site. **Mýflug Air Service,** Reykjahlíð airport, tel: 464 4400, email: myflug@myflug. is, www.myflug.is. Offers sightseeing flights around Lake Mývatn from the airfield behind the Hlíð camp site. On a clear day the 20-minute flight over the lake is stunning. They also fly over Krafla, the Jökulsá Canyon, and the central highlands to Askja and Kverkfjöll. A minimum of two to three persons is usually needed to go ahead with the flight. **Atlantsflug,** Fögrubrekku 10, 200 Kopavogur, tel: 854 4105, email: info@flightseeing.is, www.flightseeing.is. Offers a variety of sightseeing flights over the glacial tongues streaming from the Vatnajökull icecap, and over the highland interior.

*Tour Operators Abroad*

**UK**
**All Iceland,** 90 London Road, SE1 6LN, London, tel: (0) 1904 406534/0207 928 0946, email: info@all-iceland.co.uk, www.all-iceland.co.uk. Run by London-based Icelanders, this tour operator specialises solely in Icelandic holidays – everything from spa breaks to trail-running tours.
**Discover the World,** Arctic House, 8 Bolters Lane, Banstead, Surrey SM7 2AR, tel: 01737 214250, email: travel@discover-the-world. co.uk, www.discover-the-world. co.uk. A comprehensive travel and information service for Iceland. Hotel tours, camping and sleeping-bag accommodation tours, activity holidays, fly drive and independent travel arrangements, bus and air passes.
**Icelandair,** Adam House, 2nd floor, 1 Fitzroy Square, London W1T 5HE, tel: 020 7874 1000, email: uk@icelandair.is, www.icelandair.co.uk. Icelandair's in-house travel agency. Offers a broad range of escorted and unescorted programmes for groups and individuals year round, including fly-drive packages and stopovers.
**Nordic Experience,** 39 Crouch Street, Colchester, CO3 3EN, tel: 01206 708 680, www.nordicexperience.co.uk. Arrange various comfortable self-drive summer and winter packages to Iceland.

*Walking near Lake Mývatn.*

**USA**
**Distant Journeys**, PO Box 1211, Camden, Maine, 04843, USA, tel: 888-845 5781, email: journeys@distantjourneys.com, www.distantjourneys.com. Hiking and walking tours in the Fjallabak nature reserve.
**Icelandair Holidays,** 1900 Crown Colony Drive, Quincy, MA 02169, USA, tel: 1-800-223 5500, email: usa@icelandair.is, www.icelandair.us. Icelandair's in-house travel agency.

# V

## Visas and Passports

Iceland is part of the Schengen Agreement, which exempts personal border controls between 26 EU countries. EU citizens, and citizens from some other countries including Australia, New Zealand, Canada and the USA, are exempted from the need to carry a visa for a stay of up to three months in all within the Schengen area. The total stay within the Schengen Area must not exceed three months in any period of six months. Your passport must be valid for a further three months beyond your proposed departure date. You may be asked to produce evidence of funds to support yourself and an air or ferry ticket out of the country.

Citizens who need a visa can find out more from their home country's embassy or from the Icelandic Directorate of Immigration (Útlendingastofnun; Skógarhlíð 6, 105 Reykjavik; tel: 444 0900; http://utl.is).

If you intend to work in Iceland, you will need a pre-arranged job and a residence and work permit which your prospective employer applies for before you enter the country. Residents of the European Economic Area (EEA states) may stay in Iceland for up to three months without having

an air or ferry ticket out of the country and may also look for work.

Residents of Denmark, Finland, Norway and Sweden do not need a passport to enter Iceland. Residents of the following countries may enter Iceland using their national identity card: Austria, Belgium, the Czech Republic, Estonia, France, Germany, Greece, Hungary, Italy, Liechtenstein, Lithuania, Luxembourg, Malta, the Netherlands, Poland, Portugal, Slovak Republic, Slovenia, Spain and Switzerland.

# W

## Weights and Measures

Iceland adopted the metric system (SI) in 1900, so all distances and weights are in centimetres, metres, kilometres, litres, grams, kilograms, metric tonnes etc.

## What to Bring

Iceland will feel expensive for many visitors: the cost of importing goods, and a 24 per cent VAT rate on some items (reduced rate is 11 percent), means that you may pay more than at home. Bring everything for your stay in the way of clothing, medicine, camera film and other equipment. If you plan to backpack around the country, it is worth bringing in your duty-free food allowance (3kg/6.6lb, up to ISK25,000 in value) in the form of dried foods. Freeze-dried products are costly and virtually unavailable outside specialist shops in Reykjavík.

Iceland's freak wind gusts have been known to wreak havoc at campgrounds – a summerweight tent may not survive. If you bring your own tent, make sure you are able to repair bent poles, broken guy ropes and holes in canvas. Bring heavy-duty tent pegs; lightweight aluminium pegs may not be enough.

TRANSPORT
A – Z
LANGUAGE

# LANGUAGE

# UNDERSTANDING THE LANGUAGE

## ABOUT ICELANDIC

Icelandic is one of the Nordic family of languages and most closely resembles Norwegian and Faroese. Remarkably, the Icelandic spoken today has not changed greatly from the language of the early Norse settlers (see page 91).

For the foreigner, Icelandic is daunting, but most Icelanders, particularly the young, speak English fluently, as well as Danish, Norwegian or Swedish. German and French are less widely spoken, but also taught at school. Icelanders are by nature quite reticent with foreigners and not easily drawn into conversation but it will be worth it. If you can pick up a few phrases of Icelandic, it will be appreciated.

## PRONUNCIATION TIPS

Stress falls naturally on the first syllable of a word. The following examples of pronunciation are for guidance only – many Icelandic sounds do not exist in English.

### Vowels and Consonants

**Ð / ð** pronounced 'th' as in *the*
**Þ / þ** pronounced 'th' as in *thing*
**a** as in *hard*
**á** as in *how*
**e** as in *get*
**é** as in *yet*
**i** or y as in *thin*
**í** or ý as in *been*
**o** as in *ought*
**ó** as in *gold*
**ö** as in *first*
**u** as in *hook*
**ú** as in *fool*

**ae** as in *fight*
**au** between the sounds in *fate* and *oil*, as in the French *feuille*
**ey/ei** as in *day*
**fn** is pn as in *open*
**g** when followed by i (except at the start of a word) is y as in *yet*
**hv** is kf as in *thankful*
**j** is y as in *yet*
**ll** is tl as in *bottle*
**r** is always lightly rolled
**rl** is rtl as in *heartless*
**rn** is tn as in *button*
**tn** and fn when at the end of words are almost silent.

## GEOGRAPHY

The following lists show common elements in place names, the English translation and an example.
*Á* **river** Hvítá **white river**
*Borg* **rocky crag** Dimmuborgir **dark crags**
*Brekka* **slope** Brekkulækur **slope stream**
*Dalur* **valley** Fljótsdalur **river valley**
*Drangur* **column** Drangavík **rock bay**
*Eldur* **fire** Eldfell **fire mountain**
*Eyja* **island** Flatey **flat island**
*Fell* **mountain** Snæfell **snow mountain**
*Fjall* **mountain** Bláfjöll **blue mountains**
*Fjörður* **fjord** Hafnarfjörður **harbour fjord**
*Foss* **waterfall** Gullfoss **gold falls**
*Gígur* **crater** Lakagígar **cow stomach craters**
*Gil* **ravine** Jökulgil **glacier ravine**
*Heiði* **heath** Hellisheiði **cave heath**
*Hellir* **cave** Sönghellir **song caves**
*Hlíð* **hillside** Reykjahlíð **smoky hillside**
*Hóll* **hill/hillock** Vatnsdalshólar **lake valley hills**

*Holt* **hill** Brattholt **steep hill**
*Hraun* **lava** Ódáðahraun **ill deeds lava**
*Höfði* **cape** Höfdabrekka **cape slope**
*Höfn* **harbour** Þórshöfn **Thor's harbour**
*Jökull* **glacier** Vatnajökull **lake glacier**
*Lækur* **stream** Varmilækur **warm stream**
*Laug* **hot spring** Laugarvatn **hot spring lake**
*Lind* **spring** Hvannalindir **angelica springs**
*Lón* **lagoon** Jökulsárlón **glacier river lagoon**
*Mýri* **marsh** Mýrdalsjökull **marsh valley glacier**
*Nes* **peninsula** Snæfellsnes **snow mountain peninsula**
*Reykur* **smoke** Reykjanes **smoky peninsula**
*Sandur* **sand** Mýrdalssandur **marsh valley sand**
*Skarð* **pass** Kerlingarskarð **troll wife's pass**
*Skógur* **wood** Skógafoss **wood falls**
*Staður* **place** Egilsstaðir **Egil's place**
*Strönd* **coast/beach** Hornstrandir **horn peak coast**
*Tindur* **peak** Tindfjöll **peak mountains**
*Tjörn* **pond** Störu-tjarnir **big ponds**
*Vatn* **lake** Hvítárvatn **white river lake**
*Vík* **small bay** Reykjavík **smoky bay**
*Vogur* **inlet** Kópavogur **seal pup inlet**
*Völlur* **plain** Þingvellir **assembly plains**

## AT THE RESTAURANT

Most restaurant staff speak some English or other Scandinavian languages. The words and phrases below will help you order from simpler menus.

*Ég ætla að fá...* **I would like...**
*Áttu til...?* **Have you got any...?**
*Meira...* **More...**
*Ekki meira takk* **No more, thank you**
*Mjög gott* **Very good**
*Ég er grænmetisæta* **I am vegetarian**
*Reikninginn, takk* **The bill, please**
*Matseðill* **Menu**
*Forréttir* **Starters**
*Súpa* **Soup**
*Brauð* **Bread**
*Smjör* **Butter**
*Sósa* **Sauce**

### Kjötréttir/Meat Dishes

*Kjöt* **Meat**
*Lambakjöt* **Lamb**
*Nautakjöt* **Beef**
*Svínakjöt* **Pork**
*Kjúklingur* **Chicken**
*Hangikjöt* **Smoked lamb**

### Fiskréttir/Fish Dishes

*Fiskur* **Fish**
*Ýsa* **Haddock**
*Lúða* **Halibut**
*Rækjur* **Prawns**
*Lax* **Salmon**
*Silungur/Bleikja* **Trout**

### Grænmeti/Vegetables

*Kartöflur* **Potatoes**
*Franskar* **Chips**
*Blómkál* **Cauliflower**
*Grænar baunir* **Peas**
*Rauðkál* **Red cabbage**
*Sveppir* **Mushrooms**
*Gulrætur* **Carrots**
*Rófur* **Turnips**
*Salat* **Salad**

### Eftirréttir/Desserts

*Ís* **Ice-cream**
*Kaka/Terta* **Cake**

### Drykkir/Drinks

*Te* **Tea**
*Kaffi* **Coffee**
*Mjólk* **Milk**
*Sykur* **Sugar**
*Appelsínusafi* **Orange juice**
*Bjór* **Beer**
*Pilsner* **Low-alcohol beer**
*Hvítvín* **White wine**

*Rauðvín* **Red wine**
*Vatn* **Water**

## USEFUL WORDS AND PHRASES

The Icelandic language does not have an equivalent to "please". The phrase *Gerðu svo vel* is employed to invite a person into a house, to the table or to begin eating. It also translates to "here you are" when giving something to somebody. On a public notice "please" is *vinsamlegast*. For example, "please take your shoes off", a common request when entering a home or changing room is *vinsamlegast farið úr skónum*. When leaving the table or saying goodbye after a meal or drinks it is customary to thank the host by saying *Takk fyrir mig*.

**Hello/good morning** *Góðan dag*
**Good evening** *Gott kvöld*
**Goodnight** *Góða nótt*
**What is your name?** *Hvað heitir þú?*
**My name is...** *Ég heiti*
**How are you?** *Hvað segirðu gott?*
**Fine, and you?** *Allt fínt, en þú?*
**Fine** *Allt fínt*
**Alright** *Allt í lagi*
**Goodbye** *Bless*
**Yes** *Já*
**No** *Nei*
**Thanks** *Takk*
**Thank you very much** *Takk fyrir*
**Yes please** *Já takk*
**No thank you** *Nei takk*
**May I have...** *Má eg fá...*
**When?** *Hvenær?*
**Today** *Í dag*
**Tomorrow** *Á morgun*
**Yesterday** *Í gær*
**In the morning** *Fyrir hádegi*
**In the afternoon** *Eftir hádegi*
**Cheers!** *Skál!*
**How much does this cost?** *Hvað kostar þetta?*
**Come!** *Komdu!*
**Excuse me** *Afsakið*
**Sorry** *Fyrirgefðu*
**I do not understand** *Ég skil ekki*

## SIGNS

**Toilet** *Snyrting*
**Gents** *Karlar*
**Ladies** *Konur*

**Open** *Opið*
**Closed** *Lokað*
**Danger** *Hætta*
**Forbidden** *Bannað*
**Campsite** *Tjaldstæði*
**Entry** *Inngangur/Inn*
**Exit** *Útgangur/Út*
**Parking** *Bílastæði*
**Schedule** *Áætlun*
**Airport** *Flugvöllur*
**Blind summit (road sign)** *Blindhæð*
**Jeep track** *Jeppavegur*
**Police** *Lögreglan*
**Hospital** *Sjúkrahús*
**Health Centre** *Heilsugæslustöð*
**Doctor** *Læknir*
**Dentist** *Tannlæknir*
**Bank** *Banki*
**Post Office** *Póstur*
**Chemist** *Apótek*
**Co-op store** *Kaupfélag*
**Swimming pool** *Sundlaug*
**Mechanic/garage** *Verkstæði*

## NUMBERS

*Núll* **zero**
*Einn* **one**
*Tveir* **two**
*Þrír* **three**
*Fjórir* **four**
*Fimm* **five**
*Sex* **six**
*Sjö* **seven**
*Átta* **eight**
*Níu* **nine**
*Tíu* **ten**
*Ellefu* **eleven**
*Tólf* **twelve**
*Þrettán* **thirteen**
*Fjórtán* **fourteen**
*Fimmtán* **fifteen**
*Sextán* **sixteen**
*Sautján* **seventeen**
*Átján* **eighteen**
*Nítján* **nineteen**
*Tuttugu* **twenty**
*Tuttugu og einn* **twenty-one**
*Þrjátíu* **thirty**
*Fjörutíu* **forty**
*Fimmtíu* **fifty**
*Sextíu* **sixty**
*Sjötíu* **seventy**
*Áttatíu* **eighty**
*Níutíu* **ninety**
*Hundrað* **one hundred**
*Tvö hundrað* **two hundred**
*Þúsund* **one thousand**
*Miljón* **one million**

# FURTHER READING

## GENERAL

**Cod: A Biography of the Fish that Changed the World** by Mark Kurlansky. Highly acclaimed, fascinating account of a fish and an industry so vital to Iceland.

**The English Dane** by Sarah Bakewell. Readable biography about Jørgen Jørgensen, the "Dog-Days King", one of the strangest characters ever to set foot in Iceland.

**A Guide to the Flowering Plants and Ferns of Iceland** by Hörður Kristinsson. Written by the former Professor of Botany at the University of Iceland, this is a comprehensive, easy-to-use full-colour identification guide organised by flower colour and characteristics.

**Icelandic Food & Cookery** by Nanna Rögnvaldardóttir. Icelandic cookbook, for a literal taste of Iceland.

**Icelandic Bird Guide** by Jóhann Óli Hilmarsson. A practical guide to identifying Icelandic breeding birds, visitors and vagrants, including a section on identifying eggs and fledglings.

**Last Places: A Journey in the North** by Lawrence Millman. An extremely funny travelogue, which exactly pinpoints the attraction of cold, bleak landscapes.

**Letters from Iceland** by W.H. Auden and Louis MacNeice. Irreverent letters and poems sent by the two poets on a 1936 journey to Iceland, still fascinating and funny today.

**Ring of Seasons** by Terry Lacy. A good all-round overview of Icelandic history and culture from the perspective of a foreign resident.

**Studio Ólafur Elíasson** A book exploring the work of renowned Danish-Icelandic artist Ólafur Elíasson, creator of the Harpa Concert Hall's glinting façade.

## LITERATURE

**Angels of the Universe** by Einar Már Guðmundsson. This acclaimed novel won the Nordic Council's Literary Award in 1995. A disturbing and moving tale of a young man's slide into schizophrenia, based on the life of the author's brother. Also released as a film.

**The Atom Station** by Halldór Laxness. A wonderful dark comedy with a political slant by Iceland's late Nobel laureate.

**The Blue Fox** by Sjón. A short, strange fable by playwright, poet and sometime-Björk-collaborator Sjón.

**Devil's Island** by Einar Kárason. Pithy novel about the clash between poverty-stricken Icelanders and flashy American culture in 1950s Reykjavík.

**Independent People** by Halldór Laxness. The classic story of a man's struggle for independence, symbolic of the Icelandic nation, which helped to win its author the Nobel Prize for Literature.

**Tainted Blood** by Arnaldur Indriðason. A fascinating murder mystery featuring Reykjavík detective Erlendur and his team, who investigate a man's murder with help from Iceland's Genetic Research Centre. (Also published under the title Jar City, the name too of its successful cinematic release.)

**Treasures of Icelandic Verse** by various authors. An anthology of various Icelandic poems, with both the original and the translation.

**Troll's Cathedral** by Ólafur Gunnarsson. The story of a family beset by violence.

Many of Iceland's **Sagas** have been translated into English and other languages; particularly readable are Egils Saga, Laxdæla Saga and Njáls Saga, which are all published under the Penguin Classics label.

**The Sagas of the Icelanders,** translated by Robert Kellogg and also published by Penguin Classics, includes 10 sagas and seven shorter Old Norse tales.

**Burial Rites,** by Hannah Kent. A poignant novel based on the true story of Agnes Magnúsdóttir, the last person to be executed in Iceland.

**101 Reykyavik,** by Hallgrimur Helgason. A comic tale of a middle-aged loser and his bizarre love triangle written by the best known Icelandic contemporary author. The book was also turned in an award-winning film by the same title. Last Rituals, by Yrsa Sigurðardóttir. A noir criminal novel that delves deep into Icelandic psyche, old legends and history of the island.

## Send Us Your Thoughts

We do our best to ensure the information in our books is as accurate and up-to-date as possible. The books are updated on a regular basis using local contacts, who painstakingly add, amend and correct as required. However, some details (such as telephone numbers and opening times) are liable to change, and we are ultimately reliant on our readers to put us in the picture.

We welcome your feedback, especially your experience of using the book "on the road". Maybe we recommended a hotel that you liked (or another that you didn't), or you came across a great bar or new attraction we missed.

We will acknowledge all contributions, and we'll offer an Insight Guide to the best letters received.

Please write to us at:
**Insight Guides
PO Box 7910
London SE1 1WE**
Or email us at:
**hello@insightguides.com**

## OTHER INSIGHT GUIDES

More than 120 **Insight Guides and Insight City Guides** cover every continent, providing information on culture and all the top sights, as well as superb photography and detailed maps. Insight Guides covering this region include Norway, Sweden, Finland, and Scandinavia.

In addition, the pocket-sized **Insight Explore Guides** give you the best routes around the world's most exciting cities and countries.

# CREDITS

## Insight Guide Credits

### Distribution
**UK, Ireland and Europe**
Apa Publications (UK) Ltd;
sales@insightguides.com
**United States and Canada**
Ingram Publisher Services;
ips@ingramcontent.com
**Australia and New Zealand**
Woodslane; info@woodslane.com.au
**Southeast Asia**
Apa Publications (SN) Pte;
singaporeoffice@insightguides.com
**Hong Kong, Taiwan and China**
Apa Publications (HK) Ltd;
hongkongoffice@insightguides.com
**Worldwide**
Apa Publications (UK) Ltd;
sales@insightguides.com
**Special Sales, Content Licensing and CoPublishing**
Insight Guides can be purchased in bulk quantities at discounted prices. We can create special editions, personalised jackets and corporate imprints tailored to your needs. sales@insightguides.com
www.insightguides.biz

**Printed in China by CTPS**

First Edition 1992
Eighth Edition 2017

Every effort has been made to provide accurate information in this publication, but changes are inevitable. The publisher cannot be responsible for any resulting loss, inconvenience or injury. We would appreciate it if readers would call our attention to any errors or outdated information. We also welcome your suggestions; please contact us at: hello@insightguides.com

**www.insightguides.com**

**Editor:** Tom Fleming
**Author:** Fran Parnell
**Head of Production:** Rebeka Davies
**Update Production:** AM Services
**Picture Editor:** Tom Smyth
**Cartography:** original cartography Cosmographics, updated by Carte

## Contributors

This new edition of *Insight Guide: Iceland* was commissioned and co-ordinated and edited by Insight Guides editor **Tom Fleming** at Insight Guides' London office and updated by **Fran Parnell**. Fran has written guides to Iceland, Denmark, Finland, and Sweden. She loves Iron Age and Viking history, and is currently attempting to run a

marathon in each Scandinavian capital. This guide builds on the excellent foundations of previous editions of the book; key contributors have been **James Proctor**, who supplied the features on Food and Drink, Environmental Protection and Whaling, and **Tony Perrottet**, editor of the original edition of *Insight Guide: Iceland*.

## About Insight Guides

**Insight Guides** have more than 45 years' experience of publishing high-quality, visual travel guides. We produce 400 full-colour titles, in both print and digital form, covering more than 200 destinations across the globe, in a variety of formats to meet your different needs.
 **Insight Guides** are written by local authors who use their on-the-ground experience to provide the

very latest information; their local expertise is evident in the extensive historical and cultural background features. All the reviews in **Insight Guides** are independent; we strive to maintain an impartial view. Our reviews are carefully selected to guide you to the best places to eat, go out and shop, so you can be confident that when we say a place is special, we really mean it.

### Legend

**City maps**

| | |
|---|---|
| | Freeway/Highway/Motorway |
| | Divided Highway |
| | Main Roads |
| | Minor Roads |
| | Pedestrian Roads |
| | Steps |
| | Footpath |
| | Railway |
| | Funicular Railway |
| | Cable Car |
| | Tunnel |
| | City Wall |
| | Important Building |
| | Built Up Area |
| | Other Land |
| | Transport Hub |
| | Park |
| | Pedestrian Area |
| | Bus Station |
| | Tourist Information |
| | Main Post Office |
| | Cathedral/Church |
| | Mosque |
| | Synagogue |
| | Statue/Monument |
| | Beach |
| | Airport |

**Regional maps**

| | |
|---|---|
| | Freeway/Highway/Motorway (with junction) |
| | Freeway/Highway/Motorway (under construction) |
| | Divided Highway |
| | Main Road |
| | Secondary Road |
| | Minor Road |
| | Track |
| | Footpath |
| | International Boundary |
| | State/Province Boundary |
| | National Park/Reserve |
| | Marine Park |
| | Ferry Route |
| | Marshland/Swamp |
| | Glacier     Salt Lake |
| | Airport/Airfield |
| | Ancient Site |
| | Border Control |
| | Cable Car |
| | Castle/Castle Ruins |
| | Cave |
| | Chateau/Stately Home |
| | Church/Church Ruins |
| | Crater |
| | Lighthouse |
| | Mountain Peak |
| | Place of Interest |
| | Viewpoint |

# INDEX